Warm Wishes
Dr. Marji Neal. Fayemiwo

Moshood Ayenle Fayemiwo

Rave Reviews for Aliko Mohammad Dangote

"Through the eyes of the authors, the reader gets the opportunity to experience life through young Aliko's eyes and learns how he became one of the most successful and richest Black persons in the world....The authors made the story of Aliko Muhammad Dangote come alive with all of the rich background history of Aliko's family and his family's humble beginnings in Kano City, Nigeria. This book is highly recommended to anyone who enjoys learning about how different people of all walks of life become rich and successful, and what it takes to get to the top."

---*Readers Favorite Book Review, 5.00 Stars, Hawesville, Kentucky, USA.*

"A compelling book about a unique personality in Africa,"

---*Goodreads Book Review, 5.0 Stars, Santa Monica, California, USA*

"*Aliko Mohammad Dangote* is a commendable start. In a land lacking a culture of independent biography, this is a starting point, and *Dangote* -- part unauthorized biography, part history book, and part success-manual -- is a promising introduction to the fascinating and still largely unmapped universe of one of the world's richest men."

---*The Huffington Post, New York, NY, USA.*

"Aliko Mohammad Dangote is a very rich and savvy businessman, an unassuming entrepreneur, and a global icon. His emergence as the richest Black person in the world for five consecutive years is big news, considering the sclerotic corruption in Nigeria and the nation's torrid reputation of scammers and swindlers around the world. A must-read manual of success..."

---The Nigerian Voice Magazine, Flevoland, The Netherlands,

"...Flawlessly written and devoid of editing errors and typos, *Aliko Mohammad Dangote, The Biography of the Richest Black Person in the World,* stands out as a hallmark of excellent artisan- ship and knowledgeable chronicling...This is a must-read for anyone, who thinks it is not possible to become a stalwart in one's chosen endeavor,"

---Bookplex Review of Books, Mumbai, India.

ADVANCE PRAISE FOR ALIKO MOHAMMAD DANGOTE

"I am deeply impressed by this work... it is gratifying to note that the authors could come out with the first and only biography of Aliko Mohammad Dangote, the richest Black person in the world. Well done. I commend this work to all and sundry"

---- Prof. Adebowale Ibidapo Adefuye, the ambassador of Nigeria to the United States, Washington, DC, USA.

"ALIKO MOHAMMAD DANGOTE is a compelling narrative about an exceptional African entrepreneur. It traces the complicated transformation of an ambitious trader into a corporate titan. This book can be read not only as an exciting narrative about the life of a prodigious investor, but also as an inspirational account of the astonishing process of wealth-creation by the richest black man in the world. Beyond these, the book provides the familial, socio-cultural, economic and political contexts for understanding the force of character and amazing entrepreneurial vision that propelled this gutsy risk-taker - Dangote - to the position of global commercial exceptionality that he has attained...."

--- Wale Adebanwi (PhD), Associate Professor, University of California-Davis, USA, and author of "Trials and Triumphs: the Story of The NEWS."

"I must admit that I was taken aback by the enormity of the task you set out to accomplish. What a book, I must confess! I was most fascinated at the pains the authors took to trace a part of Nigeria's political and commercial history from northern Nigeria through several interim episodes to our present day's dispensation. The genealogical research that offered such a laborious detail of Dangote's ancestry was also proof of the hard work the project required. This is a book that will go a long way in answering several academic questions that students of Nigeria's history may have in mind. It is a practical guide to opportune geeks and ambitious young men and women who will grasp a clue on when and where to be push full in business endeavors. As presented in the book, Dangote's attitude of avoiding conflict with political leaders wherever possible will surely serve as a useful tip to serious and aspiring businessmen and women. Occasional hints here and there, of speculated flaws on Dangote's path to success crown the professional credentials of the project. For instance, rather than being a purely praise-singing book, efforts were also made to highlight critical positions pointing out occasional biased incentives offered by government that may have driven competitors out of the market in favor of Dangote. This is a professional narrative that easily betrays the journalistic background of one of the authors. Well readable and highly commendable..."

---Frisky Larr, radio journalist, communication scientist and author of "Nigeria's Journalistic Militantism," Bochum, Republic of Germany.

"The power of the tongue is humans' strongest weapon. Tongue produces the ability to speak and when speech is refined and properly-harnessed, it produces wisdom. Wisdom in turns teaches one has to be humble and humility is the father of greatness. This book explained magnificently how Mr. Aliko Mohammad Dangote has used this weapon to become the richest Black person in the world in thirty years. Truly a remarkable biography of a wise human being who has proved by conduct, hard work and perseverance that we are all able to prosper in any part of the globe, irrespective of skin color and past circumstances..."

--- Tammy Jane Radovanović, Head, Loita Capital Trade Office. Johannesburg, South Africa.

Aliko Mohammad Dangote

"The authors traced the history of Mr. Aliko Dangote and his larger than life personality as a business icon and perhaps the most successful business man in Nigeria and in Africa today. The book took readers into Mr. Dangote's persona; a cool headed, humble, simple and hardworking man, who has succeeded in building the largest private industrial business empire in Nigeria nay West Africa which have enriched many lives through job creation and service delivery. The authors presented Aliko as a poster boy for Nigeria's potential and a tremendous boost for morale. What is truly exciting about Mr. Dangote's wealth, as this book shows, is that he plows his business profits back into the local economy to generate more wealth and employment opportunities. That definitely distinguishes Mr. Dangote from other men and women of means in Nigeria. Mr. Dangote is presented in this book as a genuine African patriot for contributing to the industrialization of the continent. The fact that Dangote is the richest African and Black man in the world are a testament to the potentials of the African economy for investors interested in making legitimate money in the Nigerian economy. In fact, Aliko's business success presents a window of opportunity for the Nigerian government to attract foreign investors into the Nigerian and African economies. If Dangote can make stupendous profit locally, so can others who are willing to invest in the African economy. A readable book written in an easy and straight forward prose..."

---Dr Segun Oshinaga, author, coach, speaker, pastor and president, Wisdom for Winning Network, Lagos, Nigeria.

"Like any other denouements of memoir books, the last chapter is the highlight. As a reader, the denouement always takes the heavier weight of a literary merit for memoirs and autobiographies. Also the book provided a comprehensive historical account of main events in Nigeria which made Mr. Dangote of what he is today. Excellent job! The authors managed to lead the chapters of seeing the different sides of the world of business to be fascinating yet a serious path toward success---"

--- Ms. Lou Fuentes, Publishing Consultant, Trafford Publishing Company, Bloomington, Indiana, USA.

"Africana readers and political-economic policy wonks of African affairs will love this book! Moshood Fayemiwo and Margie Neal's "Aliko Mohammad Dangote" is appropriately African-centered – an attempt by an African scholar and his co-author to present Africans as the subject of history. The authors are right, "Africans must learn to celebrate their own"; and what better way to do this than through this thoroughly interesting biographical treatise of the richest Black man in the world! This superbly written biography exemplars the historical vibrancy of the Nigerian business class and debunks the notion that corruption is the core tenet that characterizes the country's socio-economic culture. You must read this "Good News from Africa" monograph; it is fashioned in a style similar to Vali Nasr's *Forces of Fortune* (Nasr, 2009), a book that comparatively documents the alternative experience of many Turkish "Capitalist Prophets of Change". Refreshingly differently, however, for Aliko Mohammad Dangote, reveals for reader-publics the agent-centric contributions of Africans' global business success in this regard- using as case study, the very rich story of Nigeria's Aliko Dangote, the world's richest African..."

---Rita Kiki Edozie (PhD), Associate Professor of International Relations, Director of African- American and African Studies, and author of " Reconstructing Africa's Third Wave of Democracy: Comparative African Democratic Politics," Michigan State University, East Lansing, MI, USA.

"Congratulations for a job well done with the first and only biography of Mr. Aliko Dangote. The authors covered the various trajectories of the quintessential Dangote and give the reader a well-written, well-researched and balanced story of how the richest man in Nigeria, Africa and the world achieved this remarkable feat. Considering the time and hard work that went into this scholarly work, there is no doubt it should win the authors accolades and awards. Mr. Dangote is a great Nigerian, and his legendary business accomplishments should be a thing of pride to Nigerians, Africans and indeed all Black people of the world. I am proud of the authors and commend them for the painstaking efforts that went into writing this seminal work. Again, congratulations..."

--- Emeka Linus Emekauwa (PhD), General Manager, and host of "African Series, Saturday 3-6pm program, WSHA 88.9FM Radio Raleigh, North Carolina, USA

"Considering that the insubstantial book culture in Nigeria and much of Africa is replete with hagiographies and vanity publications, this researched biography on Aliko Dangote by two respected authors is a most welcome replenishing of a famished bookstore. African Economic History should draw required invigoration from a human-centered narrative of how enormous fortune can be built up and consolidated by talented individuals with eyes on the main chance. I look forward to reading the entire book as well as recommending it to my students..."

> ---*Ayo Olukotun (PhD), Professor of Political Science, Lead City University, Ibadan, Nigeria and author of "Repressive State and Resurgent Media Under Nigeria's Military Dictatorship, 1988-98."*

"Since Nigeria gained her independence from the UK over half-a-century ago, the nation has been battered and abused by soldiers of fortunes and venal politicians, who are in government to serve their selfish desires rather than serving the citizens. In spite of Nigeria's abundant human and material resources, poverty is abound but as the authors of this book have pointed out, there is indeed hope for Africa's most populous nation. That hope lies with God Almighty and the few men and women who are making a difference in Nigeria and Mr. Aliko Dangote is one of such rare people. He is a prodigiously wealthy man, who is using his vast fortune to create employment opportunities instead of stashing the money away in overseas. This book is a good resource for teaching aspiring young business peoples of the world on how to start small and grow big..."

> ---*Barrister (Dr) Janet Ogundipe-Fashakin, Head and Principal Attorney, Fashakin and Associates, PC Law Firm, Queens, NY USA.*

"The life of Aliko Mohammad Dangote, the richest, black, Nigerian man, is skillfully collated by the authors, demonstrating his economic success was part of an incredible legacy of resilience and accomplishments. Unhindered by racial heritage with an unusually powerful and unique combination of sound business principles and behaviors, Dangote has trumped long held assumptions, cultural archetypes and stereotypes, to become known as a respected business man, power broker and philanthropist"

> ---*Hon Gloria Hyatt, Member of the British Empire (MBE), motivational speaker, education, coach and managing director, Teach Consultancy Limited, Liverpool, UK.*

"The strength of *Aliko Mohammad Dangote* lies in its exploration of the forces, attitudes and circumstances that shaped and still shapes Dangote's life and business -- everything from the influence of his maternal grandfather to his city of birth (Kano, commercial capital of northern Nigeria) to his absolute devotion to Islam. These and more explain his remarkable business acumen, his much-criticized closeness to Nigeria's successive governments, his unwavering belief in the economic potentials of Nigeria, and his philanthropic spirit. From *Aliko Mohammad Dangote*, we see that Aliko's life is a careful balancing game, in a country where 'politics' -- by every definition of it -- is more than everything. On the one hand is the family philosophy, established by forebear Sanusi Dantata. Aliko is quoted as saying, of his grandfather: "He always advises us that: no matter what you do, you must always respect the authority of the day. Do not fight government. You must be an obedient person. And that's something I learnt and took seriously."

--- Tolu Ogunlesi, author, writer, columnist, The Punch and winner,
2009 CNN Multi-choice African Journalism Award (Arts & Culture),
Lagos, Nigeria.

"Mr. Dangote needs to be celebrated by all Africans, black people and indeed people of other races too for his accomplishments..."

---Mr. Mohammed Mardah, President Yankasa Association of New
York, Inc. Bronx, NY, USA.

"I was in Nigeria with my father-Dr. Moshood Fayemiwo, the coauthor of this book-- in 2011 during part of the field work and research for this biography and was amazed at the interest shown by ordinary Nigerians on the story of Mr. Aliko Mohammad Dangote of Nigeria and the history of his company, the Dangote Group of Companies. It was funny that my father insisted we switched to eating some of the groceries produced by the Dangote Group of companies at our guest house: from noodles, spaghetti, yogurt, milk to macaroni, sugar, salt, fruit juice, bottle water etc. in order for him to know how popular Dangote is in Nigeria and the impact of his products on the lives of ordinary Nigerians.

Later, I became his side-kick during interviews with grocers and consumers in selected stores in Abuja, Nigeria's administrative and political capital city. The overall impression I got from the unscientific poll before we returned to the United States was that, many Nigerians who patronized Dangote products do so for three reasons: affordability, patriotism and quality. There is no doubt that Mr. Dangote's success is one of the most positive news that has come out of Nigeria and Africa in recent times. This is a book everyone should read not because I was involved, but because it is a good book,"

---Mr. Oluwafemi Emmanuel Fayemiwo, Southern Illinois University, Carbondale, Illinois; US Marine Crops Parris Island, BeaufortsSouth Carolina, USA.

"For long, the African continent seemed to have been written off by the Western media as that part of the world constantly afflicted with poverty, diseases and political instability which needed rescue from the developed world through foreign aid. But as the authors of this book have pointed out, good news and new things are indeed coming out of Africa and Nigeria's Mr. Dangote, who has emerged as the richest black man in the world, is in the vanguard of a new revolution in the continent. How he began from humble beginning and succeeded in building an indigenous manufacturing company to world standard was beautifully narrated by the authors, and the Midas touch of this billionaire was commended to any ambitious, hardworking, focused and motivated person anywhere in the world. This is a highly inspirational and engaging book on the success of a rich man. The words are superb and the narrative is engaging. This is a very motivating successful story of a focused man with a purpose and goal in his lifetime,"

---Gloria Espinosa, Adjunct Professor, Dominican University, River Forest, Illinois, USA.

"As a Haitian-American, I believe that black people are the same all over the world, whether in the Caribbean, Latin America, Asia and of course, in Africa the Motherland. It is a thing of joy to hear that a black person, who lives in the south of the Sahara, is now the richest black person in the world. This shows that hard work and focus do pay for anyone, who applies him or herself to the timeless principle of business success; irrespective of where one may be living in any corner of the world. Who knows, a black person may soon emerge as the richest person in the world. A must read book for every one willing to pay the price of success and achieve prosperity,"

--- *Ms. Marie Celestine, real estate broker r, Chicago, IL, USA.*

"Young Aliko Muhammad Dangote displayed signs of his future success at a very early age in life. Born in Kano City in northern Nigeria to his father, Mohammad Dangote, and to his mother, Mariya Sanusi Dantata, he demonstrated a fierce and a passionate love for learning early on. After his father's premature death when Aliko Dangote was still a young child, his maternal grandfather Sanusi Alhassan Dantata raised him. He was raised as a devout Muslim, and he thrived within the strict Islamic teachings and beliefs. His strong belief in his faith is what has shaped Mr. Aliko Muhammad into the man that he is today, and has helped to pave the way for all of his successes in becoming the richest black person in the world. Although Mr. Aliko Muhammad grew up in a very wealthy Nigerian family that has spawn the Dangote Group into a multimillion business, it was Aliko Muhammad Dangote's tenacity for hard work that made the successful Dangote Group the worldwide empire that it is today. Mr. Aliko Muhammad made his billions by knowing what the people of Nigeria and Africa needed to survive and then expanded on that concept. He eventually surpassed that basic idea, and turned the Dangote Group into one of the most prosperous companies in the world. I enjoyed the book *"Aliko Muhammad Dangote: The Richest Black Person in the World"* by authors Moshood A. Fayemiwo and Margie M. Neal. A highly recommended book...."

---*Ms. Sylvia Manning-Heslin, The Whistle Stop Child Development Center, San Jose, California, USA.*

"This is a well written chronological account of an achiever. To an enterprising young man, this is a manual for success. To me, this biographical account of Mr. Aliko Muhammad Dangote is a rich blend of art and entertainment, literature work, motivation and bout of challenge for the diverse readers of the book. This is more than the usual compilation of series of events in the life of the richest black person in the world, but a unique departure from stereotyped biographies. It is abundantly clear that though Mr. Dangote had a rich heritage of industry, influence, wealth and power bequeathed on him, he chose his own path to greatness. Dangote is an embodiment of timeless quality principles and character as shared by great men and women living or dead that commanded the world attention and endeared them to the vast number of the world population. Driven by passion to add value to human existence, he moved in different economic ambience to better the lots of the world around him. He came across as someone adequately prepared for every opportunity for success and maximized it. He saw opportunities and wealth where others saw obstacles and lack. His foresight and depth in commerce is unparalleled, passion and resilience in face of challenges commendable and these aren't learnt in the four walls of a school. He is a testimony of ambition, plan, team-work, value creation and fulfillment. A world proof that Africa, and Nigeria is blessed with savvy and world-class professionals, who have moved beyond their skin color, ethnic divide, geographical location and common mediocrity as global citizens in a globalized economy"

--- Mr. Olanrewaju Daodu, Principal Consultant, Megaminds Concept Group, and Regional Representative, Alternative Lifestyle Communication Nigeria Limited, Lagos, Nigeria.

"Aliko Dangote became the richest black person in the world, despite the fact that he didn't grow up with his mother. He was able to live freely with his extended maternal family members that nurtured and brought him up. He believed in delayed gratification and was never carried away by immediate gains, but by the future gains which he discovered as a result of his focus on his vision. Young Aliko discovered that life is an adventure, and therefore focused on his passion at an early age. He was able to leverage his ideas with mentors around him. His ability to identify problems and provide solutions gave him the reward of a lifetime for a job well done. He was able to face all the business challenges that he encountered, because he believes that for one to be successful in life, one should give to life rather than expect from life. If everyone could follow these simple steps, one could predict his or her success depending on our input. I urge everyone to practice success today and make it a habit, because being successful is never an act; it is what we do continuously just like young Aliko practiced. This book is another source of knowledge one needs to seek to know the experience of starting small and thinking big"

---Mr. Richard Opeyemi Fayemiwo, Head, Northern Operations, Alternative Lifestyle Communication Nigeria Limited, Abuja, Lagos, Nigeria.

"Perhaps more than any other Nigerian, billionaire businessman Aliko Mohammed Dangote represents the possibilities of entrepreneurial excellence and industry by citizens of a country often regrettably discussed in terms of her unfulfilled potentials. In this biography of "the richest black person in the world" Moshood Ademola Fayemiwo and Margie Marie Neal unravel the historical and everyday circumstances that have shaped the extraordinary career of an African businessman and sometimes controversial political player. In turns journalese and scholarly, this revealing book is a remarkable addition to the genre of biography which is often abused on the one hand by Africa's influential politicians and businessmen anxious to rewrite history in their favor, and on the other by authors eager to cash in on their vanity"

--Nduka Otiono, (PhD), Banting Postdoctoral Fellow, Institute of African Studies, Carleton University, Ottawa, ON, Canada.

"With the journalism background of one of the authors, there is no doubt this is a good book about Aliko Mohammad Dangote, the richest black person in the world..."

---Kalu Ogbaa (PhD), Professor, Department of English, Southern Connecticut University, New Haven Connecticut, USA and author of "General Ojukwu, the legend of Biafra."

"ALIKO (MOHAMMAD) DANGOTE, AGE; 54: The Nigerian businessman's fortune surged 557% in the past year, making him the world's biggest gainer in percentage terms and Africa's richest individual...with fortune worth $13.8billion..."

—FORBES MAGAZINE, NEW YORK, USA, 2011

The history of the *Forbes* magazine, which has become synonymous with wealth creation and celebration of the rich, began as an idea in 1917. The son of a local tailor and a Scottish immigrant, Mr. Bertie

Charles Forbes, born in 1880, left his native Scotland, first for South Africa in 1901, and later for New York, the United States, in 1904. He got a job with the *Hearst* newspapers as a columnist, covering finance and banking, industry, marketing, taxes, science and technology, transportation, communications, investments and entrepreneurship. After making a name for himself as a popular columnist, he left his employers at the height of World War I to start his own publication. Everyone was surprised that he wanted to take a plunge into the tempestuous terrain of publishing a magazine at such a time of uncertainty. He replied that was the real reason he wanted to start the publication: to teach people how to survive during periods of economic uncertainty. He started the publication as a bi-weekly for 15 cents per copy in 1917. He wrote all the stories himself, usually in large print. Most of the editorials were just quotes and sayings of rich men and women; on how to make money, on how to survive a hostile economic climate and on how to earn a living during periods of war. The publication, which is 96 years old today, is read by nearly 10 million readers and subscribers all over the world. The United States Publishers Information Bureau ranked it the 14th largest magazine in the world and the fourth in the United States. The Audit Bureau of Circulation (ABC) ranked it among Top 25 Magazines in the world for 2011. Mr. Malcolm Stevens Forbes, Sr. took over the magazine from his father. He piloted the publishing outfit to an even higher level and ceded the stage to his son, Malcolm Stevenson Forbes, Jr. (1947-). Steve Forbes, Jr., who succeeded his father, began the Magazine's Lists of the World's Billionaires and other similar lists in 1982.

Why is the *Forbes* magazine so authoritative, definitive and credible? It has never been sued by any reader for libelous publication in nearly a century of its existence. It has never retracted a story or editorial, except errata and corrigenda. It is the publication adjudged as the best for discovering investment opportunities in the world. With nearly one million copies in circulation as at June, 2012, the bi-weekly is one of the most successful family-owned companies in the world. Its annual revenues exceed $370 million a year, according to the *Advertising Age Listing* for the year 2004. The more than nine-decade old magazine has survived some of its competitors and emerged as finalist for the United States National Magazine Award in 1993. It is the only specialized business publishing company in the world with publishing editions in China, Korea, Russia, Dubai, Israel, Poland, and Turkey and of recent, Africa. The total assets of the global media empire are more than $1billion. The aim of Mr. Bertie Charles Forbes was to celebrate business success and financial triumph over adversities and vicissitudes of life. His grandson has remained true to that mission for 96 years. In 2010, the magazine, in its Annual Lists of the World's Billionaires published in 2011 declared

Mr. Aliko Mohammad Dangote of Nigeria, the richest person in Nigeria, the richest person in West Africa, and the richest person in Africa. With personal fortune estimated at $13.8bn, Mr. Aliko Mohammad Dangote of Nigeria is now the richest black person in the world. Although his fortune fell to $11.3 billion in 2012, he is still the richest black person in the world since Mr. Ibrahim Al-Amoudi worth $12.5 billion in 2012 prefers to claim Saudi Arabian citizenship even though he was born in Ethiopia.

This is the authoritative biography of Mr. Aliko Mohammad Dangote, the richest person in Nigeria, the richest person in West Africa, the richest person in Africa, and the richest black person in the world.

ALIKO MOHAMMAD
DANGOTE

THE BIOGRAPHY
OF THE
RICHEST BLACK PERSON
IN THE WORLD

MOSHOOD ADEMOLA FAYEMIWO
and
MARGIE MARIE NEAL

Strategic Book Publishing and Rights Co.

Book Design/Layout by Kalpart. Visit www.kalpart.com

Strategic Book Publishing and Rights Co.
12620 FM 1960, Suite A4-507
Houston TX 77065
www.sbpra.com

ISBN: 978-1-62516-808-5

Cover Photos: Courtesy of the Authors
Cover Design: Kit Foster, London, UK

First Edition: - 2013

E-Book available
Authors' Website: www.allternativecommunication.com

DEDICATION

For every human being – white or black, male or female, young or old-out there working to transform the world, this book is dedicated to you. As Aliko Muhammad Dangote has succeeded, you too will succeed with hard work, perseverance and strong determination.

Do not give up.

Note: The authors did not solicit for, and neither were they commissioned, compromised, induced in whatever form, nor offered financial assistance of any kind; either by Mr. Aliko Mohammad Dangote, his associates or any of his companies to write this book. This is a well-researched work voluntarily undertaken by the authors in Africa, between October, 2010 and January 2012 as anunbiased narrative of the story of Aliko Mohammad Dangote, the richest black person in the world.

Contents

Acknowledgements

EVERY LIVING human being on earth wants to be rich. That is a legitimate demand. But unfortunately not every person living on planet earth is rich and will be rich. Some may say everyone is rich, as long as a person has access to food, clothing and shelter; the rest are mere additions. But when we say someone is rich, the assumption is that the person has surpassed the acquisitions of the three basic necessities of life as elementary as food, clothing and shelter. There are tons of books, lectures and "theories" out there about how people can become rich. In all these literatures, certain basic "truths" run through them all and the application of these "truths" work for anyone who applies them in any environment; be it, in the United States of America, India, Australia, Russia, Asia, Europe, Africa or Nigeria. Mr. Aliko Mohammad Dangote discerned very early in his early 20's the efficacies of these global truths and applied them in his business. Today he has emerged the richest Nigerian, the richest African and the richest black person on planet earth. During our field work and research in Africa for this biography, we discovered these laws of making money which Mr. Dangote put to use to become the richest black person in the world.

The first law of making money and becoming a rich person is through God's guidance and blessing. Aliko Dangote has never failed to credit God for his success in life. There are several millionaires and billionaires in history, who have openly confessed the power of God in their business successes. These God-fearing rich men and women conduct their businesses strictly along their religious convictions and live by Godly precepts. For example, Mr. David Green, the Oklahoma-based billionaire, who is *Forbes* number 382th billionaire in the world worth

US$2.0 billion, would readily tell you that, if not for the blessing of God in his life, he would not be where he is today and he was right. How could a man begin a business with just $600 loan in 1972 just like Aliko Dangote did in 1977 and both worked their ways into becoming billionaires, if not by divine blessing? Green's business; *Hobby Lobby* involves just knocking pieces of discarded junks together and rebuilding them. Today, he has 360 retail stores scattered all over the United States and has diversified into other business ventures producing Christian movies through his son, Mart. His companies refuse to affix bar codes into their re-tooled and re-packaged arts, and also do not use middlemen and women but deal directly with customers. Like Mr. Dangote who supports many religious organizations in Nigeria, West Africa and around the world, the Greens give generously to Christian causes. Mr. Mart Green once said; "The 'why' of the existence of every one on earth is to prepare each and every one of us for eternity."

The same is true of Mr. Philip Anschutz, the Texas oil magnate, estimated by the *Forbes* magazine to be worth US$7.5 billion. Mr. Anschutz lives in Colorado and ranked as the 41st richest man in America. He lives his Christian values and opposition to evolution. Called "Billionaire Christian," he hasn't granted a press interview in more than 30 years. As his close friend, Jim Monaghan told Mark Moring of *Christianity Today* magazine, "Philip's set of values and beliefs permeate his life. He is a composite of religious values, ethics, and morals, but he doesn't wear it on his sleeve. He walks the talk."

In every forum where the secret of success comes up, Aliko acknowledges the Hand of God as his pillar. According to him; "You could be at the very top today, and the next day you are at the low places. We don't pray for that, but in case it happens, it will not be difficult to adjust." Some of today's rich men and women do not know that whatever they are today, it is God that has made them. As they say in Nigeria; "No condition is permanent." One African-American/black millionaire forgot this timeless principle in the 1990s after he made millions of dollars as a boxer. He bought fleet of limousine cars, often surrounded with bevy of bodyguards and hangers-on, spending lavishly. But he became arrogant and his millions of dollars (he wasn't even a billionaire), entered into his head. One day in the streets of New York City, he held bundles of the greenbacks for all to see and said tongue-in-cheeks; "Where is God now?" That was his downfall. Today the boxer millionaire is bankrupt. Aliko knows that without God, he would not be where he is today. In his speeches, he confesses God's favor in his life. In his lifestyle, he lives prudently, and his commitment to his religion bears eloquent testimony to this God- consciousness and the fear of the Holy One in all his undertakings.

The legendary American oil magnate, and unarguably the greatest philanthropist in American history and the founder of the Rockefeller Foundation; Mr. John D. Rockefeller Sr. (1839-1937) once confessed he would not have been able to amass his several billion dollar fortunes without the strength and power that God gave him. "I believe that the power to make money is a gift from God Almighty," he once said. Aliko Dangote owes all his successes in life to God, as he too once said; "I am a very prayerful person, I believe so much in God but you also have to condition your mind as a business person and know that today I can make quite a lot of money and tomorrow I can lose quite a lot of money."

In order to succeed in business, time is not a factor when it comes to turn-around and profit-making or financial break-through. Yes, it is good to begin at a small pace but if you are manufacturing a product or providing a service, you can make profit beyond your wildest dreams if your potential customers or clients trust you and patronize you. Thus, the second law of making money, plenty of it as the story of Mr. Dangote shows, is to know how to read events and trends instead of waiting on time.

Take a look at the amazing story of Mr. Jerry Yang, the Taiwanese immigrant brought to the United States as a 10-year old after his father died when he was a 2- year old. Born in 1967 and brought to the U.S. by his mother from Taipei, his mother was a teacher of theater arts and drama at San Jose, California when Jerry was growing up. When the young man discovered his greatest invention which over 200 million human beings use around the globe today-(www.yahoo.com)-Yang left Stanford University, Palo Alto, California and within four years (1996-2000), the young man was worth $3billion. In just four years! The Internet search engine which he co-founded with David Filo, his colleague at Stanford is worth $20billion today while Filo too has amassed a personal fortune of $3billion according to the *Forbes* list of world billionaires. *Yahoo* turned out successfully that it turned its young founders into billionaires. The two inventors made $3billion each in just four years.

Mr. George Soros, the Hungarian-American philanthropist, hedge fund investor and author made $1.1 billion in one investment in one day: Wednesday September 16, 1992. As he told Fareed Zakaria on *CNN/GPS*, no human being can predict the future, but smart people can and do predict certain trends in life. Time is not a big deal in changing life's fortunes. Aliko Dangote's fortunes increased by 544% between 2008 and 2011 to emerge the richest black person in the world at a time many rich men and women and billionaires of the world were losing money. Time is not what makes people rich, rather God's mercy and blessing on the product or service being offered to the public. The ability to read predictable trends and events in life is also crucial in the secrets of money-making.

The second law is tied to another sub-law called discernment. This is the ability to know what is happening around you. Information is life. Those who have the latest information, whether in formal or informal formats are always above the rest. As this biography would show, Aliko Dangote may not be a PhD holder, but he was certainly ahead of the curve of his contemporaries while in his early twenties to leave Kano City for Lagos, Nigeria's administrative and political capital for three decades because, he knew that was where the political and business activities were happening in Nigeria. Even today, he chooses to stay in this city of 21 million people; the most populous city in Africa, according to *The New York Times,* and the seventh fastest growing city in the world, because of the high purchasing power of its inhabitants. Today, all his business expansion follows this principle: manufacturing is the future of Africa and the continent must look inwards. With incandescent fervor for the continent's economic development, he believes importation is a headwind for the Nigerian nay African economy. In all his investments, he tells the various governments in the continent to come to terms with the reality that indigenous entrepreneurship is the way to Africa's industrialization. As Nobel Peace Laureate and Kenyan political activist, the late Ms. Maathai once said, "It is important to nurture new ideas and initiatives which can make a difference for Africa." Aliko began these new ideas and initiatives about twenty years ago.

Right now, there are many economic areas and business opportunities in Africa literally waiting to be "exploited" by smart business men and women which would create millions of jobs for able-bodied young African men and women. Unfortunately, many African business men and women are afraid, or aren't convinced about the success of such business ventures. They are afraid to take risks. But life is a risk. As *Virgin* megabrand founder, Rebel Billionaire and recipient of United Nations 2007 Citizen of the Year Award, Richard Branson, who made substantial profits from his business investments in Africa, told *TIME,* every business investment is a risk. "In the end, though, you've got to take calculated risks, otherwise, you're going to sit in mothballs all day and do nothing. Life is a helluva lot more fun if you say yes rather than no." Hear Mr. Dangote; "Nigeria is really the best place to invest. It is one of the best places to make money. You know, all over the world it is the best kept secret actually in terms of investment." But you may chuckle and snigger; "Oh yes, that's good to say when you are the richest black business man in the world and have the billions!" But Mr. Raymond Ackerman, the South African businessman, who was fired at *Checkers* Stores and used his severance pay to set up the renowned *Pick "N" Pay* Chain Stores also agreed with Mr. Dangote. According to Mr. Ackerman; "Building a successful business requires ninety percent guts and ten percent capital. I happen to be a great believer in family-controlled businesses. There aren't enough of them around anymore," in an interview with Dave Marrs of South Africa's *Business Day.*

It was the power of discernment to know that information is life that made Mr. Rupert Murdoch to enter into the US media market with *Fox News* Corporation in 1979 and currently rakes in more than $33.405 billion in revenue. Mr. Murdoch has provided alternative news platform to the left-leaning American media through the *Fox News* Corporation. That decision has led to the birth of the second largest media empire in the world next to the *BBC* with such conservative programs as, the *O'Reilly Factor, Hannity, On the Record with Greta* and others, which have enriched America's market place of ideas, thereby deepening our democracy. No matter your ideological persuasion, there is no dismissing the obvious that the *Fox News* Corporation has succeeded in creating alternative view points on socio-economic and political issues in America.

The third law of making money that Mr. Dangote put to use in Africa is the strong desire to create a need or a service. "I feel great. I'm feeling fulfilled that at least you are doing something great for your country," Aliko said when asked of his business success. As this biography would show, those who have made their marks in the world of business, either in the United States, Europe, Asia or Africa or any part of the world, did not have money as their primary motivation. No one can make a billion US dollars by mere wishing for it. As Aliko Dangote's story would show, every creative, smart and innovative business man or woman thinks of conceiving an idea and when that idea materializes, the reward for that idea in most times is financial success. When you think of Mr. Bill Gates, your mind goes to computers. Each time you see *Wal-Mart* where does your mind go? Back in Nigeria, every stupendously rich person is identified with a service, an idea that blossoms and becomes a household name. We are not talking of fraudulent business men and women here. We are talking of few African manufacturers and service providers.

Ideas are everywhere, new ideas or improvement on existing ideas; but it takes instincts, guts and risks to experiment with old or new ideas. No one epitomizes this risk-taking in the 20th century than Mr. Richard Warren Sears, founder of the *Sears* retail stores. To be sure, he was not the inventor of mail order marketing in the United States but he popularized it in 1898 as he watched the cosmopolitan changes taking place in American towns and cities. That innovative improvement to retailing became the marketing strength of *Sears*. Mr. Sears saw a need to meet the demand of rail workers who didn't have the time to waste in retail stores and met that need through mail order marketing full of coupons. His re-innovated idea has become fashionable today.

The fourth law is saving and prudence. Saving is keeping a portion of one's money aside periodically for future rainy day. Every religion admonishes sensible human beings to cultivate the habit of saving. There is a popular African saying that; "any wise person who wants to be financially-successful in life would not eat with all ten fingers." The fourth richest man in the world, Mr. Warren Buffett counsels that regular cultivation of the habit of saving and the inculcation of same mindset to kids is one of the secrets of success and one of the laws of money-making. Elisabeth "Liz" Claiborne, the Belgian-American entrepreneur, invented the famous Claiborne suit for women in New York in 1976, which later grossed over 5billion in sales, with a $50,000 start-up capital from her savings as chief designer for Youth Guild for 15 years. Liz Claiborne Inc., which changed its name to Fifth & Pacific Companies Inc. in May 2012 later, branched into perfumes, accessories and other sartorial alternatives for women. It currently trades on the New York Stock Exchange with over 15,000 employees and $301m annual revenues.

Allied to the habit of saving is the virtue of prudence in money-making and management. Prudence is a virtue that is necessary, not only in the conduct of our individual lives, but also in the lives of great business men and women and the supra-rich people of the world. At the level of personal life, prudence is accomplished by simply being cautious about the choices we make, the company we keep, and discretions on major fundamental issues of life, which dictate and impact on the trajectories of people's lives. Self-control is one of the virtues of prudence. It teaches people how to manage one's money and what belongs to others. Prudence dictates individual behaviors in society. Some people do not know that the persona of a business person reflects on the business as well as the product offered for sale or the type of service (s) offered the public or customers. Some people lack self-restrain in money management and consumption.

In many consumer nations of the world, some people value the worth of their lives by the amount of material things they own: the latest automobile, house furniture, wears and apparels, labor-saving devices at home, electronic stuffs and the like. Recall the lack of prudence on the parts of the top executives of the Texas-based *Enron* Energy Corporation led by the late Mr. Kenneth Lay of Texas? Remember how Bernie Madoff of New York made off with billions of investor's money, which he surreptitiously diverted into personal use: arts works, yachts, exotic automobiles and outrageously expensive mansions and chateaux in Florida, New York and other places? It was lack of prudence that led these men and many others crashed their careers and inflict sorrows and miseries on themselves and others. As the Italians wisely say in an old proverb; "He that has no prudence has nothing at all."

Developing a brand for a product or a service is a herculean task, which involves long years of preparation, sacrifice and needed prudence on the parts of all the stakeholders involved in building a brand name. However, just as it takes prudence to maintain customer's loyalty, so also the lack of prudence can destroy a brand name. It took prudence for Mr. Bezos and nearly a decade to nurture his "baby;" Amazon -the online retail giant- into a household name today in more than 183 countries. He believes prudence as a virtue is essential to keep the brand in its number one position because; "A brand for a company is like a reputation for a person. You earn reputation by trying to do hard things well." Prudence teaches a business person how to invest, where and when? Prudence also teaches how to juggle your business life with your other equally important commitments: family, your loved ones, your health and keeping your promises to others. The Creator (or Nature, pick your choice) - has given each of us the same 24 hours daily time allocation during our brief sojourn on earth. It's up to each of us to use these hours judiciously and productively. Prudence teaches people how to multi-task and achieve their life goals.

When Mr. Jobs, the late co-founder of *Apple* Computers bounced back in 1997 after he was eased out of the company he co-founded with Steve Wozniak, he wanted his alter-ego as a successor. He wanted someone who would also complement him, so he went for Tim Cook, an Alabama native. Cook became the chief executive officer who woke up at 4.30am every day, first by sending email to all sectional heads at the company and then planning ahead. To keep the company in its global dominant position, Tim, unlike Steve was the policy and administrative wonk of the company as a *Forbes* reporter noted; "Cook – or anyone else for that matter – is unlikely to be able to mirror Jobs' presence. However, the industry view of Cook is as an intelligent and capable leader. The consensus is that, under Cook, *Apple* is in good hands." Jobs' health had been a major concern on the future of *Apple* but with Cook at the helms, a San Francisco reporter believed that; "Like the Wizard of Oz, Jobs tries his best to hide behind a curtain, keeping a tight rein on media access and dealing harshly with friends who say too much to biographers," but Cook used the virtue of prudence to concentrate on what was essential most in the company. Those observations were made less than 24 months to Steve's death. But how did prudence help Tim keep things in proper perspective at *Apple*? Mr. Cook disclosed his secret this way: "We believe in saying no to thousands of projects so that we can really focus on the few that are truly important and meaningful to us." The two words: important and meaningful, are the keys.

Prudence entails punctuality, ability to exploit enterprising attitude for success, native intelligence, purposefulness, perseverance and the spirit of not giving up in the face of multitudes of adversities. Prudence builds professionalism, optimism, inventiveness, versatility, tolerance, sociability, agility, efficiency, patience and responsibility. As will be seen in the biography of Mr. Dangote, the virtue of prudence permeates his entire business conglomerate.

The fifth law is hard work. According to Aliko; "Passion is what drives me forward. Passion is what makes me go to bed at 2am and wake up at 6am." Billionaires work harder than the rest of us, contrary to some views that since they are stupendously rich, they loaf around and enjoy their billions. Real hard work is what drives many of the world's billionaires –now we do not include African military generals and politicians who made their money by dipping their hands into the pubic till-but we are talking of renowned business people of the world. Billionaires work harder than the rest of us, because they have conditioned themselves that way. They take pleasure in hard work, because that was how they began, so working hard is second nature to them. In his autobiography; *Losing My Virginity*, Sir Branson explained his life story;

"I was dyslexic, I had no understanding of school work whatsoever. I certainly would have failed IQ test. And it was one of the reasons I left school when I was 15 years old. And if I –if I'm not interested in something I don't grasp it." Branson explained that hard work was the secret to his success and coupled with enjoying what you are doing while doing it. So it is with Aliko Dangote, the richest black person in the world. To him; "Hard work counts quite a lot in business but at the same time you have to have luck and divine favor. Because if you don't have luck and divine favor, whatever you touch might turn out to be bad." He should know as the epitome of financial success!

The sixth law of creating great, and long –lasting wealth and attaining financial success in life is to live a life of contentment and simplicity. Aliko once said; "I am just being myself, it does not matter if you have a dollar or a million; life is very transient." Most of the billionaires in the world live by this principle. Mr. Jim C. Walton is worth $16.4billion. One of the three Walton's on the *Forbes* list of world's billionaires but he drives a 15-year old Dodge Dakota truck, a practice of simplicity he inherited from his late father, Mr. Sam Walton, the billionaire founder of *Wal-Mart*. Mr. Ingvar Kamprad, the Swedish billionaire worth $33billion and founder of *Ikea*-one of the largest producers of merchandize and household items in the world-does not fly first class. He drives his native country's most favorite automobile, a 1993 *Volvo*. He and his family have cultivated the habit of eating at home in a modest living room furnished only with the family's household furniture. When the family eats out, which is rare, they dine only in lower-tiers eateries and take-away.

It is said of Mr. Azim Premji, the $11.2 billion worth Indian billionaire that he drove a fairly-used Ford Escort automobile for eight years before he traded it in for a new Toyota Corolla. Premji, who inherited a small and fairly-successful cooking oil company from his father expanded it and used modern technology to turn it into what is today known as *Wipro*. He also inherited the frugal lifestyle of his deceased father. At the beginning of the business, Azim refused to ride a car, but preferred to walk from his house, which is just a stone throw to his factory. When asked by Indian journalists why he preferred to walk rather than ride a car, the billionaire replied he did not see any need for an automobile. When he travels, he flies economy, refuses to wear designer suits and shoes; and prefers to lodge in cheap but neat motels. He insisted guests should use paper plates to eat few years ago at his son's - Rishad's- wedding and those not ready to do so should kindly leave the wedding ceremony. Some call Azim Mr. Parsimonious billionaire but Mr. Premji is not bothered, insisting he would not allow his billions to change his usual and original simple lifestyle. "Here at *Wipro,* we don't have differentiation," he explained his lifestyle to David Smith of *The Guardian* of London. "It keeps you in touch with reality. I think there are too many chief executives who've completely lost their sense of reality and live in a different world. Their whole opportunity is in the developing world, which is completely stripped down in terms of standards of living as compared to the western world. How do they get in touch with reality?"

When Messrs. Sergey Brin and Larry Page, founders of the phenomenally successful world Internet giant; *Google* were looking for a venture capitalist to invest in their dream while at Stanford University, Palo Alto California as undergraduates in the late 1990s, they approached one of their professors, David Cheriton, who took the two "boys" to Kleiner Perkins, owners of *Caulfield & Byers.* The rest, as they say, is history. But Cheriton got $1.4billions from his former students in stocks as the "linkman" after *Google* became a success story. You would think the college professor would paint the university campus red every day. Not him! Mr. Cheriton did not allow the billions to change his normal lifestyle. He still prefers to ride his bike regularly on campus, in addition to keeping his 1993 Honda Accord car, and his 1986 Volkswagen Camper. He still lives in his 1981 house in Palo Alto,

California and says he doesn't want to waste money by going to a barber to cut his hair. Mr. Cheriton told *The Edmonton Journal* in his native Alberta, Canada in an interview during a vacation there in 2006; "These people who build houses with 13 bathrooms and so on, there's something wrong with them. I've kind of clung on to working with the people I like working with, and teaching and research and riding my bicycle and driving my ratty old cars. It may sound a little corny, but I feel like I definitely come from that background of the ordinary person."

Across the Atlantic, another billionaire lives exactly like Professor Cheriton. When asked why he cuts his own hair, buys his clothes at British retailers; *Marks & Spencer* and will not drink a three-figure wine, Mr. John Caudwell, the British billionaire worth $2.6billion, explained to Gary Parkinson of *The Independent* of London he liked frugal and simple lifestyle. "If you throw money around like confetti, it just becomes shallow and meaningless. I think it's almost a balance. If you don't have the bad life, how can you recognize the good? It's not tightness; it's about value for money. I don't like paying too much for anything or wasting it. I think that I'm more of a balanced individual rather than a dichotomy." Mr. Caudwell made his money as a former auto-repair shop owner and engineer to *Michelin Tire* Corporation. In 1987, he switched to cell-phone business-the *Caudwell* Group. The list of billionaires who live simple lives is endless.

The seventh and last law of money making is the spirit of charity and giving. Some people are rich, but pretend the money is given to them to hoard, as if they would take the wealth to heaven after their deaths. Real rich people display the spirit of charity. They give to several worthy causes and Mr. Dangote fulfills this law to the letter. His greatest wish in life according to him is to leave a worthy legacy. "After my death, I want to be remembered as Africa's greatest industrialist (and a generous giver too)." As John D. Rockefeller Sr. foremost American industrialist, the greatest philanthropist of his day and the founder of the oil company, *Standard Oil Company*, USA once said; "God gave me my money. I believe the power to make money is a gift from God Almighty to be used and to be developed to the best of our ability for the good of mankind. Having been endowed with the gift I possess, I believe it is my duty to make money and still make money and to use the money for the good of my fellow man according to the dictates of my conscience."

The reason rich people open up their hands to supporting others not as fortunate as they are and other worthy causes, is the satisfaction it gives when they see the impact of their generous hearts in the lives of others. Many rich people of the world did not have the overriding motive of making money itself when they set out to actualize their dreams. As Mr. Donald Trump, the New York real estate mogul and founder of the popular and successful TV show *The Apprentice* once said about money-making; "Money was never a big motivation for me, except as a way to keep score. The real excitement is playing the game." Mr. Ted Turner, the founder of the Cable News Network (*CNN*) and member of the elite *Forbes* world's list of billionaires worth $2billion confessed that it is not easy to cultivate the habit of generosity. According to the Atlanta, Georgia native; "Over a three- year period, I gave away half of what I had. To be honest, my hands shook as I signed it away. I knew I was taking myself out of the race to be the richest man in the world."

Paradoxically, the areas that wealthy people were greatly disadvantaged while growing up often become their passions when they become financial success. Take the late Mr. Walter Annenberg for example. He was a college drop-out from the University of Pennsylvania; while he was growing up and was pained he couldn't finish his university education. When he was 32 years old his late father, Mr. Moses Annenberg left him with a shambolic publishing company, the *Triangle Publications* which was in the red. It was one of the causes for Walter dropping out of college. At his father's death in 1942, his other seven siblings told him they did not want to have anything to do with the comatose company their deceased father left behind. Walter was the first born and only son. He had no requisite education to run newspapers, yet he plunged into the comatose business and somehow employed native intelligence to turn around the fortunes of the newspapers his father was publishing: *the Philadelphia Inquirer* and the *Daily Racing Form*. The two publications survived the Great Depression and the kerfuffle of World War II. The college drop-out soon became a successful publisher and added two other publications; *Seventeen* and *TV Guide* to the two publications he inherited from his father. He managed the company profitably for 28 years and decided to sell them in 1988 to the *Knight Rider* Company and the *Fox News* Corporation for $8billion. That automatically shut Annenberg into the *Forbes* list of world billionaires.

Now with his personal fortune estimated at $4.2 billion, he remembered his upbringing. He remembered how he dropped out of college for lack of money and vowed no one would pass through the same ordeal he went through. He went back to the University of Pennsylvania and donated nearly a billion dollars to build the university's College of Information and Journalism School named after him. He did the same at the University of Southern California at San Diego, which was also appropriately named after him. By the time he died in October 2002 at his home in New York City at the age of 94, Annenberg had given away nearly all his fortunes for the promotion of education, including generous donations to the United Negro Fund of America and the New York's Metropolitan Museum of Art, the nation of Israel and numerous worthy causes.

These laws of money-making, attaining business success and riches are not by anyway inexhaustible, but as we pored over tons of books, examined the statements and speeches of Mr. Dangote and analyzed the messages we gathered from our various interviewees, these seven laws of money making according to Mr. Aliko Mohammed

Dangote emerged. You too can apply these laws into your business and you will be amazed at their resounding success. According to the American prolific author, writer, motivational speaker, and was once described as one of the most well-known and thought-provoking motivational experts in the world, Mr. Brian Tracy, in his 2001 best seller; *"The 21 Success Secrets of Self-Made Millionaires: How to Achieve Financial Independence Faster and Easier Than You Ever Thought Possible,"* disclosed, making millions and becoming a billionaire has nothing to do with skin color, how you were born, or where you live in any part of the world. What makes a person successful in business are the things that people do. "If you consistently and persistently do the things that other successful people do, nothing in the world can stop you from being a big success also," he said. Tracy, a dynamic and an inspirational speaker and one of the leading experts on how people could harness their natural endowments and human potential for success has been invited to address employees and top executives of famous corporations like the *IBM, Arthur Andersen* and many more. He has also authored best-selling books and earnestly believes human beings can harness their God-given talents anywhere in the world and achieve business / financial success.

In writing the first authoritative biography of Mr. Dangote, we owe a lot of people and corporations our gratitude and appreciation. As usual and normal with every creative work we have written, we begin by giving thanks to God Almighty for His inspiration and blessing. It was God Almighty who put the idea into our minds as far back as 2008 when we read the *Forbes* magazine where Mr. Dangote became the first Nigerian to be listed in the magazine's list of world billionaires. We knew the rate at which the man was going in his business pursuits, sooner or later, the world would notice him and be attracted to his wealth, but we did not know he would one day become the richest person in Nigeria, Africa and richest black person in the world. Dangote's achievement is not a small achievement. It is very difficult for Africans to garner international accolade and recognition in their home land until they get to the Western world. Indeed, the proverbial saying that prophets have no honor in their land is very true of Africans, but Dangote's success has demystified this saying. He did not tag-along any multinational corporation to achieve financial success, but built his business empire from the scratch. Every black person and human being anywhere in the world should be extremely proud of this Nigerian, a great African, and an exceptional business man.

Thanks to Mrs. Aisha Hamza-Otokunrin in Abuja who assisted with the legal paper works for our American company to be licensed in Nigeria. Barrister Kunle Fadipe, Moshood's classmate and friend of over thirty years from the University of Lagos opened his office and house for our use during our time in Nigeria to conduct interviews with important stake-holders for this book. Dr Jimmy Imo of Wake Forest, North Carolina and Moshood had co-researched a book together in the past and is hereby acknowledged. Mr. Israel Ojimadu, a young Nigerian-American business man based in Raleigh, North Carolina has always been a source of support and inspiration for some of our publications and we continue to remain grateful to him. We also wish to thank Mr. Wole Olaoye, the chief executive of Diametric Nigeria Limited Abuja, who remains a good friend and senior professional colleague over the years. We thank him for his hospitality in Abuja, Nigeria.

While Moshood was publishing a samizdat magazine in the 1990s during the years of military dictatorship in Nigeria, there was a Nigerian woman activist; Ms. Alice Ukoko, an attorney and human rights activist living in London, UK who forged a personal relationship. This brave and courageous lady was instrumental in bringing Moshood's plight to global attention when he was detained at the dreaded directorate of military intelligence (DMI) detention center, Apapa, Lagos. At personal risk to her life, she traveled to Rome, Italy in 1997 to deliver a letter to the late Pope John Paul II and bombarded the Amnesty

International (AI), London, UK with paper work and photographs depicting the horrible living conditions of numerous political detainees herded in several prisons and detention cells in Nigeria during the Abacha military dictatorship. She was one of those outspoken Nigerians living overseas whose heroic efforts were instrumental to the visit of the late Pope John Paul II to Nigeria in summer 1998 to plead for the release of many Nigerian political detainees. She and Moshood have remained friends ever since and her visit from the UK to Abuja, Nigeria during the research for this book was very encouraging.

Thanks to Femi Fayemiwo, Moshood's son at Southern Illinois University, Carbondale and now in the United States Marine Corps. He became a close confidante and assisted tremendously during the visits to Nigeria for this pioneering biography on Mr. Aliko Dangote. Moshood values the tremendous support of all the members of staff of Evangelical Church of West Africa (ECWA) at Wuse II, Abuja, Nigeria, especially Mr. Hamden, who showed understanding during the nearly one year stay at the guest house. Moshood deliberately chose the guest house, because of the serene atmosphere and spiritual ambience that was conducive for writing and intellectual works. Some of the moments he cherished at the guest house were the regular Sunday Worship services and spiritually-inspiring songs which ministered to his soul. Thanks Mr. Taiye Haruna, formerly, permanent secretary, political division, office of the secretary to the Nigerian government and now of the Police Service Commission for his assistance. Thanks also to Mrs. Dupe Jemibewon, Mrs. Baker of the federal ministry of information, Abuja; Malam Shagiri of the federal ministry of women's affairs and social development, Abuja and Moshood's personal assistant, Mr. Arinze Alinnor.

During the research and field works in Nigeria, Moshood was privileged to interact with some spiritual Nigerians who assisted greatly in the success of this book through their prayers. Thanks to Mr. Joseph Abashi Yaro, who taught Moshood how to be circumspect of people; Pastors

Victor Sangbuwa, David Okoror, Tajudeen Aladesawe and numerous others, who served as our spiritual backers. Thanks also to several hundreds of our prayer buddies in Nigeria, West Africa, in the United States and around the world, who stood by us during our stay in Nigeria for this important book. Special thanks to Pastor Ms. Rhoda Musa and our co-worshippers at the Triumphant Ministry International, Silver bird Parish Abuja for their prayers. We also wish to thank Mr. Steve Agada of Office Advantage, Abuja in Nigeria for teaching me how to be wary of certain promises made by human beings. We extend our sincere thanks and heartfelt appreciation to Pastor Ugochukwu Ikpeazu, the General Overseer, of Triumphant Ministry International, Nigeria for his spiritual support, and constant encouragement and backing during the field work for this book. People like him are rare in Christendom. Thanks to Hon. Ibrahim El-Sudi, member, House of Representatives in Nigeria. We thank our numerous chauffeurs in Kano, Kaduna, Zaria, Wudil, Abuja, Lagos, Port Harcourt, Yenagoa and other numerous places we visited in Nigeria during our research and field works for this book. Moshood wishes to thank his two cousins; Princess Shade Adesunloye and Princess Toyin Adesunloye in Chicago for their encouragement and also Reverend Abiodun Ajayi and Pastor Ebenezer Adedeji also in Chicago for their spiritual support, while we were out of the United States for over a year for this book.

We thank Mr. Tom Wallace of Strategic Book Publishers, Houston, Texas for believing in this project. Thanks to Lynette, Linda, Eleanor and the rest crews at AEG Publishing Group in New York, Connecticut, Florida and Texas for their assistance and suggestions. Thanks to Jenn, Bruce and Kit for their wonderful works on the production of this book. We value the useful suggestions offered by Mrs. Lou Fuentes of Trafford Publishers, Indiana to the original draft and the revisions made by our friends and colleagues.

The co-author, Margie Marie Neal, would wish to thank the following people for their tremendous assistance during her first visit to Nigeria and those who offered encouragement during the research for this book. First, my thanks, gratitude and appreciation to my Lord Jesus Christ, who brought my husband and I together in the first place, and made it possible for us to collaborate together on a work of this nature. The Lord God Almighty has sustained us through thick and thin during our relationship as husband and wife; His Grace and Providence have continued to sustain us. It has been my desire to collaborate with my husband to write books and I thank God Almighty for giving me the strength and power to be a co-author of this important book. I want to thank Prof. Lizanne Destefanno, my mentor, adviser and Doctoral chair at the University of Illinois at Urbana-Champaign whose support and encouragement in all I do have been immensely beneficial during our more than ten-year relationship. My sincere thanks and appreciation to my dedicated and loving mother; Mary A. Neal, who believed in me and encouraged, and supported me in every step of my life. Thanks Julius W. Neal for being a dedicated father. I will like to appreciate my younger sisters; Julia A. Neal and Patricia A. Neal. Thanks to my best friends; Marie Celestine and Leona Kidd-McClendon.

We thank all those who endorsed the book. If there is anyone we have failed to acknowledge, this is not deliberate but for space constraints and we plead for their understanding. As usual, all errors, inaccuracies and mistakes in this book are entirely ours.

Moshood Ademola Fayemiwo, PhD
Margie Marie Neal, Ed.D
May, 2013

PREFACE

WHY A BOOK ON ALIKO MOHAMMAD DANGOTE?

IN 1999, Moshood Fayemiwo left Nigeria with his entire family for the United States of America, immediately after his release from the military gulag of the late General Sani Abacha, Nigeria's most brutal military dictator. He had been harassed, detained, and put out of circulation for several months when he was the publisher and editor of the defunct *Razor* magazine and *Evening News* in Lagos, Nigeria between 1992 and 1999. When the fervid atmosphere became unbearable for him to continue with his most beloved profession: journalism, he was compelled to relocate to neighboring Benin Republic in the summer of 1996 after his attorney, the late Mr. Gani Fawehinmi secured his bail from the federal intelligence and investigation bureau (FIIB), at Alagbon close detention center in Ikoyi, Lagos where he had been detained for six months (February, 16 –July 28, 1996). Unbeknown to him, the murderous goons of the late military dictator traced him to Cotonou, Benin Republic, and kidnapped him back to Nigeria on Friday, February 14, 1997. He was kept in an underground military dungeon for nearly two years during the struggle for the validation of the June 12, 1993 presidential election victory of the late Mr. Moshood Abiola (see b at link http://nigeriaworld.com/feature/ article/ report1.html). The deaths of both Abacha and Abiola in summer 1998 paved the way for the emergence of Nigeria's last military dictator, General Abdulsalam Abubakar, who ordered his release and the release of other political detainees. Shortly

41

after his release, he left Nigeria with his entire family to the United States.

On arrival here in the U.S, he decided to go back to school first, in Florida and later, in New York. The first thing he noticed during his first graduate degree program at the University of South Florida in 2002 was how insular the average American is on events around the world, especially the so-called Third World countries. He could remember a graduate student of international affairs and history, who took interest in him when she learned he was from Nigeria. They eventually struck up a conversation. She discovered she had read one of his articles in one of the local newspapers in Florida but her first question surely took Moshood aback. "Is it true that most Africans sleep on trees?" Moshood's instinct told him to indulge her ignorance with such tacky question, "Yes" but quickly added; "including the United States Ambassador in Nigeria. As a matter of fact, when President Bill Clinton visited Africa in 1998, he slept on the largest and biggest mahogany tree in Africa!" The lady was flummoxed. Later Moshood took the initiative to educate her about the African continent and the African people. Of course, the ludicrous notion that some human beings sleep on top of trees in the 21st century still exists in many parts of rural America. On another occasion, an American pastor thought he was making a facetious remark when he asked Moshood at a Tampa worship center; what do you people eat in Africa? Such silly, trashy and racist remarks from provincial illiterate Americans will make any decent person throw up and I have heard such gobbledygook remarks like these in my more than a decade of traveling around the United States, mostly in the rural villages.

Many Americans, including African-Americans- black folk- still get their news about Africa and Africans from hear-says and old legends. The Western media outlets, especially the cable television unfortunately have not helped matters; some of them have become mere mega phonic outlets for projecting the worse of Africans in the West.

After Moshood left the state of Florida for New York State for further studies, and finally re-married, his African-American wife was ignorant about Africa too. Although she read world history as a minor at the State University of New York (SUNY) for her first degree and has interacted with many Africans in Chicago and around the United States, but she had never visited Africa. There were some issues she brought up about Africa and Moshood's native Nigeria at times that Moshood had to defend. But no one could blame her, because, like the average American, most of what she knew about Africa were from hear-says, old legends, and scuttlebutts still peddled by some of the Western Media. Then, the opportunity came in 2010 when Moshood was co-authoring another book about another African personality. The book project was an opportunity for Moshood's wife to accompany him to Nigeria. It was his first visit after a decade since he left his native land, and his wife's first visit to Nigeria and Black Africa. Moshood's wife was surprised about the beauty of Nigeria as they visited Lagos, a bustling commercial city of nearly 21 million inhabitants, according to *The New York Times*. They toured Ikeja, took pictures of scenic Victoria Island and serene Ikoyi, saw Port Harcourt, Rivers State, slept in Yenagoa and ate African food in Otuoke, the Nigerian president's home town in Bayelsa State. All these scenes reminded Moshood's wife of life and the geographical beauty of the Southern Region of the United States. Of course, they flew in local aircraft like in any Western nation and had a good time in Abuja, the nation's administrative capital.

From the moment she arrived in Nigeria, Moshood's mother-in-law, father-in-law and other relations, including friends back home in the United States began to call, suggesting they were apprehensive and fearful for his wife's safety in Nigeria. Text messages were pouring in warning she should be careful of her safety in Nigeria. At one point, she received a text from a friend back home in the States asking if she was being careful as she was relaxing beside a swimming pool in Nigeria enjoying herself.

Of course, everything was not right with everywhere they went in Nigeria just like any other nation in the world. There were some ugly incidents too during her nearly three weeks visit, but were a far cry from the news some Western Press feed Americans about Africa; wars, blood-letting, poverty, famine, rape, gangland activities, tears, sorrows and blood. By the time they returned back to the United States, now Moshood knew he has an ally in convincing his in-laws and others in America to change their negative views about Africa and Nigeria. The biased news being constantly fed Americans and the rest of the world by some Western Media does not reflect the objective reality of the true situation of things in the continent. That there is a war going on in a part of Africa which, by the way, is a continent of fifty-four independent nations –with South Sudan now an independent nation in July 2011-does not mean there is Armageddon in Africa. After all, a rape is committed every day in New York City, drive-by shooting is a daily occurrence in Chicago, gangland activities and other urban crimes are part of city life in Los Angeles, murders regularly occur in Detroit, Michigan and other urban cities in the United States, according to crime statistics from the Federal Bureau of Investigation, yet the United States of America is not about to crumble. In Africa, such occurrences are blown out of proportion by a section of the Western Media. Most Americans do not even know that Africa is a continent, including President George W. Bush (2000-2008), who repeatedly referred to Africa as a country throughout his eight years in office. Africa is the second largest continent in the world; bigger than North America; far bigger than Europe and Antarctica combined.

Africa is changing. The once neglected part of the world is more than the flora and fauna; the Serengeti, the beautiful weather and natural scenery. But the change that is taking place in Africa in the New Millennium is its people.

44

Today, there are more than 1 billion human beings in Africa. These human beings need food, clothing and shelter; they will need soaps, tooth brushes and creams; computers and televisions; they will need to talk to one another-in Nigeria alone, there are 170 million users of Black Berry and other cell phones. The mobile telephone business in Nigeria in the last twelve years is an explosion. In Africa, cars are in great demand, bottle water are in high demand, so are furniture, shoes, hair shampoos, books, radios, pasta, noodles, salt, candies, macaroni, spaghetti, the list is inexhaustible. In 2006, the World Bank disclosed that Africa, with $978.3 billion Gross National Income, was the tenth largest economy in the world behind the United States, Japan, Germany, China, the UK, France, Italy, Spain and Canada. That put Africa ahead of Australia, India, Brazil, New Zealand, Switzerland, the Republic of Korea, Russian Federation, Mexico and the Nordic bloc.

Take the Irish-owned *Guinness* drink for example. Its sales have plummeted so badly in Europe that more Nigerians drink *Guinness Stout* now than Irish in Ireland prompting the company to expand its operations in Africa's most populous nation, according to the company's chief executive officer, Mr. Paul Walsh in 2007. In Africa alone, 93million people drink *Coke* daily. What is happening in Africa today is what is called "consumer safari," and the West should pay attention as Prof Viyay Mahajan of the McCombs School of Business at the University of Texas, Austin disclosed in his book, "*Africa Rising: How 900 Million African Consumers Offer More Than You Think.*" China knows and the Chinese are tapping into these vast economic opportunities. The Indians too have long established their presence in Africa, so are the Japanese and Koreans with their ubiquitous low-budget vehicles and electronic products but Americans are yet to make appreciable impact in the Dark Continent. This is ironic considering the fact we, Americans are the highest aid donors to Africa next to the Nordic and the largest importers of, crude oil from Africa (we import nearly 30 percent of our 10, 270,000 barrels of daily domestic oil consumption from Africa according to the U.S Energy Information Administration).

Another thing Moshood and his wife also discovered, as they traveled across Nigeria was the age bracket of those who are shaping the future of Nigeria. Beginning with President Goodluck Jonathan, virtually all the stakeholders they interviewed were born in the 50's. It dawned on them that a new generation of leadership is beginning to emerge in Nigeria. These were young Nigerian men and women, who were in their teens when Nigeria attained political independence from the UK in 1960. This means a new generation of Nigerians are now in charge of Africa's most populous nation; young Nigerians, who are unencumbered by the problems of ethnicity, tribalism and ethnic parochial interests which wrecked Nigeria's first democratic experiment in 1966, and plunged the nation into a three-year civil war. In short, Nigeria is changing and that optimism was confirmed by the historic election of Mr. Jonathan as president on Saturday May 16, 2011. It was a pan-Nigerian mandate which did away with moth-eaten factors that had retarded Nigeria's progress for long. Perhaps, it may be a new day in Nigeria! Although fissiparous tendencies, the menace of the misanthropic radical Islamic group, *Boko Haram*, corruption, unemployment and other socio-economic crises are still dogging the nation, The sticking point is bad leadership, which fuels corruption and has chronically debilitated Nigeria since independence, but how events finally play out in Africa's most populous nation will certainly not limit the potentials of its people.

Finally, the news from the New York-based *Forbes* magazine which declared that the richest black person on earth is a Nigerian has now made Moshood's task easier. First, as a Nigerian- American desirous of correcting the negative impression of Nigeria and the African continent in the United States; second, as a proud black man, and third, as a global citizen. If the news report that Mr. Aliko Mohammad Dangote is the richest black person in the world had come from a Nigerian or an African newspaper or magazine, many Nigerians and Africans would have dismissed the report. The reason is that, in that part of the world, it is sometimes difficult to celebrate success. But the report by the highly influential and respected *Forbes* magazine has left no one in doubt that truly indeed; the richest black person on earth is an African and a Nigerian. Who knows, very soon, the richest person on earth may be an African and a Nigerian.

Africans must love to appreciate their own. They must celebrate the successes of their country men and women wherever they may be in any part of the world. It should not have taken the Nobel Academy in Oslo, Sweden to point out to Africans, and indeed Nigerians, that its own William Shakespeare in 1986 was the great African bard, Mr. Wole Soyinka. Africans and Kenyans should not have waited for the same Oslo to give them a Wangari Maatahi as the first African woman Nobel Peace Laureate in 2004. The great Nigerian writer, Chinua Achebe should be a pride to the black race anytime and anywhere in the world. As Richard John Mapomya, the South African businessman and founder/chairman, African Chamber of Commerce during apartheid regime in South Africa noted, given a chance, a black man or woman could become successful as a white man, or woman, and be acknowledged as such. In the case of Mr. Dangote's success story, he did not wait for anyone to give him any chance; rather, he created his own chance and seized it without linking up with any white man or company in the developed world. The fact of the matter is; Mr. Dangote is an autochthonous African-made richest black person in the world. This is indeed very gratifying, for, it shows Africa is coming up on its own.

This is why this book; "*Aliko Mohammad Dangote, the Biography of the Richest Black Person in the World*" was written. It is intended to celebrate a man who started from nothing, but today has achieved fame, prominence and power. But more importantly, this work is intended to look into the secrets of Dangote's success in business and how millions of young Nigerians, Africans, indeed black men and women, and white men and women too all over the world and any aspiring human being anywhere in the world can tap into what we call; "The secrets of Dangote success" (SDS) to reach the pinnacles of their careers.

As usual, all errors, omissions and inaccuracies in this book are entirely ours. We wish you happy and pleasant reading.

Moshood Ademola Fayemiwo, PhD
Chicago, IL USA.
May 2013

Margie Marie Neal, Ed.D
Chicago, IL USA
May 2013

How Materials Were Sourced

for the book: Aliko Mohammad Dangote: The Biography Of The Richest Black Person In The World

WHY DO some Africans have aversions toward African achievers and do not cultivate the habit of celebrating African greats? Why do some black people denigrate black achievers instead of holding them high for the world to see? Why are "African prophets" not celebrated at home? Why do some black people in the world continue to perpetuate the "divide and rule" tactics erected by old colonialists to bifurcate Africans in the homeland and those in the Diaspora? As the late Jamaican Reggae Artist, Peter Tosh (Winston Hubert McIntosh: 1944-1987) once sang; "Anywhere you go, as long as you are a black man, you are an African. You've got the identity of an African." Thanks to modern technology and globalization, the world is changing and Africa is changing too. Good News is coming from the African continent!

It was the famous Atlanta-based televangelist, Pastor Creflo Dollar, who once told his congregation; "Africa is changing. Forget about all those negative reports you read in the newspapers. In Africa, you see six- lane major highways, modern airports, and the last time I visited, I was chauffeur-driven from the airport in a brand new limousine." His counterpart at Oak Park in Chicago, Pastor

Bill Winston was so mesmerized by the riches of Rev. David Oyedepo that he vowed to get himself the latest jet that Mr. Oyedepo had just acquired in Lagos, Nigeria. Mr. Aliko Dangote was once the butt of scurrilous attack by some Nigerians when he said he was a billionaire by world standard before the verdict was out by the *Forbes* magazine, which declared him the richest person in Nigeria, the richest person in Africa and, going by his estimated personal fortune of $13.8 billion, the richest black person in the world. Currently, Mr. Aliko Mohammad Dangote's personal fortune is estimated at US$11.2billion (2012) but since another billionaire, Ethiopia-born Mohammed Hussein Almoudi worth $12.3 billion does not claim Ethiopian citizenship, but prefers to be a Saudi Arabian citizen, Mr. Aliko Mohammad Dangote still remains the richest person in Africa and the richest black person in the world. "This year, Aliko's fortune climbed to $16.1 billion."

But one of the major problems confronting the black race is that, some do not believe in themselves. Black people expect alternative achievement expectations about themselves, or what award-winning Pulitzer Prize Award journalist and nationally-syndicated writer, Leonard Pitts Jr. once described as; "...the same unconscious assumptions... which is that a certain level of achievement is black and another is white." Former President George Bush called it, "the soft bigotry of low expectations, "during the 2000 presidential campaign in which black people, either in the African Motherland or in Diaspora set a bar for their achievements and what they can become in life. With such self-inflicted complex, they wait for other races to validate the best and brightest among black people before Africans/blacks recognize them as great achievers.

Why do Africans have to rely on the Paris-based *France Football* magazine to tell them that the prodigiously talented Roger Mila of Cameroon for example, is the best footballer in Africa? Why do Africans have to rely, wait and be told by other races and their media, who among African women, such as Ethiopian-born, New York-based Liya Kebede,

Nigerian-born, New York-based Oluchi Onweagba, Nigerian-born, UK-based Patti Boulaye, Sade Adu, Phylicia Rashad, Halle Berry and many others, are the most beautiful women on the face of the earth? Why should the best and the brightest brains and geniuses of Africa have to be "discovered," by other races and foreign media, for Africans / blacks to appreciate their own? As Aliko Mohammad Dangote once said; he would not agree with anyone that he is a billionaire until the *Forbes* magazine declared him as one, because he knew the mentality of Africans. This is sad and must change on the part of Africans and blacks wherever they may be in any corner of the world. Africans and black people should learn to have confidence in themselves. They should celebrate the best, brightest, and finest of African achievers anywhere they may be. They should desist from running down African/black greats and that was one of the reasons this book was written.

This is a pioneering work and for this, the authors are indebted to a lot of people who made this work a reality. As many people know, most of the business men and women of the world are always busy and are constantly on the move, more so, when you are the richest person in Africa. Mr. Aliko Mohammad Dangote is a rich man and very rich indeed. He is also a very busy man and a very busy man indeed, so tracking him down for interview for his biography was difficult. We were in Nigeria and Africa for fourteen months to conduct a research on the Aliko biography. We reached out to some of his aides to get Aliko to sit down for an interview for this book but were unsuccessful. But the good news is that, the life of the man who grew up in Kano five and a half decades ago is an open book. He is such a big fish that it is impossible to "hide" the golden child of Nigerian business, so most of the accounts of the richest black person in the world were his interviews with local and world media

The authors spent a total of fourteen months in Nigeria between the fall of 2010 and the fall of 2011 and returned to the United States in winter 2012. We visited Aliko's ancestral home in ancient Kano, northern Nigeria; spoke to those who grew up with him and knew him from his formative years. In Kano, the stories and life histories of the paternal and maternal families of Aliko Dangote are stories told and re-told in the ancient city, but gathering materials on his family backgrounds were initially difficult. We received little cooperation from some members of the extended families of both the father and mother sides of Aliko Dangote, while those who cooperated and gave us information chose to remain anonymous. We had interviews with some Kano elders who knew much about the birth, parentage and formative years of young Aliko in ancient Kano in the 50's and 60's. We approached this biography from the angle of using the objective lenses of grassroots people in Kano, the birthplace of Dangote and their narratives, rather than the usual practice of conducting interviews with acolytes whose views and assessment are open to biases.

We discarded the conventional inverted pyramid approach to our interviews and field work in order to present the "real" Aliko to Nigerians, Africans and the world. A lot of research went into reading the biographies of some of the richest men and women in the world as we tried to draw parallels between the rise of Aliko Dangote and other billionaires of the world. We looked at certain commonalities among these super rich men and women of the world. We drew out the values they hold dear, which helped them to arrive at where they are today in the world and still maintain their privileged economic power. It is not easy to make a billion dollar, not to talk of 16 billion dollars as Aliko Dangote has made and every dime he made was made in Africa. In highbrow Victoria Island, Lagos in littoral southern Nigeria where Aliko holds court, his Gangnam style of living bespeaks real money and plenty of it. At Ikoyi in the same Lagos where he has his sprawling corporate headquarters, Dangote is definitely a billionaire in every material sense of the word. He lives the life of a stupendously rich man. In Abuja too, where he has some of the most beautiful and expensive houses, his lifestyle speaks of his trillions of Nigerian Naira and billions of dollars fortunes, not to talk of mansions scattered in many cities and towns at home and abroad.

The captivating story of Aliko Dangote is that right from the day he was born, he was destined for financial success. He had the right beginning as the scion of the richest man in Nigeria at a time; the eminently successful Sanusi Alhassan Dantata (now late) as his maternal grandfather. His maternal great-grand father Alhassan Abdullahi Dantata, who sowed the acorn that became the oak of the Dantata family fortune served as source of inspiration for the fourth generation of his family. As the first grandson of Sanusi Dantata, young Aliko grew up in the right atmosphere and thrived in the most conducive climate to excel. He was introduced to money and how to make it very early in life. We traced his many footpaths. We followed his footprints; from Kano to Egypt, to Lagos and many diverse places in Nigeria, West Africa and the African continent which defined the Aliko Dangote success story.

It would be a misplaced assumption, indeed erroneous, to say Aliko Dangote's success in life was already cut out for him very early in life because of his rich pedigrees. Every cent/kobo and dime that Aliko Dangote made were as a result of his ability to put to use the opportunities that he had while growing up; opportunities that were available to some of his peers in contemporary Nigeria / Africa. By watching his uncles, cousins and other family members conduct businesses, negotiate deals, and schmooze with politicians and thereby learning how to climb the ropes, Aliko Dangote succeeded in cutting his business teeth very early in life. His lifestyle, ethical values, prudence, simplicity, ability to spot talents, the fear of God and other similar characteristics of other billionaires of the world are not hereditary but distinctly Aliko. These themes were the pivotal areas of sourced materials for this pioneering work. We looked at Aliko Dangote from afar; we conducted interviews with few people around him, spoke to ordinary

Nigerians and succeeded in presenting a balanced and unbiased portrait of the richest black person in the world.

This biography is not written as an academic book. Its genre falls within the popular culture of our time. We have not written this book as a textbook, but as a general interest non-fiction in narrative prose, easy and straightforward. Any one, man or woman, young or old, African, non-African, black or white, indeed every human being on the face of the earth should be able to read and understand how the first Nigerian billionaire and the first African person in sub-Saharan Africa began from humble beginning to emerge as the first richest black person of African descent in the world.

Aliko Mohammad Dangote

Opening Words

THE POPULATION of the world, according to the United States Census figure is put currently at 7.1 billion human beings as of 2012. Of this figure, sixty percent of human beings live in the continent of Asia alone, while both China and India contain thirty-one percent human beings on the planet earth. About one hundred, and seventy-three million children are born annually and the continent of Africa is the second most populous area on earth next to Asia. While more human beings are born annually, few human beings are dying-about fifty-three million annually – which is less than one-third of the number of babies born around the world. However, the rate of poverty in the world is not keeping pace with population growth, against the backdrop of the number of babies and the reduction in the number of deaths annually in the world.

More than two- thirds of the populations of the world live in poverty. The indices used by the United Nations for poverty estimations are; personal and disposable income, access to housing, education, water, employment, and other basic essentials of life. Human rights activists have also included other rights such as; rights to justice, gender equality, universal suffrage, power and privileges as indices of poverty estimation. Paradoxically, the two continents where two-thirds of human beings live- Asia and Africa- are the areas where the majority of poor peoples of the world live. Most of the impoverished human beings on planet earth are mostly children; 122 million of them are out of school; 2 million children die each year, because they do not have access to basic immunization; 15 million are orphaned annually through the HIV-AIDS epidemic and other frightening statistics according to the UNICEF.

There is plenty of money in the world. There are enough material resources at the disposal of the various governments of the world for every human being has access to these basic essentials of life. However, the wealth of the world is controlled by less than one percent of a class of people identified by the *Forbes* magazine as world's billionaires. The magazine has been compiling the names of world billionaires for 31 years when it began the practice in 1982. Owned by three generations of the Forbes Family of New York, since its tradition, the magazine had not deemed it fit to name an African of black descent in Africa south of the Sahara among these supra-super rich men people of the world.

The Sudanese billionaire, Mr. Mohammed Al-Almoundi, who appeared on the list usually, claimed Saudi citizenship. In 2008, the tradition changed. The *Forbes* magazine listed the name of Mr. Aliko Dangote as one of the billionaires among the list of one thousand and two hundred, and ten people of the world. The magazine reported that Dangote was worth $3.3 billion and in 2011; his fortunes surged to $13.8 billion to emerge the richest man/person in Nigeria and the richest man/person in Africa. He occupied the 51st position in the world beating well-known African and popular African-American black billionaires such as; Mohammad Al-Almoundi, who was born in Ethiopia but preferred to claim Saudi citizenship (worth $12.3 billion); Nasseff Sawiris of Egypt ($5.6billion), including the two Sawiris Brothers: Naguib Sawiris ($3.5billion); Onsi Sawiris ($2.9billion); black South African shipping magnate, Patrice Motsepe ($3.5billion), and Ms. Opral Winfrey of the United States ($2.5billion). Other names from Africa were; Mr. Mike Adenuga of Nigeria worth $2billion and Mr. Femi Otedola worth about $1.2billion the previous year. Another Egyptian on the list was Yaseem Mansour ($1.8billion), while Al Fayed, an Egyptian based in the UK completed the list of Africans with personal fortune of $1billion. Mr. Mo Ibrahim of Sudan has also made the list. Mr. Dangote has become the richest black person in the world for four consecutive years (2008-to date). "Today, Aliko is worth $16.1 billion."

For long, it was difficult for Western publications to assess the monetary worth of many African rich people. The reasons were not far-fetched. Many of the rich people in Africa were either serving or retired military generals, or rulers and politicians, who amassed much of their wealth through official pilfering. Much of the wealth were squirreled into private pockets, kept in coded bank accounts in Switzerland, Europe, the Isle of Man, Cayman Island, Monaco, Panama and other havens, considered unreachable by their home governments. For example, Zimbabwe is going through one of the worst economic crises in its 31-year existence, yet the president, Mr. Robert G. Mugabe is said to be worth $3billion.

Some world leaders and holders of elected positions and kings who are billionaires, such as former prime minister of Italy, Mr. Silvia Berlusconi (worth $20billion); Mayor Michael Bloomberg of New York City ($15billion); King Abdullah ibn Abdul-Aziz of Saudi Arabia ($21billion); Hajji Hassanah Bokia, the Sultan of Brunei ($20billion); Sheikh Khallifa bin Zayyed al Nahyan, the president of United Arab Emirates ($19billion) and the social welfare minister of Indonesia, Mr. Aburial Bakri, ($9.2billion) were formerly businessmen who had investments spread all over the world. These men owned companies quoted on the New York Stock Exchange and other stock markets, owned shares in some of the world's most reputable companies, and corporations, and their savings could be verified. Their annual tax returns are also sources that are available to verify their net worth, but in many African countries, such information is unavailable. Another reason was that many of the so-called rich Africans were not known to engage in manufacturing and their companies were privately-owned and un-quoted in their nation's stock exchanges. Another difficulty encountered by Western journalists desirous of investigating the wealth of rich Africans was the nature of doing business in the continent.

These and many other reasons had precluded the *Forbes* magazine and other "wealth-creation" publications from knowing the estimated net worth of wealthy Africans and include them on the list of world billionaires. For examples, few publications ever ventured into the net worth of some people in the erstwhile Soviet Union until after the fall of communism and the splintering of the behemoth. Today, *perestroika* (restructuring and the introduction of market economy) and *glasnost* (openness) have allowed the world to identify at least three public office holders who are billionaires in Russia: Senator Suleiman Kerimov ($17.5 billion); Senator Andrey Molchanov ($4billion) and Gleb Fetisov ($3.9billion), while two Ukrainian public office holders: Senators Rinat Akhmetov and Kostyantin Zhevago are worth $7.4billion and $3.4 billion respectively. In Europe, Senator Serge Dassault of France and Lord Swraj Paul, two members of British House of Lords are also billionaires worth $9.9 billion and $1.3billion respectively. The wealth of these individuals and sources of their riches are open books. The Saudis have oil; in fact, every public office holder in Saudi Arabia and often belong to the monarchy, have the potentials of joining the club of world billionaires like Prince Alwaleed bin Talal ($21.5billion), who is richer than King Abdullah of Saudi Arabia worth $10billion.

Some of the retired military generals in Africa, especially Nigerian military generals, are billionaires but much of their "wealth" could not be independently verified. Similarly, the sources of their wealth have not been disclosed. Most of them do not use the money for productive purposes such as; manufacturing, buying of stocks, supporting philanthropic and other worthy causes etc. so when they boast they are billionaires; the question Western journalists ask is: Show us the money? If other Nigerian billionaires, apart from Messrs. Aliko Dangote and Mike Adenuga can "own up" to the source(s) of their wealth, it would be pretty easy for journalists and writers to find out the sources of the wealth and the various investments tied to the wealth. This was the top call for some rich Nigerian and African business people, until the entry of Nigeria's Aliko Dangote into the club of world billionaires list in 2008. Mr. Dangote opened the gateway for rich Africans south of the Sahara to be celebrated, both locally and around the world. For the first time in black Africa, he has demonstrated the reward of success through manufacturing, and the establishment of industries to provide services and put millions of young men and women to work in Africa. This is remarkable. This is his story. This biography is how it all began 56 years ago. This is the biography of Mr. Aliko Mohammad Dangote, the richest black person in the world today.

CHAPTER 1
KANO: THE HOME OF BLACK ARABIAN TRADERS

"I built a conglomerate and emerged the richest black man in the world in 2008, but it didn't happen overnight. It took me thirty years to get to where I am today. Youth of today aspire to be like me, but they want to achieve it overnight. It's not going to work. To build a successful business, you must start small and dream big. In the journey of entrepreneurship, tenacity of purpose is supreme"

---Mr. Aliko Mohammad Dangote.

THE HISTORY of present-day northern Nigeria is full of records and archived materials dating back to the 10th century, when three large empires dominated the large swath of land, stretching from Sokoto in the northwest to the tip of Lake Chad in the northeast, Ilorin in the southwest, and parts of present-day northern Cameroon. The three dominant empires were: the Hausa-Fulani Empire, also known as the Sokoto Caliphate; the Kanem-Bornu Empire and the Oyo Empire. Before the arrival of the British colonialists in 1900, most of northern region was controlled by Othman Dan Fodio. He established his authority after the conquest of most of the Hausa city-states in 1808 and converted the majority of the inhabitants into Islam.

The aboriginal people of the land, prior to the Islamic conquest, were known to have migrated from the land of

Nubia between 500 and 800 CE. Like other Nigerian tribes, which traced their origins to the Near East- the Yoruba people of West Africa living predominantly in western Nigeria, traced their origin to Oduduwa, son of Lamurudu, who migrated from present-day Egypt. The Igbo-people speaking also traced the ancestry of the Ibo tribe to the Neolithic Oriental world, dating to the 9500CE, while the Hausa people traced their origin to the Far East as well. The foremost progenitor of the Hausa tribe was a man called Bayajida, the son of King Abdullahi of present-day Baghdad in Iraq. Bayajida left the ancient town of Baghdad after its conquest by a marauding army led by Queen Zigawa. He headed westwards until he reached Bornu. He was said to have found affection and love from the King of Bornu who gave his first daughter; Magira to him, as a wife. In spite of Bayajida's marriage to the king's daughter, legends had it; the king was envious and afraid of his son-in-law. He then hatched a plot to kill his son-in-law, but the plot was leaked to Bayajida by Magira. At night, Bayajida took Magira and his loyalists and fled Bornu. When they got to Garn Gabas, which is today known as Hadejia town, Magira went into labor and gave birth to Gabas-ta-Biram, the first son of Bayajida. Bayajida left his first wife behind in Hadejia and continued his journey westwards.

According to several historical accounts, which had been corroborated by Hausa mythologies and legends; prominent among these accounts, the famous *Kano Chronicles,* Bayajida arrived at Gaya town and asked the local blacksmiths there to make him a knife, which he carried as defense. He continued on his journey till he arrived at Daura town, which is in present-day Katsina State. He was thirsty and asked a local woman for water to drink. The woman told him he had to wait; the townsfolk only fetched water from the village dug well once a week, because *Sarkin* or king- a python-lodged in the well water. Bayajida was livid and asked to be taken to the well. He fought with the king python and killed it, which brought him fame and recognition.

Meanwhile, Magajiya Duarama the Queen of Daura, had issued a decree, that anyone who succeeded in killing the python would be given half of her kingdom. When Bayajida was brought before the queen, he asked for the queen's hand in marriage instead of half of the kingdom. But there was a snag; according to tradition, the Queen of Daura must not marry; instead, Queen Magajiya Duarama gave her first slave named; Bagwariya to Bayajida. Soon, Bagwariya became pregnant, gave birth, and named her son: "*Karap Da Gari*" meaning; "He snatched the entire town." This affront from a slave incensed Queen Magajiya Duarama. The queen now changed her mind, married Bayajida, got pregnant and had a son for Bayajida, who she named "*Bawo*" meaning "Give it back." These two sons of Bayajida went on different paths to produce seven children each. But because Bawo was the true legitimate son of Queen of Daura, his seven children were referred to as; *Hausa Bakwai,* or the seven legitimate sons of Bayajida, who formed seven Hausa city-states namely: Kano, founded in 998 AD; Biran, founded in 1100AD; Zazzau or Zaria, founded in 1200AD; Katsina, founded in 1400AD; Second Daura, founded in 1800AD; Gobir, founded in 1806 AD; and finally Rano. The children of Karap Da Gari were referred to as; *Banza Bakwai,* or the seven illegitimate sons of Bayajida. They were the founders of another seven Hausa city-states namely: Gwari or Gwari land; Ilorin in present-day Kwara State; Kwararafa in Jukun land; Nupe or Nupe land; Kebbi, Yauri and Zamfara. These fourteen city-states were altogether referred to, as the fourteen Hausa city-states. Of the fourteen Hausa city-states, Kano was the oldest. The historic and ancient city of Kano is located in the arid Sahel region of northern Nigeria.

According to Kano's history dating back to the 10th century in *Kano Chronicles,* the ancient town was initially controlled by splintered chiefdoms. The early settlers practiced ritual traditions, according to Nagendra Kir Singh in *International Encyclopedia of Islamic Dynasties* where most of his sources came from the famous *Kano*

Chronicles. The three most important chiefdoms in Kano were; Sheme, Dala and Santolo, The early settlers traced their origin to Dala Hill with Barbushe, as the first spiritual guardian of the ancient city. According to historical accounts, the name, Kano was the name of a man who came to Dala Hill in search of iron. In 999 A.D, Bagauda, the first son of Bayajida, the man credited with siring the seven illegitimate sons known as *Banza Bokwoi*, and another set of seven legitimate sons known as; *Hausa Bokwoi* that became the founders of the Hausa city-states, became the first king of ancient Kano. Today, the *Bagauda Lake Hotel* along Kano-Tiga-Jos Road in the outskirts of southern Kano stands as monument in memory of Bagauda, the first king of Kano. Between 999 A.D. to the period of the conquest of the town by Othman Dan Fodio, the *Kano Chronicles* reported that 39 kings ruled the ancient city. Bagauda subdued all the chiefdoms and built his political base in Sheme, but Santolo chiefdom continued to resist the dominance of Bagauda. After his death in 1094, Bagauda's son, Gijiman became king, and ruled for thirty-nine years. Gijiman moved the political base of his father from Sheme to Dala and after his death in 1134, his son; Tsaraki took over two years later and reigned till 1194. It was Tsaraki who began the modernization of Kano by building the city walls against foreign invasion. He could not finish the projects until his son; Yaji mounted the throne in 1349 and ruled till 1385. There were no historical records of what happened during the nearly two centuries between Tsaraki and Yaji. Yaji extended the city's territories to Rano and Zannayaba. It was Yaji that finally conquered Santolo, subjugated the people and completed the city walls started by his father. Santolo did not give up easily, but Yaji enlisted the help of Muslim Wangarawa and Dioula who set fire on the traditional rituals of the people of Santolo and converted the natives into Islam.

Five years after Yaji's death, Kananeji ascended the throne and was on the throne for twenty years. Kananeji extended his rule as far as Zazzau by killing the king of

Zazzau. Dauda replaced Kananeji in 1410 and was on the throne for 28 years. But, unlike his predecessor, he set his eyes eastwards and formed alliance with Bornu. During his reign, he copied a lot of cultural traditions from Bornu such as; the use of trumpets to announce the presence of the king and the introduction of titles such as; *Galadima, Chiroma, Kaigama,* and many others. Muhammad Rumfa became king from 1461 to 1499, but there were no historical accounts during the twenty-three years between Kananeji and when Rumfa became king. It was Rumfa who built Kirmi Market, the City Gate, and established the *Tara-la-Kano* or Nine of Kano as an administrative system of chiefdoms among his nine subordinates, as the ancient city began to expand. He also built *Gidan Rumfa,* or Rumfa Palace as administrative court, where he settled disputes and adjudicated justice. Rumfa was the first king of ancient Kano to celebrate the Moslem Festival of *Eid –il-Fitri,* commonly celebrated after the Islamic Holy month of Ramadan as more and more Moslems began to settle in the ancient city. But as his power and influence grew, Rumfa decided to attack Katsina in 1488 as part of his expansionist policies and territorial ambitions. He died while the war was on and the war was inherited by his successor; Abdullahi in 1499. Abdullahi ruled only for ten years and failed to annex Katsina as his father. His successor, Muhammad Kisoki, a warrior and his first son could not defeat Katsina either, and during his fifty-six year reign, he decided to eat the humble pie by setting his sight on Zaria. His forces easily and effortlessly defeated Zaria and turned the town into its vassalage. Katsina remained a hard nut to track for Muhammad Kisoko. Shortly thereafter, a more powerful foreign invading army descended on Kano.

There were no historical accounts of what happened, between the reigns of Muhammad Rumfa and Kumbari dan Sharef between 1565, and 1731, when Othman Dan Fodio's Jihadists overthrew Kumbari Dan Sharef between 1731 and 1743. Sharef fought hard to ward off the marauding Sokoto Jihadists led by the legendary Othman Dan Fodio. This lasted for nearly sixty years until 1805, when the ancient city fell into the hands of the invading Moslem proselytizers and Fodio converted virtually everyone into the Islamic religion. Historically, the aboriginal settlers of Kano were not Moslems and the original language of the people was not Hausa Language. According to historian and director general, research and documentation directorate of Kano State Government, Mr. Ibrahim Ado-Kurawa, "The earliest settlers of Kano were Hausa speaking people, whose language belongs to the Chadic Family of the Afro-Asia Phylum." Shehu Othman dan Fodio, referred to as the Islamic "*Sword of Truth*" by Hiskett in his biographical piece on the Great Jihadist titled; "*The Sword of Truth: the Life and Times of Shehu Usman dan Fodio*" (New York) explained that, the aim of the man was to proselytize all the conquered Hausa territories. Fodio then made Sokoto the administrative capital of the new city-state known as; the Sokoto Caliphate. Ironically, after dividing the conquered territories among his sons, he did not live in Sokoto, but chose to make his home in a little desert town of Gobir. At the heights of the Caliphate's suzerainty, which lasted for over a century, three other traditional states constantly challenged, tormented, and waged wars against the caliphate: Kanem Bornu, which constantly raided Daura, and parts of the districts of Katsina in the eastern flank; Zamfara State in the western flank; and occasionally Songhai State, which often used Kebbi as a buffer city to attack the Sokoto Caliphate.

In *Comparative Study of Thirty City-States: an Investigation*, Morgan Herman Hansen explained, the various patterns these rivalries played out among the city-states. Songhai, Kanem-Bornu, Zamfara and Sokoto constantly butted heads to control the heartland of what was then known as, the Hausa States, which was what the land was initially called before Fodio's invasion in 1805. It was this large swath of geographical spread that later became the core of northern region which the British Governor-General, Sir Frederick Lugard annexed with the southern part of Nigeria to be known as Nigeria in the 1914 Amalgamated Territories which gave birth to the nation known today as Nigeria.

While there were internecine skirmishes among the various city-states to dislodge the dominant Sokoto Caliphate by other traditional powers, there were also internal struggles among the Hausa-Fulani City-States. These struggles for supremacy and political hegemony were intense between Kaduna and Kano. The Kaduna City State had its political base in Zazzau. The Hausa- Fulani-Sokoto Dynasty controlled Kano for the next 99 years, until the British Colonial authorities captured Kano in 1903.

Between 1895 when King Kumbari Dan Sharef was defeated by Othman Dan Fodio forces from Sokoto and the Sokoto Fulani Jihadists were in turn defeated by the British, seven Emirs ruled Kano as a vassal state. They ruled Kano from Sokoto in what historians referred to as; the era of the Hausa-Fulani Sokoto Caliphate in northern region. The Emirs were; Emir Suleiman, who ruled from 1805 to 1819; Emir lbrahim from 1819-1846; Emir Usman from 1846-1855; while Emir Abdullah, ruled for 28 years; followed by Emir Mohammed Bello, who ruled for ten years; and Mohammed Tukur, who ruled for just a year. Emir Tukur had a running battle with his main rival, Yusufu, who also laid claim to the throne. The war of attrition between Yusufu and Tukur reached a head which led to the assassination of Tukur and thus paved the way for Emir Alitu, who ruled for nine years when the British forces arrived. Aliyu didn't give up easily. He fought hard to ward-off the invading British forces, but the superior military power of the British army finally prevailed. In 1903, Aliyu was captured in his palace in Sokoto by the British forces. He was chained and transported to the British colonial headquarters in Lokoja central Nigeria, where the Landers Brothers and Mungo Park first "discovered" Nigeria. Emir Aliyu remained in exile till 1926 where he died. The British decided to punish him for the fierce battle he engaged them, which led to the death of several British soldiers during the 1903 Sokoto Invasion and finally led to the fall of Ancient Kano to the British forces.

The British colonial authorities were not stupid not to realize that their colonial project would run into a hitch if, they abolished the Emirate altogether. Consequently, in line with their practice in other parts of Nigeria and Africa, and would remove a stubborn and cantankerous king, and they replace him with a pliant and more amenable man, usually the kinsman or brother of the deposed and exiled king. That was what happened to Emir Aliyu in Lokoja. They brought his brother, Mohammed Abbas to replace him and told him to move to Kano instead of ruling from Sokoto. Abbas was the first Emir of Kano to rule in Kano, from 1903, and was on the throne for sixteen years. Usman, who succeeded him ruled for seven years followed by Emir Abdullahi Bayero, who was on the throne for 27 years. During the nationalist struggles for Nigeria's political independence, and three years after de-colonization of Nigeria, two Emirs ruled in quick succession; Emir Muhammad Sanusi, who was the grandfather of the Governor of Central Bank of Nigeria, Dr Sanusi Lamido Sanusi, reigned from 1954 to 1963; and Emir Muhammad Inuwa, who ruled for just a year, which paved the way for the current Emir of Kano, Alhaji Ado Bayero. Today, Ado Bayero, born in 1930 and former Nigerian Ambassador to Senegal is the 13th Fulani Emir of Kano City. His father was the 10th Emir of Kano, who ruled from 1926 to 1953.

Traditionally, Kano has always been a city of commerce and bustling trading post. The introduction of the obnoxious trans-Saharan Slave Trade; though condemnable and inhuman, but paradoxically, later became an enterprise that led to the economic development of many Hausa States in the 16th and 17th centuries. One of the main lucrative slave posts was the Hausa State of Zazzau, in the southern frontiers of ancient Kano, which was an attractive local point for collection of slaves. It was here majority of the conquered slaves were exchanged for salt in Kano, and then the slaves were sold to slave traders and Saharan merchants across the desert. Ancient Kano thus became a strategic distribution center for the lucrative trans-Saharan Slave Trade, throughout much of the two hundred years of the inhuman trade in human beings. The trans-Saharan Slave Trade continued into the 19th century, even, after the abolition of the trans-Atlantic Slave Trade. This was so, because majority of the victims of the trans-Saharan Slave Trade carried out mostly in the northern Sahel were women. More importantly, the enslaved women were crudely treated, because many of the slave dealers used women for household chores, also as concubines and commercial sex workers. As disclosed by Leslie Alexander and Walter Rucker in their book: *"Encyclopedia of African-American History, Volume 1,"* sexual exploitation was one of the features of the obnoxious trans-Saharan Slave Trade. Even today, the award-winning documentary of modern-day slavery; *"The Freedom Project: Ending Modern-Day Slavery"* by the Cable News Network (*CNN*) reported that there is "illegal" slave trade still going on in many countries in the Saharan region of North Africa, of, which many of their victims are exploited young girls and women, mostly used as commercial sex workers.

After the formal abolition of the obnoxious trans-Saharan Slave Trade, Kola nut trade became the next most lucrative trade in the northern region. The trade in kola nut was popular in many parts of the outlawed slave routes such as; Air, Kano, Chad Basin, Gold Coast (now Ghana), Awlad in Songhay; Tafilalet in Morocco, and other parts of Near East. As J.F. Ade Ajayi disclosed in his popular *magnum opus, Africa in the Nineteen Century until the 1880s,* kola nut supplanted slavery after its abolition. Kola nut became a lucrative article of trade for several reasons. First, kola nuts have religious, traditional and spiritual purposes. Second, the chemical composition contains caffeine, which makes kola nuts serve the twin purposes of social stimulant and coffee substitute. Thirdly, kola nuts were lucrative and in high demand, which shifted traders' attention from slavery.

Another precious article of trade ancient Kano was

noted for was leather business. Animal hides, and skin were also popular articles of trade in Kano during the period. Other lucrative businesses and trades were also conducted in gold, salt, and henna. The most prominent article of trade that Kano was later noted for was the popular groundnut pyramids. Leather business in ancient Kano was one of the most thriving businesses and crafts in the city's "informal economy." The type of leather manufacture in Kano was autochthonous to the city made of tanned and dyed goatskins known as; morocco leather and nut of an acacia, which ensured the Kano type was attractive to buyers. It was a lucrative business carried out in large streets and compounds in certain areas and families, who displayed their wares in the city's popular Kurmi Market. Many leather traders also came from neighboring Bilma in northern Kano in today's Niger Republic. Today, the largest tannery company; Fata Tannery Company in Africa, is located in Kano. Over the years, the leather business has been taken over by Lebanese, Pakistanis, and Asian business men. They are found mostly in Sharada estate, Kano.

Salt was also a lucrative article of trade that ancient Kano was noted for in the 15th and 16th centuries. At a time, salt was even used as medium of exchange and after cowries supplanted it, salt became a veritable source of export to far places like Morocco, Tunisia, and Tripolitania. According to Houtsma in his book, *E.J. Brill's First Encyclopedia of Islam, 1913-1938,* Kano was the most important lucrative town throughout the political and economic dominance of the Sudan Empire in the 16th century. Other important articles of trade which put the ancient city of Kano on high economic pedestal were; gunpowder, iron-monger and cotton goods of European origin; large quantities of sugar, mostly from Egypt; and many of the first Arab settlers from Ghadames in the Nalut district, Fezzan region in today's south-western Libya brought ivory as article of trade as well.

Henna business, which is the fashionable way most Hausa-Fulani women make themselves beautiful from time immemorial, has traditionally become a lucrative art in ancient Kano. It was mostly practiced in the Old City, where women adorned their bodies with beautiful tattoos and haute couture. Farming was also widely practiced, because of the fertility of the land in Kano, as reported by the famous African historian; Leo Africanus. R. Brown in his book, *"Leo Africanus,"* disclosed that the great historian; Leo Africanus (c.1494-c.1554?), said he observed large cultivation of rice, sorghum, maize, cereals, and millet during his historic visit to Kano in the 16th century. In addition to cash crops such as indigo, tobacco and *durra (sorghum vulgate),* there were also other activities such as; cattle grazing and animal husbandry.

The opening of Kano City to the rail road from Lagos in 1912 by the British colonial authorities, two years before the Amalgamation of the Northern and Southern Protectorates to become what is known as present-day Nigeria by Sir Frederick Lugard, accelerated the commercial and socio-economic development of modern Kano. Prior to the arrival of the British colonialists and the introduction of the political system known as; Indirect Rule system and policy of governance, virtually all the fourteen Hausa city-states operated independently without a centralized political or commercial center. This was reversed by the early British colonial administrators, who made Kano their administrative capital and seat of government. According to Dr. Shehu Tijjani Yusuf, History teacher at Bayero University, Kano and author of; *"The Impact of the Railway on Kano Emirate, c. 1903-1960s: the Case of Madobi and Kwankwanso Towns,"* The establishment of the railway by the British six years after they defeated the Sokoto Caliphate, and established their administrative post in Kano in Northern Nigeria definitely accelerated the rapid economic transformation of the ancient city." He cited two adjoining cities to Kano where the rail road had much significant economic impact: the two groundnut cities of Madobi and Kwankwanso. To him, "The impact of railway on the rural settlements of Madobi and Kwankwaso in Kano emirate is a study of the legacy of the British imperialism in Northern Nigeria. The railway... played an active role in the entrenchment of British colonial interests in Northern Nigeria and elsewhere in Nigeria. As the cases of rural settlements of Madobi and Kwankwaso in Kano Emirate shows, the establishment of railway stations in Northern Nigeria was closely tied to the indigenous groundnut economy. This, inadvertently, required a new, fast, and efficient haulage system, which the railways satisfied."

The railway also enabled Kano merchants to have access to two important seaports, because the rail line entered Kano City from the northern flank of Kaduna, thus linking Kano City to Lagos and Port Harcourt. These twin cities were economically important as they became two strategic cities with large seaports in both pre-and post-colonial Nigeria.

Of all the articles of trade that made the ancient town of Kano an important trading post in the 19th century, the trade in kola nut was the most lucrative. Kola nut was the crude oil of the day, not only in Kano, but across the West African sub-region. Kola nut became the gold, which led to constant interactions between and among the traders. Kano thus became the place to go just as the discovery of gold in California between 1848 and 1855 led by James W. Marshall of Coloma, California led to the Gold Rush to the Continental United States. In short, everyone wanted to be a part of the action; in Kano, the Hausa States down to Ghana and Niger, including, Lake Chad, and other remnant parts of disintegrated Songhai and Mali empires.

One of the major traders in the booming kola nut business was Malam Madugu Abdullahi, born in Danshayi near Kano. Danshayi in the 1880s was a border town between Kano and another town, Gonja in the south-western part of Kano. History had it that the grandfather of Madugu Abdullahi was originally from Katsina, who migrated to Kano during the trans-Saharan Slave Trade. During his trading activities, he met and fell in love with a woman trader called Fatimata and they settled at a town called Bebeji, near Kano. Bebeji in the 19th century was also another lucrative trading town, but not as big as Kano, but what stood Bebeji out was the cosmopolitan nature of the small town. Bebeji had large number of traders from other Hausa city- states such as; Gwari, Nupe, Jukun, Agalawa and others. While visiting traders from other Hausa states went to big Kano to trade, small Bebeji was the small Kano to retire to; for whatever could be found in the former invariably existed in the latter. Traders also preferred Bebeji, because it was small and life there was fun. There is a local Hausa saying, which captured the relationship between, Kano and Bebeji; *"Birni tana da goro goma, ke Bebeji kina da bari 20"* meaning *"If Kano has 10 kolas you are sure that Bebeji must have 20 halves."* It was here that Fatimata gave birth to Abdullahi's first son in 1877, who they named Alhassan.

Meanwhile, because of his trading activities, Abdullahi was shuttling between Bebeji and another trading post called Madobi, but on returning to Bebeji, he died there. Fatimata could not bear the sudden death of her husband, so when she re-married, she decided to move from Bebeji with her new husband, who was a peripatetic kola nut trader with his base in the present West African nation of Ghana (then called Gold Coast) town of Accra. In Accra, Fatimata gave birth to other children, but she did not take her first son Alhassan Abdullahi named after his father along with her, instead, left the tot in Bebeji with a nurse named Tata. It was Hajiya (Madam) Tata that nursed, catered and cared for little Abdullahi. Consequently, as the young Alhassan grew up, there was only one person he knew who nursed and brought him up, so he decided to bear the name "Dantata" or, literally in Hausa Language; "Son of Tata." When he grew up, he chose to be called Alhassan Dantata. Family records had it that Alhassan was born with a twin brother, who was said to have died at birth. This Alhassan Abdullahi Dantata was later to become the maternal great grandfather of the man, who later became the richest black person in the world.

Alhassan Abdulahi Dantata grew up in his native

Bebeji near Kano. He went to school at Madrasah Koranic School in the ancient town and later moved to Gonja where most of his father's businesses were located. He did not see his mother until 1892, when he travelled to Accra and was introduced to his half-siblings: Shuaibu, Jaji, Bala and Sidi. Alhassan Dantata did not stay in Accra, but preferred to be shuttling between the trading posts of the various towns in West Africa: Bebeji, Kano, Accra and Lagos after he had mastered the tricks of the trade from his inherited father's business. A chip off the old block, Alhassan learned quickly and soon expanded the little trading company that his father left behind. Alhassan began to trade in gold, necklaces, peanuts and other articles and within a decade, had become the largest exporter of kola nut, between Kano and Accra. By 1913, when the British colonialists opened the first rail road from Lagos to Kano, Alhassan seized the opportunity and became the first merchant trader to transport his kola nuts from Kano to Lagos by railway. Soon, he was exporting his articles of trade through the Lagos and Port Harcourt sea ports. In 1915 during World War I, Alhassan got married to his first wife, Umma Zaria who gave him his first son Sanusi that year. He soon built a palatial house in Koki Quarters of Kano, while shuttling between his Kano residence and Bebeji. A year after the birth of his first son, and shortly after the end of World War I, the fortune of kola nut as the main article of trade nose-dived giving way to groundnuts. Alhassan quickly adjusted, and in that year, the British Royal Niger Company was looking for a major agent of groundnut supplier. It was not difficult for the multi-national company to appoint Alhassan as the company's sole agent and supplier in the entire northern region of Nigeria.

This was during the legendary booming era of the groundnut pyramid. By the 1920s, the millions of pounds began to pour in and in that decade, Alhassan performed *Hajj* or Holy Pilgrimage to the Holy Land of Mecca and Medina in accordance with the Islamic injunction. On his way back to Nigeria, he had a stop-over in England and negotiated with the Royal Niger Company, which had changed its name to United African Company (*UAC)* and persuaded them to team up with him to establish a bank in Kano. His efforts yielded fruits with the establishment of the British Bank of West Africa in 1929 with him as the largest shareholder. He married his second wife, Maimunat and his second son Mahmud was born. Two other male children; Aminu and Ahmadu came in quick session. There were other daughters too sired by Alhassan Abdullahi Dantata. The era of the groundnut pyramid was the apogee of Alhassan Abdullahi Dantata business success. By the 1930s, in spite of the economic kerfuffle that engulfed the world during the Great Depression, Alhassan had become the richest person in Kano. His distant competitors were two Kano trading merchants: Messrs. Umaru Sharubutu Koki and Maikano Agogo. By the time he died on August 17, 1955-five years before Nigeria gained political independence, Alhassan was reputed to be the richest person in West Africa. A deeply religious man, he made his sons: Sanusi, Mahmud, Aminu, and Ahmadu and - other sons he sired through other women in accordance with his religion - to sign an undertaking that upon his passing, they would work together as one family and would not divide his business empire.

The sons kept to their promise. They honoured their deceased millionaire father by handling different aspects of the multi-million dollar thriving family business. Of course, there was enough for the children in the pie, and the large conglomerate had several arms: retailing, farming, merchandising, distribution etc. As the first son and eldest child, the siblings deferred to Sanusi to occupy their father's driver's seat, while they supported him to run the flourishing family outfit. But Ahmadu decided to play politics instead of being part of the family business and was the first to die five years after the death of their father. The second son, Mahmud, born in 1922 died in 1983 leaving Sanusi and Aminu (1931-) to preserve the family fortunes. The rest sons took their different trajectories of lives according to their callings, while the women moved into their husband homes.

Mr Sanusi Alhassan Dantata took over immediately after his father's demise in 1955. He built the family outfit to greater heights, and even, surpassed the family patriarch. Upon Nigeria's independence in 1960, Sanusi quickly built his political connections using his younger brother, the late Ahmadu as the arrow-head. It was like the late Nigerian multi-millionaire, Mr. Alhassan Abdullahi Dantata took a page out of the life of the late John Davison Rockefeller Jr., the Ohio-born chairman of Standard Oil USA and the richest American of his day, who left his fortunes in the hands of his five sons: John D. Rockefeller III (the eldest); Nelson Aldrich Rockefeller, David Rockefeller, Winthrop Rockefeller and Laurence Spellman Rockefeller. One of the Five Rockefellers; Nelson, later grew up to become the vice-president of the United States of America in 1974 following the resignation of President Richard Nixon over the famous Watergate Scandal and the resignation of vice-president Spiro Agnew earlier on over bribery allegations. President Gerald Ford, who succeeded Richard Nixon as president appointed Mr Nelson Rockefeller as his vice-president. Another son of the Rockefellers – Winthrop – became the governor of the state of Arkansas. But, in spite of their engagements in other areas of life, they did not abandon the family business empire. Sanusi Alhassan Dantata took his father's flourishing business empire into the next level in the 20th century as did the Rockefellers.

Mr. Sanusi Alhassan Dantata was born in 1915 as the eldest male child of Alhassan Abdullahi Dantata in Bebeji, Kano. His mother was Uma Zaria, the first wife of the richest man in Nigeria during his day. Mr. Sanusi Dantata assumed the new patriarch of the Dantata family business, branching into far flung areas of modernized agriculture, livestock, merchandize and distribution. Since his father had opened the Lagos annex of the family business, he decided to focus on Lagos by deploying some of his father's able lieutenants to that part of Nigeria immediately Nigeria attained political independence. His younger brother, Aminu also weighed in and joined in the rapid transformation of the family business. Sanusi did not abandon his late father's businesses of leather, kola nuts, hides and skins, salt, sugar etc. rather, he expanded the distribution networks employing more agents by looking beyond the shores of Nigeria. Neo-colonialism might have Balkanized the West African sub-region and opened up the large swath of land from Senegal in the west across the sand dunes of the Sahara Desert via Mali, Ghana, Tripoli, Chad and Niger to the Cameroons in the north and south; yet the age-old religious, linguistic and kinship ties that bonded Moslems and Hausas together during pre-colonial era still exist. With these in mind, Sanusi and his brother, Aminu extended their trading activities to all the newly-independent West African countries, especially where Hausa Language is spoken. Of course, Hausa Language still remains the most populous language spoken by nearly half of the inhabitants of the West African sub- region. Today, it is still the second most populous and widely-spoken language in Africa, next to Swahili accounting for nearly 50 million native speakers. The Dantata Boys were not deterred by the new colonial languages of French and English; in addition, they relied on the family name "Dantata," which had become a household name in several important markets and commodity trading routes throughout Wes Africa.

It appears it has always been the tradition among billionaires; rich people, that when they have amassed fortunes, they normally live behind strict instructions that their wealth must never be divided among their children. Many billionaires do not even write wills, especially those of them that are monogamists. The polygamists among them often have firm grips on their fortunes and how to look after such fortunes when they passed on. For examples, Forrest Mars Sr., the American inventor of *Mars Chocolate* known worldwide and the owner of the renowned *Uncle Ben's Rice* lived to the ripe age of 95 in 1999. He was once ranked by the *Forbes* magazine as the 30th richest man in the United States with personal fortune of S\$4billion.

Married to his sweet heart, Chicagoan Ruth Meyer for nearly forty years, Mars left standing instructions that his three children; Forrest Jr., John, and daughter Jacqueline, should run the family business empire between them and his fortune must not be divided. The same tradition Mr. Sam Walton, the founder of *Wal-Mart* left for his wife and four children before he died in April 1992. His wife, Helen of nearly fifty years, was worth $16.4 billion before she died in 2007 and their children: Samuel Robson, John Thomas, James Carr, Alice and Louise once had the enviable distinctions of holding five billionaires sports on the *Forbes* list of world billionaires until 2005, when one of them died in a plane crash. The two daughters of Mr. Walton preferred to hold minor shares in the world's renowned chain store. Today, the remaining two sons and the widow of the first son, who died in a plane crash, appear annually on the *Forbes* list of world billionaires. The list of billionaires that adopted this type of tradition to their inheritance seemed to cut across nations and tradition. In Nigeria, this was exactly what Mr. Alhassan Abdullahi Dantata did when he was about to die.

The late Alhassan Dantata, the planter of the seed of wealth had left a note on how the family business should be conducted after leaving the scene which ran something like, "Dantata's Family Business Codes." First code; hang together and be united. The shrewd businessman from Bebeji made all his children to swear, while on his death bed that they would never bicker or fight over his business empire after his death, even though they were from a polygamous family. Although he did not leave behind a formal and legal will as we know today, but he asked them to swear by the Holy Qur'an that his business empire would remain intact, and his businesses would not be divided. It is a tradition that has percolated to the rest Dantatas now in their 5th generation. No Dantata blood refers to any business as; "my own" rather; "our own." This has ensured the dominance of the Dantatas in many business areas. This clan solidarity simply means a threat to one of the

Dantatas is a threat to the whole clan. They practice a neo-patrimonial system of business relationship, which is a way of ensuring dominance. Basically, a neo-patrimonial system is building solidarity through clientele and crude ascription of loyalty as advocated by the German political economist and philosopher; Max Weber. The system is old-fashioned and archaic, but it is an effective and legal strategy to make fanatics out of your supporters.

Each of the thousands of agents and distributors that worked for the Dantatas were made to think, behave and feel that he or she was part of "our business." This mentality translates to collective interests. In other words, all Dantata's interests are our interests too, for, a threat to the Dantata's interests is also a threat to every associate's collective interests. It is a political variant of building fanaticism out of political supporters used by Adolf Hitler during Nazi Germany.

The third rule is; do not discriminate against anyone, who comes from either far or near to make a fortune out of the Dantata seed of wealth as long as the person is a Moslem, or is ready to become one. Fourth, discharge all your religious obligations: pray five times daily (*Sal 'at*), observe the holy month fasting for 30 days (Ramadan); give generously and cheerfully (*Zakat and Zadaqat*) to the propagation of the religion of Islam, and the needy, and observe *Hajj* or Holy Pilgrimage to Mecca and Medina. In addition, use the Dantata wealth to sponsor as many Moslems as possible that want to fulfil this injunction. Use the power of filial solidarity for both support and advantage. Any "outsider" who wants to marry a Dantata must be ready to be a part of the family business and abide by these principles. Finally, live simple, unassuming and frugal life and steer clear of politics, but support the government of the day.

All Dantatas have imbibed these rules like the Holy Grail for nearly five generations. These templates were later to be employed more effectively by the great- grandson of Alhassan Abdullahi Dantata to emerge as the richest black person in the world, although he tweaked with the Dantata Codes to suit modern business ethics. For example, inside the behemoth Dangote Group, Christians and Muslims are labels you tuck inside your pockets once you come on board and tribalism is an anathema in a nation of 250 tongues and tribes. But forty and fifty years ago, things were different.

The Dantatas knew where to concentrate their business energies and maximize their competitive edge and potentials. They left the southern Nigerian markets to two strong competitors: Mr. Timothy Adeola Odutola (1902-1995) the Ogbeni-Oja of Ijebu-Ode, the multi-millionaire business magnate and tire merchant that controlled western Nigeria; and the stupendously rich Ibo multi-millionaire, Sir Louis Odumegwu-Ojukwu (1901-1966), who controlled and dominated the business of importing, exporting, merchandizing, and haulage trading in much of eastern Nigeria. But no Nigerian businessman would avoid Lagos completely. Lagos was where the business Titans normally converged. Lagos was where the action was (and still is); because the city was the commercial, social and economic hubs of modern Nigeria both in pre-and post-independence eras. Like New York to the United States and world economy, Lagos is the commercial heartbeat of Nigeria. As the locals say, it is the way Lagos goes that Nigeria goes.

In Lagos itself in those days, there were other important business players such as; Mr. Shafi Lawal Edu, the chairman and chief executive of Shafi Lawal Edu & Sons, who was reputed to be one of Nigeria's early indigenous multi-millionaires. There was the legendary Da Rocha family, which settled in Lagos from Brazil, and later built its multi-million business empire that stretched across the whole of West Africa and beyond. Known as *Baba Olomi* or the water man, Mr. Da Rocha was credited with building the first indigenous water corporation in Lagos, which supplied the city of Lagos from where he made much of his fortunes. The company was later taken over by the Lagos State Government at Adiyan Water Works near Oke-

Aro, a border town between Ogun and Lagos States in north Lagos. Sir Mobolaji Bank-Anthony was also one of the early Lagos multi-millionaires, including Ade Tuyo, who controlled the city's pastry and baking industry. Mr. Akintola Williams, Nigeria's first indigenous chartered accountant and Adebayo Braithwaite, who was the youngest-only 36 years old- and the owner of Nigeria's first indigenous insurance company, African Alliance Insurance Company. There was also Mr. Emmanuel Akwiwu, the Lagos-based attorney turned oil magnate. Others were the famous Benson family and Mr. Sule Oyeshola Gbadamoshi (S.O.G) of Ikorodu, and many indigenous Nigerian businessmen and women. However, the Dantatas up-north had the whole of the northern region and Sahara Desert virtually for their operations. Any aspiring business man or woman wanting a piece of the action in that part of Nigeria would have to pay homage to the Dantatas of Kano. Those who could not slug it out with the Dantatas often entered into business relationships with them.

In its September 1965 edition, TIME did a cover story on the rise of indigenous African business in the then 31-newly-indepedent African nations that had just attained political independence. The magazine discovered that Nigeria, with 55 million populations was not only the most populous, but also the most prosperous independent African nation with a-4.5 per cent annual growth rate. Additionally, Nigeria was the African nation with the largest number of African millionaires. The first Nigerian millionaire was unarguably Mr. Sanusi Dantata, who dominated Nigeria's peanut business improving on the traditional business of his father: retailing. At the age of 46, he emerged as the nation's richest multi-millionaire in 1965 followed by then 63-year old Mr. Timothy Adeola-Odutola, who had just acquired a- 5,000 acres of rubber plantation worth $1,700,000 in 1964. The third richest Nigerian was then 66-year old Sir Odumegwu-Ojukwu and the first president of the Nigerian Stock Exchange. In 1964, Sanusi exported 84,000 tons of peanuts to the United

Kingdom and was paid cash, the first and only largest business transaction by any businessman in black Africa of his day.

Before he died on April 15, 1997; Sanusi sired several children from his wives and began to put them in charge of the family businesses, while they shared the pies with their half-brothers and cousins in the Aminu side of the clan. There was Abdulkadir Sanusi Dantata, his first son and eldest child; Usman Amaka Sanusi Dantata, the 3rd child born in Saudi Arabia in 1950 and the owner of one-time largest poultry farm in Nigeria, the *Anadariya Farm* located in between Bagauda Lake Hotel and Tiga Village where one of the authors of this book-Moshood Fayemiwo-worked briefly as a high school graduate in 1980. Others were Ahmadu, Aminu, Mahmud, Halima and Mariya, his daughter and the mother of the first grandson of Mr. Sanusi Alhassan Dantata called Aliko. It should be noted that Moslem names are given to children from generation to generation, thus, while Sanusi Dantata had a half-brother called Ahmadu, he also had a son called by the same name; so also his half-brother and another of his son bearing the same name of Aminu.

THE BIRTH OF ALIKO MOHAMMED DANGOTE

The life journey of the man who would become the richest person in Africa began in the mid-1950s. Mr. Sanusi Alhassan Dantata had many business associates as the richest man in Kano and Nigeria. But with all his wealth, he steered clear of politics until the 1930s when he seriously became involve with the Islamic Sufi sect known as the Qadriyya Sect in Kano. Mr. Sanusi Alhassan Dantata attended an Islamic school in Kano known as madrasa just as his late father Alhassan Dantata, who grew up in Bebeji Town. The school taught strict Islamic teaching based on the *Qadriyya* sect popular in many of the West African nations bordering on the Sahara Desert such as; The Sudan, Ethiopia, Mali, Somalia and Algeria. Adherents of the sect are also found in India, Spain and Turkey.

Founded around the 1119 CE by a respectable Islamic cleric; Abdulkadir Gilani, who was one of the foremost followers of the respected Abu Sa'id al-Mubarak Mukharrami of old Baghdad, the sect has some distinct worship features such as; rose color of green and white, wearing of black felt hat, the belief in the Holy Prophet Mohammed (SAW), and also belief in sheikhs as Allah's messengers. The *Qadriyya* adherents are mostly Sufis given the freedom to interpret the *Hadiths*, or Saying and Doing of the Prophet. Other beliefs of the sect are; initiations of believers, those that are 18 years and above, while the Five Pillars of Islam are to be respected. The *Qadriyya* sect followers use other Islamic texts in addition to the Holy Qur'an of which the book; *Futuh al-Ghayb* or *"Revelations from the Invisible World"* is a prominent one.

Believers are taught to exercise strict religious and moral instructions which tame the body, and suppress human ego. Humility and respect for constituted authorities by Allah and man is one of the features of members. Self-abnegation concerning food, consumption, and attitude to wealth is also encouraged. Young initiates from the age of 18 are normally encouraged to live in *"tekke"* or "commune" where they are mentored by *Qadriyya* sheikhs, who ask members to recount their dreams, trances and visions as forms of spiritual development.

According to Islamic scholars in the ancient city of Kano, Mr. Sanusi Dantata became a member of the *Qadriyya* Movement in Kano when a religious leader he met in Kumasi, Ghana preached to him during one of his several business trips to the former Gold Coast. His great grand-father and his father also traced part of their heritage to Ghana and with his encouragement; the leader of the sect in Kumasi named Ali was brought to Kano. As a rich man, Mr. Sanusi Dantata supported the religious works of Sheikh Ali Kumasi (born 1902-?), who, his numerous followers referred to as Sheikh Ali Kumasi. As many Kano indigenes know, especially Islamic scholars, the religious politics in the ancient city is always intense as different Islamic sects and their leaders or sheikhs jostle for supremacy and popularity among faithful. When the richest man in a religiously-charged city such as Kano gave his support to one of the leading Islamic scholars in town, it was bound to attract publicity and intense debate among the Islamic community. Soon, as Mr. Sanusi Dantata used his money to support the religious activities of the *Qadriyya* sect led by Ali Kumasi, his support soon invited friction among the religious followers of another prominent Islamic scholar in Kano, Sheikh Muhammad Nasiri Kabara.

Like Sheikh Ali Kumasi, whose parentage was from the Sahel area of West Africa, Sheikh Nasiri Muhammad Umar Kabara, born in 1912 in a village called Guringuwa in the outskirts of ancient Kano, originally hailed from the Republic of Mauritania. His great grandparents historically were from a town called Kabara in the ancient town of Timbuktu. His father migrated from the West African town in the 18th century and settled at Adakawa City in Kano. Later on, the family moved from Adakawa to another town founded by them, which was also named Kabara in Timbuktu between Mali and Mauritania after the patriarch of the family Mallam Kabara, hence, the name of Sheikh Nasiri Muhammad Umar Kabara. The grandparents and parents of Nasiri Muhammad Umar Kabara were strictly members of the Islamic Sufi sect right from their ancestral home of Kabara in Timbuktu Kingdom, Mali and Mauritania. When the parents of Nasiri Muhammad arrived in ancient Kano around 1787, it was said that the first Islamic school in Kabara Village was built by them to spread the Islamic religion. The school called; Zaure Islamic School was a sort of home school, which held in the living room of the patriarch and involved teaching of students by rote by learned Islamic scholars composed largely of the Kabara family members. The school, which is regarded as one of the oldest Islamic schools in Kano, and northern Nigeria has now been absorbed into the *Darul Qadriyya* School which is still functioning in Kabara Village.

According to Dr. Abdullah Uba Adamu, a professor of Islamic Religious Studies, and an authority on Islamic History of Kano at the Bayero University, Kano, who has conducted research and written extensively on the rise of the *Qadriyya* Sect in West Africa, little Nasiri had displayed thirst for Islamic Knowledge very early in life, while growing up in Kabara Village. It was disclosed by members of the sect that, the man, who was later to become Sheikh Nasiri Muhammad Umar Kabara did not read the Holy Qur'an from modern-day book form, rather he read it from the *Allo Qur'an* School in Timbuktu. Those who attended the school read the Qur'an from wooden plates as the Holy Book was handed down to followers by the original compilers of the book, before it was modernized through printing machine as we have it today. He was said to be highly versed in Islamic Jurisprudence and Linguistics using his high fluency in Arabic Language to memorize by rote great Islamic books such as; *Bad'ul Amli* and *Murshida*-two ancient Islamic books, which deal with the Unity of Allah, or what is called *Tauhidi*. Young Nasiri Muhammad Umar Kabara was also credited with the ability to memorize three other Islamic books: *Ahlari, Iziyya* and *Ishiriniya* which deepened his knowledge of Belief in Allah and His Holy Prophet, Salat, Zakat, Hajj, Ramadan-Five Pillars of Islam- and other teachings of the religion, including poetry in praise of the Holy Prophet Mohammed.

These important books were later translated into the Hausa Language, which became popular in many Qur'anic schools in Kano, and other parts of northern Nigeria. Many of those that later became the followers of the revered Islamic scholar in Kano said his prodigious appetite for Islamic Knowledge put him ahead of his peers that only few people of his age could compete with him. Similarly, it was said that many of his contemporaries were even coming to him for knowledge, which soon qualified him to enter into the elite group of *Tafsir* at his early age. According to Naqshbandiya Foundation for Islamic Education-one of the most authoritative compilers of the History of Qur'anic Education in Northern Nigeria-there were five Islamic schools of knowledge in Kano in the 1920s when Nasiri Muhammad Umar Kabara was growing up. These five renowned schools could be regarded as the pre-university institutions in Kano namely: Mallam Ibrahim Qur'an School in Yakasai Ward ran by the Chief Judge of Kano; Malam Mustafa Qur'an School located in Kurawa Ward organized by the Bichi Circuit Judge; the Qur'an School in Daneji Ward owned and ran by the Deputy Imam of Kano Central Mosque; Sheikh Mallam Sambo Abdulkarim Qur'an School located at Ciromawa Ward, and lastly; Mallam Inuwa Qur'an School ran by the Chief Imam of Mayanka Ward. According to some records, Nasiri Muhammad Umar Kabara as a young Islamic scholar visited all these five Qur'anic schools and devoured all the books in their libraries.

Other Islamic scholars, who came across young Nasiri Muhammad Umar Kabara during the 1920s in Kano came away impressed with his vast knowledge, and deep understanding of the Islamic Knowledge. According to Dr. Adamu of Bayero University in Kano, by the 1930s, ancient Kano was bustling with knowledge, especially among young Islamic scholars, who had just graduated from the renowned Al-Alzhar University, Cairo Egypt-the first university in Africa-and had returned home to put their knowledge to use. Aliko Dangote was later to attend this university. Young Nasiri Muhammad Umar Kabara joined them and took them up on several debates concerning the religion of Islam. They too were wowed by the young man with such analytical mind, who had successfully combined his Timbuktu ancestry-another important center of Islamic Knowledge in the Arab world even credited by some historians as the site of the first university in the Arab World-with his Kano knowledge. By the mid-1930s, the 16-year old Nasiri Muhammad Umar Kabara as a revered Islamic scholar continued to keep every Islamic scholar guessing which of the Sufi's sects he would eventually pitch his religious tent. In 1937 at the relatively young age of 18, the *Qadriyya* Sufi Sect in Kano got its foremost scholar.

The entry of Nasiri Muhammad Kabara, even though he was in his late teens changed the profile of the *Qadriyya* Sect in Kano. He introduced new ideas and festivals into the teaching of students studying in the sect's Qur'anic schools in Kano. He brought radical reforms to the *Tariqa*- he introduced a festival in celebration of the birthday of *Shaykh Abd al-Qadri al-Jilani,* which had been abandoned by Islamic faithful for long, and instituted the use of *Bandiri* in Kano City and throughout Hausa land in northern Nigeria. In spite of his vast knowledge in *Sufism,* and his intellect, many older scholars within the movement still considered him a young man and at 18-yeras old, he was not accepted into the leadership of the sect, but was only given the *Wazifa* or Recitation of the Holy Qur'an. The apogee of his learning and thus, recognition occurred during the reign of Mr. Abdullahi Bayero, the Emir of Kano, between 1926 and 1953, and the father of the current Emir of Kano, Mr. Ado Bayero; the 13th Emir of Kano. When Emir Abdullahi Bayero was embarking on Holy Pilgrimage to Mecca and Medina in the 1930s, Nasiri Muhammad Kabara sent a letter through the Wali to the Emir requesting him to get an *Ijaza,* who would become his *Muqaddan* of his own *Zawiya.* These are words in Islam that non-Muslims may not understand so here are their meanings in the story of Nasiri Muhammad Kabara and connection to Aliko Dangote as will be seen shortly. *"Ijaza"* is a permission given to an Islamic scholar by an Emir designating that particular person as an authority in interpretation of some portions of the Holy Qur'an. It could also be interpreted as the power to be conferred or adjudged as an authority on certain textual portions of the Holy Qur'an. "Ijaza Mujarada" or "Narrative Permission" as one Islamic scholar explained at Bayero University, Kano could be granted by the Emir to an individual designating that particular person as an authority on a specific text or group of texts in the Holy Qur'an.

It could also be Group Permissions by the Emir in council to a particular person in that order, or a group of Islamic scholars, who have proven by conduct and deep knowledge of certain textual portions of the Holy Qur'an as correct interpreters. Other types of Ijaza that have been identified by Sheikh G.F. Haddad in *"Living Islam, Living Tradition"* include *"Ijazatu al-'umum"* or universal permission for all the Muslims; *"Ijazatu majhul"* or permission to an unknown; *"Ijaza mu 'allaqa"* or conditional permission, *"Ijazatu al-ma'dum"* or permission to the nonexistent, *"Ijazatu ma lam yatahammalhu al-mujizu li-yarwiyahu al-mujazu idha tahammalahu al-mujiz* or permission to narrate what the giver of permission has not given himself permission, and several others. *Muqaddam* is a title adopted by Islamic nations, usually as an Arabic title designating an Islamic scholar as a leader in an Islamic community, who normally is the spokesman of that particular Moslem community. Such a title is traditionally given to early converts of Islam and is supposed to exercise powers over both religious and at times secular aspects of the Moslem *ummah* (faithful). In some Arab nations, the title confers military functions to the holder of the title, and the use of the title is popular among the *Tijaniyah Sufi* sect of whom the *Qadriyya* community is a part of in Kano, and other parts of the Islamic world in West and North Africa.

Tafsri in Islam is very important in determining scholarship, and playing leadership roles among Muslim *ummah* or believers. In Islam, the way and manner the Holy Qur'an and other books were written contain some coded and secret meanings, which require spiritual inspirations to de-code such hidden and spiritual meanings. Scholars believe there are some Moslems gifted with the knowledge to interpret the meanings of words, phrases, parables, thoughts, and other figures of speech. Other competencies that *Tafsri* require are the exact interpretations of some Islamic rulings, and laws especially in communities that are governed by *Shar'ia* or Islamic

Law. Majority of Islamic scholars believe that the Prophet Mohammed was the first person to lay example on how *Tafsri* should be done by reciting the verses of the Qur'an to his followers, and follow up with exact interpretations. Any Islamic scholar who engages in this act of Qur'an teaching, according to Moslem scholars in the city of Kano could be said to be engaging in *Tafsri* or simply called *Tafsri* once he has been adjudged as very proficient or divinely inspired to indulge in such act.

The *bandiri* in its exact meaning is a piece of drum used among Sufi adherents in Islam. It is a ritual for receiving trances or visions from the super-natural world. The drum can also be beaten to inspire super-natural dreams by Sufi believers. According to Brian Larkin in *"Bandiri: Music, Globalization, and Urban Experience in Nigeria"* while detailing his research works in northern Nigeria; " Bandiri singers are Hausa musicians who take Indian film tunes and change the words to sing songs praising the prophet Muhammad." *Jubbahs* is a way of dressing among Islamic scholars to distinguish them from other people. It is a flowing robe that is presented to a *Muqaddam* as an instrument of religious authority. There is nothing spectacular about the dress, according to some religious analysts and Islamic scholars, because any Moslem or ordinary man in the street can wear it. In some Arab nations, similar attire such as *Hijabs, Jibabs* etc. are commonplace and the *Jubbahs,* in particular is supposed to be worn by honorable Muslim sheikhs and scholars for distinguishing and identification purposes.

The letter that Nasiri Muhammad Kabara wrote to Emir Abdullahi Bayero confounded the respected emir, who was surprised that such a young man with deep knowledge and penetrating insight into the Holy Qur'an lived in Kano. Consequently, before the emir departed for Mecca and Medina, he sent *jubbah* and a cap to Nasiri Muhammad Kabara designating him the emir's *Muqaddan.* That appointment raised the public profile of the young Islamic scholar, and to solidify, and cash in on his new recognition, he, Nasiri Muhammad Kabara as the new *Muqaddan* to Alhaji Abdullahi Bayero, Emir of Kano decided to embark on his Hajj or Holy Pilgrimage to Mecca and Medina immediately his boss returned from his own Hajj. In 1949 at the age of 30 years, Kabara decided to embark on Hajj, and when he was preparing to embark on the Holy Pilgrimage, he contacted one of his popular students/followers in one of the Sufi's madras and his near age-mate. His name was then Malam Sanusi Dantata; a 32-year old Kano merchant, who sources said, bankrolled the entire pilgrimage.

The Holy Pilgrimage of 1949 afforded Nasiri Mohammed Kabara the opportunity to further deepen his knowledge as he had stops-over in many ancient Islamic centers along the route to the Holy Lands of Mecca and Medina during his return journey back to Kano. He met the popular Sheikh Muhammad al-Fatih of Sudan, and had discussions with Sheikh Qarib Allah Khalifa, leader of the Samaniya Sect of Sudan, and went back to the ancestral homes of his ancestors in Mauritania, where he was warmly received by Sheikh Hashim Muhammad, the newly-installed Khalifa of Mauritania. With these extensive backgrounds, contacts and voyages, Nasiri Muhammad Kabara returned to Kano to warm embrace of his supporters, and soon became the undisputed leader of the Qadriyya Movement in Kano and the whole of Nigeria. Among those who used to come to the Dantata Family House in Kano City during this period was a young man known as Malam Mohammad Dangote. Meanwhile, Mr. Sanusi Dantata used the occasion of his own return back from Hajj to have a stop-over in Ghana. It was during this period that he met Sheikh Ali Kumasi (born in 1902), who was the leader of the *Qadriyya* Movement in Ghana. Few years later, Ali Kumasi relocated from Ghana to Kano City, and that strained the existing relationship between the two learned Islamic scholars: Sheikhs Nasiri Muhammad Kabara and Ali Kumasi. Naturally, Mr. Sanusi Dantata was caught in between his friendship with his two Islamic brothers, who had become rivals in Kano.

Meanwhile, Nasiri Muhammad Kabara was becoming more popular and powerful, and was soon appointed into the council of the advisers of Emir of Kano, Abdullahi Bayero; a council which also had the wealthiest Kano man, Sanusi Dantata as a member. Mr. Mohammed Dangote, who was a business associate of Mr. Sanusi Dantata and a member of the *Qadriyya* sect, too sided with Sheikh Ali Kumasi which cemented his business relationship with the Dantatas. But Mohammad was also a politician. The Dantatas are renowned business men and women and the family patriarch, Pa Alhassan Dantata had left a strict warning to all his children just like Mr. Sule Oyeshola Gbadamoshi (S.O.G) of Ikorodu, Lagos "commanded " all his children: have nothing to do with politics, but befriend politicians, because you may need them in the future. During this period, the children of Sanusi had begun to come up of age, and his two daughters among his many children were very attractive. In the early 1950s, Mohammad Dangote, who had been ogling at one of the daughters of his friend, Mariya, summed up courage and told of his feelings for the young lady to her father, Sanusi Dantata, his business associate.

Marriage in Islam is very different from other types of marriage and among the *Qadriyya* Sect; there are stringent procedures to be followed before a marriage is consummated. There are certain characteristics that Sufi Moslems want or expect from an ideal wife when considering marriage according to *Sura al-Nisa, 4:34*. Among *Qadriyya* adherents, issues such as the age, manners, wealth, beauty, family status and, of most importance, the religion of the would-be bride are important. Since a man is expected to support a woman, he should be economically well-off than his prospective wife, because if it is the other way round, she may dominate him. She must be a Moslem believer, for, as one Islamic teacher in Kano disclosed, quoting Prophet Muhammad; "You should marry a religious woman; otherwise you will be a loser. Do not marry women off for their comeliness; their comeliness may lead them to perdition. Do not marry them off for their possessions; their possessions may lead them to dominate. Marry them for their religion. A Black, believing slave is better than a beautiful free woman who does not believe. The woman should not be tall or gaunt, short or ugly, or have bad manners. She should not be old or have a child from a previous marriage. She should not be a slave if the man can marry a free woman."

Normally, the man should be far older than his would-be wife, and some Islamic scholars expect the woman to be between 14 years and 20 years of age, and by 30 years, should be matured and all the children she wants to bear should cease by 40, because of health reasons for her and her children. It is *haramic* or sacrilegious, and condemnable for a Moslem bride-to-be to lose her virginity before marriage. She must not have been previously married and have a child out of wedlock. In addition to these characteristics, a would-be bride should have the ability of conception. A Moslem marries a woman, who is able to conceive and gives him offspring so that humanity can be preserved. All these qualities Mariya possessed, and even more so, Mohammad Dangote was madly in love. He accepted all the conditions that his future father-in-law gave for the marriage to be consummated when he confided in his business associate, and friend, the lady's father, Sanusi Dantata.

It did not take long for Mr. Sanusi Dantata to make up his mind after Mohammad Dangote had informed him of his interest in his daughter. "I'll rather give you my daughter than someone else. I know you, we are business partners, we attend the same mosque, and you have been my business acquaintance for years, so I know Mariya will be safe in your hands," Mr. Sanusi Dantata was quoted as saying. But there was one concern that the rich man had about his future son-in-law: Mohammad Dangote was a politician. According to his first son by Mariya, who later became the richest Black person in the world, Aliko recounted, "My father, Mohammad Dangote was a business man and a politician. He was a member of the Northern House of Assembly." The two men were prepared to work around the snag, and Mr. Sanusi Dantata had the upper hand so he set the rules. Since his friend Mohammad Dangote had other wives, his eldest daughter; Mariya would still live with him at his sprawling mansion in his house in Koki, Kano. "Mohammad, you have other wives and I love Mariya so much that I don't want her to experience any heartbreak," Mr. Sanusi Dantata told his friend. "In addition, you're a politician; who may not have the time to stay at home, and I will not allow my precious daughter to live Kano for Lagos, so if you want her, she must continue to live under my roof." Mr. Mohammad Dangote agreed to the terms set by his friend, and so on a Glorious Friday at the Sanusi Dantata Family Mosque in Kano City in the mid-1950s, Mr. Mohammad Dangote and young Mariya Sanusi-Dantata were joined in holy matrimony at a *Nikai* (wedding) ceremony officiated by Sheikh Ali Kumasi. All the friends of the Dantatas were present with a special representative of the Emir of Kano, Mr. Abdullahi Bayero; the 11th Emir of Kano. Mr. Mohammad Dangote was far, far older than his young beautiful bride, but in the religion of Islam, age is no barrier to love and marriage. Mohammad Dangote, the bridegroom / husband did not deviate from the agreement he had with his father-in-law. At any rate, he was very busy with his political activities. He had his family in Kano, but his base was in Kaduna, which was the political and administrative seat of the Northern Peoples Government.

Less than two years after the consummation of the marriage, Mr. Mohammad Dangote was in Kaduna in 1957 when news reached him that his wife, Mariya Sanusi-Dantata-Dangote had put to bed in the famous family house of the Dantatas in Kano City. It was on Wednesday April 10, 1957, and the baby boy weighed about 3.1kg. Immediately news reached Mr. Sanusi Dantata that his daughter had given birth to a bouncing baby boy, he left everything he was doing and went to see the new addition to the Dangote-Dantata Family. He was elated when he saw the boy; he took some features from his father, and the built of his mother, but Mr. Sanusi Dantata made up his mind to give his own brain to this kid. The reason was because; he was his first grandchild, and a boy, who would take the touch of the legendary Dantata Family fame to the fourth and fifth generations of the Dantatas.

On Wednesday April 17, 1957 at a quiet but elaborate ceremony inside the private mosque of Mr. Sanusi Dantata in Koki quarters in Kano City, the *Sunna* or naming ceremony of the first grandson of Mr. Sanusi Dantata was held. The rest Dantatas were present, while Mr. Mohammad Dangote, the proud father, sat by his wife, Mariya, who was holding the new born baby. Mr. Sanusi Dantata, as usual, was calling the shots. He had already chosen a name for his first grandson: Aliko. The proud father said his new son should be named after him, so the child was christened Aliko Mohammad Dangote. At the naming ceremony of the first grandson of Mr. Sanusi Alhassan Dantata, kola nuts and other edibles were plenty in abundance. The officiating Sheikh Ali Kumasi, the Chief *Imam* or priest went to the main business of the day immediately all the guests had settled down and the new name for the new baby boy had been chosen. His maternal grandfather said he saw something different in the birth of the boy and said he wanted him to be named "Aliko" which means "The defender of humankind."

If Aliko were to be born in America, his name would probably have been Alexander, for the name "Aliko" has its origin in Greek history. The name was after the legendary Alexander the Great, who lived in the 4th century and ruled over Macedonia and the Greek world. At the relatively young age of 30, Alexander had conquered the whole world of his day as a great military general. His conquests and military prowess earned him the distinguished honor of having the popular Egyptian city of Alexandria named after him, and historians refer to him as Alexander the Great.

In other words, Pa Sanusi Alhassan Dantata saw something in his first grandson, which no one in the family saw, and which was highly prophetic. The child's parents, especially the father wanted his first son by Mariya Dantata to be his *"tokora"* or namesake, which is the practice in Islam, so he wanted the child's middle name to be taken from the father's first name which is "Mohammad." Of course, the name, "Mohammad," is usually given to a male child and it means; "The Glorified One" - the name of Prophet Mohammad, the founder of the Islamic religion. The first and eldest grand- child of Pa Sanusi Alhassan Dantata and the great, grand-child of Pa Alhassan Abdullahi Dantata was thus named; Aliko Mohammad Dangote or Aliko Dangote for short.

Sir Ahmadu Bello, first indigenous premier of northern Nigeria with Emir Sanusi of Kano, Aliko's hometown when the going was good in the 1950s until both parted ways. © Kano Museum, Kano

Mr. Abubakar Tafawa-Balewa, the Prime Minister of Nigeria in 1960 with President Dwight Eisenhower of the United States at the White House. Behind middle is Chief Theophilus Olawale Shobowale Benson, Nigeria's Minister of Information. Photo Credit State Department, Washington DC, USA

Nigeria's first prime minister, Abubakar Tafawa-Balewa visited President Dwight Eisenhower at the White House in 1960 shortly after Nigeria attained independence from Britain. Among Balewa's entourage was Mr. Theophilus Olawale Shobowale (T.O.S) Benson, Nigeria's minister of information. Bello preferred to hold court in Kaduna rather than Lagos but he (Bello) was the one running the show from Kaduna © US State Department, Washington, DC

The founding fathers of Nigeria (L-R) Obafemi Awolowo, Abubakar Tafawa-Balewa, Ahmadu Bello and Nnamdi Azikiwe Photo Credit Federal Ministry of Information Nigeria

Obafemi Awolowo, premier of western Nigeria, Tafawa-Balewa, first prime minister of Nigeria and Ahmadu Bello, premier of northern Nigeria: Mohammad Dangote, Aliko's father belonged to the same political party with Tafawa-Balewa and Bello.

Alhaji Ado Bayero, Emir (King) of Kano 1963- where Aliko was born Photo Credit Kano Museum

Emir Ado Bayero, the Muslim king of Kano, Aliko's hometown and Alhaji Alhassan Dantata (1877- 1955).

o Alhassan Abdullahi Dantata (1877-1955) Aliko Dangote's maternal great-grandfather Photo Credit: Family File

Aliko's maternal great-grandfather and the richest man in Kano in the 1950s. . © Kano Museum, Kano

CHAPTER 2
GROWING UP IN THE LAND OF BLACK ARABIAN MERCHANTS

NIGERIA WAS at the ferment of political and nationalistic agitations when Aliko Dangote was born. Nigerian historians and political humorists commonly assert that, prior to 1960 when the British colonial authorities ceded the political stage for the local politicians to govern themselves; Nigeria was sitting on three legs. The western region was administered by the Action Group (AG), led by the late Mr. Obafemi Awolowo; the eastern region was controlled by the National Citizens of Nigerians and the Cameroons (NCNC), led by the late Mr. Nnamdi Azikiwe, while Mr. Ahmadu Belo led the Northern People's Congress (NPC). Mr. Awolowo ruled western region with administrative capital in Ibadan, Azikiwe held court in the coal city of Enugu, while Bello ruled in the northern region's town of Kaduna.

The seat of the federal government was in commercial Lagos. Between 1887 and 1900, the British colonial authorities brought all the disparate towns, villages, cities and regions in the areas known as Nigeria together under British colonial rule and divided the large swath of land in the north and south into what is referred to as; the

Dangote

Northern and Southern Protectorates of Nigeria. In 1903, the British colonial authorities conquered the Hausa-Fulani Caliphate based in Sokoto, which had in turn conquered much of what eventually became northern Nigeria during the Jihad waged by the legendary Othman Dan Fodio. Three years later, Lagos was annexed to become part of Southern Protectorate of Nigeria just as Sokoto became part of Northern Protectorate of Nigeria.

Following the outbreak of WWI, the British colonial authorities were concerned about the costs of the global war and dwindling budgetary allocations to run and administer their foreign colonies. This necessitated the merging of the Colony of Lagos and the Southern and Northern Protectorates together as the Protectorate of Nigeria. The 1914 annexation and unification of both the north and south were later referred to as; the Amalgamated Territories of Nigeria. Conscious of the impact of WWI on the psyches of peoples of the world toward foreign domination and imperialism, the British colonial government in Nigeria began to chart ways to disengage from Africa so the natives could govern themselves. This materialized in the next three decades after several outspoken Nigerians; especially the early educated elites, who studied in the United Kingdom, the Americas and other parts of the world led the nationalist struggles for political independence. In the next three decades, the British colonial authorities took Nigeria through five constitutional arrangements and tried successfully to weld all the centrifugal and centripetal territories of Nigeria into a single whole.

In 1922, the Clifford Constitution was born and allowed the natives to stand for elections as legislative members for Lagos Council. The signals that the British colonial government gave that it was preparing Nigerians for self-government coupled with the push on the path of the early Nigerian nationalists led to the formation of the Nigerian Youth Movement (NYM) in 1936. For administrative convenience and to ensure autonomy of the constituents' parts of Nigeria, Governor Bernard Henry Bourdillion (1935-

1943) successor to Mr. Donald Charles Cameron (1931-1935) in the fall of 1935 divided southern Nigeria into two separate entities known as; western and eastern regions in 1939. Seizing on the political ferment in the country, some southern politicians coalesced around the great Nigerian orator, journalist, philosopher and the *bête noire* of the British colonial administration, Mr. Nnamdi Azikiwe to float a political party known as the National Council of Nigeria and the Cameroons in 1944. Notable foundation members of the NCNC were: Mr. Herbert Macaulay who co-founded the NCNC-Nigeria's first political party with Mr. Azikiwe, Messrs. Theophilus Olawale Shobowale Benson, Adeniran Ogunsanya, Patrick Nwakama Ottih of southern Cameroons, Harold Dappa-Biriye, Kenekueyero B. Omateseye, and Mrs. Funmilayo Ransome-Kuti, the first treasurer and women leader of the party among several notable leaders. In 1946, a new colonial governor-general of Nigeria was sent from Britain, and a new constitution known as Richard's Constitution named after Sir Arthur Richards (1943-1947) was passed into law. Seizing the initiative of their southern counterparts that had formed a political party five years earlier, politicians in the northern region of Nigeria met in Kaduna and formed the Northern People's Congress (NPC) in 1949. The main movers behind the formation of NPC, which began, first as a cultural organization, before it became a full-fledged political party were Messrs. Ahmadu Bello and Abubakar Tafawa-Balewa. Other notable foundation members of the NPC were; Mr. Maitama Sule, Mr. Shehu Shagari, who was to become Nigeria's first executive president (1979-1983), and others. Gov. Richard left Nigeria and was replaced by Mr. John Stuart McPherson in 1947. The latter was instrumental in setting the stage for regional elections in Nigeria a year later.

Three year later, a political magus in the western region who had just returned from the United Kingdom as a lawyer, just 41 years old, rallied all traditional rulers, the intelligentsia and elites in the western region of Nigeria to form a political party known as the Action Group (AG). The young attorney was the legendary Mr. Obafemi Jeremiah Awolowo and the launching of the political party took place in April 1951. The AG was initially a cultural association called; *"Egbe Omo Oduduwa."* Other foundation members of the AG were Messrs. Samuel Ladoke Akintola, Adekunle Ajasin, Bode Thomas, Oba Olateru-Olagbegi of Owo, Oba Samuel Akinsanya, the Odemo of Ishara, Oba Moses Awolesi, the Akarigbo of Remo, Anthony Enahoro and others. As if the British colonial authorities had clearly read the political mood of Nigerians aftermath of WWII, in 1951, Mr. Macpherson passed a new constitution into law and elections were held in the three regions of the north, west, and east. The 1951 regional elections were held in the three regions with the British regional governors as chief electoral officers. In the northern region, Mr. Bryan was the governor and twenty out of the ninety seats allocated to the northern region were to come from Kano alone. The NPC controlled most of the seats in the northern house of assembly and among some of the notable members were; Messrs. Abubakar Tafawa Balewa, Ahmadu Bello, Ibrahim Imam of Yerwa representing the Bornu Youth Movement, Muhammadu Mustapha Made Gyan, A.A. Agogede, Iya Abubakar, Malam Mukhtar Bello, Mr. Shehu Shagari, Mr. Ado Bayero, Bello Malabu, Malam Bashir Umaru, Malam Ibrahim Mwa, Alhaji Usman Liman, Malam Ibrahim Musa Cashash, and Malam Mohammed Dangote, the father of Aliko who was to become the richest person in Nigeria sixty-two years later.

The 1951 regional elections in the northern region and the other two western and eastern regions of Nigeria laid the foundations for the constitutional conferences that were held in London between July 30 and August 22, 1953 on how a future independent Nigeria would be governed. Gov. McPherson left Nigeria in 1955 and Mr. James Robertson replaced him and prepared Nigeria for independence in 1960. At the epoch-making event attended by equal representatives of the three regional governments of NPC-northern Nigeria, AG-western Nigeria and NCNC-eastern Nigeria, the AG and NCNC jointly canvassed for a federal government. On the other hand, the NPC listed a-10-point political agenda, which should govern the future federal arrangement in an independent Nigeria namely: higher education, defense, power (electricity), insurance, foreign trade, water control, and central court of justice, industrial development, external relations, and the issue of southern Cameroons. The delegates from the southern Cameroons informed the conference they wanted to opt out of future Nigeria but were told to submit the request for a referendum when they returned home. The referendum eventually passed and southern Cameroons joined with the northern Cameroons to become today's nation of Cameroon. Following the successful conclusion of the London Constitutional Conference, a new constitution known as the Lyttelton Constitution came into effect in 1954, which retained the political restructure of the country as it was fashioned out under the Macpherson Constitution three years earlier: 184 members in the federal legislature in Lagos with a speaker, and three ex-officio members; 92 members from the northern house of assembly, eastern and western regional houses of assembly had 42 members each and 6 for southern Cameroon and 2 for Lagos. At the regional houses of assembly, 90, 80 and 84 legislators were in Kaduna, Ibadan and Enugu in the north, west and east respectively.

The year 1957 when Aliko Dangote was born, the British colonial authorities were preparing to depart Nigeria for Britain, preparatory to Nigeria's attainment of political independence in 1960. There were flurry of conferences in Britain by the various stake-holders toward working out modalities among the various ethnic and tribal groupings that make up modern Nigeria on the future independent nation. The British Government sent Mr. Westray Gawain Bell (1909-1995) to serve as the governor of the northern region that year and mandated to stay in his position till Nigeria attained political independence, but after independence, Mr. Bell stayed till 1962 and Malam Kashim Ibrahim (1910-1990) took over as the governor of the northern region. Meanwhile, the indomitable and legendary Mr. Ahmadu Bello (1910-1966), who had won the April 1954 regional elections was holding forte as premier and his administration had the following cabinet ministers: Mr. Ali Monguno, minister of agriculture; Malam Mua'zu Lamido, minister of animal and forest resources; Mr. Hedley H. Marshall, minister of justice and attorney-general and Malam Abdullahi Danburan Jada, minister of northern Cameroon affairs. The northern part of Cameroon was initially slated to be a part of independent Nigeria, but when a referendum was conducted in that part of Nigeria, the Nigerians inhabiting that geographical area chose to be a part of independent Cameroon rather than be with Nigeria in 1960. Other ministers in the administration of Mr. Bello were: Mr. Isa Kaita, the *Madawaki of Katsina* as minister of education; Mr. Abba M. Habib, minister of trade and industry, the minister of works was Mr. George U. Ohikere; the minister of finance was Mr. Aliyu, the *Makama Bida;* Mr. Abdullahi Maikano Dutse was minister of local government affairs, while Mr. Ahman, the *Galadima of Pategi* was minister of health; and Malam Shehu Usman, the *Galadima of Maska* was minister of internal affairs; Mr. Michael Audu Buba, the *Waziri of Shendam* and Mr. Ibrahim Musa Gashash was minister of land and survey.

In order to bring governance to the grassroots level and involve all important stake-holders in the Nigerian People's Congress (NPC) administration of northern Nigeria before the attainment of political independence in 1960, first class traditional rulers were constituted into a ministerial council without portfolios: Sultan Abubakar III of Sokoto; Emir Muhammadu Sanusi of Kano, Emir Usman Nagogo of Katsina; Emir Sulu Gambari of Ilorin; Atta Ali Obaje of Igala and the chief of Wukari, Mr. Atoshi Agbamanu. Six ministers of state were equally appointed namely: Mr. Abutu of Obekpa; Malam Muhammadu Kabir, the *Ciroma* of Katagum; Mr. Samuel Aliyu Ajayi; Malam Umaru Abba

Kaam, the Wali of Muri; Mr. D.A. Ogbadu and Mr. Aliyu, the Turaki of Zazzau. In the October-November 1956 regional elections which produced the Ahmadu Bello Administration, 134 members were elected into the northern house of assembly and the region's minister of justice and attorney-general, Mr. Hedley. H. Marshal became an un-elected ex-officio member.

The political activities in Kano were contentious and acrimonious during the 1950's leading up to the granting of political independence in 1960. To understand the complex political situation, especially between the Sultanate and other northern Nigerian emirates, especially Kano, one must understand the religious differences between the various emirates. Although Othman dan Fodio had succeeded in annexing virtually all Hausa lands and converted the people into the religion of Islam, there were still two broad "houses" of beliefs in the religion: the *Tijaniyya* Moslem and the *Quadriyya* Moslem sects, which often create tensions between the Sultan of Sokoto and other emirs in the northern region. These religious differences are often played down by the larger interests of the Moslem brotherhood; nevertheless, the difference normally polarizes the Hausa-Fulani Moslem dynasty. This was exactly what occurred in the late 1950s shortly after young Aliko was born and three years into Nigeria's political independence when Aliko was 6 years old. It was during the reign of Malam Muhammadu Sanusi, the 11th Emir of Kano in 1953-two years before the death of Pa Alhassan Dantata-the richest man in Kano and Nigeria at the time, according to the London-based *West Africa* magazine and four years before the birth of Mr. Aliko Mohammad Dangote.

How Emir Muhammadu Sanusi quickly fell out of favour three years after Nigeria attained political independence had been attributed to politics. After all, he could be referred to as one of the founding fathers of Nigeria, because he was a member of the northern region delegates to the Nigerian Constitutional Conference in the United Kingdom on July 27, 1953. Another London Constitutional Conference was again held between May 23 and June 31, 1957, the year Aliko Dangote was born. The two conferences were charged with the task of deliberating on the political structure of a future independent Nigeria. Among the delegates that attended the conferences were: the Action Group delegates (western region); Mr. Adesoji Aderemi, the Oni of Ife; Messrs. Bode Thomas; Samuel. L. Akintola, Arthur Prest, and Obafemi Awolowo, who was then western regional minister of local government. The following people were chosen as advisers to the western region delegates: Messrs Rotimi Williams; S. O. Shonibare, Mr. Samuel. O. Awokoya, the western region minister of education; Mr. Anthony Enahoro, Justice Latifu J. Dosumu. Mrs. Tanimowo Ogunlesi; G. C. Nonyelu, Mr. Alfred O. Rewane; Mallam Mudi Sipikin; Olateru- Olagbegi II, the Olowo of Owo, who was western regional minister without portfolio and the Obi of Idumuje Ugboko.

The National Council for Nigeria and the Cameroons (eastern region) delegates were led by Mr. Nnamdi Azikiwe comprising; Messrs. Kingsley Ozumba Mbadiwe, E. O. Eyo, Esq., Mallam Bello Ijumu and Mr. Kolawole Balogun. The following were chosen as advisers to the NCNC delegates: Messrs. Mbonu Ojike, T. N. P. Birabi, V. A. Nwankwo.; N. N. Mbile, L. P. Ojukwu; E. G. Gundu and Dennis C. Osadebe.; Mrs. Margaret Ekpo; Mr. H. Omo Osagie; Mr. Yamu Numa, and Mr. F. S. Edah. The Northern People's Congress (northern Nigeria) had the smallest number of delegates led by Mr. Ahmadu Belo, who was the northern region minister of local government and community development. Other members were; Messrs. Abubakar Tafawa Balewa, the central minister of works and transport; Aliyu Makaman Bida, the northern region minister of education and social welfare and, Emir Usuman Nagogo, of Katsina, who was the central minister without portfolio. The following people served as advisers to the NPC delegates: Messrs. Abba Habib, Ajiyan Bama; Pastor David Lot, from Benue-Plateau; Mallam Ibrahim Imam from Bornu; Mallam Saladu Alamanu, Mr. G. U. Ohikere,; Benjamin Akiga, Mohammadu Ribadu, the central minister of natural resources, mines and power; Mallam Dauda Kwoi; Mr. Shehu Ahmadu, Mallam Sarkin Shanu and Mallam Nuhu Bamalle.

To demonstrate that ancient Kano had always acted independently from the northern region political mood, the people of Kano traditionally registered their political uniqueness by voting for the Northern Elements Progressive Union (Northern Nigeria, Kano) or NEPU. At the constitutional conference in London, they demanded, and got a separate delegation led by one man; Mallam Aminu Kano. He came with his only adviser: Mallam Abubakar Zukogi. The northern Cameroon was still a part of Nigeria and was equally represented by one delegate and one adviser: Mr. E. M. L. Endeley, the central minister of labour and Rev. J. C. Kangsen, respectively.

The south-eastern people, or those referred to as the Niger Delta had always claimed and still claim that they are a distinct people from their Ibo eastern Nigerians and thus canvassed for a separate delegation. They got their request at the second London Conference: two delegate leaders under the aegis of a minority party; the National Independence Party (NIP). These were: Messrs. Eyo Ita., who was eastern regional minister of natural resources, and A. C. Nwapa, who was the central minister of commerce and industries. Three delegate advisers: Messrs Okoi Arikpo, the central minister of lands, survey, local development and communications. Jaja A. Wachuku and E. U. Udoma completed the pack.

The deliberations of the Second Independence Conference in London led to the 1959 general elections, which eventually formed the basis on which the federal and regional governments ruled Nigeria at independence on October 1, 1960. The elections at the three regions of the north, west, and east produced three premiers for the region, but at the federal level, the inability of any of the three dominant parties of NPC, NCNC, and AG to win a simple majority led to a government of national unity. It was mooted by the NPC as a form of government of national unity with the NPC as the senior partner, but the AG rejected any form of alliance, while the NCNC joined the NPC invitation to form an alliance. That alliance led to Mr. Abubakar Tafawa-Balewa becoming the prime minister while the outgoing colonial governor-general, Mr. James Wilson Robertson handed over to Mr. Nnamdi Azikiwe of the NCNC as the governor-general-a sinecure post in a parliamentary system of government-of Nigeria in November 1960.

Meanwhile in Kano, there was intense politicking involving the views and political activities of the reigning Emir Muhammadu Sanusi of Kano. An outspoken traditional ruler who did not hide his political views from his subject; and sooner or later, he ran into trouble with the NPC-led government of Mr. Ahmadu Bello, the region's powerful premier. Another issue that complicated Sanusi's position was his open profession of *Tijaniya surfi* sect, which runs against the Sokoto Caliphate's adherence to the *Quadriya surfi* sect. The differences between the *Tijaniya* and *Qadriyya* Moslem Sects caused the problems of Emir Mohammadu Sanusi seven years before Nigerian attained political independence and three years after the British colonial power departed the political scene. The crisis that engulfed the city of Kano in 1963 following the deposition and eventual banishment of Emir Muhammadu Sanusi affected relationships among friends and between relatives and unsettled the royal family. Born in 1907-four years after the deposition of Emir Muhammadu Abbas, the son of Emir Abdullahi-who was deposed by the British colonial authorities, Sanusi was the elder son of Emir Abdullahi Bayero who reigned between 1926 and 1953.

The tenth Emir of Kano was installed as Emir of Kano following the deposition of his father and banishment to Lokoja. Sanusi had a younger brother, Prince Ado Bayero, who is now the current Emir of Kano. Sanusi worked with the Kano Native Authority between 1926 and 1947 after his education at the Kano Provincial Primary School and Kano Native Middle School. He was a member of the northern house of assembly prior to his ascension to the throne in 1953. He was also made the district head of Bici, while simultaneously holding the powerful title of *Ciroma* of Kano. Following his installation as Emir in 1953, Emir Sanusi was appointed into the northern region assembly and given a ministerial position without portfolio. He was among few northern leaders that participated in the constitutional talks in London, UK, which led to the granting of political independence to Nigeria in 1960. Following the banishment of Emir Muhammadu Sanusi, many prominent northern politicians were said to have died in mysterious circumstances.

According to those that were old enough to witness the crisis in the 1960s who spoke to the authors, the deposition of the respected emir caused many untoward events and strange happenings in the ancient city. Among one of the politicians that died during the crisis was Malam Mohammad Dangote, the father of Aliko Dangote. According to Dangote, "At the time he died, he was a member of the federal house, here in Lagos. He was a member of northern house of assembly in Kaduna. From there he came to Lagos. I was just eight years old when he died. I know (sic) him, but not very, very close, because I was raised by my maternal grandfather."

The problems Emir Sanusi had could not be unconnected with the age-long struggle and rivalries between the house of Othman dan Fodio in Sokoto and the ruling house of Kano. The Jihad that brought the Sultanate under Sokoto lasted for more than a century, until the British colonialists came and whittled down the power of the Sokoto Caliphate. Hitherto, Sokoto was in the habit of influencing the succession to the throne and, who became the Emir of Kano. It was not unusual for Emirs in Kano to shore up their power base by marrying daughters of the Sultan, including currying favors from the Sultanate. The practice stopped in 1905, but the house of Othman Dan Fodio was not about to give up easily its power and influence over Kano. Mr. Ahmadu Bello himself had fought hard to become the Sultan of Sokoto in 1938 but had failed. To compensate him for his lose to his cousin, Mr. Siddiq Abubakar III (1903-1988), who was installed the 17th Sultan of Sokoto, Abubakar created the title; "*Sardauna*" literally meaning "War Leader," hence the name Mr. Ahmadu Bello, the Sardauna of Sokoto. The title; "*Sardauna* of Sokoto," was a new title that never existed in the history of the Sokoto Caliphate. Emir Sanusi took the "independence" of Kano too far through his utterances and blunt criticisms of the NPC-led government of Mr. Ahmadu Bello in northern Nigeria. By 1960 when Nigeria attained political independence, the NPC government of Mr. Ahmadu Bello quickly exploited its power and in 1963, spurious allegations were brought against Emir Sanusi. Subsequently, he was banished to Azare never to return to the throne of his forefathers.

Below is a short political history of the ancient city of Kano featuring the various emirs and their ruling houses between 99A.D and the formation of the ancient city up to the present. The short history of Kano and its emirs are as follows: 99AD: Hausa State founded and Kano too. The Hausa city-states and ancient Kano were a loose federation and autonomous entities without central administrative unit. In 1670-1702, Muhammd Dadi Dan Bawa assumed power in Kano. Between 1702 and 1730, the eldest son of Dadi; Muhamman Sharefa mounted the throne as ruler of Kano. Muhamman Kumbari took over from his father in 1730 and ruled till 1743. Kumbari ceded the stage for his eldest son, Kaber, in 1743, and Kaber was on the throne for ten years. Muhamman Yaji, his eldest son replaced him in 1753 and was on the throne till 1768, when he died and his eldest son, Baba Zakin was made king. When Baba Zakin died in 1776, he was replaced by his son, Dauda Asama II who was on the throne briefly for four years. Muhamman Alwali ruled from 1781 to 1807, and then the Othman Dan Fodio invasion occurred.

Beginning from 1807, Fodio's conquest of Kano led to the era of Moslem Hausa-Fulani suzerainty in the ancient town and in many parts of northern Nigeria. Emir Sulaiman Abahama reigned between 1807 and 1819. He descended from the Modibawa Dynasty, and married the daughter of Sultan Muhammad Bello of Sokoto State. There was no record of him siring a male child as successor to Alwali, who was removed by the invading army of Fodio. He died on August 22, 1819. He was the first Moslem emir of Kano following the inauguration of the Sokoto Caliphate. Ibrahim Dabo mounted the throne in 1819 and reigned till 1845. His great, grandfather had earlier ruled Kano. He descended from one of the earlier rulers of Kano that had converted into Islam. His mother was Halima and became the second emir of Kano. He consolidated his rule through two powerful marriages to first, Maryam, the granddaughter of Othman Man Dan Fodio, and another wife who was the daughter of the Waziri of Sokoto. Before he died on February 9, 1846, he positioned four of his boys to succeed him namely: Usman Dan Ibrahim Dabo, Dan Lawal, Dan Ibrahim Dabo, Abdullahi Dan Ibrahim Dabo, Muhammadu Bello, and Dan Ibrahim Dabo. In 1846, Usman I, Dan Ibrahim Dabo became the third Hausa-Fulani emir of Kano. He died on August 26, 1855.

The monarchy changed from hereditary in 1855; instead of Usman's son succeeding him, his younger brother, Abdullahi, from the same father was made fourth Hausa-Fulani emir of Kano. He used his grandfather's formula to consolidate his hold on power by getting married to the daughter of Sultan Aliyu Babba of Sokoto, the great grandson of Othman Dan Fodio. Before his death on September 8, 1882, he positioned four of his male children for the throne and gave out his daughter in marriage to the first district head of Rabah and the seventh Sultan of Sokoto, Sultan Abu-Bakr II, Ibn Muhammad Bello (1873-1877). His children; Yusuf Galadima dan Abdullahi, (died in 1894), Aliyu Babba dan Abdullahi, Muhammad Abbas dan Abdullahi, Usman dan Abdullahi Zainab binti Abdullahi, married Sultan Abubakar II ibn Muhammad Bello and successfully used religion and marital ties to struggle for the throne.

In 1882, the system reverted back to monarchical hereditary as Muhammed Bello; the son of Ibrahim Dabo became the sixth emir of Kano. He sired four male children before he died on November 25, 1893 but only one later became emir of Kano. His four male children were; Muhammad Tukur dan Muhammad Bello, Ibrahim dan Muhammad Bello, Zakari dan Muhammad Bello, and Abubakar dan Muhammad Bello. He died in 1893 paving the way for his first son who ruled for two years (1893-1895). When he died on March 16, 1895, he left no male child behind. His other brothers could not present a common candidate to lay claim to the throne paving the way for a neutral candidate, Aliyu Baba, the grandson of Abdullahi, the fourth emir of Kano to mount the throne. The seventh emir of Kano, who was on the throne when the British Colonialists took over northern Nigeria resisted British colonialism and was dethroned. He was subsequently banished to Lokoja where he died in exile in 1926. The British colonial authorities changed the rules of the succession game in 1903. Henceforth, Sokoto was denied the power of dictating succession to the throne, and the ancient town of Kano got the autonomy to decide its emir / king.

Following the deposition and banishment of Aliyu Baba in 1903, Muhammad Abbas became the first emir to be appointed by Frederick Lugard following British colonial conquest and the first to be given the title; His Royal Highness by the British colonial authorities. He was the eighth Fulani emir of Kano. The British stopped the idea of the Sultanate sending or appointing an emir for Kano. Before he died on May 1, 1919, Abbas positioned his two surviving sons as future emirs: Abdullahi Bayero dan Muhammad Abbas, and Muhammad Inuwa Abbas. His Highness Emir Usman II became ninth emir but ruled for just seven years (1919-1926). Emir Abdullahi Bayero mounted the throne in 1926. The tenth Emir of Kano and the second longest reigning emir in Kano history, he was the father of Ado Bayero, the current Emir of Kano. His two male children; Muhammad Sanusi and Ado Bayero were later to reign as emirs in quick successions. He died on December 25, 1953). Muhammad Sanusi mounted the throne in 1953. He was the first and only emir of Kano to be knighted by the Queen of England. He was a member of the northern region delegation to the Nigerian Constitutional Conference in London in the late 1950s which led to the independence of Nigeria in 1960. He was deposed in 1963. He died in 1984 at Azare where he was banished to by the NPC government of Mr. Ahmadu Bello. He left a son, Aminu Sanusi whose sons could lay claim to the stool in the future. One of his prominent grandsons is Mr. Sanusi Lamido Sanusi, the current governor of the Central Bank of Nigeria. Between February, 1963 and October, 1963, Muhammadu Inuwa replaced Sanusi as Emir of Kano.

Emir Inuwa was born in 1901. He was the Turakin Kano between 1927 and 1939 and also the district head of Dawakin Kudu. He was ill when he was crowned as emir in February 1963 following the deposition of Emir Muhammadu Sanusi. He died nine months later on October 8, 1963 and was the shortest reigning emir in Kano history. His Highness, Ado Abdullahi Bayero became the thirteenth Hausa-Fulani emir of Kano in 1963. His reign is the longest reigning emir in Kano history to date. He was at his diplomatic post in Dakar as Nigeria's Ambassador to Senegal when he was chosen as emir.

Following the deposition of Emir Sanusi in 1963, there were demonstrations and riots all over Kano. Many houses were set ablaze and some people lost their lives in the orgy of arson and civil disobedience precipitated by the crisis. Many supporters of the deposed Emir Sanusi believed he was removed by the NPC-led government of Mr. Ahmadu Bello, the premier of northern Nigeria, because of his political outspokenness. In order to douse the raging inferno, the NPC government hurriedly chose the then district head of

Dawakin-Kudi, Malam Muhammed Inuwa Abbas as the new emir of Kano. Coming less than two months after Emir Sanusi was deposed; the charged political atmosphere in the ancient city of Kano reached a boiling point. Mr. Abbas took ill and his illness was visible to everyone that he would not be able to discharge his traditional and religious duties as emir. Nevertheless, the NPC government went ahead and installed him as the emir of Kano. On October 8th the same year; barely nine months after his installation, Emir Abass died. His reign was the shortest in Kano history. About forty-five days later, Prince Ado Bayero was installed as the 13th Fulani emir of Kano. Two years later, Mohammad Dangote died and a year after, the first military coup d'état took place. Mr. Ahmadu Bello, the premier of northern Nigeria and other political leaders were assassinated and the era of military regime began in Nigeria.

It is also historically significant to trace the three generations of British explorers and army British generals that shaped the history of Kano, northern Nigeria where Aliko was born and the history of modern Nigeria. The Scottish explorer, Mr. Mungo Park was the first to embark on a voyage to West Africa in his desire to discover the legendary River Niger, which serves much of Nigeria and West Africa today. He later died at Bussa near Lokoja in what later became central Nigeria and present-day capital of Kogi State. His colleague, Mr. Hugh Clapperton took over and extended his discovery to much of the whole of northern region, reaching Kaduna, Zaria, Katsina, Sokoto and Kano. In June 1826, he managed to reach ancient Kano, but contracted a strange disease. He was not deterred until he reached Sokoto, where he was detained by Sultan Bello and where he died in April 1827. The Lander Brothers; Richard and John, took over from the two deceased Scottish explorers. Mr. Richard was the first to arrive in Badagry near Lagos and was later accompanied by his younger brother, Mr. John Lander. They navigated the routes established by both Messrs. Park and Clapperton, but on getting to present-day Kogi State, they were attacked by African tribesmen. Mr. Richard died from arrow wounds shot at them by the villagers before he and his brother could reach New Bussa to see the tomb of Mr. Park. Mr. John Lander died on his return to England from a disease he had contracted in Africa. Historians said the disease that killed him was probably malaria fever.

The pioneering efforts of these British explorers almost two centuries earlier helped the invasion of the present-day Nigeria, when Lagos Colony was annexed by the British in 1806 and the Sokoto Caliphate was similarly conquered in 1903 by General Kemball, who established his garrison in Sokoto and gave Kano semi-autonomy outside Sokoto. He handed over to his fellow military commander, General Frederick Dealtry Lugard, who assumed office as the governor-general of both the Northern and Southern Protectorates in 1912. Lugard, after consultation with his mistress and later wife, Ms. Flora Shaw (1852-1929), who was a foreign correspondent and colonial editor for the *Times* of London newspaper on a vacation at Borgu where Lugard was stationed suggested the name "Nigeria" to the two territories of north and south. Ms. Shaw based the new name on the Niger River or Niger-Area, which was later shortened to "Nigeria." In 1914 as WWI broke out, Lugard quickly united both the Northern and Southern parts of Nigeria, including southern Cameroons into one nation. Reproduced below was the report/article that Ms. Shaw sent to the *Times* of London making a case for the name; "Nigeria," as the appropriate name to call the Northern and Southern Protectorates of the British in pre-1914.

(DAME FLORA LOUISA SHAW LADY LUGARD (1852-1929) THE BRITISH WOMAN WHO NAMED "NIGERIA" IN 1897 GIVE THE NEW NATION, "NIGERIA" AND NOT "ROYAL NIGER"

By: Flora Louisa Shaw

"... Nearly two months have elapsed since the dispatch

of additional British officers and war-like stores to the territories of the Royal Niger Company prepared the public mind for probable military operations in those districts' Sir George Goldie, the governor of the company, left England on December 4, and reached Lokoja, the military capital of the Company, on New Year's Day. It is to be expected that his arrival will be shortly followed by a decision as to any active policy which it may be thought desirable to pursue, and in countries where the fighting season is short action follows swift upon decision. Therefore, if fighting is to take place, it is probably that news of it will be not long delayed. A force of from 800 to 1.000 trained Hausas well provided with military equipment and well led by British officers constitutes an instrument for war which, though small in comparison with the vast crowds in arms commanded by local chiefs of the native Niger States, is still sufficiently important to arouse considerable interest in its proceedings. Various rumors have been current as to the object against which the force is to be directed. The fact that its military base will be at Lokoja combines with, what is known from other sources to give assurance that the operations will be confined wholly to the internal affairs of the territories over which the charter of the Company extends. Border difficulties may be dismissed from consideration. While we wait for definite information it may, therefore, be worthwhile to consider briefly what is known about the general situation in the Royal Niger Company's territories.

In the first place, as the title "Royal Niger Company's Territories" is not only inconvenient to use but to some extent also misleading, it may, be permissible to coin a shorter title for the operation of pagan and Mahomedan States which have been brought by the exertions of the Royal Niger Company within the confines of a British Protectorate and thus need for, the first time in their history to be described as an entity by some general name. To speak of them as the Central Sudan, which is the title accorded by some geographers and travelers, has the disadvantage of ignoring political frontier-lines, while the word 'Sudan' is too apt to connect itself in the public mind with the French Hinterland of Algeria, or the vexed questions of the Nile basin. The name "Nigeria" applying to no other portion of Africa may, without offence to any neighbors, be accepted as co-extensive with the territories over which the Royal Niger Company has extended British influence, and may serve to differentiate them equally from the British colonies of Lagos and the Niger Protectorate on the coast and from the French territories of the Upper Niger.

"Nigeria," thus understood, covers, as is well known, a thickly peopled area of about half-a million square miles, extending inland from the sea to Lake Chad and the northern limits of the empire of Soot, bounded on the east by the German frontier and on the west by a line drawn; southwards from Say to the French frontier of Dlahomey.

The frontier lines have for 10 years been the subject of discussion with our European neighbours on either side. The northern limit was definitely settled by the Anglo-French treaty of 1891; the eastern boundary was determined by the Anglo-German treaty of 1893; and certain vexed questions on the western frontier were for practical purposes brought to a close last year, when the Royal Niger Company completed in the neighbourhood of Bajibo the erection of forts which it judged necessary for the legitimate maintenance of its authority.

Within these limits "Nigeria" contains many widely differing characteristics of climate, country, and inhabitants. Its history is ancient and is not wanting in dramatic elements of interest and romance. The country has been vaguely thought of as a country of swamps and forests, inhabited by pagan natives of low type who, as was lately demonstrated after the outbreak at Brass, had not finally risen above the cannibal stage. This is true of the immediate neighbourhood of the coast, where the Niger runs to the sea through mangrove swamps and a population demoralized by the use of bad European spirits display their barbarous vices to European observation. Nothing could be more misleading than such an impression of the general character of the distinct hill question. As the country slopes inland it rises in successive waves. The first drops to a valley three or four hundred miles inland through which run in opposite directions the two great rivers of the district. The Benue, lowing west by south from the German frontier, and the Middle Niger, flowing east by south from the French Sudan, meet at Lokoja, and the double flood, turning at that point at a right angle, forms the waterway of the Lower Niger to the coast. This is the entrance passage of the Company's territories.

Everything desiring to enter "Nigeria" from the sea must pass this way, and it is therefore not surprising that this is the most generally known portion of the territory. The most important territories of "Nigeria" lie beyond the boundary of the two rivers. North of the valley, traced in an irregular semi-circle from east to north-west by the basins through which they run, the ground rises again in another and more considerable wave, reaching a height of 2,000 feet and maintaining a plateau level of from 1,700 feet to 2,000 feet which does not appear seriously to decline until the northern boundaries of Sokoto are reached. On the further side of two great rivers the ground rises so rapidly as to overhang the flood in some places with hills of which the summits are forest-crowned, while in other parts beautiful views are offered of open and diversified landscape. At this time of the year portions of the riverbanks are covered with masses of flowering creepers, which hang to the water's edge. Scarlet, yellow, pink, and mauve tints prevail. Rare lilies and orchids also abound, and the European travellers who have seen it to rank with the picturesque beauties of the world have held the scenery on some points of the river.

The country of the northern plateau appears to be generally open, and in its natural condition to consist in many parts, like a large portion of the bush country of Australia, of roughgrass lightly timbered. It is well watered, abounds in natural products, and offers evident facilities for cultivation. In the northern parts of the territory connecting the towns of Kuku, Kano, Wurnu, Sokoto, Landu, & co, where, by proximity to the principal seats of native authority, the maximum amount of order and security may perhaps be looked for, the country has been described by a recent traveller as resembling, wherever it is. Not subject to devastation by marauders, a continuous garden. The methods of agriculture are simple, but the fertility of the soil appears to supply the place of more scientific treatment. Hedges of castor oil plant, which grows luxuriantly, divide the cultivated, land. The principal crops raised are Guinea corn, Indian corn, wheat, and other cereals, cassava, rice, onions, cotton, indigo, peas, beans, sweet potatoes, ground nuts, and kitchen vegetables, and the Hausa native of the interior attributes the great superiority in strength which he possesses over the native of the coast to the superior food on which ho lives. The pagan coast native lives chiefly on cassava and bananas, to which gin may perhaps now unfortunately be added. The Hausa of the interior lives chiefly on Guinea corn, and uses neither tea, coffee, nor habitually any stimulant, except the kola nut, which he chews, and which, notwithstanding its disagreeable taste to Europeans, is immensely valued as a native luxury.

The Royal Niger Company, unable to prevent the consumption and importation of alcoholic liquor in the territories of the coast, took the precaution in the early days of their administration of absolutely prohibiting the introduction of European alcohol in any form into the territorys of the interior. Throughout the central region economic trees abound. Conspicuous amongst thorn are India-rubber, shea-butter, tamarinds, date and other palms, besides bread fruit, kuka, and many of which the nameless are less familiar to English ears. The banana and the papaw are among the native fruits, and wherever the pomegranate flourishes the climate is said to be suitable for white habitation. Tobacco grows wild through-the whole region. Towards its eastern boundaries the plateau of "Nigeria" rises into mountainous. Regions, where amid rocky fastnesses and fertile valleys the aboriginal pagan inhabitants of the country defend their liberties as they can from the advancing slave-raider. The mountainous districts alternate with forestland still the home of the elephant, and with regions of extraordinary fertility where cultivated crops flourish. Wild fruits land flowers are plentiful, and extensive tracts are described as being covered with rich sweet herbage full of violets in various parts of "Nigeria;" iron is found and has been worked for centuries. Silver is known to exist in considerable quantities, and the waters of the Benue are reputed by the natives to wash down gold. The whole plateau is diversified by occasional mountain ridges. Towards the west, where it fattens into a region of extensive cotton fields, it stretches across the valley of the Niger to the comparatively little known but interesting kingdom of which the name is variously given as Barbar, Boussa, and Borgu. Near Blajibo, on the boundary of this State, the flood of the Niger is broken by rapids which impede the course of navigation from the sea and have been the scene of the death of more than one distinguished traveller. Borgu has successfully withstood the advance of Mahomedan power, and is one of the few large States which is wholly independent of Sokoto. It is usually counted among the pagan States, but the inhabitants repudiate the description of themselves as pagans and claim to be of the religion of "Issa, the Jew who died for men." A sort of spurious Christianity, largely mixed with pagan superstitions and rites, is held by some travellers to be the religion of the people of Borgu, who are also believed to have some racial affinity with the Berbers of Northern Africa. The populations of "Nigeria" are, like the country which they inhabit, widely diversified. Tribes distinguished by most interesting and remarkable peculiarities occur. The body of the population may, however, fairly be classed in three main divisions. These are pagans, Hausas, and Foulahs. The Pagans are the indigenous inhabitants now driven by successive tides of foreign conquest to take refuge in the mountains or in the countries of the Lower Niger and the coast, where they have sought the protection of European Powers. They are still very numerous, and they represent the lowest civilization of the country.

The Hausas, who are generally regarded as forming the most interesting of the races which inhabit the country, are believed to number as many as 15 millions. At the beginning of this century they were conquered by the Mahomedan Foulahs, who for about two hundred years had been gradually establishing their domination in the Sudan. The Hausas at that time were pagans, but their civilization claims to be quite as old as that of the Foulahs themselves, and they also came originally into "Nigeria" from the north, travelling, according to their own traditions, across Africa from Asia. In "Nigeria" they either drove out or enslaved the original pagan inhabitants and founded several States known geographically as Hausaland. Their principal town of Kano, which is now the commercial capital of Sokoto, has flourished as a centre of government, commerce, and art for nearly 1,000 years. It was founded at about the period when William the Conqueror was engaged in building the Tower of London. Its marketplace is said to be the largest in the world. Kano-made cloth is sought by the Arab populations throughout the north of Africa, and Kano workers in leather and iron have maintained the fame of their district for centuries. The pure-bred Hausa is perfectly black, but is, of course, of a far higher type than the ordinary negro, and differs from him especially in the fact that he is naturally active, persistent, and industrious. He is essentially a man of peace as the Foulah is a man of war. The Hausa of today is Mahomedan, having in the matter of religion yielded to the superior enthusiasm of his conquerors. The Hausa language has, however, conquered the language of the Foulah, and is the Court language of Sokoto.

The Foulah is a Mahomedan Arab, relatively light coloured, of the well-known type. The Foulah domination over various Hausa States in Nigeria was established in the first instance rather by military than by religious superiority, and gradually rulers of the Foulah race began to take the Place of the Hausa Kings. But in the year 1802, a religious war was proclaimed against the Hausa populations, and resulted in the establishment of a certain Sheikh Othman as Sultan of Sokoto, then, as now, the dominant State. Within a few years all the petty Kings of the Hausa States were replaced by Foulah Emirs, and the Foulah race was definitely established in the position which it holds today as the dominating race of the entire district. On the death of Othman one of his sons inherited the sovereignty of Sokoto, and one the sovereignty of Gandu. Gandu has, however, always recognized in some degree the supremacy of Sokoto, and Sokoto has remained the supreme native power of Nigeria. All other Hausa States within the borders of this district pay tribute to it, the so-called pagan State of Borga forming a notable exception. The principal fact in regard to the payment of this tribute with which the administration of the Royal Niger Company is likely to be concerned is that it is largely paid in slaves. The Emir of Adamawa, whose territory lies towards the eastern boundary of the Company, is said to contribute no less a number than 10,000 annually. Nupe, Muri, Bautshi, Zaria, and other States contribute in their degree. Slaves are raided for not only among the pagan populations of the mountains, but by every Foulah King amongst his own Hausa subjects.

Slaves are the currency of the country for all large sums as well as for Imperial tribute, and whenever a petty ruler is pressed for money he raids on whom he dares. So numerous is the Hausa population, and so general is the practice of slave-raiding amongst the Mahomedan Foulahs, that it has been calculated that of the whole population of the world one in every 10 is a Hausa-speaking slave. To proclaim a general war against the practice of slave-raiding over an immense-district through- out which slaves constitute so important a source of wealth would inevitably rouse all the Foulah States to arms, and would be a task far beyond the strength of the government of the Royal

Niger Company. The Company has endeavoured to pursue its work in the territories under its influence with the friendly co-operation of the constituted authorities. No Foulah administration has more constantly oppressed its subject populations in this respect than that of Nupe, whose territory stretches along the northern bank of the Middle Niger from the neighbourhood of Lokoja to the frontier of the western province of Borgu, and whose Emir claims to extend his rights southward over the pagan States upon the other bank. Nupe was one of the latest of the Hausa States to fall under the Foulah yoke. It was conquered about 1818, and the Hausa populations within its borders, who were among the most civilized of the country, have more than once since then risen against their oppressors. On the latest occasion of such a revolt, when the Hausa populations of the kingdom of Nupe rose in 1882 against the then reigning emir, the help of the Company was given to the Mahomedan domination. But help has always been given with conditions.

It has been the practice of the Company to endeavour to protect certain peaceful pagan populations. To the south of the two rivers who have appealed to them for assistance. In a personal interview between the Governor of the Company and the late Emir of Nupe, held at Bida so lately as January of 1892, it was clearly laid down that Nupe should not raid for slaves across either the Niger or the Benue in countries which are under British protection. The Emir of Nupe was definitely warned that slave-raiding south of the river would constitute a casus beli with the Company. The warning has been disregarded, not only by the Emir Maloke, who died last year, but by his successor, the present Emir Abu Bokhari. A force of Nupe soldiers numbering about 1,000 cavalry and 10,000 infantry have been for some months concentrated to the south of the river in the neighbourhood of Kabba waiting only for the season to permit of the beginning of slave-raiding operations.

The latest news which has been received from the territories is to the effect that this force has been further strengthened by the presence of the Emir himself with the remainder of the Nape army, bringing the whole to an approximate strength of 2,000 cavalry and 18,000 to 20,000 infantry. If the Company should judge it necessary in vindication of their authority to enter into armed conflict with this body of troops, the operation will be more considerable than any which has yet been attempted by them, and, whether success or failures attend their arms, the consequences cannot fail to be proportionately far-reaching."

(Culled un-edited from the *Times* of London, January 8, 1897)

CHAPTER 3
ALIKO MOHAMMAD DANGOTE'S PARENTAGE

THERE IS a unique wisdom that comes with longevity, especially those that live long to see their grandchildren and the children of their 3rd generation. Is it because some grandmothers and grandfathers are not so much emotionally attached to their grandchildren that they can see their potentials more than the biological parents of such children? Take some of the world's rich people and billionaires for examples. Why was it that the parents of Jeff Bezos did not detect his potentials very early enough, but it was his grandfather? In an interview with the *People* magazine in 1999, the mother of the creator of the world's largest online retail outlet; *Amazon.com* disclosed that as early as the age of 3, she noticed something in Jeff that brought out his interest in computers and machines.

The Bezoses left Cuba for the United States when Fidel Castro staged the 1959 revolution. The family settled in the predominantly Cuban-American community in southern Florida in Miami called; Little Havana. Jeff Bezos was born few years after and as Mrs. Jacklyn Gise Bezos explained in the interview, she witnessed one particular incident when Jeff was demanding to be moved from his crib to a bed. Now, no responsible mother would do that to a 3-year old, so she gave him a pacifier as a restraint. At night, the tot took a screwdriver and successfully got out of the crib to the bemusement of her mom. Sensing the creativity in the boy, Jeff was enrolled in a Montessori pre-school. His teacher reported that the little kid was always fixated on anything mechanical that he had to be literally removed from other toddlers.

His father, Miguel Bezos; an executive with an oil company in Miami did not want his son to have anything to do with computers or mechanics. But for his grandfather, who was a retiree living in Cotulla, Texas; perhaps, Jeff's talents would not have been discovered. He asked Jeff's parents to send the young lad to him during summer vacation and few days together, the older Bezos called the parents in south Miami and told them their son – his grandson – was going to be a computer whizz kid. He began to encourage his grandson by filling his car garage in Cotulla with things like; screw-drivers, castrate cattle, junk machines, arc welders and other machines each summer the little boy was with him. By the time Jeff entered Palmetto High School near Miami, he had become so good in the Sciences that he emerged the class president and valedictorian; which ensured him a place at Princeton. At the Ivy League institution, he won honors where he was one of the best students in electronic and electrical engineering. Just as his grandfather predicted, Jeff eventually grew up to become a computer whizz-kid.

How about Oprah Winfrey, the first African-American and black woman billionaire? How did a young African-American daughter of freed slaves, who grew up in poor Kosciusko, Mississippi make it? The state of Mississippi in the South was one of the poorest, if not the poorest state in the South in student enrolment and the highest in student drop-out, especially for African-Americans/black in 1954 when Oprah was born. Even today, Mississippi is one of the five states at the bottom in student enrolment in the United States. Nothing prepared Oprah in her upbringing and parentage to become the most famous TV hostess later in life in the United States. For starters, she was born out of wedlock and her parents separated before Oprah's second birthday. The first school for African-

Americans in the State of Mississippi was not established until 1860. Today, Mississippi ranked 50th in student enrolment and achievement in the nation. Schools in Mississippi were segregated, until 1954 following Brown versus Board of Education ruling by the United States Supreme Court banning school segregation in the state. But Hattie Mae Lee, Oprah's grandmother did not let this institutional obstacle deter her from raising her grandkid. Hattie took the little girl into her home and began tutoring her how to read very early in life beginning at age 2. She would wake her up as early as five in the morning and began to read to her. She also gave her assignments in English. Her efforts were successful that Oprah was so good in English that she skipped kindergarten and was promoted to first grade, and again, she got double promotion to third grade. By the time she was 9, she had become the best debater in her secondary school in Milwaukee, Wisconsin where she had relocated to and had become the best "talker" in her church. Her "first paycheck" in life was a - $500 cash award she won while visiting a cousin during summer holiday in Nashville, Tennessee. She won the cash award during a church poetry and debate competition. In 1966, at the age of 12, when asked what she would like to become later in life, young Oprah answered rather unhesitatingly; "I want to be paid to talk!" Paid to talk? Where did the idea of being paid to talk come to a-12 year old? That confidence was built into her by her grandmother.

Human beings are the only creations of God Almighty that can think, talk, and build relationships rooted in the family system. Sometime, somewhere, and somehow, there is someone, who is always around to help each and every one of us in the journey of life. No human being can live in Robinson Crusoe's Island. Great people in life, including the phenomenally rich, will tell you of someone who gave them their first break in life. God Almighty put these people in our lives so that when we reach the pinnacles of our lives, we too can assist others to live their dreams. Take Richard Branson, the British billionaire and creator of the *Virgin*

Group of Companies as another example. His mother was the first person, who gave him the initial capital-$6.00-he and his boyhood business partner; Johnny Gems, needed to start their first business venture, *Student* magazine in the 1960s. The same could be said of Berry Gordy. His break came in late 1950 after he had hit financial low when he returned to his native Detroit, Michigan from New York. Gordy had left home to New York with the determination to become a successful musician. But things turned sour. At 28, the idealistic man, who would later become the discoverer of *Jackson Five* and other R & B music stars returned home and took a job as a laborer at *Ford Motors*. As his life story was told by Jeanette Delissa in her book; *"The Songs of Berry Gordy: The Music, the Magic: the Memories of Motown,"* Gordy was determined to make a success out of music and entertainment. While at *Ford Motors*, he was also looking for money to re-launch his music career. As he later disclosed, "I was broke (in New York), even with the hit records in certain cases. By the time the records would be hits, I would get the money, but my end of it would be so small that I'd always be broke. When the (music) companies finally paid me, it was three months later and I owed money out to the family." Mr. Berry Gordy re-calibrated and decided to set up a music company and produce his music rather than going to recording companies. But his efforts failed and he was flat broke again in Detroit. It was Anna, his sister that assisted him with a -$700 loan. It turned out that the loan became what was later known as *Motown* Recording Company, which at a time was the largest recoding company in America.

There are certain similarities among billionaires in their formative years. Again, take Mr. Richard Branson for example. Just as Richard started demonstrating his entrepreneurial instincts very early in life in England in his teens as a student at Stowe boarding school, so young Aliko began to display his entrepreneurial spirit in the 1960s as a student in Kano, northern Nigeria. Richard co-founded *Student* magazine with his pal Johnny Gems, at the age of 15. As he disclosed in his autobiography; the magazine was set up "...to serve as an alternative culture of the hippies in England in the 1960s." Young Aliko, who was five years younger than Richard may not be a publisher of a student magazine in Kano, but the same entrepreneurial spirit was unmistakable: the early consciousness of selling and making money in the process. Aliko disclosed this entrepreneurial spirit very early in his formative years, "I can remember when I was in primary school, I would go and buy cartons of sweets (candies), and I would start selling them just to make money. I was so much interested in business. Even at that time, I was very used to buying and selling. It is in my mind all through. I did that on a part-time basis. I usually bought packets of sweets (candies), and gave some people to sell for me. I would join them whenever I closed from school. I would collect my profit and give them something out of it. And we continued like that."

Every successful person in any area of life; academics, politics, sports, music, engineering, business, you name it; would always credit somebody, who charted their ways to success and prominence. In other words, no one can easily be said to be self-made. As long as every one of us on earth passes through some other human beings as parents, family members, good peer groups, even neighbours; and interact with them; these fellow human beings act as influences on our lives. Just as these people we meet and interact with can be forces for good in our lives, so also they can be forces for ill or bad too. The influences these people have on our individual lives and what we become later in lives is how we use such influences. Take Eldrick Tont Woods, who the whole world knows as Tiger Woods for example. Whatever he becomes today must be traced to his late father, Earl who, as an amateur golfer while living in Cypress, California introduced his son to the sport as early as when the kid was just 2. How about the Williams Sisters: Serena Jameka and her elder sister, Venus Ebony Starr; both later grew up to become the greatest duo in the tennis world? Their parents; Richard Williams and Oracene

Price, deliberately left Saginaw, Michigan when their daughters were only four years old for Crompton to Los Angeles, California so that the tots could be exposed early in life to playing professional tennis near Haines City. They were home-schooled by their parents and both eventually grew up to become the best in the sports. Even today, Richard Williams remains the chief coach of Serena, the Number One in the world as at 2010.

The world has heard about the amazing, incredible and transformative life story of, unarguably the greatest orator of the 21st century, Mr. Barack Hussein Obama. How did this son of a Kenyan immigrant man and a white lady from Kansas grow up to attend some of the best universities in the world and hold the record of "the first" in the history of the black race? Read his two best-selling books: *"Dreams from My Father: A Story of Race and Inheritance,"* and *"The Audacity of Hope"* and the forces that shaped his life, which made him become the first African-American (black) president and editor of the *"Harvard Law Review Journal,"* the only African-American lawmaker to be sworn into office in the Illinois State Senate in January 2005, the first African-American (black) presidential candidate of the Democratic Party, the first African-American (black) president of the United States of America, and the first African-American (black) president to win a second term as president of the United States of America. As he recalled; "In no other country on earth is my story even possible," and three factors could be credited for President Obama's success: God Almighty, his late mother, Dr Ann Dunham, and his maternal grandparents: Stanley Armour and Madelyn Dunham. He learned the art of public speaking, elocution and oratorical prowess when his late mother would wake him up at 5 am to teach him how to read and speak, while they were in Indonesia. "Each time I complained that he had disrupted my sleep," Obama recalled, "my mom would say; 'do you think I enjoy it buster!"

The richest man in the world today, Mr. Carlos Slim Helu, the Mexican billionaire of Lebanese descent, is also another example of the powerful influence of parents in people's lives. The man, who edged out American Bill Gates from the number one position as the world's richest person would tell you he learned how to make money from his parents as early as when he was 12 years old in 1955. His father, Khalid Slim Haddad was born in Lebanon, but left the war-torn country in 1902 at the age of 14. When he got to Mexico, he changed his name to Julián Slim. It was while he was living in the heavily-populated Lebanese-Mexican community in Mexico that he met a fellow Lebanese-Mexican lady, Linda Helú; who would become his future wife and Carlos mother. The couple began by setting up a retail outlet that Slim called; "*La Estrella del Oriente*" (The *Star of the Orient*) which flourished. This made his wife, Linda set up a small, but thriving publishing business which was the first Arabic Language newspaper in their new community, though both were Christians. Young Carlos watched his parents managed these business outfits. From them he learned the business ethics of discipline, prudence, focus, ambition and drive; virtues he put to use later in his adult life to emerge as the richest person in the world. According to James Bone of *The Times* of London, David Luhnow of *The Wall Street Journal*, Ginger Thompson of *The New York Times*, Stephanie Mehta of the *Forbes* magazine, and other writers that have chronicled the life history of the richest man in the world; Carlos imbibed the Spartan discipline of money-making from his parents. As the richest man in the world disclosed in; "*Carlos Slim Helu: a Biography;*"-one of his numerous biographies: "With good perspective of history, we can (have) a better understanding of the past and present and thus a clear vision of the future." To pay tribute to his father (deceased), and express appreciation to his mother, Carlos decided to combine his father and mother's name as his name, hence the name; Carlos Slim Helu.

The list of rich and successful people in the world that developed their world views and cut their future successes from the tutelage of grandparents, parents, or that who act as father or mother figures and served as sources of inspirations are many.

Mr. Sam Walton, founder of the global retail giant, *Wal-Mart* learned how to trade and cultivate the virtues of commerce from his mother, who owned a small milk delivery store to support the Walton family in Missouri in the 1920's. He learned his strong entrepreneurial spirit when he was only 8 as a newspaper vendor. He set up his own newspaper routes when he reached the seventh grade. He continued till he entered the University of Missouri where, almost expectedly, and predictably read Business Administration. While in college at 19, he ran out of money. Sam began to sell rabbits and pigeons to pay for college tuition during the Great Depression in the 1930's. That knack for business success led him to found *Wal-Mart* later in life, and today the largest public corporation in the world worth $258 billion.

In Nigeria and other parts of Africa, the continent's early industrialists, great rich people attributed their business acumens in life to some father-figures, uncles, grandfathers and mentors. Take Mr. Timothy Adeola-Odutola (1902-1995), one of the richest persons in pre-independent Nigeria as classic example. He was born to the famous Prince Sanni Odutola Seyindemi of the Moloda ruling house of Odogbolu and Madam Sabinah Otubanjo Odutola Seyindemi. His father was a Moslem, while his mother was a converted Christian. Young Timothy was only 13 when he lost his father in 1915. Following that tragic incident, Mr. D.R Otubusin took the young half-orphan into his home and taught him tailoring and drapery crafts till 1933 when 31-year old Timothy was able to stand on his own. Pa Otubusin later became the *Awujale* or king of Ijebu-Ode in 1933. In his biography, the late Mr. Adeola-Odutola paid glowing tribute to this father-figure, who set the young man's feet on the path of business career. The same could be said of the richest man in Owo, Ondo State in western Nigeria in this century, the great industrialist and cocoa magnate; the late Reverend Johnson Olajide Fagboyegun

(1925-2008). The founder and chairman, JOF Group of Companies and first Pro-Chancellor, Adekunle Ajasin University, Akungba-Akoko, Ondo State was neglected by his biological father when he was growing up in Uso near Owo. He was said to be so malnourished, and unkempt that sores covered his two legs until his uncle, who was a trader, Pa Daniel visited Uso village, and confronted his brother on why little 'Jide was neglected. Pa Daniel took the young man under his wing, and brought him to Owo where he taught him how to trade in cocoa business. That mentoring altered the life of Olajide Fagboyegun forever. Before he died in October 2008 at 82, the industrialist described by *The Financial Times* of London as " Nigeria's foremost cocoa magnate" and the man, *Africa Today* journal published by Indiana University, USA called "foremost indigenous produce buyer in Nigeria" had built a conglomerate spanning cocoa, retailing, banking, real estate, import and export, manufacturing, auto business and many more. He could not have built the phenomenally successful *J.O. Fagboyegun & Sons Group* without the mentoring of his uncle, Pa Daniel.

It is not surprising therefore that the man, who later grew up to become the first Nigerian billionaire, the first richest Nigerian, the first richest man in West Africa, the first richest person in Africa and the first richest black person in the world began his life with someone who shaped his life. Aliko Dangote's upbringing began with his maternal grandfather, the late Mr. Sanusi Alhassan Dantata. For starters, young Aliko was not old enough to know his biological father. Aliko's father, Mohammad Dangote was not born in Kano; his parents were originally from Kura, in Kura local government area (LGA) of modern day Kano State. He was a business associate of Sanusi Dantata but was also a politician. A peripatetic politician always on the go and didn't have time to look after his children. In the years leading up to the independence of Nigeria in 1960 when little Aliko was 3, his father was involved in many political activities. Mr. Mohammad Dangote was a member of the northern regional government of the Northern People's

Congress (NPC) led by Mr. Ahmadu Bello. According to Aliko, "He was a member of the northern regional government here in Lagos. I barely knew him. I was not close to him; I was brought up by my maternal grandfather, late Sanusi Dantata." Other members of the Northern People's Congress (NPC), who were Mohammed Dangote's colleagues at the House of Representatives in Lagos at independence, were; Malam Ahmadu Rufai Daura, Messrs. Umaru Gumel, Baba Darara, Rilwanu Abdullahi, Abubakar Koguna among others from the then Kano province.

A particular incident out of several events occurred out of many following the deposition of Emir Muhammadu Sanusi of Kano in 1963 which affected Mr. Mohammad Dangote. Mr. Muhammadu Sanusi, crowned the 11th emir of Kano in 1953 had a running battle with the politicians in charge in northern Nigeria. According to those who spoke on the issue in the ancient town of Kano and wished not to be named, Emir Sanusi had been having problems with the northern regional government and the British authorities even before he became the emir of Kano. That he was a politician was an open secret. He was the Ciroma of Kano prior to becoming emir. He also worked in the native authority. Upon assuming the throne, he became a member of the northern delegation to the United Kingdom during the Nigerian Constitutional Conference prior to the granting of political independence in 1960. He was knighted by the Queen of England, alongside many of the northern delegates to the conference, but his outspokenness led to his removal by the Bello administration in 1963.

According to sources, his disagreement with the Sultan of Sokoto as a *Tijaniyya* Moslem leader in Kano also contributed to his falling out of favor with the first post-independence indigenous government. He routinely criticized the Sardauna Administration as a minister without portfolio. The last straw that broke the camel's back was the allegations of financial impropriety leveled against him in 1962 as the overseer of the affairs of the Kano Native Authority. The investigation continued into 1963, which eventually led to his banishment to Azare where he was effectively put in seclusion. The financial allegations, many argued, were mere smokescreens, but avenues to "deal with him," because of his political influence over Kano northern legislators in Kaduna, the then seat of the northern regional government. After his deposition in 1963, young Aliko was juts 6 and lived with his maternal grandfather, Mr. Sanusi Dantata and did not have premonition of the impending death of his biological father.

According to some Moslem scholars and historians in Kano, these three areas of disagreement between Emir Sanusi and Premier Bello; political differences and different religious interpretations of the role of women in an Islamic society and the strengthening of the authority of Kano as an independent traditional town from Sokoto after the latter fell to the British in 1903 caused instability in the town. Like the Northern Element Progressive Union (NEPU) party, Emir Sanusi favored strengthening women power and representation in political and traditional affairs. The conservative Northern People's Congress (NPC) held contrary position under the veil of strict puritanical interpretation of the Holy Qur'an. Emir Sanusi was a member of the NPC until he fell out of favor with Bello and the NPC orchestrated his removal in 1963. The removal of Sanusi as emir led to the formation of the Kano People's Party (KPP) in May 1963. The KPP didn't conceal its mission: return Sanusi to power or install his son, Ado as the new emir. The KPP was called by many names: "*Jamiyya Mutanem,*" (Party of Kano People), "*Jamaiyya Sanusi,*" (Sanusi People) or "*Al-Umma Kano,*" (The Kano People). The KPP wrote its manifestoes in Hausa and listed seven grievances against the Sardauna-led NPC government in Kaduna namely: *mulkin mutum daya* (struggle against one-man rule); *yanchi* (autocratic rule), *yandara* (deception in government), *darga* (struggle for religious freedom), *munafunci* (fight against hypocrisy), *son kai* (fight against selfishness or self-centeredness), and *tsortaswa* (end to reign of terror).

Many of the members openly rained curses and abuses on the Sardauna and were arrested and jailed by the northern region government. Coming so soon on the eve of the federal elections in 1964, the KPP became the arrow-head for Kano nationalism by local politicians who defected from the NPC and either pitched their political tents with the new KPP or the NEPU, the *"talakawa"* (masses) party. By July 1965, many of the KPP members were forced to register another political party; the Kano State Movement (KSM) upon the clamp down by the NPC. The KPP was decimated by the Bello government and many of their members, who narrowly escaped imprisonment morphed into the KSM. The new KSM strengthened its Kano nationalistic fervor with the central aim of fighting for Kano's political autonomy from the overbearing Sokoto Caliphate which Bello epitomized, even as a political leader and premier. Six months later, the Nigerian military staged a coup d'état on January 16, 1966 and assassinated Bello in Kaduna, and the prime minister, Mr. Abubakar Tafawa-Balewa in Lagos.

According to sources, Mr. Mohammad Dangote was a supporter of the deposed Emir of Kano, Malam Muhammadu Sanusi. Malam Muhammadu Inuwa Abbas was crowned the 12th emir of Kano in 1963 following the deposition of Emir Sanusi, although there were concerns about his health. Nevertheless, the Sardauna Administration and the dominant stake-holders moved him from his traditional position of district head of Dawakin- Kudu to the position of the emir of Kano. Less than 10 months on the throne, Emir Abbas passed, which opened the stool again to other contestants. The succession battle which began in 1963, according to sources in Kano, brought Aliko's father, Mohammad Dangote into the whole picture. One of the contestants was from Kura town who slugged it out with five other contestants. Kura was the native town of Mr. Mohammad Dangote. There were many casualties of the political intrigues that followed the deposition of Emir Sanusi in 1963 and the death of his successor, Emir

Abbas. Those knowledgeable about local politics in ancient Kano, but would not like to be quoted said Aliko's father was one of the casualties of the emir succession tussle. As it is customary in Nigeria and many African countries, politics and traditional institutions constantly butt heads as elites fight for power and privileges. Often times, the use of native voodoo and native charms could not be ruled out in such power tussles.

The news of the death of Mr. Mohammad Dangote filtered into the family compound of the Dantatas in early 1965. He had not taken ill and had not been diagnosed for any known ailment so the family was shock by his sudden death. It was difficult for the authors to obtain much information about Aliko's father as many elderly politicians in Kano avoided the topic. He left behind young Aliko, Sani, Bello and their younger brother, who later died in a plane crash with Mr. Ibrahim, the first son of the late Nigerian head of state, General Sani Abacha in 1996. There were other children too from his other wives that Mr. Mohammad Dangote left behind. The death of Aliko's father in his early 1950's left Aliko's mother, Hajiya (Madam) Mariya to become a widow. Mariya's life in Kano today is shielded from journalists. She has refused to be photographed, but instead has chosen to devote her life to philanthropic and charity causes. Consequently, the responsibility of bringing up young Aliko fell on the shoulders of his maternal grandfather, Mr. Sanusi Alhassan Dantata. Aliko was only 8 year old when his biological father died.

"The way the twig is bent so the tree grows," is a popular saying that could be applied to the upbringing of young Aliko by his maternal grandfather. But the twig begins to show very early in life what it would eventually become. Those who were forced to grow as the twig was being bent in their lives have borrowed the age-long wisdom of Appius Claudius Caecus, the Roman politician, and the Censor of Rome between 312 BC and 308 BC, who gave the world the famous saying; "Every man (and every woman too) is the architect of his (or her) own fortune."

Take Sir Winston Leonard Spenser Churchill (30 November 1874 – 24 January 1965), two-time prime minister of the United Kingdom: (1940 to 1945) and (1951 to 1955), who led the UK through much of WWII and the first prime minister of the UK to be made a honorary citizen of the United States as an example of that aphorism. He began to demonstrate his leadership qualities very early in life. Born into British aristocracy, Winston had little relationship with his father, who died early in life at 45. Winston's mother literally abandoned him in three boarding schools. Compounding his boyhood woes were his speech impediment and childhood rascality in school. But as author Robert Tarbell Oliver disclosed in his book; *"Public Speaking in the Reshaping of Great Britain,"* Churchill later overcame his adversities. "My impediment is no hindrance" he said. He grew up to become Britain's foremost statesman, artist, writer, greatest orator, and the only prime minister of Britain to win the Nobel Prize in Literature.

Theodore Roosevelt, the 26th and youngest president of the United States in history (1901-1909) was also another classic example. The youngest president of the United States-was 42 years old when he became president in 1901-began showing his leadership qualities very early in life, in spite of his asthmatic health condition and fragility. According to William Roscoe Thayer in his 1919 biography; *"Theodore Roosevelt: an Intimate Biography;"* Teddy began to show compassion for little things at 9. While growing up in the largely Dutch community Gramercy section of New York in the 19th century, he would help animals in difficulties by keeping them in a museum with the assistance of two of his cousins. He opened a small museum as a teenager which he called: *"The Natural History of Insects."* His love for animals was evident when he decided to read Biology as a homeschooled graduate. This also showed later in his presidency, when he sent to Congress and got pass into law; the Meat Inspection Act; and the Pure Food and Drug Act of 1906, the precursor to today's Food and Drug Administration (FDA). His love for animals, the flora and fauna continued in his post-presidency years, when he became the first US president to embark on a month long safari round eastern and central Africa. He came back with nearly two thousand animals and insects, which were distributed to many museums in the United States, including the Smithsonian Institution, the National Museum, the American Museum of Natural History and other zoological institutions in the nation. All these qualities he began to display in his formative years.

In Africa, Julius Kambarage Nyerere (1922-1999), the first democratically-elected president of Tanzania has been described as one of the most corrupt-free, forthright, and progressive leaders in the continent. Known as the second African leader after Nigeria's Nnamdi Azikiwe to earn a university degree outside the African continent, this great African visionary had trouble going to school in his formative years. His father was a tribal chief among the Zanaki tribe in Butiama on the eastern shore of Lake Victoria in the north west of Tanganyika in what is today the Republic of Tanzania. For six years, young Julius walked 26 miles every day to an elementary school in far-away Musoma. No wonder when he became president of independent Tanzania in 1962, Mr. Nyerere decided to focus his energy on the development of education in Tanzania. According to the great Nwalimu (or Teacher as he was called during his life time as president) in; *Julius K. Nyerere, Development is for Man, by Man, and of Man: The Declaration of Dar es Salaam"* edited by Budd L. Hall and J. Roby Kidd in *"Adult Education: A Design for Action,"* "Man can only liberate himself or develop himself. He cannot be liberated or developed by another. For Man makes himself. It is his ability to act deliberately, for a self-determined purpose, which distinguishes him from the other animals. The expansion of his own consciousness, and therefore of his power over himself, his environment, and his society, must therefore ultimately be what we mean by development. So development is for Man, by Man, and of Man. The same is true of education. Its purpose is the liberation of

Man from the restraints, and limitations of ignorance, and dependency. Education has to increase men's physical and mental freedom to increase their control over themselves, their own lives, and the environment in which they live. The ideas imparted by education, or released in the mind through education, should therefore be liberating ideas; the skills acquired by education should be liberating skills. Nothing else can properly be called education. Teaching which induces a slave mentality or a sense of impotence is not education at all — it is attack on the minds of men."

As it is in politics, so also is the application of the bending of the twig early in life and how people are the architects of their own fortunes in other areas of life, including business. Rich people that have made it to the exclusive realm of billionaire club did not suddenly find themselves in the elite club. They had begun to demonstrate their business acumens early in their formative years. Those who grew up with them could sense and see the signs of love for hard work, knack for business and money-making activities. If there was anyone in his day that epitomized the veracity of the aphorism that morning shows the day, it was Mr. Henry Ford, the founder of *Ford Motors*. In his case, little Henry was both the twig and also the one who bent his twig the way he wanted it. He eventually became the inventor of one of the most important inventions in human history: the automobile.

Born in Greenfield near Dearborn, west of Detroit Michigan, little Henry grew up in a dairy farm. Naturally, his parents expected him to follow in their footsteps. In a family of nine, Henry was the eldest. His parents expected him to take care of the chickens and the animals in the barn. He was supposed to be a shining example to his six siblings but, as Henry Ford later noted; he loathed farming like plague. To him, "Chicken sucked and they are for hawks," while; "Milk is a mess." In 1875 when he was just 12, little Henry lost his mother; Mary Litogot Ford (1839–1876) born in Michigan of Belgian heritage. The death shifted more of farm responsibilities to the young boy, who had to join his father; William Ford, to care for his other equally young six siblings, the youngest being only 3years old. But Henry did not want to be a farmer; his interest was anything mechanical and engineering. At night, while his father and his siblings were asleep after farm work, he would hide in the family kitchen secretly learning how to repair wrist watches on his own. At times, he would assemble mechanical junks and try his hands on dismantling them. Several times, his father caught him and gave him the beating of his life.

On July 30, 1879 at 16, he told his father and younger siblings he was leaving home for good. Henry left without a dime in his pocket and walked some miles from Greenfield Township to Detroit where he landed two jobs; one at a mechanical workshop as an apprentice in a steam engine assembly plant; and the other; a watch repairing vocation at night. They paid him $2.50 and $2.00 eighty hours a week respectively. The man, who later gave the world the popular *Ford Motors* on June 16, 1903 at 40, had little or no formal education. Before his invention, he endured numerous business failures which, according to him; "is a chance to begin again more intelligently" (because failure) "is just a resting place (since) we learn more from our failures than our successes." Henry died at 83 in 1947 and left behind a- $181.1 billion company known all over the world today. His passion for, and his interest in anything mechanical and engineering began at the age of 8. His father wanted to bend him to his own taste but little Henry had his own vision. He eventually wrote the history of his life based on his vision.

Little Aliko began to display his knack for entrepreneurship and talent for business acumen very early in his formative years. The Yoruba peoples of western Nigeria and West Africa have an old saying which goes like this: *"The child that would be clever and smart in life always shows, and demonstrates his or her smartness and cleverness very early in his or her formative years."* This popular Yoruba proverb could be applied to young Aliko as he began his early education in the ancient city of Kano. He enrolled at the elite primary school, the Kano Capital Elementary School, Kano in 1964 and his business acumen began to show. In those days when little kids pester their school mates for candies and "sweets" (as he called them) on the playground or in the lunch room, young Aliko would come to the rescue. He would bring candies and "sweets" to school and announce to his classmates that anyone interested could have some for a penny. But young Aliko's business acumen also extended beyond Kano Capital Elementary School. Those who knew the Dantata family clan very well at Koki Quarters said they lived in one large expanse compound in that part of Kano. It was here that the family business was conducted. There were many servants going out and coming in so, Aliko bonded with those servants too, and usually enlisted them into his candy business too. He disclosed he often gave out merchandize of his own to the servants to sell and they would report back the sales to him with hefty profits and commissions to them as cuts.

The Koki Quarters where the Dantata clan occupied in ancient Kano, northern Nigeria was like a company on its own. This was in contrast to the atomization of most families in Nigeria today. In the 1950's down to the 1970's, Aliko disclosed that the Dantata clan operated like a commune. "Everything was owned jointly. You could go to any room to sleep, go to any parent, wife, brother, sister, cousin and uncle, you name it, for anything. We looked after one another. Life was fun in those days when I was growing up. I doubt if there is any family living like that anymore in Nigeria today," he reminiscences.

A look at the expansive Dantata family from the first generation to the fourth generation demonstrates this communal lifestyle. The family tree of the Dantatas is reproduced below-:

NAVIGATING THE GENEOLOGY OF THE FAMOUS DANTATA FAMILY THE MATERNAL FAMILY OF ALIKO DANGOTE

- Originally from Katsina
- 1700
- Baba Talatin
- Moved to Kano and gave birth to Madugu Abdullahi
- Madugu Abdullahi gave birth to twin boys
- Alhassan Abullahi * Alhussaini Abdullahi (Died at birth)
- Other children of Madugu Abdullahi (Shuaibu, Jai, Bala and Sidi)
- Alhassan Abdullahi Madugu became Alhassan Abdullahi Dantata

ALHASSAN DANTATA FAMILY TREE

Alhaji Alhassan Dantata
(1877-Wednesday August 17, 1955)

− Ahmadu Dantata (1916-1960)	− Sanusi Dantata (1915-1997)
− Mahmud Dantata (1922-1983)	− Aminu Dantata (1931-)
− Abdullahi Dantata	− Almu Dantata
− Safiyan Dantata	− Nura Dantata
− Bebe Dantata	− Jamilu Dantata
− Mudi Dantata	

ALL MALE CHILDREN OF ALHASSAN DANTATA

− Aishatu Dantata	− Rakiya Dantata
− Bara Dantata	− Hussina Dantata
− Kaltume Dantata	− Juda Dantata
− Kulu Dantata	− Amina Dantata
− Fatima Sharubutu Dantata	

ALL FEMALE CHILDREN OF ALHASSAN DANTATA

Sanusi Alhassan Dantata (Aliko's grandfather)
(1915-1997)

Sanusi Alhassan children

- Mahmud
- Amaka
- Nasiru
  (1945-2012)
- Mariya
  (Dangote's mother)

- Abdulkadir
- Hassan
- Bashir C
  (1950- 2009)
- Halima (Female)

Four other children were also sired by the late Sanusi Alhassan Dantata but they are hardly known thus making a total of twelve children left behind by Sanusi Alhassan Dantata. His second wife, Mario Sanusi-Dantata also gave birth to other children, the eldest being, Abdulkadir who died in early 2012.

Aliko Dangote (Fourth generation of the Dantatas from his maternal side)

ALIKO DANGOTE PATERNAL FAMILY

- Mohammad Dangote
  (Father)
- Sani Dangote (brother)

- Aliko Mohammad
  Dangote
- Belo Dangote
  (Brother)

Aliko Dangote's children

- Zainab Aliko Dangote
- Halima Aliko Dangote
- Salma Dangote (All female)

Some other children of Aliko are Fatima, Aisha and Sadia who are also female.

(In all, Mr. Aliko Dangote has about fifteen children from four wives (women), although in official records; he claims to have three children, probably from his current wife. The authors could not obtain the photographs of the three previous women (wives) of Aliko Dangote during the field work for this biography in Nigeria. Similarly, unlike in the western world where alimony payments are documented, Nigeria does not have such a clause in its family law and customs, so we could not obtain documents from public records on the three previous divorces of Mr. Dangote. If there is any law on alimony in Nigerian common law and custom, such law is rarely enforced. As a Moslem, Mr. Dangote is entitled to a maximum of four wives, but has chosen to maintain a serial monogamist relationship, rather than maintaining polygamist relationships).

The above are the first, second, third and fourth generations of the Dantata family clan beginning with the patriarch of the clan; Alhassan, where Aliko's maternal family could be traced. Mr. Alhassan Dantata sowed the acorn that became the billion oak of the Dantata family fortunes. He sired twenty children: eleven boys and nine girls. As it is the custom in most religions, including Islam, the female children were not given prominent positions in the family business, although they were taken care of by their male siblings. The second generation of the Dantata continued with the male children. The second born son, Ahmadu as noted above died in 1960-five years after his father passed on.

Mahmud Alhassan Dantata, also known as Mahmuda was the second male child. He was involved in politics, and also ran hotel/tourism business before he died. He was a NEPU sympathizer, and while Malam Aminu Kano, who later became the leader of NEPU, lost his election in 1954, Mahmud used his family clout to win a local government seat in Kano under the NEPU. Earlier on in 1948, he had teamed up with Messrs. Haruna Kassim and Ibrahim

Gashah to establish the West African Pilgrims Agency or WAPA, hence his nickname, "Mahmud WAPA." Basically, the WAPA was a travel agency, which handled the traveling, accommodation, logistics, and other needs of Moslem pilgrims traveling from Kano, or any other parts of northern Nigeria, and West Africa to the Holy Land of Mecca and Medina during Hajj or Pilgrimage. The organization was also involved in hotel business. Mr. Mahmud Dantata also started a business relationship with Mr. Mohammed Rago Kura to set up arguably, the first modern day *bureau de change* in Kano. The currency exchange outfit handled the currencies of intending Moslem pilgrims before the pilgrims arrived at the holy lands of Mecca and Madina.

Mahmud served eight year prison sentence in Kano in November 1957, when he was caught with fake currency; the West African Pounds £998.00. He was released by the Northern People Government (NPC) in July 1964. He changed from NEPU to NPC and ran against Malam Aminu Kano, leader of the NEPU and won. He withdrew from active politics after the Nigerian military took over government in Nigeria's first coup d'état in 1966. His son, Majtaba took over his tourism business. He abolished WAPA, cashed out, and since his father owned the building where WAPA was holding its activities, he converted the building into a night club. Those who spoke to the authors in Kano said Majtaba closed down WAPA in 1960, because the northern Nigerian government had officially taken over the activities of Moslem and Christian pilgrimages to Mecca and Jerusalem respectively. Mr. Mahmud also left behind a thriving printing press before he died in 1983.

The first male child of Pa Alhassan Dantata was Sanusi, who distinguished himself. He was also the most prominent. He divided the business empire left behind by their father with his fellow male brothers: Mahmud and Aminu. Not much is known about the remaining brothers and their siblings so the next/second generation continued with Mr. Sanusi Alhassan Dantata, where the mother of Mr. Aliko Dangote descends. Mr. Aminu Alhassan Dantata, born in

1931 is still alive. He has four wives and twenty seven children. The first two sons; Bashir and Ummulkhair are dead leaving the eldest, Tajudden Aminu-Dantata to take charge of the vast business empire of the fourth son of Alhassan. Other children of Aminu Dantata are; Amna, Surayya, Nabila, Rufai (deceased), Zainab, Batool, Hafsi, Sadiq, Aliya, Sadiqa, Hassan, Jamila, Fatima, Bara, Alawiyya, Bilal (deceased), Maryam, Bashir, Hussain, Faisal, Munira, and Mohammed.

Mr. Sanusi Alhassan Dantata's family line is as follows: Mahmud Dantata (Mujaba), Abdulkadir Sanusi, Usman Amaka Sanusi, Hassan Sanusi, Nasiru Sanusi, and Bashir Sanusi. There were the six male children of Sanusi Alhassan Dantata. Halima Sanusi and Mariya Sanusi were the two female children of Sanusi Alhassan Dantata making a total of eight children. According to family records, Mr. Sanusi Alhassan Dantata; the maternal grandfather of Aliko Dangote, had a total of twelve children; but the above were the ones we were able to gather information on during the research for the biography of Africa's richest person, and the richest Black person in the world. The mother of Aliko Dangote is one of the two daughters, while Halima Sanusi Dantata is the other of the two female children. She is currently the chairperson of Redstar Oil and Gas Nigeria Limited with office on Club Road in Kano. Aliko stayed with her briefly when he was growing up in Kano in the 1960's. Mariya, Aliko's mother is the younger of the two female children.

In the Dantata clan, everything was shared communally and no child was left behind. Aliko had fond memory of such communal living and how it shaped his teenage years "...when I was born, I was taken over to him (my maternal grandfather). I never really lived with my father. I was taken away when I was six months old. It is a common practice in the north (northern Nigeria) for kids to be taken away from their biological parents, and to live with step-parents or uncles or aunties. Sometimes, I can go and live with my stepmother. It would take some time before you even realize that this is your mother. I found that as a really good idea, because it brings a bond into the family, where you don't see too much segregation. There wouldn't be that in-fighting and trying to say: "This is my son's own or whatever." Right now, I don't think it exists because everybody is fighting for himself right now. But then, I know that there are some of my step-brothers that were raised by my own mother. That was the tradition in the north. I am not sure it is still being practiced. The people I became used to were my grandparents, and my aunties. I even lived with my auntie— the senior sister to my mother. And I thought she was my mum up till a certain point. It was much later that I realized that she was only my auntie, because I have never lived with my mum."

While Mr. Sanusi Dantata wanted his first and eldest grandson to acquire Western education, he was also mindful of developing his spiritual life. When little Aliko returned from Kano Capital School, he was also expected to join his other siblings at the Madrasa School run by Sheikh Ali Kumasi at the Dantata Mosque. But more than Western education, Mr. Sanusi Alhassan Dantata gave other things to his first grandson following the death of Mohammad Dangote in 1965, when Aliko was only 8 years old. First, the inculcation of sense of family unity and family values into the young boy from the very first day he came to the world. To say little Aliko saw the power of money in the lives of people first hand would be an understatement. Mr. Sanusi Alhassan Dantata gave love to his grandson. The provision of basic necessities of life such as food, clothing and essentials of living are things that made impressionable impact in the life of the young half-orphan Aliko. Sense of security pervaded the environment Aliko grew up in Kano. The value of work ethics that made Aliko what he is today was fudged in the family compound of his grandfather. He had an upbringing that emphasized empathy for the weak, respect for constituted authorities, and obedience to seniors. The value of free enterprise, the fear of God, religious education, and moral instructions were all virtues Aliko learned from Mr. Sanusi Dantata.

For a young boy growing up without a father, it must have been too hard on the young boy's psychological development. As Aliko later disclosed, he could count the number of times he saw his father when he was growing up in Kano. There is no person that could substitute the place of a loving father in the life of a child, especially a male child, according to child and human psychologists. The place of a man, especially the presence of a father in the home during the formative years of a child is very critical and essential in the child's development in life. As Mrs. Robin McGraw, wife of Mr. Phil McGraw, host of the popular TV show, *Dr Phil* told Kate Coyne of *Good Housekeeping* magazine in an interview, raising a child requires the joint efforts of both father and mother because, there are vital things that a father knows about a child that a mother cannot understand. The sense of family that Mr. Sanusi Dantata gave to his grandson assisted young Aliko to value the power of family later in life. He was supported by cousins, uncles, nieces, and other family members, who poured all their love into the first member of the fourth Dantata Generation. The family, according to the great Chinese sage, Confucius, is the nucleus of the modern society, for as he said, the integrity of a nation is derived from the integrity of its home. This is true, for as the family goes, so the society goes.

The death of Mr. Mohammad Dangote may have had a negative psychological impact on young Aliko when his father passed on in 1965. But the family set-up and arrangement put in place by the patriarch of the maternal family, Mr. Sanusi Dantata, cushioned the effects on his grandson. The presence of grandparents, and other members of the family on the growth, and upbringing of young children; especially those who did not have intimate relationship with their biological fathers/parents were demonstrated in the lives of prominent people of the world. President Obama narrated how his formative years were shaped through the love and support his grandparents poured unto him when his mother, a young 18 –year old white woman born in Kansas became pregnant by an international student from Kenya studying at the University of Hawaii on scholarship. "My grandparents poured everything they had into me; love, affection and all," Obama said.

Ms. Louis Ciconne, the famous American singer who we know as Madonna, described by the *Guinness Book of Records* as "the most successful female artist of all time" reportedly worth nearly $1 billion was raised in Bay City, Michigan by her grandmother, Madam Elsie Mae Fortin. Mr. Eric Bishop also known as Jamie Fox, a man of prodigious talents; music, comedy, acting, *Grammy* Award winner, *Academy* Award winner, *Golden Globe* Award winner, *BET* Awards winner, the first black person to be nominated for two *Oscars* the same year and recipient, 2013 NAACP Entertainer of the Year Award was brought up by his grandparents; Mr. and Mrs. Mark and Estelle Talley in Terrell, Texas. See what the world would have missed in one of the greatest comedians of our time, Mr. George Lopez, the genius behind the *George Lopez* Show on *ABC* if his grandparents; Mr. Refugio and Mrs. Benita Gutierrez of Mission Hills, California had not taken him in when, at two months old, his father abandoned him and his mother too deserted him when young George was only 10? When the birth of popular American actor, Jack Nicholson was mired in controversy in 1937 when he was born in New York City, according to Jack's biographer, Patrick McGilligan, his grandparents; Mr. John Joseph Nicholson and Mrs. Ethel May went to the Big Apple and brought their grandson to Manasquan, New Jersey and raised him. The list is endless. In the chronicle of Hall of Famers, these grandparents should be celebrated. Aliko Dangote recognized the monumental impact his grandfather played in his life. "All I am today and I have become, I owe it to him," he said.

Thank God for these great grandparents that raised some of the best and prominent individuals in the world. There are several of such cases around the world; the kind grandmother who has to care for her grandkids after their parents died of the scourge of AIDS in Kenya; the poor grandmother in the Congo, who has to shoulder the responsibility of taking care of her grandkids, because their parents had been killed by rebel forces or their mother was raped to death by rebel soldiers in Goma.

Financial security was another thing that Aliko got from his grandfather. The first fear that strikes into the mind of a kid anywhere in the world when that devastating news of the death of the breadwinner is broken is: who will provide for our basic needs now? It is not mere cliché that fathers are referred to as the "breadwinners" of their families. True, most fathers bring the bacon home, but the presence of a man in the family not only ensures sense of psychological security, but financial security as well. In many areas of the world, especially in Africa, many men are struggling and working their butts off to put food on the table for their families. Young boys that are growing up look first unto their fathers for financial and psychological supports. When death snatches a father very early in life as it happened to little Aliko, it could be devastating. But with the wealth of Mr. Sanusi Dantata, Aliko saw money, plenty of it, in Koki Quarters while growing up in Kano in the expansive family house of the legendary Dantatas. He did not have to wake up in the morning wondering where his next meal would come from; nor begin his day starring at the ceiling looking for money to buy lunch at school. The basic essentials of life that make little kids sure of their futures were readily available for little Aliko in the 1960's. "I lacked nothing as a young boy while growing up in Kano," Aliko disclosed.

The environment of money, the making of money and the power money confers on people, who own plenty of it pervaded the Dantata family house in Koki Quarters in Kano, in the 1960's, and the 1970's when Aliko was growing up. The little boy saw how business deals and transactions were made. He saw the wealthy come and go; and political leaders; politicians, power brokers, powerful traditional rulers sauntered into the Dantata house at night. He saw beautiful and expensive cars and automobiles parked everywhere and saw first-hand, an ambience oozing of money. Anyone that grew up in such environment of non-deprivation would love to maintain such atmosphere. You do not appreciate the power of money and wealth until you need money. Poverty is not good and those who have tasted the power of money very early in life, especially in their formative years normally swear that they would ensure they keep wide berth with poverty. In the Dantata family compound in Koki Quarters in Kano where little Aliko had his formative years, he lacked nothing. During that time, Mr. Sanusi Alhassan Dantata, according to the influential *Time* magazine, was referred to as the richest man in Nigeria in 1965 at the age of 46. He was followed by Mr. Adeola Odutola, the Ogbeni-Oja of Ijebu-Ode and Mr. Louis Odumegwu-Ojukwu, the father of Mr. Emeka Odumegwu-Ojukwu, the late Biafra war lord.

Mr. Sanusi Alhassan Dantata set the feet of his first grandson, not only on the path of financial success in life; but also quality Western education and well-enriched Islamic upbringing. It is not enough for fathers or parents to ensure that their children and grandchildren succeed financially in life and their material comforts are guaranteed; their souls should also be saved through the inculcation of fear of God and love for one's Creator into them. By blending Western education at the nearby Kano Capital Elementary School and supplementing it with Islamic education in the evening at the Sanusi Dantata family mosque, Mr. Sanusi Dantata was raising a well-rounded young man. Going to school in those days was not easy, especially for poor young boys and girls, who lacked the family stability and financial wherewithal to acquire Western education.

Lastly, one vital element needed in life for one to succeed that young Aliko received from his maternal grandfather was obedience to constituted authorities, submission to the powers that be and conformity with the laws of the land. To nurture a child to become a rebel is the worst that can happen to a family. It is not the role of parents, and grandparents to nurture their children, and wards into rebels; that is the duty of the school. Aliko Dangote praised his father for this vital element of life later when he became a billionaire. As he told Mr. Samuel Awoyinfa of *The Sun* newspapers in Nigeria; "I happened to be the first grandson of Sanusi Dantata. So the person I truly see as my father is my late grandfather, Sanusi Dantata. I learnt a lot from his hard work, from his simplicity. People always talk about my humility, but nothing can compare with him. When you see him you would think he doesn't have anything. He is always a respecter of authority. He always advises us that: No matter what you do, you must always respect the authority of the day. Do not fight government. You must be an obedient person. And that's something I learnt and took seriously. I inherited my business skills from my grandfather. They were also business people—the Dantatas. Having come from a rich family doesn't give you an automatic license to riches (though). You just have to create your own idea and work hard. I have never seen any Nigerian that has really made money from inheritance. It is very, very difficult. And that is why I would always encourage my own children to work very hard especially when it comes to making their own money. I am not saying that they shouldn't rely on the fact that yes, they come from a rich home. But sometimes, it can be a great disadvantage. Because there are some certain businesses that you wouldn't like to do because you name is so and so."

Aliko Dangote has an ally in that philosophy: Mr. Warren Buffett, the fourth richest man in the world. As the Sage of Omaha told the *CNBC* in an interview, "He-referring to his first son, Howard-is not entitled to any preferential treatment. He has to get his own money. Is it because he's Buffett's son? No, it doesn't work that way. I have told my three children to work for their money. All I have will go to charity when I'm gone." Mr. Buffett has started that already; he has given out $30.7billion to the Bill and Melinda Gates Foundation as at 2006.

On his paternal side, the Dangote family initially hailed from Kura town, a sleepy town of less than 10,000 people; about 45 minutes' drive from Kano City. Late Mr. Mohammad Dangote had other wives and sired other children before he died in 1965. Some of these half-brothers and sisters of Aliko work for the *Dangote* Group today.

Auntie Rakiyyat Dantata, Aliko's maternal sister © Family File, Kano

Alhaji Alhassan Dantata (1877-Wednesday August 17, 1955). Aliko's maternal great-grandfather.

Abdullahi Dantata, one of many Aliko's uncles © Family File, Kano

Aliko's maternal uncles clockwise: Ahmadu (1916-1960), Sanusi (1915-1997) Aliko's grandfather, Mahmud (1922-1983) and Aminu (1931-) © Family File, Kano

The rest uncles of Aliko born to his great grandfather by other wives: Almuda, Safiyan, and Nura, © Family File, Kano

The rest uncles of Aliko born to his great grandfather by other wives: Bebe, Mudi and Jamilu © Family File, Kano

The rest aunties of Aliko born to his great grandfather by other wives: Rakiyyat, Aishatu, Bara and Hushima © Family File, Kano

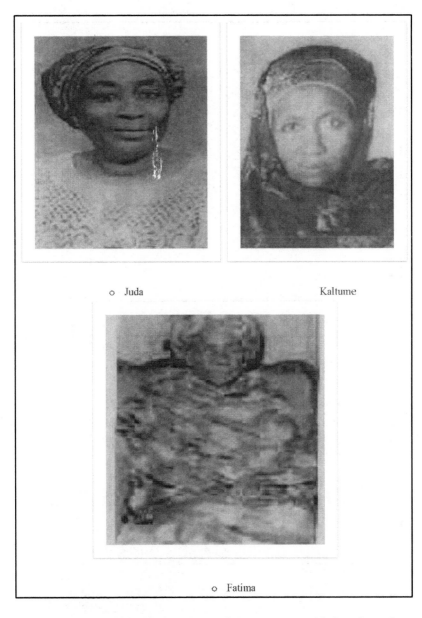

○   Juda   Kaltume

○   Fatima

The rest aunties of Aliko born to his great grandfather by other wives: Juda, Kaltume and Fatima © Family File, Kano

Aliko Mohammad Dangote

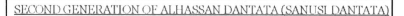

SECOND GENERATION OF ALHASSAN DANTATA (SANUSI DANTATA)

o   Sanusi (1917-1997) Aliko's maternal grandfather
SANUSI DANTATA'S CHILDREN

o   Abdulkadeer (1945-2012)

Sanusi (1917-1995) Aliko's maternal grandfather and his junior maternal uncle, Abdulkadir Sanusi Dantata (1945-2012). © Family File, Kano

OTHER MEMBERS OF ALIKO DANGOTE'S EXTENDED FAMILY

o   From top Aminu Dantata, Aliko's uncle and elder sister to his mother, Second row from left; Sayyu Dantata, Muzail Dantata; both cousins of Aliko and Dr Fatima Gaji-Dantata, Aliko's niece, former education secretary in Kano State and wife of former Governor Ibrahim Shekarau of Kano State. Bottom row, Tajudeen Dantata, eldest child of Aminu Dantata, Abdu Garba Dantata, another cousin and Sani Dangote, Aliko's brother Photo Credits Dangote Group, family file, Starcomms Company, Nigeria.

○ Aliko at a social event in the late 1980s   Picture Credit: The Source Magazine

○ Aliko Dangote in Kano Picture Credit: Photo File

162

O Aliko in the 1990s Picture Credit: Private File

o Aliko Dangote, the consummate businessman Photo Credit: Photo File

CHAPTER 4
THE UNIVERSITY YEARS IN EGYPT

THE FAMOUS British educational psychologist, analytic philosopher, and mathematician, Mr. Alfred North Whitehead (1861-1947) once said, education is not limited only to formal institutions designated as "educational institutions" and called; "schools," "colleges," or "universities," to acquire, rather "education is life." The former president of the world Aristotelian Society-one of the greatest philosophical organizations in the world- and the great mind, who supervised the doctoral dissertation of Bertrand Russell, among several of his protégées- further affirmed that the greatest relationship between social groups and individuals often give birth to commerce. He said that there are no absolute truths in the world and how individuals construct their worlds are derived from social interactions between and among human beings as members of social organisms.

In analyzing the different life trajectories of many of the world's billionaires; the when, where, and how of their education encompassed their entire life. Many of the rich men and women of the world continue to grow after formal education. There are four phases in the educational lives of the rich and successful of the world. The upbringing of the rich; the life experiences of the world's billionaires; the deprivations they experienced, either directly while growing up or the deprivations they saw others went through, which gave birth to their passions and their motivations. In addition, the abilities of the rich to spot a need in their immediate environments and their responses to the anguishes of peoples in their communities are part of their education. Finally, the earnest desires of those who grow up rich to solve problems plaguing the human race. These are all essential parts of what constitute their education. These educational experiences are not taught in formal institutions called; "colleges and universities." The abilities of the billionaires and the richly successful of the world to learn from these informal institutions account for the unique perspectives they uncovered to make money where most of the rest of human beings would not understand or fathom. In other words, attending formal colleges and universities are not the only institutions that shaped the education of world billionaires.

In tracing the educational careers of the few billionaires of the world, including Nigeria's Aliko Dangote, one would realize that these smart people learned a lot outside the four walls of formal educational institutions. For example, how could Bill Gates, the richest man in the world for thirteen consecutive years drop out of Harvard at 19 and five years later became a multi-millionaire? And a decade later; at the relatively young age of 36 became the richest person in the United States? What was missing in Harvard that young Gates could not find? Why did he decide to forgo a four-year "waste" at one of the "best" elitist educational institutions in the world? Why would Mr. Branson, as a dyslexic young man able to discover that formal education at Stowe was not his calling very early in life, while growing up in London, England? Why did he give college education a wide berth, but ended up amassing fortunes beyond his wildest dreams, while no one hears about any of his classmates becoming a billionaire? How could a college drop-out end up becoming a billionaire whereas; some educational geniuses find it difficult to make ends meet? It was the late Mr. Ray Kroc, founder of the world's famous eatery; *MacDonald's* who once said; "The world is full of educated derelicts." He may be right. After all, Mr. Kroc, a salesman with a high school diploma used native wisdom to build what is today a-$36 billion business conglomerate worldwide. Now, no one should dismiss the value of formal education. After all, virtually all of the world's billionaires went to school, and ninety percent of them at least, had their first degrees in their chosen fields. But that was not the only "college/university degrees" these superbly rich people acquired. There were also other life's educational experiences they acquired in addition to what many young men and women of today are being told to go for as pre-requisites for life's success. Good, quality, and nice education with chains of college diplomas, certificates and university degrees need to be supplemented by real life experiences. Take Aliko Dangote for instance. He became a trader first before he went to Al-Azhar University, Egypt to read business administration in the 1970s. While at Capital School as a high school student, he was selling merchandize to his class mates, friends and neighbors. The question is; which other "educational institutions" did the rich attend that a large majority of people did not attend?

The educational upbringing of the rich people of the world at home has been identified as one of the "schools" that today's billionaires attended. They quickly learned from these "home colleges" that other people did not avail themselves of the same opportunity. The idea of a home when a young man/woman is growing up is a place where father and mother-parents- live harmoniously to provide for their kids and nurture them to adulthood. Some grown-ups were fortunate to have both parents in the home to assume the joint responsibilities of the nurturing process in their formatives years. Some weren't fortunate, which should not be a hindrance. But there is a general agreement in every functioning and civilized society that the home is an "educational institution."

This is where work ethics, honesty, compassion, self-confidence, and other traits needed in nurturing ideas, discovering talents, and running successful companies, and corporations are taught. Those who learned and imbibed these virtues of hard work; virtues, which they later tapped into in adult lives, often etched out than the rest. These are virtues that all translate to making money, plenty of it, later in life. Such enduring acts of punctuality, kindness, hard work, submission, and respect learned at home in formative years are attributes that come in handy in later life for running successful businesses. For example, where did Shelton Jackson Lee, who the whole world knows as Spike Lee, get the inspiration to become a film maker? Born in Atlanta, Georgia in the south at the height of the civil rights movement the same year Aliko Dangote of Nigeria was born in Kano, northern Nigeria; Shelton's parents: Bill and Jacquelyn Lee left Atlanta for Chicago. Spike-as his mother used to call him-was six months old. His mother was a school teacher, while his father was a jazz composer. The city of Chicago didn't offer much attraction to Bill so he headed for New York. He was determined to take his first child and boy to the Big Apple for him to learn music composition and film making. What did Bill see in little Spike which his three younger brothers; David, Chris and Cinque, did not have as a future film-maker? What made their father enroll Spike in Manhattan jazz club lessons and inculcate love for musical plays, museums and art galleries into young Lee? If you have watched the 1990 film; *"Mo Better Blues,"* you would understand how parents, brothers, siblings, friends, playmates, grandfathers and grandmothers, and those we grew up with could be our first teachers in life.

Some human psychologists taught us that young children have tabula rasa brains while growing up, but what they observed in their environments is important in their adult lives. These observations often shaped their character and personality in life. Some of the rich people of the world have disclosed they learned these virtues at home: ethical values such as; good work ethics, hard work, the power of money, and how to make it, and the significance of role models who epitomize persistence very early in their lives at home. They learn hard work, using money for prosecuting social causes, virtues of giving and philanthropy, the spirit of healthy competition starting in youngster's life as early as for example, encouraging siblings competing for parental approval, the power of instincts and gut feelings and other essential entrepreneurial skills needed in adult lives of future millionaires and billionaires. The Sawiris Brothers of Egypt, and the only distinguished and unique family in Africa and a handful of such families in the world, whose three brothers make the annual list of world's billionaires, according to the *Forbes* learned the rudiments of trading and negotiations while being raised by the patriarch of the family; Onsi. Mr. Onsi Sawiris, who made the bulk of the money and the first billionaire among the Sawiris Dynasty, taught his three sons how to become billionaires. Although Mr. Buffett once said he didn't believe in "dynastic wealth," yet scions of rich people, who are smart and well-brought up often surpass their parents.

Mr. Onsi Sawiris, a corporate attorney in Cairo, Egypt abandoned the legal profession in the early 1950s and went into agriculture and manufacturing. Born in 1930 when the global effects of the Great Depression were ravaging much of the world; he knew that self-sufficiency in food production was the key to making money in North Africa and the Middle East. He plunged into massive agricultural investment across Egypt and succeeded in making a fortune. By the early 1950's, Onsi began to have problems with the Nasser regime. He left Egypt briefly for Libya and only returned to his native land during Anwar Sadat's regime. His three sons; Naguib, the eldest, and his two younger brothers; Nassef and Samih, grew up and attended some of the world's best universities in the West. But as they would later admit, their first education was growing up with the patriarch of the family fortune, their father, Onsi. He taught them how to run and manage business ventures. With combined estimated family fortunes of nearly $10billion, the Sawiris epitomized the potent power of good family education and upbringing.

Aliko Dangote's first "education" as he disclosed, began with watching his maternal grandfather, Sanusi Alhassan Dantata conduct business transactions in the expansive Dantata family business in the ever-busy Koki Quarters in the ancient city of Kano. He saw first-hand, how merchandize were bought, goods were exchanged, credit facility approved, defaulters were treated, and how merchants and traders came from far, and near to conduct businesses with the famous Dantata family of Kano. According to him, "All my business acumen and instincts I inherited from my maternal grandfather. As his first grandson, he poured his business wizardry into him. I would not have been where I am today and what I am without him; a very great man, loving and caring man."

The second level of "educational institutions" that great rich people entered that shaped and prepared them for money-making are the "universities of life experiences." In these informal institutions, which all of us also pass through in our multifaceted life trajectories, the superbly rich used their experiences for business making and reaped plenty of money in return. Many of today's striplings failed to utilize such experiences. In fact, life experiences do cut both ways. They can spur us to action and push us to achieve the unthinkable, or weigh us down and keep us perpetually prostrate. As Henry Ford, the great American auto inventor aptly remarked, "Failure is a chance to begin again more intelligently. It is just a resting place. We learn more from our failures than our successes." How did Mr. Kroc, the Chicago native founder of *MacDonald's* know that you could build a fast eatery chain of businesses into a global business empire, while Messrs. Mac and Dick MacDonald's, the two brothers, who began the business could not fathom the prospects of such a business success? It was because of the late Kroc's life experience as a traveling salesman. A former truck driver, an ambulance driver and a salesman, Kroc "wasted" his first 26 years in France before returning to Illinois, the United States after WWI and was hired as a salesman with a company called *Lily Tulip* Company. His job was to distribute the company's products of drink shakes across the United States. He was on his dreary job for seventeen years till he clocked 53 years. He had noticed there was a particular restaurant in California that recorded higher sales than any other restaurant where he made his deliveries, so he decided to check the owners out. In his famous book *"Grinding It Out: The Making of MacDonald's,"* published in 1998 after his death in January 1984, he explained how the idea of the world famous food giant came about. "It was in San Bernardino, California, and my largest purchasers were running a restaurant; two brothers; Mac and Dick MacDonald. I had to see what kind of operation was making forty malts at a time. The first thing I noticed was that they had people standing in line clamoring for those 15-cent hamburgers."

Mr. Kroc was a salesman. He knew from his experiences traveling across the nation and making deliveries that such a restaurant would be popular with people like him-those on the go. These are people who wanted to eat as they travel. They had no time settling for long hours in traditional eateries and so-called standard restaurants. He approached the two brothers with a proposal: how about opening more branches across the nation like the one in California? He volunteered to run it for the two brothers. But the brothers told him they were just small town folk who preferred to remain in their little cocoons. Dick, the younger told Mr. Kroc: "See that house up there," pointing to their home in Sam Bernardino "That's home to me and I pretty like it up here. If Mac and I open new branches or a chain as you wanted, we 'd never be home." Ray Kroc disclosed that his entrepreneurial adrenaline was running and he knew this was an opening for him to make history. According to him: "I can't pretend to know what it is-certainly it's not some divine vision; perhaps it's a combination of your background and experience, your instincts, and your dreams. Whatever it was, I saw it in the *MacDonald's* operation and in that moment, I suppose I became an entrepreneur. I decided to go for broke." What Kroc did next explained the revolutionary power of using one's life's experience to financial success. He returned to Illinois, opened the first *MacDonald's* food chain in Des Plaines, Illinois and the rest, as they say, is history. At his death on January 19, 1984, Mr. Kroc was worth more than $1.2billion, while his food chain was worth more than $36 billion a decade later. During his life time, Kroc was asked about his life's philosophy. "Press on," he said. "Nothing in the world can take the place of persistence. Talent will not; nothing is more common than unsuccessful men with talents. Genius will not; the world is full of educated derelicts. Persistence and determination alone are important."

What life experiences teach us is far greater than what any human being could learn in the four walls of a college, university or educational institution. That does not mean Western education should be discounted, but it is not enough. No wonder many of the rich people of the world went to some of the best universities in the world. Jeff Bezos went to Princeton; Bill Gates cut his technological teeth as a computer whiz kid at Harvard where he first developed the programming language; BASIC, even though he dropped out two years later. John H. Johnson, the late publisher of *Ebony* magazine-the pan-African American news publication based in Chicago and the first African-American/black businessman to appear on the *Forbes* list of American millionaires, obtained a scholarship to attend the University of Chicago and acquired further education in business at the School of Business at Northwestern University in Evanston near Chicago. Spike Lee had his first degree at the famous Morehouse College, Atlanta, Georgia and was the best graduating student in his master's class at the New York University's Institute of Film and Television. Sam Walton, the founder of *Wal-Mart* earned a business degree from the University of Missouri School Of Business in St Louis, Missouri and the list continues. In keeping with the tradition of some of the world's rich people, Aliko Dangote acquired the best university education to prepare him for his business success in life; the prestigious School of Business, Al-Azhar University in Cairo, Egypt.

Founded by the Fatimid Dynasty, that believed in the succession of the daughter of Prophet Mohammed to the priesthood, Al-Azhar University began in 975 A.D as a Madras Islamic school charged with propagating the religious philosophy of the Islamic *Sunni* sect. Ranked as the first university in Egypt and probably the first in the Oriental world, it remained a purely Islamic citadel for nearly 800 years until the military regime of General Abdel Gamar Nasser approved the university and converted it into a modern Western-style educational institution in 1963. That year, it was granted a charter by the Nasser regime to operate as a full-fledged educational institution open to all Egyptians and foreigners alike. That year, five schools of studies were opened: the school of medicine, college of pharmacy, school of agriculture, the school of economics and the school of business. Aliko Dangote was admitted to the school of business where he held his own and within three years, earned his first degree and returned home to his native Nigeria. He did his mandatory national youth service (NYSC) with his family company, the Dantata Organization in Lagos.

From there, he began to learn how to climb the business ropes in commercial Lagos with his uncle, the late Mr. Usman Amaka Dantata, one of the richest among the Sanusi Dantata family business empire. But unlike most young men and women of his time, young Aliko set his eyes on business first before going to Cairo, Egypt to earn a business degree. The business instinct in the young man convinced him to move from Kano to Lagos in 1977 at the height of Nigeria's so-called oil boom. That move would pave the way for the emergence of the future richest black person in the world as would be seen shortly. It is indeed difficult to piece together this period of Aliko's life, as little evidence showed when exactly Aliko graduated from Al-Azhar University, Cairo, Egypt. Did he attend the university as a traditional student staying on campus for the duration of his four or five years as a business student or as an external student? He could not have attended the university while in Kano before 1977 when he relocated to Lagos, because he was just 20 years old. No record exist that he went to Cairo after 1977 when he arrived Lagos to live with Uncle Amaka Sanusi Dantata to cut his business teeth. But be that as it may, young Aliko obtained a bachelor's degree in business administration from Al-Azhar University, Cairo, Egypt for the record and ventured headlong into business thereafter. That is as far as the authors could gather in Nigeria.

CHAPTER 5
HOME AWAY FROM HOME: THE STRUGGLING YEARS

THE YEAR 1977 was very significant in the life of Nigeria as a nation, but more so in the life of young Aliko. Nigeria was seventeen years old as an independent nation. After a bloody civil war during the Nigerian-Biafra War of 1967-1970- four years after political independence from Britain, and a *coup d'état* on January 15, 1966, and another counter coup six months later; Nigeria seemed to be lurching from one military regime to the other: (Major-General Aguiyi-Ironsi regime of January 15, 1966-July 1966; General Yakubu Gowon (1967-1975), and General Murtala Ramat Muhammad (1975-1976). The baton of military power changed from General Murtala Ramat Muhammad, who was assassinated in an abortive coup on February 13, 1976 to General Olusegun Obasanjo that replaced the slain general. General Obasanjo decided to change the face of the Nigerian infrastructural landscape through massive injection of government funds into road construction, bridges, modern highways, and housing. The height of the government public expenditure occurred between June 1976 and June 1977, when the military regime decided to host the world in a cultural re-awakening of all black peoples of the world known as; " World Black and African Festival of Arts and Culture" or *Festac.*

The history of *Festac* started in Paris, France in 1956,

when a group of African intellectuals usually gathered informally at the Pan-African Cultural Society in the French capital. The thrust of their discussion centered on how Africans, scattered across the world as a result of the obnoxious trans-Atlantic Slave Trade could come together in an African nation to revive the African culture. It was an idea, centered on the theme of African cultural revival. There were only two black African nations that had gained political independence during this period: the Republic of Guinea in 1957 under Ahmed Sekou Toure and Ghana (formerly called Gold Coast) under Mr. Kwame Nkrumah. Ethiopia was the only African nation that had not been colonized, although she was briefly controlled by Italy. The rest of Africa was controlled by foreign powers as a result of the Berlin Conference of 1884 in Germany. This was a period when *Negritude* or re-awakening of black consciousness was popular among African cultural irredentists. The African cultural revivalists met with Mr. Leopold Sedar Senghor (1906- 2001), who eventually became the first democratically-elected president of independent Senegal. In 1959, the black scholars met again in Rome, Italy, where they continued further discussions on how to bring their ideas into reality. It was in Rome, Italy that the African thinkers came up with the name; "World Festival of Black African Arts and Culture," or *Festac* as an acronym.

In 1960, Senegal became independent from France and Mr. Senghor was sworn in as president. He had promised to give vent to the crusade of his black scholars-friends, who had met him in Paris, France prior to becoming president. True to his promise, in 1966, the First World Festival of Black African Arts and Culture or *Festac* was staged in Dakar, Senegal with much fanfare. Nigeria which was just six years old and the most populous nation in Africa was conspicuously absent, because of the existential kerfuffle of 1966-1970, which shook the newly-independent African nation to its very foundation. To "compensate" Africa's giant for not participating in the maiden edition of *Festac*, the organizers of the event in Dakar, Senegal decided to give Nigeria the opportunity to host the event instead of Ethiopia, which had already been promised to host the second edition in Addis Ababa.

The head of state, General Yakubu Gowon, acquiesced to the invitation extended to Nigeria to host the second edition of the global cultural event. His regime was determined to host the event in order to fulfill its promise to the African and black scholars, both at home and in the Diaspora; unfortunately Gowon had the urgent task of uniting a badly fractured nation that had just passed through a bitter and gruesome 30-month civil war. His 3Rs of national reconciliation encapsulated in: reconciliation, rehabilitation, and reconstruction were uppermost in the general's plate after cessation of hostilities in 1970 aftermath of the Nigerian-Biafra Civil War. The second edition of the event was again pushed forward twice: 1970, because of the fratricidal war of 1966-1970, and in 1974, because construction works were still going on in some of the venues for staging the proposed event. By the time General Gowon was contemplating staging the global event, he was unexpectedly removed in a *coup d'état* in July 1975, while on a state visit to attend the annual summit of the Organization of African Unity (OAU, now AU) in Kampala, Uganda in East Africa. Gowon's ouster had been announced by his fellow kinsman and chief of staff, the late Brigadier Joseph Garba, who was eventually appointed minister of external affairs by General Murtala Ramat Muhammad, who replaced deposed General Gowon as head of state. Gowon went into exile in the United Kingdom after he was toppled.

His successor, General Muhammad put on hold all construction projects going on in the country for the intending hosting of the event. However, six months after Muhammad became head of state, he too was toppled in a bloody coup which paved the way for his military deputy, Lt Gen Olusegun Obasanjo, who was the chief of staff to become the new military head of state on February 15, 1976. Immediately Obasanjo was sworn as Muhammad's successor, there were sundry calls from many quarters that the *Festac* should be hosted by the Obasanjo military regime. On the other hand, many Nigerians also voiced their opinion against Nigeria hosting the event, chiefly among those Nigerians was the late Afro-beat legend, Mr. Fela Anikulapo-Kuti.

There were criticisms that trailed the decision of the Obasanjo military regime in accepting to host the *Festac* in Nigeria in January 1977 and some of the reasons were the enormous costs and state resources that would be expended on the event. The costs could be justified on both sides of the argument; costs expended would lead to economic transformation of the nation's infrastructural development and the fact that it had economic value for the country. The spokespersons of the Obasanjo military regime countered the criticisms, insisting that, as the most populous nation in Africa, and the black world, Nigeria should live up to her expectations to lift up the black race through promoting African art and culture. In addition, both the minister of finance and the minister of arts and culture during the Obasanjo regime (1976-1979) insisted that the nation's economy was solvent enough to absorb the financial costs of hosting the global event. Major-General James Jaiyeola Oluleye, the minister of finance (1975-1979) and also a member of the ruling supreme military council (SMC)-the highest decision-making organ of the junta- defended the government's action in staging the festival. He disclosed that the Nigerian economy was buoyant to stage the event, while the minister of special duties, Mr. Ochegomie Promise Fingesi coordinated the planning committee of the event.

Other members of the Obasanjo regime justified the enormous benefits that Nigeria would gain from hosting the cultural fiesta. After listening and analyzing the two sides of the argument in the media for, and against the hosting of the *Festac,* the Supreme Military Council (SMC) chaired by General Olusegun Obasanjo and his deputy, the late General Shehu Musa Yar'Adua, who was the chief of staff, passed a resolution in 1976, which gave the go-ahead for Nigeria to host the *Festac* the following year in 1977. Other members of the supreme military council (SMC) that took the decision for Nigeria to host the *Festac* in 1977 were; Brigadier Theophilus Yakubu Danjuma - chief of army staff; Commodore Michael Adelanwa - chief of naval staff; Col. John Yisa Doko - chief of air staff, Alhaji Mohammed D. Yusuf, the inspector-general of police; the general officer commanding 1st Division, Brigadier Alani Ipoola Akinrinade GOC, 2nd Division, Brigadier Martin Adamu GOC, 3rd Division; Brigadier Emmanuel Abisoye; L.G.O., Brigadier John Obada; Colonel Joseph Garba; Brigadier James Oluleye; Colonel Ibrahim Babangida; Lt. Col Muktar Muhammad; Colonel Dan Suleiman; Captain Olufemi Olumide (Nigerian Navy); Captain H Husaini Abdullahi (Nigerian Navy); Mr. Adamu Suleiman, commissioner of police, Lt. Col. Alfred Aduloju, and Lt. Commander Godwin Ndubuisi Kanu (Nigerian Navy).

The *Festac*, which was held in Lagos between January 15, 1977 and February 12, 1977, has been described as the largest and most expensive event in the history of Nigeria. It witnessed a cavalcade of the largest number of Africans in Africa, and Africans in the Diaspora, and black people ever assembled in one gathering in the history of the black race. In Dakar, Senegal and Lagos, Nigeria, where the first and second editions of the World Black and African Festival of Arts and Culture took place in 1966 and 1977 respectively, great African artists and black in the Diaspora were fully represented. From Mestre Patinha-the Capoeirista of Bahia; Duke Ellington, Alvin Ailey and Arthur Mitchell of the American Negro Dance Company to Marion Williams, and the then Queen of Samba, Clementina de Jesus. Other popular artistes were; Stevie Wonder, Donald Byrd, and Sun Ra from the United States; Gilberto Gil from Brazil; the Orchestra Afrisa International from Congo, Tabu Ley Rochereau and Ray Lema, who accompanied OK Jazz to the celebrated festival. Others were Bembeya Jazz from Guinea, Mighty Sparrow from Trinidad and Tobago, Miriam

Makeba, Dudu Pukwana and Louis Maholo, who came from black South Africa, because of the apartheid regime in South Africa, while African aboriginal singers and performers came from Australia and New Guinea to add color to the festival. Indeed, it was Africa and the black race at its best. Mr. Fingesi, the chairman of the organizing committee told foreign journalists covering the event in Lagos that, "Nigeria is no longer a Third world, but now we are the First World."

Mr. Randy Weston, African-American/black Jazz legend, who was in Lagos, Nigeria for *Festac' 77* remembers the cultural awakening thirty five years ago. "The Nigerian government reportedly put up huge amounts of oil money to stage this event. The whole idea is that we are one African people; that were the goal of FESTAC. No matter if we're in Mississippi or Havana or Australia, or wherever...They invited about 20,000 artists from across the globe. I only wound up playing once, at least officially, though I did jam with Fela... Sun Ra was there and he played once. There was so much great artistry at this conference that you didn't need to play more than once. Representatives from the entire black world organized this thing. They hosted colloquiums throughout FESTAC on everything from education to health to music, all things involved with African people. It was designed to develop a sense of global unity. The *Festac* lasted for one month, throughout January. I stayed most of the month, because I had come individually on my own; I didn't come with the American delegation because I was living in France at the time."

The Jazz great remembers the names of popular African-American/black activists, musicians, writers, authors etc. that were in Lagos, Nigeria for, unarguably the greatest cultural event that brought all black peoples of the world together for the first time under one roof. "The array of folks there was incredible. For example I'd have breakfast and my tablemates might be Louis Farrakhan, Stevie Wonder, Queen Mother Moore, and a heavy *Sufi* master named Mahi Ismail. Imagine me hanging out with those cats! When he arrived, Stevie came into the hotel with his guitar, walked in the lobby, sat down and started singing and playing his guitar."

The mission of *Festac*, according to the organizing committee, was to celebrate the "individuality, the antiquity, and the power of the Black and African World. "General Olusegun Obasanjo and Head of State of Nigeria, who was also the grand patron of the organizing committee of the cultural jamboree, told the world. He said the mission of Nigeria in staging the event was to bring all Africans in the Motherland and in the Diaspora together as one people. "To succeed, we must restore the link between culture, creativity, and mastery of modern technology and industrialism ... to endow the Black Peoples all over the world with a new society, deeply rooted in our cultural identity, and ready for the great scientific, and technological task of conquering the future," Obasanjo added. On the opening day of the festival, Gen Obasanjo poured palm wine and broke kola nuts to summon African gods and goddesses to the event, in the presence of King Oyekan of Lagos, King Moshoeshoe of Lesotho, President Siaka Stevens of Sierra Leone, and Sir President Dauda Jawara of The Gambia. The kola nuts were distributed to all the guests present at the National Theater. The gods and goddesses- the demons- heard the prayers of Mr. Obasanjo as hundreds of people died on the opening day of the cultural fiesta, because of exhaustion and over-crowdedness. However, before the event began proper, the Obasanjo military regime had to construct blocks of apartments and houses, including condominiums to house the large retinues of black people of the world coming for the global event. The regime had less than nine months to put the remaining structures in place to ensure a successful international event between February, 1976, and January 1977. Some eminent Nigerians were appointed as members of the organizing committee of the staging of *Festac* in Nigeria in 1977. The local organizing committee liaised with black peoples in the United States, the Americas, and other parts of the world, who equally set up regional staging committees to ensure a successful cultural jamboree.

To build houses and the venues in Lagos, which are now referred to as *Festac* Town, and the National Arts Theater Iganmu in central Lagos, mouth-watering contracts for the constructions of such houses and venues were awarded. The main venue of most of the cultural events; the National Arts Theater at Iganmu in central Lagos, which is 31 meters tall and occupied about 23,000 square meters space in a reclaimed marshy landscape was constructed by a Bulgarian Construction company called; *Technoexportsroy* at a cost of about $23billion in today's market during the toppled Gowon military regime. The national theater, with capacity for 5,000 guests and another 1,500 interpreters in eight of the world's major languages, was opulence stretched beyond imagination. If you sat down watching stage performances at the main hall and wanted to go to the rest room, all you needed do was push a button and closed-circuit television sets to relay every move without you missing any part. That was in 1977! Black scholars from 43 nations in Africa, North America, Latina America, the Caribbean, Southeast Asia and Australasia were on hand to present 269 papers called; African Colloquiums, which had as chairman, Col. (Dr) Ahmadu A. Ali, the federal minister of education under Gen Obasanjo. In addition, contracts were also awarded for the importation of long vehicles known as; Leyland luxury buses into the country needed to convey the various contingents of participating African and black nations from the various venues to their houses at Festac Town known as *Festac Village* in the outskirts of south-west, Lagos. Other venues used for the jamboree were; the University of Lagos, Yaba College of Technology (now City University, Lagos), Lagos City Hall, and other important places such as; the then popular Hotel Bobby on Ikorodu Road, Race Course in Ikoyi which was later renamed, Tafawa Balewa Square (TBS), Lagos etc.

Another city outside Lagos that also played hosts to the contingents was Kaduna where the Festival Durbar took place. Mr. Andrew Young, the first African-American/black to be appointed by President Jimmy Carter as US

Ambassador to the United Nations was conspicuously present. The contingents for the jamboree came from the Caribbean, South America, the United States, Australasia, Latin America and all nations in Africa, except South Africa, and Zimbabwe (then known as Southern Rhodesia). Needless to add that many of the contingents remained behind and refused to go back to their countries after the cultural event, especially those from the Caribbean and Latin America, including the Americas, after savoring the hospitality of Nigerians. For many of the contingents from the Americas and African black sisters and brothers from the Diaspora, the festival was more of a home-coming. Some of the black sisters got married to some Nigerians and fellow black brothers during the jamboree.

But beyond the cultural glitz and the razzmatazz that *Festac' 77* was supposed to be were the mouth-watering contracts and money spent on the jamboree. Many Nigerian contractors exploited the opportunity to make money out of the Nigerian nation. For example, one Mr. Tatari Alli, who later became governor of Bauchi State collected ₦403,000 (about $503,000 in 1977) as survey costs of *Fesatc Village* more than the amount actually spent. Another contractor, one Mr. G.A Dada was awarded ₦459,000 (about $559,000) for "artistic dressing?" The sum of ₦244, 625 (about $363,290) was budgeted for Nigerians sent to France for French Language courses for three weeks so they could serve as interpreters at the event. The late Mr. Tony Enahoro was indicted for collecting the money to buy a house for himself in Victoria Island, Lagos rather than paying for any French Language courses. In Kaduna, one of the venues of the *Festac'77*, Mr. Umaru Dikko, who was then commissioner for education in the old north central state and supervisor of the Durbar Festival during the event, was reported to have spent ₦500,000 (about $750,000) on "logistics, committee meetings and mobilization." A group of contractors were reported to have collected ₦12.6 million (about $20million) to clear the weeds and road at Iganmu in central Lagos, where the national theater was to be built for the event. The contract sum of ₦18million (about $30million) was awarded to British Leyland motors in the UK for the importation of luxury buses for the event and two Nigerian officials demanded and got ₦286,000 (about $402,000) bribes.

The sum of ₦608, 218.96 (about $918,410.52) was paid for non-existent contracts to a Canadian firm through the Barclay's Bank International of London for prefabricated houses for the event which were never delivered to Nigeria. The $10,000 fee paid by each of the fifty-four participating nations for the event, which raked in over $600,000 could not be accounted for and the external auditors' report concluded that it was mismanaged. The *Festac* did indeed revive African culture, but it was also an opportunity for some fat cats to feather their nests.

It was during this period that young Aliko-a- 20- year old business man- had his break. He approached his maternal grandfather, Mr. Sanusi Dantata for a loan to enable him import cement into Nigeria for some of the construction works going on at the *Festac* Village in Lagos and aftermath of the jamboree. Aliko Dangote explained how he became a part of the business elite of the event, before and after. "For me, I started small as a trader in cement. Then I left cement around 1978. Because there was this armada and cement was very difficult to get at that time. I had my own money, which my grandfather gave me free, but then he gave me also an additional loan of ₦500,000 which was big money in those days. With ₦500,000 in those days, you could buy yourself ten Mercedes Benz cars. Mercedes Benz car then was ₦5,000 naira. I am talking about Nigeria in the year 1978. Volkswagen Beetle was sold for ₦900 to ₦1,000. It was a substantial amount of money then. It was a loan that I was supposed to pay whenever I was okay— probably after three years or four years. But I paid the money (the loan) back within six months."

In the 1970's and up to the early 1990's; especially during the military regimes that governed Nigeria, there was a policy known as import license. The import license spelt out the process through which foreign goods could be imported into the country and there were many Nigerians who made lots of money during that era. But in addition to the one-month long *Festac* cultural celebration which gulped several millions (billons in today's currency), there were other development projects going on across the nation during the Obasanjo military regime (1976-1979), which required large-scale construction works across Nigeria. In addition, the energy crisis of 1973/1974 actually affected the price of crude oil, which ushered Nigeria into the era of oil boom. Furthermore, the year 1977 also coincided with era the international oil cartel known as, the Organization of Petroleum Exporting Countries (OPEC) became so powerful, of which Nigeria became a member shortly after the civil war in 1971. The OPEC soon became a bulwark against the efforts of the Western world to lower the price of crude oil as the new oil bloc leveraged the cost of their products to their advantage. Today, the 12- members OPEC comprise; Iran, Saudi Arabia, Kuwait, Iraq and Venezuela as foundation members that signed the original documents of its founding in Baghdad in September 1960 and the remaining seven nations that later joined were; Qatar, Indonesia, Libya, UAE, Algeria, Nigeria, Ecuador and Angola which joined in 2007. Gabon suspended its membership in 1975. But of all the 12 OPEC nations, Nigeria was (and still is) the most populous. This gave Nigeria more power within the oil cartel.

The three years that Lt-Gen Obasanjo was on the saddle also coincided with the implementation of Nigeria's third national development plan began by the slain General Murtala Muhammad which Obasanjo had to complete. The newly-created states of Ondo, Oyo, Ogun, Benue, Imo, Cross River, and Bauchi had to be developed and several government ministries had to be created, including the construction of numerous administrative and government offices. Furthermore, the military regime had just approved the establishment of what later became the nation's second-tier universities namely: University of Calabar, University of Ilorin, University of Maiduguri, University of Jos (which was a college campus of the University of Ibadan); University of Sokoto (now renamed Usman Danfodiyo University, Sokoto), and the University of Port Harcourt (formerly, an arm of the university college of the University of Ibadan). All these various construction projects going on across the nation needed something very vital to constructions of buildings and housing complexes: cement. In addition, the population of Nigeria had begun to increase. Nigeria contained about thirty five million people at political independence in 1960, but within a decade, the population of the country had jumped to nearly fifty million in 1970, and the population continues to grow since then. These Nigerians need to be fed, housed, and clothed. It was a no brainer that any smart, prescient, and clever business person would concentrate on these three vital areas of people's needs: food, clothing, and shelter to cater to the ballooning population of Africa's most populous nation.

When economists say there are three basic necessities of life: food, clothing and shelter, every economic analysis, studies, and even the way we live, seemed to corroborate this truth. Consequently, any business person or company that focuses business goals and ideas on any, or all of these three basic needs of life that are in demand will reap bountifully. Take the largest economy in the world for example; the United States of America. The United States has the largest Gross Domestic Product (GDP) of $14.660 trillion, more than 100 nations of the world combined, in addition to her military might and technological superiority. But what most people do not know is that, half of the GDP of the United States is derived from agriculture. The United States produces half of the grains in the entire world. She supplies and exports more than fifty percent of the world's grain and food products across the globe. This is why the United States of America has been a force for good around the world. For example, America produces almost two-thirds of the entire world output of wheat and the same amount in fertilizer production. In the United States alone, the Department of Agriculture reported in 2009 in its Consumer Expenditure Survey that the United States Average Consumer Unit, which measured consumer spending habits annually are centered on the three basic human needs of; food, clothing and shelter. An average consumer in the United States spends 25.34 percent of his or her income on food and food-related needs; 34.43 percent on housing either rented, owned, or mortgage payments; while 15.26 percent goes into clothing and clothing-related needs. That means every year; an American spends 75.03 percent of his or her income on food, clothing and shelter. No wonder, more branches and franchises of *McDonald's, Arby's, Burger King, Checkers,* and *Subway* etc. are springing up daily across the United States, and around the world. Imagine what eateries such as *Papa John's, Pizza Hut, Dominos* etc. make annually from selling pizzas either online, on the drive-through or home deliveries, in spite of the tanking economy. Why *Family Dollar, Dollar General, Dollar Tree* and such eateries are springing up all over the United States, is because they are tailored to meet these three basic needs of life. For example, the United States National Coffee Association reported that 54 percent Americans spend $9.2 billion annually on coffee alone. No wonder the Seattle-based, *Starbucks* founders and owners; the troika of Gordon Bowker, Jerry Baldwin and Zev Siegl of Washington State are worth billions.

It is no wonder then why Aliko Dangote of Nigeria later emerged as the richest Nigerian, the richest African, and the richest black person in the world, three decades after he built the phenomenally successful business conglomerate known as the *Dangote* Group. Nearly ninety-five percent of his businesses are centered on food, clothing and shelter. No matter what you do in any corner of the world, whatever your status in life, and whoever you are as a human being; you cannot do without these three essentials of life: food, clothing and shelter. As the African adage says, "I ate yesterday does not concern hunger." Aliko Dangote could be said to be ahead of the curve among his peers to be able to understand this reality of life. He has built his business empire on food, clothing, and shelter, which made his company to emerge, three decades later as the largest indigenous business outfit south of the African Sahara.

Prior to the 1977 *Festac* contract bonanza, young Aliko had been privileged to be under the business watchful eyes of his uncle and one of the children of his grandfather, Mr. Sanusi Alhassan Dantata. The name of the uncle was Mr. Usman Amaka Sanusi Dantata. Now deceased, but during his lifetime, Usman impacted the life of young Aliko in profound ways. If the business acumen of Aliko Dangote were inherited from his maternal grandfather, Mr. Sanusi Dantata; and Koki Quarter, Kano was where he inherited those traits; kudos should be paid to the late Mr. Usman Amaka Sanusi Dantata, who provided the opportunities for Aliko to experiment with those learned and inherited traits.

The 1960's and early 1970's provided huge business opportunities for several indigenous Nigerian business men and women. The Dantatas seemed to have monopolized the entire business life of northern Nigeria, although there were also other important business players who competed for the business pies in the region. Prominent indigenous business men such as; Messrs. Muhammad Agigi Sharubutu, Maikano Agogo, Umaru Sharabutu, Malam Salga MaiGoro, Madugu Kosai and several others, were major players, but none could be compared with the famous Dantata Family. The third generation which inherited the phenomenally successful business empire; *Alhassan Dantata & Son's* conglomerate left behind by the patriarch; Pa Alhassan Dantata operated like virtual monopolist. Another edge which the Dantata family had over other business competitors was that the deceased Dantata, who began it all, put in place a magnificent succession strategy among his numerous children. This ensured his business empire continued even after he died on Wednesday August 17, 1955-two years before Aliko was born.

According to family sources in Kano, immediately he knew he was about to pass to the other side, Pa Alhassan Dantata called his chief financial controller, Mr. Garba Maisikili to assemble all his children so he would leave behind his last and final words. First, he warned his children not to bicker over his wealth. Second, he instructed them to take the expanse business empire to the next level. Third, the big family should consort among themselves in order to maintain the wealth in the family. They should not enter into business mergers with any other family business outfit. Finally, no Dantata man or woman with the genes in his or her veins should be a rebel, an *enfant terrible* or lead opposition to constituted authorities and government.

His eldest son, Mr. Sanusi Alhassan Dantata, who took the baton of the family business conglomerate, adhered strictly to these rules. By the time of Nigerian independence, he dispatched his son, Usman Amaka Sanusi to go to Lagos and extend the family business empire. On May 27, 1977, four weeks after his 20th birthday, Aliko's first wife was specially chosen for him by a consensus of his mother and other uncles. The *Nikai* (wedding) ceremony took place at the family compound in Koki Quarters, Kano. Thereafter, he was brought to Lagos by his maternal grandfather and Usman Amaka Sanusi Dantata was asked to look after him. Uncle Usman took little Aliko under his business wing and developed him into a formidable business magus. When young Aliko arrived in Lagos in early 1977, he was living with his uncle, Usman Amaka Dantata at 29A Probyne Street in Central Lagos. The house was later sold to Dr. Umaru Mutallab, former chairman of First Bank of Nigeria Limited and father of Mutallab, the *Al-Qaeda* terrorist serving life imprisonment in the United States for attempting to bomb an airline in December 2010 in Detroit, Michigan.

Born in 1950 in the holy city of Mecca in Saudi Arabia as one of the six male children of late Sanusi Alhassan Dantata and the younger brother of Hajiya Mariya Sanusi-Dantata-Dangote, the mother of Aliko, Usman was the quintessential chip off the block of the Dantata family. He was a prodigious business mogul and amassed great fortunes during his life time before he died in July, 2009 at the age of 59. He taught young Aliko Dangote the type of company a savvy business person should keep in the course of conducting business deals. When he stormed the Lagos business scene in 1972 after his father told him to leave Kano for the then nation's administrative hub and economic nerve, young Usman knew he would be viewed with suspicion. After all, his reputation had preceded him as the scion of the famous Dantata family before he arrived at the Lagos business scene. Usman Amaka was only 22 years old when he got to Lagos but he had the mind of an adult. At 27 years old during the celebration of *Festac,* he had forged business relationships with the Nigerian military establishment.

The first business deal young Usman landed was the importation of rice into the country following the cessation of hostilities between Nigeria and the break-away eastern region of the defunct Republic of Biafra. The Nigerian-Biafra Civil War required that veterans that were returning from the 3-year fratricidal war needed to be taken care of by the military regime of General Yakubu Gowon. The Nigerian Ports in Lagos were heavily congested and all manners of goods and merchandize were jostling for attention. Three years later when Usman Amaka Dantata arrived Lagos, General Yakubu Gowon was toppled in a coup and a Kano home boy; General Murtala Muhammad became the nation's new helmsman. The first attention of the new military ruler was to de-congest the Nigerian Ports in Lagos. Mr. Usman Amaka and another wealthy Lagos businessman, the late Mr. Wahab Iyanda Folawiyo won the contracts. The two business men did excellent jobs in clearing the congested Lagos Ports. Government recognition soon came from the new military regime. Later, Usman became a top federal government contractor. Of course, needless to mention they made a lot of money from the haulage and decongestion contracts. By the time his young cousin, Aliko Dangote joined him two years later, the baton of the nation's leadership had changed; General Muhammad had been assassinated and

General Obasanjo was in the saddle. While Obasanjo was the military head of state between 1976 and 1979, the military strong man who was actually running the show underground was the chief of staff, the late General Shehu Musa Yar'Adua, who was the vice-president of the military junta.

The Katsina prince was 34 years old and was the first and only Nigerian to become a full military general at such a relatively young age. He was given double promotion from a Colonel to a Major-General, skipping the rank of Brigadier. As the chief of staff in charge of the supreme headquarters in Doddan Barrack, Obalende in central Lagos in the Obasanjo military regime, he was the *defacto* vice-president. Among the business elites that the young military general assembled, mostly of northern region, young Usman Amaka Dantata was a member of these industrial-army/military complex. Mr. Atiku Abubakar, then a top shot at the Nigerian Customs, who later became vice –president of Nigeria; Malam Liman Ciroma, the then head of service, Dr. Dele Cole, who later became an ambassador, Dr. Raymond Dokpesi, lured home from Poland, and later was to become a media magnate, late Dele Giwa, late Dr. Stanley Macebuh, and a host of others whose paths were later to cross with Aliko Dangote were all cutting their business teeth, professional interests and forging political alliances. Mr. Usman Amaka Dantata took his young cousin along in many of the nocturnal business meetings in Lagos where contracts were discussed, deals were made and terms of rewards were elaborately trashed out. Aliko Dangote was only 20 years old when he moved to Lagos in 1977. Uncle Usman was 27 years old and a multi-millionaire. From such a relatively young age, young Aliko had known and met some of Nigeria's political power-brokers and economic wheeler-dealers.

Although young, Aliko Dangote began to learn the art of business negotiations from his uncle in Lagos. He was exposed to the Lagos elites, even though he had lived all his life in his native Kano, he began to blend into the Lagos social, business, religious and political circles. He began to schmooze with members of many Lagos business clubs of the 1970s and other social clubs in the Lagos social circles. Many of the influential Lagos big boys were also Muslims; the Animashauns, the Edus, the Gbadamoshis, the Lawals and many of the popular Lagos names, that dominated the then nation's seat of government. Gradually, young Aliko began to learn how to speak the Yoruba Language. Through his activities at the Apapa Road office complex where his uncle had his sprawling haulage, importing and exporting businesses, young Aliko also began to forge business relationships with young Ibo business men, who were later to come on board his future Dangote business train. While Usman was making waves in the business world in Lagos; he did not take his eyes off Kano. He had always been interested in manufacturing and farming, so he went to Tiga near Bagauda in Kano and acquired large expanse of land for poultry farming and animal husbandry. The massive farms known as *Anadariya* Farms were at a time the largest farming and animal husbandry companies owned by a single individual in Nigeria and West Africa. By watching his uncle diversified his business exploits in farming, manufacturing, haulage, import and export, young Aliko learned the business sense of not putting all of one's business eggs into the proverbial single basket. But the spirit of diversification, which young Aliko learned from uncle Usman, was later taken to higher level, thanks to technology and globalization. Not only did Aliko learn from the traditional masters of indigenous Nigerian business, he was later to surpass and outshine them all. Where the young and early indigenous Nigerian business guys were content with doing businesses within Nigeria, Aliko went back to the business templates used by his maternal great-grandfather, the legendary and iconic Papa Alhassan Abdullahi Dantata. These traditional, but highly effective business templates accounted for the old man's phenomenal business success across the large swath of land then known as West Africa. Aliko Dangote updated and improved on them, using today's modern technology and globalization for maximum effects. Soon, and very soon, young Aliko Dangote was unstoppable.

From his first break-out business deal in cement importation for 20-year old Aliko where he made a fortune, some said it was worth about $4million in 1978, the up-starter soon began to dream big dreams.

The late Pa Alhassan Dantata conducted his business the old fashioned way by using mainly Hausa traders. Traditionally, most of the Hausa local traders dominated the kola nut business, importing, and exporting trading activities across the West African trading zone. Even when there was no easy transportation and free movement of people and goods; somehow, the man used his native intelligence to his advantage. For example, in his thought-provoking piece for the defunct London-based *West Africa* magazine in the 1950's, Mr. J.H. Price, in a tribute to Alhassan Dantata's business wizardry, disclosed that the man's death was first broken to the magazine in Freetown, Sierra Leone by a group of Hausa merchants waiting to conduct business with the famous business mogul. In the piece, Price, a senior editor with the magazine disclosed that, " Alhassan, whom I knew well, was possibly the richest man of any race in the whole of West Africa, and was in himself, a living rebuttal of the allegation that Africans, as a race, have no commercial aptitude, an example to his fellow - countrymen of what a man can rise to even without education and a wealthy background" (See *West Africa* magazine, October 29, 1955; Special Edition devoted to the death of Mr. Alhassan Dantata).

Mr. Aliko Dangote revived these old time's business success tips of his iconic great grandfather and masterfully adapted them to our modern business world. Uncle Usman gave more to his cousin; he taught him how to maintain administrative discipline and deal with subordinates. A classic example was the rude behavior of one Mr. Mehta, an expatriate manager working with Usman whose insubordination nearly caused a rift between uncle and cousin. The Indian expatriate was tongue-lashed and put in his place, because in the Dantata clan, no external person should be allowed to break the bonds of filial solidarity and family unity. Young Aliko was gradually coming up and learning the business ropes rapidly to the bemusement of other hangers-on in the sprawling Dantata business empire. As young Aliko was learning how to cut business deals, learn the art of negotiations, dispense with sound business ethics, and conduct himself among important political leaders and business elites; uncle Usman was also pushing his cousin to continue to network. Although these years were generally referred to as the struggling years for young Aliko; nevertheless, they were years of ample opportunities for him to begin to oil his business machinery.

By the tail end of the Obasanjo military regime in 1979, Aliko Dangote, at the relatively young age of 22 had read the nation's economic "blue-print" and where the future was heading: manufacturing. He read the Nigerian future quiet correctly, for while the few business guys of his age and day were consumed with getting their own pies out of the black gold: oil; Aliko Dangote was unperturbed. The young, savvy, ambitious, highly-motivated and shrewd business man knew the future, definitely belongs to food, food and food; edibles, groceries, commodities, clothing and shelter. Future events in Nigeria, West Africa, Africa and the world proved him right. Where the first world-recognized billionaire in Nigeria, the richest man in West Africa and the richest black person on the planet earth would make his money would not be oil, the black gold; rather, the everyday needs of all human beings and people, whether poor, rich; young or old around the world. People must eat, large populations must be fed and millions of Nigerians leaving for the urban centers daily, in what later became known as; Nigeria's rural-urban migration, must be housed and clothed. When the petro dollars arrive from overseas; when the politicians are done purloining the treasury, when the professors and students are done with their high sounding clichés and discourses; when the civil servants finish their agitation for more pay, when the military generals award mouth-watering contracts for members of the civilian-military industrial complex and pocketed half of the contract money, when the commentariats are done with their media analyses and spins;

somehow, they cannot escape from spending the money on these three basic essentials of life: food, clothing and shelter.

It took Aliko Dangote's business genius and wizardry to discover food must be put on the table, the kids must be clothed, including the aged parents in the villages and the adult city-dwellers. He saw ahead of other business moguls in his native country that houses must be built even, when some Nigerians must have to sleep under the bridges in Lagos, because of over-population and city congestion. Somehow, the Nigerian government and individuals would soon come to him for the cement to build both the houses and the bridges. Only few in Nigeria discovered this sure road to business success and billion dollar land. No wonder, Aliko Dangote once said, Nigeria is a secret to business success that is yet to be discovered, and many of such discoveries are waiting for geniuses. He discovered this secret when he was only 20 years old! It was this prescient genius that made him to approach his maternal grandfather, Grand Pa Sanusi Alhassan Dantata for a loan.

The story of the loan that Mr. Aliko Dangote obtained from his maternal grandfather has been written and talked about in all accounts of his business success, yet it was not the loan *per se* that paved the way for Aliko's ultimate business success. It was what he did with the loan. He saw beyond his contemporaries in Kano and Lagos, and invested the money on cement importation. Today, Aliko Dangote has become the cement king of Africa. It is also instructive to note that Aliko Dangote did what other smart rich people in other climes did on their paths to riches: borrowing money from close relatives and friends to create more money. The publisher of the *Chicago Defender* newspaper in Chicago, Robert Sengstacke Abbott obtained a $25 loan from his landlady in 1905 to establish one of the most successful African-American/black newspapers in the United States. Mr. John Johnson, the founder of *Ebony* and *Jet* magazines, two of the most successful African-American / black magazines in the world also did the same: he founded his publishing outfit from a $500 loan from his mother in

1942. Richard Branson borrowed $6.00 from his mother in London to establish the *Student* magazine in the 1960's and followed it up with the *Virgin Group*; Berry Gordy borrowed money from his sister to start *Motown* Records in 1960, and Aliko obtained a loan from his uncle in 1977 and built the *Dangote* Group. See the pattern? All these men borrowed money to start their own businesses and became millionaires and billionaires.

Mr. Aliko Dangote. the richest man in Nigeria and Africa Photo Credit: Author File

The many faces of the world's richest black person.

World Black and African Festival of Arts and Culture" or *Festac* in 1977, Nigeria when Aliko made his first million Dollars at the age of 20. In the pictures are General Danjuma then chief of staff, Mr Promise Fingesi, minister of special duty, General Shehu Musa Yar'Adua, chief of general staff, Col. Ahmadu Ali, minister of education/chairman, organizing committee and General Olusegun Obasanjo, head of state in 1977.

CHAPTER 6
THE UNEXPECTED
BREAK

IN EARLY 1995, a young Cuban-American businessman was reading a magazine in his office in Wall Street and something important caught his attention. In the article, the writer revealed that, with the exponential rise in the quantum of information in the world today, the trend in information manufacture and delivery would inexorably move to the Internet and the World Wide Web. The writer further disclosed that the percentage of computer usage had grown by 23,000 percent annually-the first of its kind in the use of any medium in human history- and concluded that the future of information delivery would henceforth be dictated and controlled by the computers, the Internet, and the World Wide Web. The writer described in the article what he called, the beginning of the Information Age. That revelation kept the young Wall Street executive thinking. He got home and began to mull the idea of how information could be delivered via the new technological barracuda of our time. After obtaining more information on the article he had read, he found that, sooner or later the world of Adam would give way to the world of chips, bits and bytes. He seemed to have found the future! He went back to his office and tendered his letter of resignation. His fellow Wall Street executives were flummoxed. They thought he was crazy, but he was undeterred. The young Wall Street executive had seen and discovered something that no one else had discovered, even though it was obvious some other people, including his colleagues in the office had read the same article.

Next, the young man got home and told his wife it was time they relocated from New York City to the Far North West of the Continental United States. He figured that was the ideal location for the business he had in mind. His wife trusted him. They sold their home in the Big Apple and moved into a rented apartment with a big car garage in Seattle, Washington. They bought few lap tops and engaged the services of young university graduate computer whiz kids to help them develop computer programs of book titles by approaching two of the nation's largest book wholesalers, which were the two reasons they chose Washington State in the first place. In July 1995, the world renowned online book store known as *Amazon.com* was born. The brain behind the phenomenally-successful company was Jeff Bezos. Today *Amazon.com* sells about 57,000 books a day and serves over 13 million customers worldwide. The company is worth over $48billion, while the *Forbes* magazine listed the personal net worth of Bezos at $25.2billion.

In the UK, there was a 16- year old boy, who was fed up with formal education. He was dyslexic and frustrated by constant harassment from his colleagues. He knew college was not for him. When he dropped out of school, many of his classmates thought he was a loser and avoided his company. Although dyslexic in speech, his keen sense of awareness of his surrounding and the mood of his days were sharp. He decided to give expression to what he observed and saw. For a young boy growing up in the mid-60's, he observed that young boys and girls wanted freedom; they wanted to "do their thing unmolested." In America, it was the era of the hippies and the Gen Xers. In Europe especially England, it was called the "era of alternative culture." He sold an idea to a friend that a student magazine to create a platform for the then prevailing "alternative culture" would not be a bad business. They approached their parents and raised money for the publication aptly named *Student* magazine. They made $10,000 in advertisement revenue and sold 50,000 copies in their maiden edition. If you have read Mick Brown's *Richard Branson: the Authorized Biography,* it would be pretty clear how Sir Branson, the owner of the eminently successful *Virgin* Group estimated by the *Forbes* to be worth $4.6billion began his journey to billion dollar land.

In Nigeria, the story of the late Mr. Mobolaji Bank-Anthony was also inspiring. Born in Kinshasa in present-day Democratic Republic of Congo (formerly Zaire) to the famous Aleshinloye-Williams family of Lagos, young Mobolaji returned to Nigeria with his parents in the 1900's. After completing his secondary school education in 1923, he was employed by the defunct Postal and Telegraph Company (P & T Nigeria). As a postal worker, he discovered that as Nigeria moved toward political independence, there was one sector the government would spend heavily on: education. He contacted a foreign company that specialized in fountain pens and applied to become their local representative in Nigeria. Mr. Mobolaji Bank-Anthony was right in his prescient move, because he soon became the sole distributor of pen in Nigeria, especially in the western region during the free education program of the Action Group (AG) government of the defunct western Nigeria in the '50's to the '60's led by the late Mr. Obafemi Awolowo.

Finally, another Nigerian millionaire who knew how to read the mood of his day and cashed on it was the late Nigerian Ibo business man, Sir Louis Odumegwu- Ojukwu. He began by importing dried fish in large quantities, as early as the '30's and instead of selling them through middlemen and women, he preferred to cut them off and sell directly to consumers. While at his dried fish business, he heard many Ibo market women traders complained they would love to expand their trading activities beyond defunct eastern Nigeria and travel to other parts of Nigeria, especially commercial Lagos to trade, but had been hampered by reliable transportation. Louis Odumegwu-Ojukwu quickly went to England and began importing trucks, which Ibo market women later named; "mammy wagons"-referring to them-the market women passengers. The list is endless of astute business people, who were knowledgeable enough to see into the future and find out a need. Whether in New York during the Generation X or Washington State in the Internet Age, in England during the era of alternative culture or in Nigeria of the '50's when Mr. Bank-Anthony built his fountain pen business empire, or Odumegwu-Ojukwu's mammy wagon; three factors contributed to the business success of many of the world's millionaires and billionaires.

The first is the power of information. The person with the latest information is obviously above his or her peers. All religions of the world emphasize the power of information, which is termed knowledge. The Holy Bible exhorts every human being to seek for knowledge wherever one may find it. The Book of Hosea beautifully captures it when it said; "My people are destroyed from lack of knowledge" (Hosea 4:6). The man with the latest information in the community rules over others. Ditto the Holy Qur'an enjoins Moslems to search for knowledge. In the United States in the 19th century, thousands perished from the Anglo-American Civil War of 1812 unnecessarily, because information arrived late in the South that American and English forces had ceased hostilities and reached a ceasefire in the north. General Andrew Jackson, the commanding general of the US forces and his men were still fighting the English forces, while their counterparts in New York were celebrating, embracing and drinking. The telegraph message announcing cessation of hostilities was slow in reaching General Andrew Jackson in the south. No one had the latest information on the battlefields in the south and so the warring parties continued to kill themselves unnecessarily because of lack of latest news and information.

Many youngsters nowadays believe that the possessions of chains of university degrees will guarantee them success in life. On the contrary, experiences have shown from the lives of successful business people that knowledge triumphs education. Education is the world's formal way of giving information to young people through kindergarten to the tertiary level. Those who have passed through the same pedagogy referred to as teachers, lecturers, and professors come in at specific hours of the day and impact information to mentees or students, who are given pieces of paper known as diplomas, certificates and degrees at the conclusion of these monotonous exercises. But real education lies outside the four walls of these formal institutions. The ability to tap into such "undiscovered" information is what is known as knowledge. How you use education and knowledge to change your little corner of the world or the entire world is known as wisdom. The life of the richest man in the world for thirteen consecutive years, the co-founder of *Microsoft* Mr. Bill Gates whose story is a household one, epitomizes this ability to discover knowledge and mix it with education to produce wisdom. Of course, formal education is important, but any young person who thinks staying in college for four or eight years and earning a bachelor's, master's or doctorate will turn you into a billionaire must be joking. What formal education does is to open your eyes to information that will enable you unlock your potentials and tap into hitherto undiscovered terrain. Mr. Steven Spielberg, one of the most successful film producers in the world and Hollywood powerful man was rejected twice by the School of Theater, Film and Televisions at the University of Southern California. He moved on with life and succeeded in producing some of the highest money-grossing movies in human history and became a billionaire worth $3.2billion.

The second factor is the ability to spot a need. As Jeff Bezos told Ms. Winfrey on the *Oprah Winfrey Show* in November 1999; "I've always been a super nerd, but I'm really super-passionate about computers and how they can make life better." At 16, Branson couldn't speak eloquently, but he had the sense to create a need for his peers and those making fun of him that they needed a voice in *Student* magazine. Mr. Fountain Pen, which later became the name of Mobolaji Bank-Anthony, was not the only postal worker at the defunct Post & Telegraph (P&T)

in Marina Lagos, but was the only one who was clear-headed enough to see the future and quickly cashed in. And lastly, these millionaires and billionaires, born at different times, at different eras, and different circumstances displayed similar behavioral dispositions; they acted on their intuitions and gut feelings.

Bezos left a million dollar job behind in Wall Street, because he knew the sky was the limit, if he became his own boss. Branson contacted a friend and they borrowed money to start a successful magazine, which energized the adventurous young men to proceed to greater things. Mr. Mobolaji Bank-Anthony quit his P&T job and Sir Louis Odumegwu-Ojukwu trusted his gut feelings that "mammy wagon" would be a success. In other words, there was one word missing in the lives of these successful businessmen: procrastination.

No one knew whether 22-year old Aliko Dangote read the life history of any of these successful men, but as would be seen shortly, he followed their footsteps and because they succeeded, he too succeeded. He not only made it by following in the footsteps of the masters, but he put to use the native wisdom of his great-grandfather, Pa Alhassan Dantata, the Oracle of Bebeji-Kano. He combined it with the love of his grandfather, Mr. Sanusi Alhassan Dantata and mixed both with the business wizardry of his uncle, Mr. Usman Amaka Sanusi Dantata. In 25 years, he amassed a personal fortune of $16.1billion to become the richest black person in the world. In early 2012, Mr. Dangote's net worth was estimated at $11.2billion, yet he still retains the distinguished honor of being the richest black person on planet earth worth $16.1 billion today.

By the year 1978, Aliko Dangote had become accustomed to the inner workings of government in Nigeria. Even though he was 24 years old, he was learning rapidly as he watched his uncle's nattering style with politicians, military generals, and the wheeler-dealers in the nation's inner power circle. Young Aliko soon discovered that politics and business are closely related. In many parts of Africa and especially

Nigeria, there are certain values that politicians and business people hold very dear. Such values are; showing appreciation for services rendered; demonstrating loyalty to people in government, or what is often referred to as "support for constituted authorities," which Pa Alhassan Dantata, his maternal great grandfather, had passed on to the family. These are values that had been imbibed by his offspring and have become family tradition that Mr. Sanusi Dantata had in turn, passed on too to his children and scions. Aliko Dangote religiously holds unto these family and business values; "He (Dantata) is always a respecter of authority. He always advises us that: no matter what you do, you must always respect the authority of the day. Do not fight government. You must be an obedient person. And that's something I learnt and took seriously," Aliko reminiscences.

With that mindset very early in his formative years, all the military generals and political power-brokers that his uncles and other family associates had brought him in contact with saw three traits in young Aliko namely: humility, respect and appreciation. One of these powerful Nigerians whose activities were to have serious impact on the future of Aliko Mohammad Dangote and his fortunes in life is the military general, who administered Nigeria between February 13, 1976, and September 30, 1979: General Olusegun Obasanjo. The paths of General Olusegun Aremu Obasanjo and that of Aliko Dangote first crossed in the early 1970s, when General Obasanjo was the federal minister of transport during the military regime of General Yakubu Gowon. Obasanjo was 36 years old then and a brigadier, while young Aliko was working with his uncle, the late Usman Amaka Sanusi Dantata.

In 1975, following the military *coup d'état* that toppled General Yakubu Gowon, Brigadier-General Olusegun Obasanjo was one of the beneficiaries as the new military head of state, Gen Murtala Ramat Muhammad chose Obasanjo as his chief of staff supreme headquarters, which at that time was equivalent to the position of vice president. Again, the relationship between General Obasanjo and

Dangote became closer when General Olusegun Obasanjo became the head of state and commander-in chief of the armed forces of Nigeria on February 14, 1976, following the assassination of his military predecessor, General Murtala Ramat Muhammad in the abortive *coup d'état* of Friday February 13, 1976 spearheaded by the late Col. Sukar Bukar Dimka. Though a young man watching the nation's business climate, young Aliko didn't leave anyone in doubt he was in the Nigerian business world to make it, and make it big. But he would learn from the masters; display humility and respect to the big shots and pay his dues where and when expected of him. He would bid for government contracts just like other Nigerian business barons, but he set his mind on something more than contracting; manufacturing, which would not make him beholden to any regime, government or administration. Aliko wanted to be an avant-garde in local manufacturing where he can pride himself as the pioneer galvanizer of authentic indigenous manufacturing minus the hubris of course, thus he steered clear of getting a piece of the oil action, which is the springboard for the wealth of most Nigerian moneymen and women.

In 1979, the military administration of General Olusegun Obasanjo kept faith with the Nigerian people and successfully prosecuted the transition-to-civil rule program initiated by his immediate predecessor, late General Murtala Muhammad. General elections were conducted and all the tiers of government were occupied by elected civilians. At the federal level, Mr. Shehu Usman Aliyu Shagari, the presidential candidate of the defunct National Party of Nigeria (NPN) was pronounced the winner of the presidential election by the then federal electoral commission (FEDECO) headed by late Mr. Michael Ani. On October 1, 1979 at the Tafawa Balewa Square in central Lagos, Mr. Shehu Shagari was sworn in as the first executive president of Nigeria by late Justice Atanda Fatai-Williams, the then Chief Justice of Nigeria. Aliko was only 22 years old but his experience and business connections belied his age. He had developed sharp business instincts and keen sense of the power of political patronage as a businessman.

When you are born into a big family and come from rich pedigrees and move among big people, who have made it big and watch them do big things, it is very easy to dream big dreams, especially if you are smart, wise, and very quick on the uptake about your surroundings. From the time he was born and growing up in the largely rich Dantata family, it was part of the tradition passed unto the future generations that no Dantata must play politics. The Dantata family had an ugly experience with politics, which claimed the life of Pa Alhassan Dantata's second son, late Ahmadu Dantata who dabbled into politics. The ugly experience occurred in 1960, when Mr. Sanusi Dantata lost his younger brother, Ahmadu Dantata in 1960. According to family sources, Ahmadu Dantata lost his life as a result of the political turbulence that rocked the ancient city of Kano during the reign of Emir Abdullahi Sanusi of Kano between 1953 and 1963. As the story is told in the Dantata clan, those who engaged in local politics and succession battles to the throne when they are not princes often end up losing in the end. Following the death of his younger brother in 1960, who was also Aliko Dangote's uncle and the death of Aliko's own father, Mr. Mohammad Dangote in 1965 when Aliko was only 8 years old, Aliko Dangote made up his mind very early in life that he would never be a politician. Aliko's uncle and the elder son of his great- grandfather, Mr. Ahmadu Dantata was a member of the Kano Legislature in the NPC and was chairman of the discipline committee in 1950 in the NPC region government. He was also the treasurer of the Northern Amalgamated Merchants Union and member of the Kano NPC provincial executive. He was the first member of the second generation of the Dantatas to lose his life five years after the patriarch of the family, Pa Alhassan Dantata passed on in 1955.

Although Aliko knows the intersection between politics and business and the reality of the avoidance of both crafts, nevertheless, he would confine himself to business. A businessman, who would use his wealth to dictate the political direction of his environment; instead of playing the game of politics directly; he would stay in the background pulling the political strings. Later in life when he became the richest man in Nigeria, Aliko disclosed the reason he would be interested in the political future of Nigeria: he does not want "bad" politicians to control power and enact anti-investment policies that would make him poor. "I do not want Nigeria to be another Zimbabwe so I am concerned about the political direction of my country, because if bad and inexperienced politicians control power in Nigeria, my wealth may turn into poverty and I am not ready to become a poor man." Aliko's reference to Zimbabwe was the way and manner President Robert Mugabe expelled white farmers from the Southern African nation and how tragically they lost all their investments in that nation. Some of the white farmers were later relocated to Nigeria during the administration of Dr. Bukola Abubakar Saraki of Kwara State, central Nigeria, between 2003 and 2011, a move that was said to have been promoted by Aliko Dangote. The decision of Aliko Dangote not to participate in Nigerian politics directly was a family tradition and a personal one as a business man. That decision has paid off although Aliko is not politically agnostic, but has successfully avoided the gossamer slippery banana peel of combining both crafts in Africa.

The civilian administration of President Shehu Shagari in 1979 instituted an era of what became known as the importation of "essential commodities." The global state of Nigeria's foreign exchange earnings at the start of the civilian administration of Shagari was very impressive. Nigeria reaped bountifully from increases in the prices of crude oil, which raised the financial profile of Nigeria. Another era of "oil boom," which had occurred in the 1970's during the military regime of General Yakubu Gowon played out again toward the tail end of the 1970s and early 1980s. According to available statistics, the Nigerian nation earned between $20bn to $25billion between 1979 and 1983 from sales of crude oil when Mr. Shehu Shagari was in power. With Nigeria awash with petro-dollars, the administration began a regime of importation of items such as; milk, sugar, rice and other consumables. Like other Nigerian business men and women of the period, Aliko Dangote's company; Alco Company was among the companies involved in the importation of what the Nigerian media referred to as, "essential commodities."

The Shagari administration essentially opened the nation's borders to importation of all manners of goods. The nation's currency was strong, indeed stronger than the American dollars; the Nigerian Naira exchanged at 60 kobo to one American dollar. In its first year in office, the nation's import bill had climbed to N1.2billion, which was about $1.8 billion going by the exchange rate. Suddenly, Nigeria became the next point of destination for all manners of business people from all over the world. For those in commodities trading, the importation of baby food, frozen fish, rice, vegetable oil, flour, granulated sugar, aluminum sheets, batiks, tires and motor spare parts, which Aliko Dangote focused on were money-spinning deals. The decision of the Shagari Administration to keep faith with its election promises of constructing housing estates, which later became known as the Shagari housing estates, also created booming business for a cement importer like Aliko Dangote. In 1981, unable to handle most of its large cement demands for construction projects across the country, Aliko Dangote entered into a limited joint business venture with a friend and a Kano native; Mr. Dandawaki. Dandawaki Ventures and Aliko Dangote General Business Ventures temporarily began to take deliveries of imported goods at the Nigerian Ports of Lagos, Apapa to cater to the rising demands of their customers and numerous clients, mostly the Nigerian government and the various state governments.

The apogee of the Shagari Administration business bonanza was when the administration announced it was committed to developing the nation's inchoative new federal capital city of Abuja. Conceived by the Murtala Muhammad military regime in 1975 as the future capital city of Nigeria, Abuja was chosen by the Akinola Aguda commission as Nigeria's new seat of federal government, against the backdrop of the ballooning population of Lagos. The movement of the seat of the federal government of Nigeria from Lagos to Abuja was expected to be in phases and estimated between 15 and 20 years depending on the nation's financial state. President Shehu Shagari thought otherwise, and within two years of military disengagement from governance, the civilian government began to award mouth-watering contracts for the development of Abuja. The first two ministers of the federal capital territory, Messrs. John Kadiya and Iron Dan Musa were saddled with the tasks of commencing new constructions at the nation's future administrative and political city. Aliko Dangote, like other Nigerian business men and women of the era was part of the drive to develop the nation's future federal capital city.

Other socio-economic and industrial transformation efforts of the Shagari Administration were the establishment of steel rolling mills, river basin development authorities and several construction projects that smart Nigerian business men and women benefitted from as part of the nation's rapid economic drive. Like the *Festac* jamboree five years earlier, the politicians turned the development of Abuja into another national bazaar. Every politician, especially of the ruling National Party of Nigeria (NPN), became emergency building contractors overnight. There were mouth-watering construction contracts awarded to boyfriends, girlfriends, concubines, hangers-on, delcredere jobbers and all manners of shady characters in the construction of Abuja. Many of the contractors collected mobilization fees-which was 10 percent of the actual amount of building contracts- and simply disappeared with the money. Nigeria was on corruption steroid, or what Mr. Ray Ekpu, a Nigerian journalist described as "the era of Sodom and Gomorrah in Nigeria," in his column in the defunct *National Concord* newspapers. But the bonanza did not last. Four years after the Nigerian military dis-engaged from governance, they were back again in power. Before the military struck and removed the venal politicians from power, the Shagari Administration attempted to rein in the excesses of the politicians and the large scale public waste through another regime called, "austerity measures," but the economic mismanagement had run deep. The national slide had to be arrested and perceptive Nigerian political analysts knew the days of the Shagari Administration were numbered. The political and economic situations in the country were further exacerbated by the election rigging that brought President Shehu Shagari back to power for his second term in office on October 1, 1983.

On December 31, 1983, the Nigerian military staged a *coup d'état* and removed the "the lootocrats" to borrow the word of Mr. Chinweizu, a popular Nigerian kibitzer, which ended the nation's second attempt at representative government. A new military head of state took over the reins of governance. General Muhammadu Buhari, the new military strongman decided to put a stop to the wholesale importation of all kinds of goods and essential commodities that the displaced Shehu Shagari administration had instituted for four years. Essentially, the new helmsman was saying that the national party and lootocracy were effectively over. Some of the politicians were herded into detention facilities across Nigeria. A new regime of economic belt-tightening was put in place. The Buhari military regime put a halt to the maddening construction works going on in Abuja, the federal capital territory, Nigeria's future administrative and political capital. Like other business men and women in the country, there were no doubts that Aliko Dangote and his circle of friends were not happy with the new economic policies, but like the patriot he is, he understood the mood of the nation. General Buhari through his minister of finance, Mr. Onaolapo Soleye, an economics professor at the nation's premier university; the University of

Ibadan and his counterpart in the ministry of trade, Mr. Mahmud Tukur decided to implement trade by barter economic policies which did not go down well with a majority of Nigeria's business class.

The politics of import licensing was also very contentious as many companies that had been issued import licenses prior to the coming of the Buhari military regime had their licenses revoked. Many other economic policies such as; the restriction of foreign exchange and currencies , aggressive export promotion drive and import restriction policies affected the conduct of domestic and international businesses. Although the exchange rate of the Nigerian currency, the Naira, firmed up impressively against other world currencies such, as the American dollar which exchanged for $1.00 to Nigeria's ₦00.75 Kobo and the British Pounds which exchanged £1Pound to Nigeria's ₦1, yet it was a headache for many business people to exchange the nation's currency at these official rates. The nation's apex bank, the Central Bank of Nigeria was saddled with the responsibility of granting approval to business men and women that wanted to purchase foreign currencies to conduct international businesses, but the guidelines were too stringent. The policy was afflicted by the usual Nigerian traditions of cronyism and influence peddling. The CBN demanded for all manners of papers and conditions that would frustrate even the most persevered and resilient Nigerian businessman or woman. Many desperate Nigerian business men and women, who needed foreign currencies for urgent transactions, had to resort to "illegal" foreign exchange and underground channels, which could be dangerous and punishable under a draconian decree promulgated by the regime.

Even among some of the multi-national corporations operating in the country, there were complaints about the economic policies of the regime, which they described as harsh and stifling for legitimate business transactions, especially among the manufacturing ones and those with

subsidiaries in Nigeria. For example, one of the policies of
the military regime was a directive to foreign subsidiaries
that henceforth, they must use alternative raw materials
sourced locally to manufacture their products. From
nationalism and patriotism perspectives, the directive was in
order. However, the regime did not give enough time for the
foreign corporations to source for such alternative local raw
materials. This requires long years of research to accomplish.
Many of the chief executives of such affected companies
which relied on their factories at their head offices in their
home countries tried to persuade the regime to relax the
directive, but were rebuffed. The affected corporations
threatened to close their manufacturing plants as a result of
the directive and pulled out of Nigeria. Meanwhile, other
events were taking place at this period, which pushed the
nation on the edge. By the middle of 1985, the political class
in Nigeria had liaised with their business counterparts to
effect a change in the political direction of Nigeria under the
Muhammadu Buhari regime. Like the savvy businessman he
is, Aliko Dangote didn't find it difficult to change his business
methods during the Buhari-Idiagbon military regime as the
military dictatorship later became known, as the two top
shots of the dictatorship; General Muhammadu Buhari and
Major-General Tunde Idiagbon, the head of state and chief of
staff supreme headquarters, respectively were said to have
epitomized the iron-fisted regime. It was during this period
that Dangote General Textiles Products Enterprises was
born. It specialized in exporting local products such as;
calico, cashew nuts, gun Arabic, cotton, ginnery and textile
products. The total annual worth of the company later rose
to $15million by 1989. It was a great credit to Aliko's fertile
business mind of the ability to shift with the economic
policies of successive Nigerian governments.

Mr. Dangote's shift to manufacturing occurred during
a visit to Brazil in the late '80s. He was surprised that the
Latin America nation was able to sustain home-grown needs,
in spite of the crushing weight of its foreign debts estimated
at $111billion-the largest debt of any nation in the world-

in 1986. Aliko observed that, even as the economy of Brazil was hemorrhaging under the crushing weight of her ballooning foreign debts in the '80s, the manufacturing sector was active and buoyant. He visited a manufacturing chain called *Arisco Produtos Alimenticios SA* located in the Arisco region of Brazil. *Arisco* at that time could be regarded as the *Wal-Mart* of Brazil. *Arisco* manufactured canned and household goods, grew foods, and groceries, and concentrated on the three essential human needs of food, clothing and shelter, ranging from salad dressings, tomato products, canned soups, mayonnaise, seasonings, ketchups, noodles, to deserts, bouillons and many more. Today, the Brazilian food chain has been acquired by Unilever Best Foods Holding Corporation. The visit to *Arisco* in Brazil was an eye-opener to Mr. Dangote. He reasoned that if *Arisco Produtos Alimenticios SA* could do it in South America, he too could jump start local manufacturing in Nigeria and Africa. He returned to Nigeria and began to re-position his companies to what he called "backward integration toward manufacturing instead of importation." With dauntless persistence against overwhelming odds in a nation awash with petrodollars and government imports virtually everything, Dangote began to adjust to local manufacturing, instead of importation.

On Friday/Saturday August 27, 1985, the military regime of General Muhammadu Buhari was toppled by his chief of army staff, General Ibrahim Badamasi Babangida. The new Babangida military regime decided to liberalize the nation's economic policies encapsulated in its structural adjustment program (SAP). The policy was crafted by two former World Bank executives appointed by the new regime: Dr. Kalu Idika Kalu, who was finance secretary and Dr. Chu S.P Okongwu, the secretary of national planning. The SAP, which some economic analysts said was instigated by the World Bank and the International Monetary Fund (IMF) came with mixed-blessings. To Keynesian laissez fair economists, the government should have minimal participation in running businesses, because experience has shown that such government-owned, and government-run public institutions are usually badly run and often mismanaged. In Nigeria, many of such government-owned and government-run public institutions such as; electricity, telecommunications, water, transportation, airways etc. fall short of good and efficient performances. In most cases, they have become conduits for waste, avenues for defrauding government and draining tax-payers. When such public corporations are privatized and sold to private corporations, they are run efficiently. They also provide reliable, efficient and stable services to the people. In addition, competition among corporations for service supply ensures higher productivity, efficiency and robust economy. This type of economic system is what obtains in the United States, Japan, South Korea, India, Malaysia and other advanced capitalist states and liberalized economies of the world.

On the other side of the spectrum is the alternative ideological paradigm, known as the welfare or socialist / communist economic viewpoint. The latter argues that privatization, or the act of selling public-owned companies to private business men and women is tantamount to selling-off the commonwealth to money bags whose sole aim is profit-making. In addition, this school of thought insists that there are some essential services that should not be privatized, because of the harmful impact on the poor, who will not be able to afford the costs of such services when controlled by private individuals. In Nigeria, one of the foremost advocates of the latter economic policy view point and ideological school was the London-trained economic professor, the late Mr. Samuel Adepoju Aluko. He had in his column many other left-leaning Nigerian academics such as; Edwin Madunagu, Eskor Toyo, Akin Oyebode, late Bala Usman, Alhaji Balarabe Musa, late Comrade Ola Oni, Dipo Fashina, late Bade Onimode, Ayodele Awojobi etc.

By the time the Babangida regime rolled out the four ingredients of SAP namely: import restriction and substitution; export promotion; trade liberalization and realistic value of the nation's currency, the Naira; Aliko

Dangote, and few other Nigerian business men and women, that had the prescient inkling that the economic future of Nigeria largely depends on private enterprise took the gauntlet and began aggressive manufacturing drive. In a nutshell, Babangida's SAP became the engine that ushered Nigeria into the road to a private-driven economy, where only those products that are so crucial to the survival of Nigeria would be allowed into the country under an import restriction policy regime. Since people like Dangote and other business men and women largely involved in commodity trading were already in that field, rolling out aggressive export promotion drive was necessary. The establishment of the Nigerian Export Promotion Council (NEPC) was a logical corollary of this policy. By trade liberalization, the military regime relaxed the economic space, which broadened economic participation, especially in the banking and finance sectors, and other vital areas of the nation's economy. The proponents of Babangidanomics, in their wisdom believed that unnecessary restrictions and bureaucratic bottlenecks would stifle private initiatives and harm the nation's economic future. Consequently, the obnoxious and draconian policy of criminalizing possession of foreign currencies was abrogated. The economic space was open for currency trading in licensed *bureau de change* outlets and in merchant banks. Lastly, the Babangida regime announced that the nation's official exchange rate of the Nigerian Naira to the US Dollars and other foreign currencies were artificial considering the nation's domestic manufacturing base. Consequently, the only way to truly determine the realistic value of the nation's currency; the Nigerian Naira, was to allow it to "float" with its counterparts, rather than through arbitrary military ukase. By the '90's, Aliko Dangote and other smart Nigerian men and women got the message going around the world that the zeitgeist now were two words: *glasnost* and *perestroika*.

In 1989, Aliko Dangote was on economic sprint. He floated Dangote Textile Products and had his eyes on giving the Nigerian textile mills a run for their money. In 1992, the seed that he planted at Kankara Ginnery Plant was waiting for harvest, which was to sweep the nation's government-owned epileptic textile industry. In 1990, he floated the Liberty Merchant Bank with an imposing edifice in Victoria Island, Lagos. He put his younger brother, Belo Dangote at the helm. A year later, with a paid-up share capital of ₦ 30million (about $25million) the bank made an after-tax profit of ₦18million ($15million). That was the beginning of how 38-year old Aliko Mohammad Dangote began the journey to dominate and rule the Nigerian economy. Next, he set his eyes on cocoa, cashew, calico, palm oil, sugar, salt, vegetable oil and cement. He brought another brother, Sani Dangote on the board of the Dangote business train. By the ignominious end of the Babangida military regime in summer 1993, Dangote was on a roll. He had his business hands in all the cookie jars of the Nigerian economy: transportation, commodity trading, banking, finance, textile, fishing, haulage, real estate, aluminum business, farming, cement, auto business just name it. But even at this time, Aliko Dangote was just warming up, but makes no mistake about it, the Aliko Mohammed Dangote business train was warming up to depart from the station and corner Nigeria's domestic market.

Mr. Babangida abdicated governance in controversial circumstances aftermath of the controversial annulment of the June 12, 1993 presidential election won by the late Mr. Moshood Abiola. The debilitating national crises led to yet another *coup d'etat* by the chief of staff, late Sani Abacha, who erased all the democratic structures put in place by erstwhile military dictator, Babangida and Abacha returned Nigeria to a full-blown military autocracy.

The 5-year dictatorship of General Sani Abacha began in 1993 following the annulment of the June 12, 1993 presidential election considered one of the freest and fairest presidential elections in Nigerian history. Unknown to many Nigerians, the late Mr. Moshood Abiola met with Aliko Dangote to solicit for his support before the June 12, 1993 presidential election. Aliko Dangote, a humble and unassuming businessman hardly mentions it. As a rich business man, he is passionately interested in ensuring that good men and women, who have liberal economic policies, occupy political offices in Nigeria. His town man, Mr. Othman Tofa, the presidential candidate of the defunct National Republican Convention (NRC) and Moshood Abiola's opponent in the 1993 election also solicited Aliko's political support. At the end of the day when the election was annulled and the political crises began, Dangote was among those powerful and influential Nigerian elites operating in the background to resolve the debilitating crises. Again, unknown to many Nigerians, he surreptitiously funneled money through third party to some pro-democracy organizations during, unarguably one of the most critical periods in Nigerian political history.

CHAPTER 7
ALIKO THE YOUNG BUSINESSMAN

THE DICTATORSHIP of General Sani Abacha came to a tragic end in summer 1998, when the general died and Nigerian stake-holders met to chart a new way forward for Africa's most populous nation. For the larger part of Sani Abacha's 5-year iron-fisted regime, Nigeria was practically on the edge and everyone was apprehensive, including the international community about the future of Nigeria. The deaths of Abacha and his chief political rival, Mr. Moshood Abiola a month later cleared the political fog that had enveloped the country. The chief of defense staff, General Abdusalam Abubakar became the new head of state following the deaths of both Abacha and Abiola. The new military strongman immediately set up a transition to civil rule, which terminated in May 1999. General Abubakar governed Nigeria for 10 months (July 1998-May 1999), and successfully handed over to a democratically- elected administration.

Immediately Mr. Olusegun Obasanjo was sworn in on May 29, 1999 as an elected president, Dangote knew the likely economic policies of the new administration. Aliko was among the rich men and women in Nigeria that contributed heavily to fund the political campaign of the retired general during the 1999 presidential elections when the retired military general was chosen as the presidential flag bearer of the People's Democratic Party (PDP). Mr. Obasanjo has had an enviable military career in the Nigerian

Army and successfully handed over the reins of governance to a democratically-elected government in 1979-a rare feat in Africa in the '70s-thus his public profile and international reputation remained unblemished. The paths of Messrs. Obasanjo and Dangote had crossed as far back as the early 1970s; consequently the second coming of the retired military general to power was advantageous to Aliko Dangote. Similarly, the vice-president, Mr. Atiku Abubakar was also a close chum of Aliko Dangote. The paths of Atiku and Aliko had also crossed as early as the '70s when Mr. Abubakar was at the head of the Nigerian Customs. As one of the nation's largest importers of commodities and goods, Mr. Dangote had several encounters with the retired customs boss.

In 1999 when he became Nigeria's second executive president, Mr. Obasanjo did not hide his aversion toward government waste as it has been the usual practice in Nigeria. The retired general now-turned elected president committed his administration to aggressive privatization policy with a view to either resuscitating the comatose government-owned corporations with good management team, or out rightly sell off those that could not be revived. In the wisdom of top administration officials, government-owned companies were a drain on tax-payers; because of the slip-shod manner most of them were being managed. The Nigerian media characterized these badly-run public corporations as "drain pipes "on the Nigerian economy. Consequently, the Obasanjo administration established the Bureau of Pubic Enterprise (BPE) to oversee the sale of such non-performing public enterprises. It was through this open bidding for non-performing government-owned companies that Mr. Dangote put his power of negotiations to work. From textile, agro-allied, cement, sugar to other areas of the economy, the Dangote Group systematically acquired these moribund businesses and turned them around.

Aliko Dangote, as the one of the chief supporters of government of the day also played a prominent role in ensuring the election victory of the late President Umaru

Musa Yar'Adua in 2007 after term limits forced President Obasanjo to step down. The patriotic role of Aliko Dangote continued in the installation of Mr. Goodluck Jonathan as acting president in 2010 and later as elected president. In 2011, there was no doubt that the richest person in Nigeria would continue to play a significant role in the administration of the fourth executive president of Nigeria. While Mr. Jonathan was the vice-president under the deceased President Umaru Musa Yar'Adua, there was a close rapport between the twain. During the crisis ignited by the way and manner the illness of President Yar'Adua was handled by administration officials, Aliko Dangote and other rich Nigerians were involved in dousing the attendant tension and anxiety in the Nigerian polity, at least behind the scenes. As events later played out, Vice-President Jonathan was made acting president by the National Assembly and later confirmed as President of the Federal Republic of Nigeria. Today, Aliko Dangote is one of the pillars behind the Jonathan Administration.

ALIKO IN THE BOARDROOM

IN NIGERIA'S tough and tumble world of boardroom politics, how does one edge out rivalries and etch out? How does a businessman or woman build household brands from scratch to household name in a consumer nation? How does an indigenous entrepreneur compete with multi-national corporations for share of the Nigerian market-unarguably the largest market in black Africa? This is where Aliko shines most.

Aliko is a shrewd businessman. He is a calculating investor. His mantra is that, avoidable risk is not a recipe for success in business and in life. Fact is; Dangote is a risk - taker any time, any day. When he relies on his gut feelings in most cases, he threads where many Nigerian entrepreneurs dread. Mr. Akin Osuntokun was a public relations adviser to the *Dangote* Group few years ago. He described the Dangote exceptionalism in Nigerian business ambience this way; "The crucial difference between Aliko and other Nigerian entrepreneurs is his bold and courageous faith in the Nigerian economy. Risk, of course, is Aliko's second name and his third name is who dares wins. Out of the comfort zone of commodity trading he diversified full time and full throttle into the cruel vagaries of industrialisation in what essentially was a casino economy." Osuntokun, who later became an administration insider during President Obasanjo Years (1999-2007) and later managing director of News Agency of Nigeria (NAN), further explained that, the culture of stashing illicit money abroad by Nigerian pilferers in public office did not deter a man like Dangote to re-invest in the Nigerian economy. By taking such gut-risky moves, Mr. Dangote has succeeded in building household brands to leapfrog the Nigerian economy from primitive accumulation of capital to manufacturing.

OLUSEGUN OBASANJO, THE MIITARY GENERAL (1975-1979), OLUSEGUN OBASANJO, THE PRESIDENT (1999-2007) AND THE UNTOLD UNDERCURRENTS OF PRIVATIZATION AND ALIKO MOHAMMAD DANGOTE'S WEALTH

The year 1975 was indeed a turning point in the history of Nigeria's economic growth and the building of primitive accumulation of indigenous capital. Young Aliko was just 20 years old in a population of 80 million Nigerians, but he was keenly aware of economic and investment opportunities in his native country. The Gowon military regime began the implementation of its Second National Development Plan in 1970 and 1975. By 1975, Nigeria was awash with petrol-dollars, which Gowon capitalized upon and increased the salaries of all Nigerian workers by 100 percent under what was known as Udoji Salary Award chaired by Mr. Jerome Udoji. In 1975, the Nigerian military awarded contracts for the importation of 30 million tons of cement, while the Nigerian ministry of defense alone placed orders for 20 million tons of cement. With 105 ships berthing at the Nigerian Ports full of cement, the cement armada went crazy with 45 ships a day of which 300 ships alone were full of cement vessels. The Nigerian government was paying $4,100 daily on demurrage for each cement vessel after the grace period of 10 days. In 1975 alone, 3,500 thousand metric tons of cement were imported, with Lagos, Ibadan and Umuahia topping the list with 682.9, 470.1 and 259.2 thousand metric tons of cement respectively. Other cities and towns where various construction works were going on and needed cement badly were: Enugu: 233.2 thousand metric tons; Kano: 194 thousand; Akure: 189.5 thousand; Port Harcourt: 185.2 thousand, Calabar: 176.5 thousand; Sokoto: 145.3 thousand; Ogoja: 127.1 thousand, and Maiduguri: 106.8 thousand tons of cement. Besides Akure and Ogoja, constructions of new federal universities were taking place in the rest cities and towns, while all the cities and towns, except Ogoja became administrative capitals of the newly-created states the following year.

Lt. Col Shehu Musa Yar'Adua, the federal commissioner for transport was a Hausa-Fulani man like Mr. Usman Amaka Dantata in 1975 shortly after the *coup d'état* that removed General Yakubu Gowon, and at the federal ministry of transport, Usman Dantata was very close to Mr. Yusuf Gobir who was the powerful permanent secretary. There were other important players that were instrumental in advancing the business interests of Dangote's uncle in 1975, which opened great opportunities for Mr. Dangote himself. Many years later; roughly two years later in the short run and twenty-four years later, some of these military officers were later to return to power after eventful military careers, this time as politicians. The friendships forged almost quarter century earlier came in handy for a smart business man like Aliko Dangote. The young 38-year old military head of state, Lt-Gen Olusegun Obasanjo in 1975 later became an elected civilian president in 1999. He brought his federal commissioner of education, Col Ahmadu Ali back as the chairman of the ruling People's Democratic Party (PDP). The chief of army staff then, Lt-Gen Theophilus Danjuma was brought back as defense minister. Major-General Abdulahi Mohammad, now retired, who was the head of the Directorate of Military Intelligence in 1975 in Lagos, and a close friend of the late Gen Shehu Musa Yar'Adua, and one of the master minds of the *coup d'état* that overthrew Genera Yakubu Gowon in 1975 became Mr. Obasanjo's new chief of staff between ,1999 and 2007. General Yar'Adua, the planner of the 1975 *coup d'état* was Mr. Obasanjo's chief of staff in 1976. The late Yar'Adua himself had been Obasanjo's *defacto* vice-president in 1976, and his brother, the late Mr. Umaru Musa Yar'Adua was later anointed as Mr. Obasanjo's successor in 2007. President Umaru Musa Yar'Adua died in 2010 but the 24-year military-civilian complex worked to the advancement of Nigeria's capitalism of which Aliko Dangote was and still is a magus. Dangote revealed this as much when he disclosed that his maternal and paternal families had been dealing with successive Nigerian governments since 1960 when Nigerian attained political independence from Britain.

"I don't like to boast, but let me tell you something. I was born into money. Both my fathers—from my mother's side and also from my father's side—they have always had money. So, it's not that I just came and picked up something from this thing. But it does not mean also in the family that everybody would be rich. I don't know any of my family members—both from my mother's side and my father's side—that has ever had a deal with anybody in the government." Mr. Dangote may not be saying the truth on the latter assertion. The Dantata family members have been in and out of government, especially in his home state of Kano during both military and civilian administrations in Nigeria. Mr. Aminu Dantata, Aliko Dangote's maternal uncle was once a treasury secretary in his home state of Kano. Aliko's late father was a politician. Of recent, his niece, Dr. Fatima Dantata was education secretary in the civilian administration of Mr. Ibrahim Shekarau and eventually became the fourth wife of the governor. Again, Mr. Dangote's cousin, Tajudeen Dantata was one-time in charge of department of housing and urban development in Kano state. Another cousin currently heads the state's department of tourism. But family connections, political patronage and government-assisted programs alone are not enough to make a business entrepreneur amass $16.1billion dollars. Aliko shrugs off any insinuation of exploiting family connections to make wealth.

According to Mr. Dangote, "My story is the story of a man and a brand Nigerians have come to know, to love and to accept. Nigerians are investing in us because they believe in us, they believe in the name Dangote. Apart from believing in us, we have a track record which we have actually shown. If you look at all our factories, they have grown steady and gradually to where we are today. In all modesty, we can say we have done very well. There is no business that we are in and we are not No.1. The worse one that we have, maybe we have a second position. That in itself is our business strategy. We aim to dominate our market, to lead in every market segment. They have all been run efficiently and professionally by people who really know the business very well. We have a very good brand name, and that is part of what many people are actually investing in. They are not really investing in Aliko Dangote only. They are investing in the Dangote brand. They believe in my own business acumen, but it is not the only thing that people are investing in. They are investing in the Dangote brand. Right from the beginning of our business, we have always been very conscious about what we give to the consumers. Because once you start on a wrong footing, that's it. You've missed it. It's almost impossible to go back and convince (the) people."

The history of the privatization of public-owned companies and the wealth of Aliko Dangote continues to generate controversies and hear-says in Nigeria. The questions are; did the Obasanjo administration favor Dangote in the sales of government-owned companies in the administration's privatization exercise between 1999 and 2007? Were the sales and transactions clean and transparent? Were officials of the Bureau of Public Enterprise (BPE), which oversaw the privatization exercise compromised by bidders and buyers of who, Mr. Aliko Dangote was a major beneficiary?

From 1960 to 1999, successive Nigerian administrations, both military and civilian, reportedly expended about ₦ 800 billion (about $6billion) of tax payers and oil money on the provision of subsidized services to Nigerian citizens. These services range from rail, water, electricity, bridges, postal, oil, insurance, banking to education, printing, housing, to name just a few of such government-owned but publicly-subsidized services under the sun. The military administration of General Ibrahim Babangida decided to take government out of these services in 1988 through privatization and appointed late Mr. Hamzar Zayyad as head of the privatization exercise in 1988. Mr. Zayyad and his committee identified one hundred and eleven companies and corporations that should be sold to private entrepreneurs. By 1993, eighty-eight of these corporations had been sold. In 1999, Mr. Olusegun Obasanjo became a civilian president and decided to sell off the remaining public companies to private entrepreneurs. The list of such corporations is long, but they included the following; Nigerian Telecommunication, Nigerian Electric Power Authority, Ajaokuta Steel Complex, Nigerian Fertilizer Company, Aluminum Smelter Company of Nigeria, Federal Savings Bank, Afri-Bank, Federal Mortgage Bank of Nigeria, Nigerian Sugar Company at Bacita, Nigerian Machine Tools, Oshogbo, Nigerian Paper Mills at Jebba, Iwopin and Oku-Iboku, Ashaka Cement, Sunti Sugar Company, Nigerian Insurance Company, Nigerian Re-Insurance, Benue Cement Company, Assurance Bank, Steel Rolling Mills at Oshogbo, Calabar Cement, Leyland Company, Peugeot Automobile of Nigeria, Volkswagen of Nigeria, Jos Steel Rolling Mill, Katsina Steel Rolling Mill, National Iron Ore and Mining at Itakpe, Nigerian Uranium Company, Nigerian Television

Authority, News Agency of Nigeria, Nigerian Port Authority, New Nigerian Newspapers, Daily Times of Nigeria, Nigerian National Petroleum Company, Eleme Petrochemicals, Kaduna, Warri and Port Harcourt Refineries, Nigerian Gas Company, Petroleum and Pipelines Manufacturing Company, African Petroleum, Unipetrol, National Oil, Dresser Nigeria Limited, Baker Nigeria, Federal Housing Authority, and Nigeria's twelve water basin authorities.

Other public corporations which the Nigerian government fully or jointly-owned, and similarly slated for either full privatization or commercialization included: Ore oil palm, National park board, Nigerian postal company, Nigerian airways, Festac '77 hotel, Nigerian Industrial Development Bank Limited, Nigerian Bank for Commerce and Industry Limited, Federal Super Phosphate Fertilizer Company Limited; United Bank of Nigeria, and many more. At the end of the privatization exercise, substantial numbers of these corporations were sold to both local and foreign investors in Nigeria. Mr. Richard Branson of *Virgin* Group for instance, bought Nigerian Airways which he later re-sold to Mr. Jimoh Ibrahim, another Nigerian rich man who renamed it *Air Nigeria.* Ajaokuta Steel Complex, valued at $1.5 billion was sold to an Indian businessman for $300 million. Aladja Steel Complex at Warri in eastern Nigeria was sold for 20 percent less than its actual price. A Russian company bought Nigeria's aluminum smelter company at Ikot-Abasi in eastern Nigeria for a song; ₦5.5 billion (about $35millin) compared with its actual price of ₦ 480billion) (about $3billlion). The sales of the Nigerian steel rolling mills in Oshogbo, Jos and Katsina were also mired in controversy between the Ispat families of India: Messrs. Pramod K. Mittal and Lakshmi Nivas Mittal of India, who were slugging it out with the Nigerian government over who legally owned the Ispat family-owned business in India among the warring family members.

According to Mr. Sanusi Mohammad, the secretary-general of African Iron and Steel Association, the whole privatization exercise in Nigeria was not transparent. He told investors and business leaders in Doha, Qatar at a conference that privatization started and ended with slogans in Nigeria. "There are three public steel rolling mills at Jos, Oshogbo and Katsina which have been liquidated some three years ago. The companies were subsequently sold to private entrepreneurs at ridiculous prices. The Katsina Steel Rolling mill is the only one that has been producing epileptically, and has never exceeded 10% of capacity utilization following the privatization exercise. Oshogbo and Jos have not commercially produced 1 kg of rolled products till date," he informed the business executives gathered at the conference.

A sordid account of the privatization exercise saw an Indian company running away with $17 million out of $200million they raised from Nigerian banks to bid for and win a steel rolling mill in the country forcing the Nigerian government to set up an inquiry in 2008. Mr. Isola Sarafadeen, Nigeria's minister of mines and steel subsequently set up a panel under the chairmanship of Mr. Magaji Inua but the findings of the panel, which indicted the Indian investors, are yet to be implemented almost half-a-decade after the scandal. According to Mohammad; "The privatization exercise in Nigeria has been so full of lack of transparency and beclouded in corrupt practices that the post- 2007 government is now re-nationalizing some of the enterprises including the Nigerian National Petroleum Company's Kaduna refinery and Port Harcourt refinery, the Nigerian Telecommunications (NITEL), and Nigerian Insurance Company (NICON)."

The same heated arguments and controversies trailed the privatization of the Daily Times Newspapers of Nigeria, the oldest and largest newspaper company in black Africa founded by a group of Nigerian-British consortium in 1925. The military administration of Gen Murtala Muhammad forcefully acquired the media company in 1975 and destroyed the largest media company in Africa. The same could also be said about cement production in Nigeria.

Nigeria had nine functioning cement companies in 1978 before Mr. Dangote emerged as the cement king of Africa. These were; Nkalagu cement at Anambra state in eastern Nigeria established in 1954 by Mr. Smidth, a Danish national; Ewekoro in Ogun State managed by the West African Cement Company founded in 1959 by Mr. Wickers-Armstrong a Briton in conjunction with the Action Group government of the late Obafemi Awolowo in the defunct western region of Nigeria. In 1962, a German national, Mr. Ferrostahl went to Sokoto and establish the Sokoto Cement Company, which he ran with the Northern People's Congress administration of the late Mr. Ahmadu Bello. The Okpella Cement Company in the defunct Bendel State now Edo state was established by an Austrian, Mr. Caro Continho in 1965, while another German national; Mr. Polysius went to Calabar in 1964 and partnered with the eastern regional government of Mr. Michael Okpara to establish the Calabar Cement Company. The West African Portland Cement Company opened another factory in Sagamu in 1975 while a Swiss national, Mr. Cementina went to Gboko in central Nigeria the same year to establish what today is known as Benue Cement Corporation. In 1978 as the Olusegun Obasanjo military regime was putting finishing touches to disengage and return power to elected civilian government, Mr. Smidth went to Onigbolo in Benin Republic and opened another cement factory following WAPCO's move three years earlier to open a branch of its cement company in Ashaka in Benue state. The Onigbolo Benin cement factory was a consortium between Nigeria and its western neighbor, the Beninese government.

All the cement companies were operating at full capacity before their full privatization. Most of them have been sold to Mr. Dangote under the privatization program of Mr. Obasanjo when he came back to power in 1999 as an elected civilian president. Were these mere coincidences that Mr. Dangote had his first break as a cement importer in 1977, when Mr. Obasanjo was a military head of state and again, in 1999 when Mr. Obasanjo returned as an elected president and then Mr. Dangote became a billionaire?

Many political analysts in Nigeria said Mr. Dangote was indeed fairly favored by the post-military civilian administrations in Nigeria during the nation's privatization exercise and that has accounted for the quantum leap in Mr. Dangote's personal wealth between 1999 and to date.

Several diplomatic correspondence from the United States Embassy in Nigeria to the State Department in Washington, DC have revealed backhand deals in the privatization exercise carried out by the Obasanjo Administration between 1999 and 2007. According to one of the diplomatic correspondence, "The Bureau of Private Enterprises oversaw the privatization of many government-owned businesses, including sugar, steel, rice and other sectors. It is widely believed that the privatization exercise benefited both the President, through Aliko Dangote, and the Vice President, (Mr. Abubakar Atiku) through various agents." Many Nigerian analysts are betting that the relationship between Messrs. Olusegun Obasanjo and Aliko Dangote run deeper than just mere coincidences in 1978 and 1999. Could Mr. Dangote be fronting for former President Olusegun Obasanjo of Nigeria?

Mr. Ochereome Nnanna of Nigeria's *Vanguard* newspapers scolded Mr. Dangote for his sharp business practices, "Dangote is seen as a government-made billionaire," he wrote. "More than any other Nigerian entrepreneur, his (Dangote) group is reputed as having enjoyed generous Federal Government freebies, such as waivers and uncommonly favorable terms that drove co-competitors out of the market. The controlling power Dangote wields over cement, sugar and flour puts Nigerians at the mercy of its pricing mechanism. It required a presidential ultimatum for Dangote to crash the prices of its cement products from ₦2, 500 to ₦1, 500 in May this year, (2011) only for the product to skyrocket again to ₦2, 800 in August in parts of the Lagos metropolis."

In 2011, the United States Embassy in Abuja, Nigeria

sent another cable message to the State Department in Washington DC about Mr. Aliko Dangote. "Alhaji Aliko Dangote (Dangote) is founder, president and CEO of Nigeria's largest national company, Dangote Group of Companies (the Group). Dangote's wealth and prestige are based on his family connections and political friendships yet he is esteemed by many Nigerians for his business acumen. He has led the Dangote Group of Companies to unprecedented success in Nigeria, starting the company as a trading entity in 1977, and growing it to an estimated $700 million manufacturing or semi-manufacturing behemoth that it is today." The cable continued: "The Group is a household name in Nigeria and comes closer than any Nigerian company to market domination in many sectors. The Group employs roughly 10,000 Nigerians and turns over a profit estimated at $1.3 billion. It runs 15 manufacturing, and bagging facilities nationwide, and has operations in industries as wide ranging as cement, sugar, wheat, textiles, polypropylene sacks, and property leasing. Part of the Dangote business strategy is to focus on provision of basic human needs: food, shelter, and clothing."

The confidential cable message from the United States Embassy in Nigeria continued; "In part, because of this shared dream, the (Nigerian) Government has been very supportive of Dangote. We know the company at one time or another held exclusive import rights in sugar, cement, and rice using such advantages to do volume business and undercut competitors. In a December 1996 interview, Aliko Dangote admitted that a government mandate once forced him to import so much rice that the local market crashed by almost 80 percent. The direction of Government of Nigeria trade barriers also suggests preferential treatment. High tariffs or outright bans on imported items favor the Group in nearly all areas in which they do business, including wheat flour, cement, certain textiles, sugar and pasta. Further, the Government of Nigeria is normally slow in privatizing state-owned production facilities. Yet the Dangote Group swiftly won bids on Government of Nigeria-owned manufacturing installations such as the Benue Cement Company and the Savannah Sugar Company, and constructed its own berth at Government of Nigeria-owned Apapa port in Lagos where ships with production inputs offload directly at the Dangote Group factory."

The highly-classified cable concluded that Mr. Dangote was not operating according to market forces, but like an insider-trading environment in which the Nigerian Government was his agents, disclosing that "Dangote's obvious unfair advantage and support from the Government of Nigeria are disturbing for US companies wanting to enter a market with over 130 million consumers. Conversely, some US companies indirectly benefit from Government of Nigeria restrictions protecting the Dangote Group of Companies, adding complexity to the Dangote paradigm. For example, Dangote allegedly receives unfair, preferential treatment to import bulk commodities. However, he is a loyal U.S. wheat customer and buys millions of dollars' worth of other US products. General Electric makes much of Dangote's machinery and the Group will buy about 300 used trucks (mostly made by International) from the US this year. Further, the Group secured a U$D 310,000 grant from the Trade Development Agency in 2000 and aspire to a future Export-Import Bank loan."

A classic example of how Mr. Dangote had used his influence and government-backed connections to corner juicy government-owned corporations during the privatization exercise of the Obasanjo Administration between 1999 and 2007 was the intense acrimony and fight over the purchase of Bacita Sugar Company. According to sources in Nigeria, the authors gathered that when the sugar company located in Kwara State in central Nigeria was slated for privatization in 2004, Mrs. Josephine Oluwadamilola Kuteyi was among the bidders. Born in Ondo Town in Ondo State, western Nigeria, Ms. Kuteyi had been in the sugar business for twenty five years and was hell bent in buying the sugar plant at all costs, but Mr. Dangote was also determined to buy the company. It got to a stage that Mr. Dangote had to go and see Pastor Enoch Adeboye, the popular Nigerian televangelist and general overseer of the Redeemed Christian Church of God when he learnt that Ms. Kuteyi was a senior member of the mega church. "Dangote thought it was Pastor Adeboye that was using Ms. Kuteyi as a front when in actual fact, the amiable man of God didn't have any clue about the transaction," a source informed the authors in Nigeria. According to investigations in Nigeria, Mr. Dangote was prepared to propose to the woman and make her his next wife, if only he could buy the sugar plant at Bacita but the snag was that, the woman, although a divorcee was a born-again Christian." Aliko Dangote's sexual advances hit the rocks on account of religious difference. The lady was able to raise the down payment of ₦2.5 billion (about $20million) for the sugar company. Aliko Dangote backed down when the woman paid for the sugar company in 2006 and Ms. Kuteyi began to run the company with her sons. The lady was later to die in a plane crash in summer 2011 when she was flying in her private jet from her sugar plant in central Nigeria to her hometown in Ondo town in western Nigeria.

As the New York-based *Sahara Reporters*-an online muck-raking magazine that has become the *bête noire* of Nigerian corrupt officials- disclosed in 2010; "The Kano-born Dangote was a commodity trader, but he obtained his massive wealth during the regime of President Olusegun Obasanjo, who encouraged the sell-off of state-owned corporations, presidential aircraft and government properties to Dangote and other questionable businessmen. Essentially, Dangote's wealth is the equivalent of 7 percent of Nigeria's gross domestic product (GDP). Manipulating his unfettered access to those in the seat of political power in Nigeria, Mr. Dangote seized virtually full possession of the cement market and swept up some of the highest import quotas of all local companies. He also received lavish import and export waivers from the Obasanjo, Yar'adua and now Jonathan regimes. Mr. Dangote's style has been to ignore allegations of cement price-fixing, over-inflated IPOs and resale of Broadband licenses. Apart from his generous handouts from various regimes, the 53-year-old Dangote also serves on government boards and operatives within shady political campaign groups that raise unrestricted funds for presidential campaigns and elections. In 2009, Mr. Dangote was involved in a share manipulation scam involving African Petroleum (*AP*) Plc, a company owned by Femi Otedola, his alter ego and erstwhile friend. Mr. Otedola accused Dangote of precipitating a sharp drop in the shares of *AP* in order to erase Mr. Otedola (name) from the *Forbes* billionaires' roster. The ambitious Dangote says he expects his firm to have a market cap of $60 billion within five years. Mr. Dangote is currently on Mr. Goodluck Jonathan's Presidential Campaign Council." Yet, whatever may be said or written about Mr. Dangote's enormous wealth, his wealth was legitimately earned as the *Economist* magazine of London noted, in spite of his cozy relationship with Nigeria's soiled political class.

Mr. Dangote rebutted point-by-point to all rumors and criticisms on his relationship with former and current Nigerian leaders, especially two-time Nigerian military and civilian leader; Mr. Olusegun Obasanjo, the privatization program and sundry issues. "Number one, we didn't just get up and went to them (the companies) and said: "Okay, this is how much we are going to give you." There are bidding process that took place during the privatization exercise. The papers are there." He explained that his companies put in bids for the comatose government-owned companies in an open system like other interested buyers, Chinese, Indian and other foreigners as well, and the *Dangote* Group won some and lost some bidding. He cited three examples of how the privatization exercise was conducted into three Nigerian companies; the Nigerian oil refineries, the steel plants and the aluminium companies.

"How much did the government spend in 1989 to build these refineries? Obviously there would be depreciation after these many years. Here is something that was run down. You don't now go and recover your money. We paid the price of $1.1billion, because the $561million we paid for Port Harcourt is 51 per cent of $1.1billion. We didn't buy the whole refineries. The government still owns 49 per cent. We only bought 51 per cent. And 51 per cent of $1.1billion is only $561million. That's how we arrived (at) $561million. In the case of the Kaduna Refinery, the Chinese which Nigerians don't mind, if it goes to a foreigner, the Chinese were given juicy oil blocks. The day that they signed the production sharing agreement that was the day that they said: "We are not bidding, unless we sign and collect the oil blocks." These guys signed and collected the oil blocks and they still priced the refinery at $102million. And they vowed they would not pay more than $102million. Then we said, fine, rather than allowing this thing to decay like that, we wrote to say we were interested also in bidding. The price that they gave was far below the reserved price. And now, we gave 60 per cent more than the Chinese. And the Chinese said they were not going to put a dime more than $102million."

Mr. Dangote continued; "We bought at $160million with all the challenges. But I thought this same refinery was given to Shell, to Chevron, to Texaco and they rejected them, saying they don't want to even run them for nothing. And we have now paid over ₦100billion (about $50million) and people are shouting. I believe people should focus more on shouting about Eleme Petrochemical. Government spent almost $1.5billion and it was sold for $200million. And we bid. And we lost. And people didn't see that. We bid for the same Eleme Petrochemical with a company that has never ever visited Nigeria. But because they are foreigners, they bought not even 51 per cent, they bought 75 per cent. And they were hailed. And they paid. And they got it. We lost as Dangote. And we spent more than $5 to 7million doing things like bringing experts to come and check and (follow) due diligence and all that. We lost our money and time. But Nigerians didn't say anything because these are foreigners. That is by the side."

He condemned the way some commentators singled out his companies for criticism over the privatization exercise and the manner some Nigerians read meanings to an exercise that was open and transparent. "Look at the way and manner foreigners bought Ajaokuta" referring to his nation's largest steel complex located in central Nigeria. "Ajaokuta almost made Nigeria bankrupt. The government of Nigeria spent $4.4billion on Ajaokuta. And all these foreigners don't bring their money in here. Majority of the money they borrowed locally. They didn't bring fresh cash. And these same people paid a paltry $300million for 60 per cent of a plant that government spent $4.4billion. Nigerians are not complaining about that. Instead they are complaining about our own, because people don't have interest in the steel industry. Delta Steel, government spent $1.45billion, then renovated it with ₦45billion (about $42million) and they sold it for $30million to be paid over three years. This one was also sold to an Indian company. They don't have anything in Nigeria, but people now are not complaining. I am not complaining about the price these things were sold. What I am complaining about is that, if you have to complain; then complain about foreigners taking our assets."

Similarly, he took swipes at the sale process of Nigeria's aluminium smelting company that was sold to a Chinese company as well "At ALSCON the smelting company, government spent $3.4billion. The Russians that have never ever visited Nigeria bought the company at $200million, with the condition that it is after the government dredges the river they would pay the $200million. And the cost of dredging the river is $260million. So you can see that government had to give out $60million out of their pocket to get rid of ALSCON. Because if not, the place would continue to go down, people would go and start cannibalizing the place. So government now said, "We don't have any more money to sink in. Rather than continuously have these assets go under, it is better we even give them out for peanuts."

On the allegation that he is too close to the Nigerian government, Mr. Dangote fired this volley at his critics; "There is no one in the world who would have investments and be fighting government. It doesn't matter where you are, whether you are in Russia, whether you are in (the) UK, whether you are in America. You would not have investments and say, fine, my number one enemy is government. Do people who accuse me of being close to the government of Obasanjo expect me to say my number one enemy is government? It is not possible. There is no business that has no link with politics. None and I challenge anybody to contradict me. Because you either say to a government in power, "ok, fine I am for you." Or "I am against you." And obviously, a right thinking business person would say, I am for you. If you need both the government and the people of the country, that is what you would do. That is where the issue of corporate governance and social responsibility comes in. You are not going to fold your arms, because you are operating within the environment. If you are operating within the environment, why do you want to make the government your enemy?" Aliko makes no bones about his support for Any Government in Power, or AGIP as the locals call it.

Again, he rebutted the allegation that successive Nigerian administrations- at least since 1999 when the soldiers ceded the stage-have tethered to the interests of the plutocratic class, of whom he's a topmost magus. He reiterated the symbiotic relationship between government and business, the private and public sectors including their joint participation in the economic development of Nigeria. "Government does not have the capacity to employ every one; indeed, the private sector is the engine that drives the economic direction of any nation, Nigeria inclusive," he said.

Mr. Dangote dismissed out rightly all insinuations of any sinister relationship with Mr. Obasanjo other than moving Nigerian economy forward in the right direction. "Former President Obasanjo and I became closer because his government is purely for people who would add value to the economy. If I wasn't adding value to the economy, I can assure you that I wouldn't be as friendly as I am with Obasanjo. Eighty-five per cent of my relationship with Obasanjo has to do with the economy of the country. Even when we sit down, 85 per cent of the time is spent discussing the economy. How do we move the economy forward? And I think I have to be really grateful." On the allegations by critics he is operating like a virtual monopolist and a ruthless businessman, Aliko was unabashedly unapologetic. "Managing a company in Nigeria is challenging. Nigeria is the place to separate the men from the boys. It is where you separate a good manager from a bad one. It hasn't been easy attaining number one position. We haven't always started as number one. Often, we start as a challenger, taking on a dominant player. Take the case where in the year 2000 we started to enter a market where some people have been there forty years before us. And we still went into the market, and we fought our way in to become number two. And we are on the verge of getting to number one. The product is flour. We fought our way up into that market using the power of the Dangote brand and offering quality. Quality customer service, and also the capacity, because if you don't have capacity, even when your market is good, you can't do much... To meet capacity, we invested heavily. Apart from investing heavily, we made sure that our quality is good and consistent with the former quality when we used to import flour. We used to be basically just importers. We were just importing and then we would market the goods and sell. In the beginning, we sold cement. Today, we manufacture cement. Today the best cement in Nigeria—you can go and take the samples and check—is coming from our one billion dollar factory at Obajana. And what we have there is 97 per cent local raw materials. The only thing we lack is the gypsum. Even this, we buy some of it from Gombe area (in central Nigeria) which we mix with the foreign ones. But everything is there in one location. And it is the best cement compared to the one we are importing from Taiwan, Europe and China." He waved off the allegation he rocketed to wealth through Obasanjo. "We've been at this thing for the past 30 years; go and check the books."

Mr. Dangote has had a spat with the Nigerian government over sale of government industries during his nation's privatization program. In May 2007, he tussled with the late President Umaru Musa Yar'Adua shortly after his swearing in as Mr. Obasanjo's successor. The late president seized the two Nigerian-owned oil refineries in Kaduna and Port Harcourt that were earlier sold to Mr. Dangote. The total capacities of the refineries were put at 300,000 barrels. Mr. Dangote sucked it up and moved on. He is now planning to build his own private refinery-the first in Africa- in Lagos after the seizure of the two refineries. Nigeria has only four refineries operating at below full capacity. On his part, ex-President Olusegun Obasanjo has fired back at critics of cozy relationship between him and Dangote. "Anyone who is onto trading in Nigeria does not add value to the Nigerian economy. There is no way Nigeria can develop without industrial base," he said.

Back to back, Obasanjo has been a reliable bookend to Aliko in their dyadic vision of indigenous entrepreneurial drive. Given the lacerating nature of doing business in Africa, especially the onslaught by foreign investors that continue to flush Nigeria with tawdry products, Aliko's white-hot enthusiasm about Nigeria's nay Africa's economic prospects through indigenous manufacturing is reflexive. Although he sways few Nigerians he's not a prop of his nation's retired military-civilian industrial complex, yet he continues to receive plaudits and raves from the continent's commentariat. Obasanjo, Nigeria's longest ruler as both military dictator and elected civilian president envisions a neo- African chutzpah in Aliko Dangote, who hinges the path to Africa's economic growth on indigenous manufacturing. "If after 50 years Nigeria does not get it right and in four years Dangote was able to get it right, then Dangote deserves to be supported by (the Nigerian) government," he said. Perhaps, the sleepily sleazy privatization program jumpstarted by Mr. Obasanjo in which Mr. Dangote cornered juicy government-owned corporations for himself during their sales may be a part of this economic nationalism.

CHAPTER 8
INSIDE THE BILLION DOLLAR ALIKO BUSINESS EMPIRE

"I always make sure I hire people that are smarter than me"
---*Mr. Aliko Dangote*

THERE ARE three basic necessities of life: food, clothing and shelter. After these three fundamental needs of life, modern man has leapfrogged from those basic life's essentials to modern technology which has made life better and enjoyable. In between these three basic needs are the service sectors of human living, which add more value to human life. Every successful entrepreneur in life made money from either of the two sectors: providing food, clothing, and shelter to others, or engage in activities that help others in maximizing the great potentials of modern technology and in the process become wealthy. A thorough analysis of the *Forbes* list of billionaires in the world bears testimony to this fact. The late Mr. John Johnson, publisher of *Ebony* and *Jet* magazines of Chicago, and the first black person to be listed in the *Forbes* list of 400 millionaires in the United States made virtually all his fortunes from communication: the media. The first human being to be the first richest man on earth consecutively for thirteen years-Mr. Bill Gates- made his wealth through technology. The first black man to be listed on the *Forbes* list of world billionaires in 2001-Mr. Bob Johnson- the owner of *Black Entertainment Television: BET:* which he later sold, made his money from the media. The first black woman billionaire, Ms. Oprah Winfrey also of Chicago made her wealth from media business. The late Mr. Sam Walton, the founder of *Wal-Mart* made his billions from retailing: food, clothing and shelter.

A look at the fortunes of Mr. Dangote revealed they are either related directly to food: sugar, pasta, noodles, and flour mills, salt; or directly related to clothing: textile, or; shelter: cement, real estate and so on. Like *Wal-Mart* every human being on earth must eat as a local African adage says, "I ate yesterday does not concern hunger." No matter how poor a person is, even those that are mentally-disturbed, society makes sure they are clothed so as to protect our human decency. No wonder, clothing is the second business of most of the world's rich people. The power of shelter as a money-making business is as legendary as the human origin right from the Garden of Eden. After these three basic necessities of life, investment in the media and technology businesses are money-garnering ventures across the world. From *Google, Yahoo, Apple, Microsoft, General Electric, Dell* to *CNN*, etc. that are worth billions of dollars and other social media companies associated with them: *Face book, Twitter, My Space, You Tube,* mobile phone, ITunes and many more that have revolutionized the way human beings live and interact with one another. Some of the largest and richest companies in the world today are in media technology.

The list of *Fortune Global 500 Companies* revealed that, either directly, or as part of their ancillary services, half of the companies are involved in food, clothing and shelter. The world's largest oil companies such as; *Royal Dutch Shell* of Netherlands, *Chevron, Exxon-Mobil, Petrobras-Petrleo* of Brazil, *Total, Conoco-Philips, China National Petroleum,* and *BP,* may be known for oil production and marketing, but part of their profits come from agricultural and farming-related products. Imagine what motorists do after pumping gas into their vehicles? Most motorists enter the stores owned by these oil companies in their fuel stations to buy something to eat. *Wal-Mart,* the largest company in the world provides the food, clothing and shelter needs of its customers in all its store outlets all over the world. The *Agricultural Bank of China* which makes the list of the *Forbes* Top 25 Companies in the World caters exclusively to making money available to Chinese farmers. In other words, in addition to telecommunication and oil, the next money-yielding sector in the world today is agriculture. It is no wonder the *Dangote Group* is concentrated on these three essentials of life: food, clothing and shelter.

The world first heard of the billion dollar fortunes of Bill Gates, the world's former richest man for thirteen years, which all came from *Microsoft.* But that was four years ago. It may interest the world to know that Bill Gates now makes $44 billion out of his mouthwatering $67billion fortune from food beverage. He is now the largest stock holder of *Femsa* and *Grupo Televisis* the two main *Coke* bottlers in Mexico. Food beverage has now taken over telecommunication as Mr. Gates wealth. The Huang Maori family's $1.8 billion-worth companies in the Republic of Belize deal mainly in food and retailing. The same for late Colombia's Julio Mario Santo Domingo, the second richest billionaire in his native country and the 108th billionaire in the world assessed to be worth $8.4billion. He made his entire fortune from food: beer. Of all the 13 billionaires in Africa, over 60 percent of them made their fortunes from food, clothing and shelter. Of the seven billionaires from Egypt, five of them are into hotel business, construction and retailing; including the Sawaris Brothers; except one, who is into telecommunication. In South Africa, except the DeBeers family and lawyer-turned investor Mr. Patrick Motsepe, the remaining two: Messrs. Johann Rupert and Christofell Wiese made their $6.6 billion and $3.5 billion respectively from consumer retailing. Mr. Mohammed Al-Fayed and family made their $1.4billin fortune from consumer retailing, and of course, Mr. Aliko Dangote of Nigeria. Ironically, except Mr. Mike Adenuga of Nigeria, who made part of his $4.7billlion fortune from banking and oil, no African billionaire listed on the *Forbes* list made his or her fortune from banking.

But Mr. Dangote stands out. He is the only African/black billionaire, who made virtually all his billion dollars fortunes from indigenous manufacturing. Furthermore, he is the only world billionaire to make his entire fortune solely from local manufacturing in the area of the world known, and called; the Third World. This is very important in several respects. First, Dangote has proved that a Nigerian, or an African does not need to be an agent to a multi-national corporation or a distributor to a company in the metropolitan world to be successful. This was the point stressed by former President Olusegun Obasanjo when he explained his support for the *Dangote* Group during his eight-year presidency. Local trading will not develop Nigeria or Africa, but only indigenous manufacturing. A lot has been written and said about the dislocations in the economies of African nations, and many under-developed countries, and one of the main causes of the dislocation is, because of the dependent capitalist system that makes the economies of Third World nations mere appendages to the multi-national corporations of the West. Take *Coca-Cola* for example, Dangote supplies the sugar that the conglomerate needs for local production in Nigeria, and in virtually all the countries in the West African sub-region instead of the usual practice in the past when *Coco-Cola* imported its sugar needs from abroad. By developing and building virtually all its subsidiaries from local manufacturing, Mr. Dangote has succeeded in building an autochthonous business empire. Secondly, Aliko Dangote has proved to Africans and other developing nations that the futures of their economies certainly rest on indigenous manufacturing. No nation, or a group of people can develop, unless they are able to feed themselves, provide shelter for their masses and clothing for their citizens.

Thirdly, Aliko Dangote has proved that a Nigerian and an African can stay in that part of the world often neglected or under-reported and use his or her God-given talents and business acumen to start, manage, and build a company to world standard. Those Nigerians and Africans that believe until they come to America, go to Europe, China or Asia to learn business ethics, they cannot succeed in business may have a re-think after studying Dangote's formula for business success in the world. Fourthly and lastly, Aliko Dangote has shown the power of native intelligence, Spartan discipline, charity, and the ability to spot a need to amass fortune instead of using templates for business success from Harvard, Yale, or London Business Schools which sometimes do not work in Africa.

The many branches of the largest business conglomerate in Nigeria, the largest employer of labor in Nigeria, and the largest business empire in the West African business sub-zone are testimonies to the phenomenal success of the *Dangote Group*. With presence in virtually all nations in West Africa and other parts of Africa, including Cameroon, South Africa, Uganda, Ethiopia, Rwanda, Algeria, Morocco and Zambia, the *Dangote Group* is a conglomerate that is set to conquer not only the black world, but the world's global business scene. When a company announces that its vision and mission, "is to be a world-class enterprise that is passionate about the living standards of the general populace and 'ensure' high returns to stake-holders," one begins to wonder what the company will do to accomplish such an open vision. The *Dangote Group* provides an answer; "To touch the lives of people by providing their basic needs." In Nigeria, the basic needs of the people are food, clothing, and shelter. In Africa, the basic needs of the people are; food, clothing, and shelter; and in every nation of the world, the basic needs of the people are also basically the same; food, clothing, and shelter. A peep into the Dangote Group would reveal the resolve of Aliko to conquer the business world by an African entrepreneur.

The Dangote Cement Company is the largest in Nigeria, in West Africa and one of the largest in the African continent. In 1973, Nigeria had five functioning cement companies, partly- owned and operated by the Nigerian government with non-Nigerians, while the Nigerian and Beninese governments jointly-owned one at Onigbolo near Cotonou in Benin Republic. As with most government-owned companies that were badly-run, the cement plants were either shut down because of unprofitability, or sold to private corporations because they were running at a loss. The problems of epileptic power supply, bad road network and other infrastructural debilities forced the Nigerian government to shut down the cement plants. The *Dangote Group* moved in and injected capital into the cement plants and turned them around under the privatization policy of the Nigerian government. Mr. Dangote brought in some of the best cement scientists from around the world, paid them handsomely and soon emerged Nigeria's leading cement manufacturer. Today, the *Dangote* Group controls 60 percent of Nigeria's cement market. With the able leadership of the man at the helms and supported by cement experts from home and abroad, Aliko Dangote systematically built a cement corporation that now has branches and manufacturing plants in virtually all nations in the West African sub-regional market and other parts of Africa.

Mr. Devakumar Edwin, an Indian and one of the pioneer staffers of the company is currently the group's executive director for projects and industries. His reminiscences on how it all began; "I joined the group about 20 years ago. It was a trading company at that time but they had the ambition to venture into manufacturing. Our first venture was into textiles in late 1991. Up till 1997, we did not grow much in manufacturing, except that we had one textile unit in Kano, and one in Lagos. And then we decided to go further into manufacturing. We decided to start with four plants simultaneously: the pasta plant, salt refinery, flour mills and the sugar refinery. We have taken over the Benue Cement Company and we started the Obajana project. We also acquired the Savannah Sugar Mills to make our entry into the production of sugar easy. What we did was to begin manufacturing those products which we are trading. We already had the market, the customers, the distribution network and the warehouse. All we had to do was produce instead of going into trading. We began local production of cement. Now, we have been going beyond Nigeria. We have been moving into other African countries. We are putting up a sugar refinery in Algeria and also a cement plant in Senegal... New cement plants are about to take off in Zambia, South Africa, Tanzania, Republic of Congo and Ethiopia."

Today, the Dangote Cement Company plant at Obajana in Benue State, central Nigeria is the largest cement producing plant in Nigeria and in West Africa. Commissioned on Saturday May 12, 2007 by former President Olusegun Obasanjo, Dangote Cement Plant at Obajana in Kogi State, central Nigeria estimated to be worth $1billion at inception is the largest cement plant in Africa. The Dangote Group currently has four of its subsidiaries listed on the Nigerian Stock Exchange (NSE). They include; Obajana Cement Plc. (Dangote Cement Plc.)/Benue Cement Company Plc. (BCC); Dangote Sugar Refinery Plc, Dangote Flour Mills Plc. and National Salt Company of Nigeria Plc.)

The five four mills at the Dangote Flour Mills Company control nearly two-third of the local market. They are located in Apapa in southern Lagos; another one in Ikorodu in the outskirts of northern Lagos; three other plants are in Ilorin, Kwara State in central Nigeria; one in Dangote's home town of Kano in northern Nigeria, and the last in the south eastern city of Calabar in Cross River State, eastern Nigeria. The flour mills produce semolina, a nutritious food for consumption and have total production capacities of 4,500Mtpd. These total annual production capacities increased to 8,000Mtpd in December 2009.

Mr. Rohit Chaudry is the managing director of the Dangote Flour Mills. He disclosed that the company, in spite of its setbacks when it was suspended from the Nigerian Stock Exchange (NSE) few years ago, has taken its expansion drive to new frontiers. According to him; "The increase due to inflationary pressures are part of the challenges faced by the competition vis-à-vis the likelihood of potential new entrants and the rising cost of raw materials company," adding however, that between 2009 and 2011, the *Dangote Group* injected over ₦7.5 billion (about $48million) into the arm of the group to boost production. Today, the company's plants at Apapa, Lagos, Kano, Calabar and Ilorin in western, northern, south-eastern and north-central Nigeria respectively have total daily production of 7,000 metric tons compared with their pre-2009 4,500 metric tons daily production. According to Chaudry; "The Ilorin mills have additional 500 metric tons per day, while Apapa mill expanded to 2,500 tons from initial 1,000, Calabar mill increased from 1,000 to 1,500 tons, while Kano mill has absorbed the rest." The company is also into the production of new wheat meals such as Semolina (Danvita) and Alkama. Although the nation's epileptic power supply is affecting operational expenses as the company spends a fortune daily to source for alternative reliable and regular power supply, Chaudry disclosed the company is poised to reach greater heights.

The import and export division of the Dangote Group is another money-spinning arm of the conglomerate. Mr. Dangote is seriously and aggressively tapping into the West African sub-region market. In addition to establishing cement manufacturing plants in many of the West African nations, creating employment opportunities is his secondary goal. For example, Chaudry disclosed that the injection of over ₦7.5billion (about $48million) into the company in 2009 has increased production from 4,500 tons to 7,000 daily. Consequently, the domestic market has led to rise in the exports of wheat meals such as' Semolina and Danvita to neighboring Chad, Niger and other West African countries. As Mr. Dangote disclosed; "If we export from Nigeria to any of these countries, we will collect 30 per cent export incentives and when we get into those countries, we are not to pay local duties. So, it is okay for the company. The export is in view of the group's envisaged excess for local demand and the huge demand for the products in the sub-region. The new strategy will increase the company's bottom-line as well as the returns on shareholders' investment." In its drive to exploit the incentives created by the Nigerian government to boost export drive and shift Nigeria's dependence on crude oil, the Dangote Group is aggressively spreading its tentacles to the West African sub-region market in other areas such as; salt, noodles, rice, cement and other household goods and commodities.

In London, Mr. Dangote told *Reuters* during the world media's *News Makers Forum* in 2011 that the group would issue Global Depository Receipts (GDR) to be listed on the London Stock Exchange by the year 2014. According to him, "The only thing that we need to do is quickly to create that avenue of exporting cement rather than importing cement. And the third phase now, which we will do within the first quarter of next year, (2013) will be the other African assets which are owned by Dangote Industries that will be taken over by Dangote Cement. This will take us to about 46 million tons by 2015." He disclosed that the Global Depository Receipts (GDR) will be beneficial to his companies because; "The structure is much better for us, it is a market (London Market) that we understand very well," adding that the New York-based Morgan Stanley would be one of the three investment banks that would advise on the GDR.

The Dangote leasing arm of the conglomerate has its headquarters at the Tin Can Island near Apapa Port in southern Lagos. It leases out about 2,000 vehicles and industrial equipment to private and industrial concerns in Lagos and other parts of the country. Dangote Transport and Leasing Company are patronized mostly by corporations wishing to save money through planned overhead expenses. There are 1,000 suburban vehicles of all models in the fleet. What distinguishes this arm of the company from other leasing outfits is that, locally-trained vehicle engineers and mechanics attend to customers in case of breakdown of the leasing vehicles. Mr. Busari Abdul-Razak is the workshop manager at the Dangote Transport and Leasing Company

Lagos. The remaining 1,000 heavy duty vehicles are available for lease to manufacturing companies.

Another favorite product from the *Dangote* Group is its noodles. After watching the Nigerian food market, and sensing that it was ripe for Dangote to give the Indian manufacturers a run for their money in the noodles business, Dangote Noodles hit the Nigerian market in grand style. Mr. Rohit Chaudry is the group managing director of Dangote Flour Mills; manufacturers of Dangote Noodles. "We are the first to come out with a range of three unique brands, and it is the first brand that comes with natural chicken extract and to this end we buy real chickens from around the country as part of our quality push approved by NAFDAC," he disclosed in Lagos. NAFDAC is Nigeria's equivalent of the Food and Drug Administration (FDA), which regulates food and drug quality control in Africa's most populous nation. Dangote Noodles come in three different flavors: instant noodles, snack variant and ready-to-eat flavors. Continuing on the unique advantages of Dangote Noodles to extant brands in the market, Chaudry added that, "The materials when revealed are targeted to relate with the entire family, because Dangote Noodles provides wholesome nourishment to the entire family..."

Like everything that Mr. Dangote does, the company followed up the introduction of the Dangote Noodles into the market with strong aggressive marketing strategy, especially newspaper, radio and television commercials. "Bringing the international class experience akin to other markets here, is the connect we wanted as the core business remains the white noodles, and with this ,we did not stop at product value but the youth which is up to half of the population of the country. We are also the only brand with nutrient fortification and all these put us in a unique class compared to the mass market," the group managing director further added. Its famous and populous television commercial; "What is cooking" instantly became a hit in many Nigerian homes, especially with little kids. The group poached capable and good hands from the noodles industry hitherto dominated by the Indians. The spirit of competition is good for customers, and as Aliko has demonstrated in Nigeria and Africa, taking on the "leaders" in an existing market is good business. What is required is the ability to play the game square and fair by attracting customers with new ideas. Mr. Dangote borrowed the business ethics of other astute business men and women who had excelled in their trades. For example, Mr. Walton worked for *J.C Penney* for 22 years (1940-1962) before he left to found *Wal-Mart*. Mr. James Cash Penney himself who founded *J.C Penney* Stores in 1912, a native of Missouri as Mr. Walton worked for defunct *Golden Rules* Stores for 14 years before he went on to establish his own retail store. Today, both *J.C Penney* and *Wal-Mart* compete to the benefit of their customers. After all, the spirit of competition is at the core of American capitalism. In Nigeria, Mr. Dangote is definitely competing like a typical American capitalist.

The Dangote pasta, another local brand is located at Ikorodu near Lagos. The pasta division engages the services of nearly 500 production crew and other ancillary workers. Established in 2000, it currently has the capacity to produce 6,000 tons of pasta annually. Mr. Palati Sai-Prakash was the managing director of the company, while Mr. Wale Dangote is the head of treasury at the Dangote Pasta Limited at Ikorodu, Lagos. Sai-Prakash disclosed that the pasta products from the Dangote stable have tremendously improved to add value to the dietary needs of Nigerians. "As always, we would continue to strive to ensure that our product is accessible and affordable. We would like to maintain international best practices in our operations which has (sic) made us earned the NIS/SO award for system quality from the Standard Organization of Nigeria (SON). We are expanding our operations to meet the demands of our customers." He said the improvement in Dangote pasta has not created any dent on the customer's purse as the prices of the pasta remain the same. The consumers of Dangote pasta still get value for their money, in addition to the new addition of minerals and vitamins known as *actilease* that the company uses as additives. According to Sai-Prakash, "The Dangote Pasta

Company has come a long way in the delivery of quality and affordable meals to Nigerians and touching the lives of Nigerians and we want to assure our various stake-holders of value innovation, continuous product improvement in our spaghetti. As a market leader, we have pioneered the introduction of multi-vitamins and minerals into our products (which) ensure complete absorption of these additions into the body system."

Early in 2012- Sai-Prakash relinquished his position to Mr. Oladeinde Brown as managing director. Brown was moved as personal assistant to Mr. Aliko Dangote from the corporate head office in central Lagos to oversee the newly-improved Dangote Pasta Company in Ikorodu, Lagos.

The Dangote Salt Company encompasses its salt refining plants in industrial Oregun area of Lagos, Apapa in northern and southern Lagos respectively. Other plants are in Port Harcourt, Rivers State in south eastern Nigeria, the National Salt Company of Nigeria, Ota, Ogun State, western Nigeria, Dangote Salt Processing plants in Calabar, Cross River State. The plants have total daily production capacities of 2,000 million tons (Mtpd).

Other areas of the multi-billion dollar Dangote Group include; Blue-Star Services Company, Dangote Agro-Sacks Company, Dangote Ginnery Limited, Nasal Insurance Company, and Alsan Insurance Company among others.

Greenview Development Company Limited is also another arm of the group. Established as a haulage and cargo-handling outfit, Greenview Development Nigeria Limited entered into partnership with the federal government of Nigeria under the port concession program of the government. Since the 1960s, the Nigerian Ports Authority had been battling with port congestion and the inability of the agency to handle the fleet of cargoes passing through, unarguably one of the busiest ports in West Africa. In addition to the bottleneck of port congestion, government too was also losing much-needed revenues. This forced many Nigerian port users to look elsewhere for the importation of their goods and wares.

Consequently, the federal government of Nigeria decided to involve private business men and women to assist it in transporting goods and imported wares at the Apapa Port in Lagos. This involves the Dangote Group taking possession of "Terminal E" point at the busy port complex. Cargoes such as; fertilizer, cement, salt and other containers are the specialties of Green view Development Nigeria Limited. Billed as a lease that would last for the first 25 years (2006-2031), the entry of the company into the clearing and forwarding business has completely ameliorated the ubiquitous port congestion in Apapa port, Lagos, Nigeria. The national distribution arsenal of *Dangote Group* across Nigeria contains nearly 2,000 trucks and tractors, and its launch of a ₦1 billion (about $7million) national distribution scheme tagged: *"Your Truck Scheme"* has also boosted the conglomerate's efficiency in port clearance and de-congestion. Truck drivers and handlers of the distribution services have also benefited from the scheme, which makes them vital stake-holders with the opportunity of owning each of the distribution vans, trucks and tractors worth ₦5.5million (about $35,000.00).

The Dangote Properties and Leasing Company is the real estate arm of the *Dangote Group*. It includes chains of apartment complexes, and luxury flats and condominiums scattered across major cities and towns in Nigeria. For example, there are 41 of such complexes in his ancestral home of Kano catering to eclectic tastes of the nouveau riches and the well-heeled. The commercial hub of Nigeria, Lagos, and the nation's political hub, Abuja, also have such modern complexes; owned and managed by Dangote Properties. Luxurious condominiums in highbrow areas such as; Ikoyi, Victoria Island, Lekki in Lagos; Maitama Districts and Central Business Districts of Abuja in the federal capital city; Kano City and Port Harcourt, Kaduna, and other cities, and towns are what make the group the largest business empire in Nigeria, and West Africa, and among the First Three in Africa. With over 200 apartment buildings in its fold, Dangote Properties and Leasing Company are collaborating with the

Nigerian government in making housing cheaper and available to many Nigerians, especially the upper and middle income classes in Africa's most populous nation.

In Mr. Dangote's vast business empire, he stands sure-footed like the rock of Gibraltar. As a savvy business man, he enters into joint ownership and mergers when business success dictates such partnerships. Recently, when approached by a group of Nigerian investors to come on board Blue-Star Consortium which was bidding for majority shares of both Kaduna and Port Harcourt oil refineries in northern and south-eastern Nigeria respectively, Dangote brought his financial muscle into the deal and became major owners of the oil companies. He had been wary of moving into the lucrative oil and gas sectors of the Nigerian economy for several reasons until he was convinced recently that he should be a big player too. But the administration of late President Umaru Musa Yar'Adua later revoked the bidding of Mr. Dangote's stakes in the two oil refineries. The action confirmed Dangote's wariness in entering into business mergers and partnership in Nigeria. "I prefer to mind my own business," he said. "When you enter into business partnership with any one, there is always room for suspicion. When you buy a new car, your partner's wife would tell him it is the business money and company funds you have used. This is why I don't enter into business partnership."

While much has been known and written about how Mr. Dangote became the cement king of Africa, little has been written about his sugar oligopoly in Nigeria. The Dangote Sugar refinery at Apapa, south-west Lagos; Dangote Sugar refinery plant in Hadejia, Jigawa State; and several plants in other parts of Africa are money-spinning ventures contributing to the economic developments of the African continent. The apex body that regulates sugar production in Nigeria is the National Sugar Development Council (NSDC). It was established by the military regime of General Ibrahim Babangida by a decree in 1993, which was ratified by the Nigerian National Assembly in 2004.

Mr. Usman Bello is the executive secretary of the council

which is under Nigeria's department of commerce and industry. According to him, Nigeria's domestic consumption of the energy product is far from being met, and there are wide opportunities for would-be investors in the sector. "There are about 170 to 180 billion tons of sugar productions worldwide, and out of these global demands; Brazil alone has 5 million hectares of land for sugar-cane production which ranks Brazil and Australia the world's major player in the sugar trade," he said. Nigeria only has 30,000 hectares of land devoted to sugar-cane production whereas; the country needs about 300,000 hectares of land for sugar-cane production to meet local demands for sugar consumption. The Nigerian government lacks the capacity to meet these local consumption needs after the sugar factories in Bacita, Lafiagi and others were privatized. This is where Dangote Sugar Company has been playing a vital role in the production and supply of sugar needs in Nigeria

Sugar is one of the staple products in the world. The total world production of sugar increased from 160.569 million tons in 2010 to 168.045 million tons in 2011, and production has not kept up with the demand and consumption of sugar in the world. Some of the world's largest producers of world sugar consumption are; Brazil, which controls 14.6 % of world production; Australia, which controls 10 % of the world market; Thailand produces 10% of world sugar production, India, China and Cuba, Mexico and Guatemala, are also major players in the world sugar production. But of recent, weather conditions such as, cyclone, rain, heavy snow and other natural disruptions have affected sugar production in the world market. For examples, countries like Australia, Brazil and India have been major suppliers of sugar to the European Union, China, the Asia Pacific and the Americas. But a massive cyclone which hit the Aussies recently has affected the capability of Australia to meet the needs of its traditional buyers. While Brazil is using its local production for ethanol to save energy and is also coping with the exceptional dry weather in the South American nation, China world sugar output has plummeted by about 300,000 tons in the last two years alone, because of heavy snow and frost. Russia, Kazakhstan and Belarus are reeling from drought too, thus necessitating the three nations which collectively are the three largest consumers of sugar in the world to look elsewhere to meet local demands. These conditions in many parts of the world have pushed up demand for sugar across the world. For examples, the EU recently announced it would increase quotas to non-EU countries willing to export sugar to the community. While Japan is yet to recover from the last devastating tsunami, the country is in dire need of sugar. It is against this backdrop that Dangote Sugar Refinery (DSR) Company stands to benefit from such world need for sugar and especially in other parts of Africa too.

The company has traditionally been the major suppliers of the product to multi-national corporations such as the *Coca-Cola, Nigerian Bottling Company, Seven-up, Pepsi-Cola* and other companies in Nigeria and West Africa in need of sugar for their products. Dangote Sugar Processing Company supplies 70 percent of local sugar market in Nigeria, and the high demand of the product, and falling production definitely works to the company's advantage. In Africa, the United States imports the bulk of its sugar needs from Angola, Botswana, Egypt and Ghana; while major sugar demands in nine African nations: Congo Brazzaville, Democratic Republic of Congo, Cote D'Ivoire, Egypt, Madagascar, Malawi, Mauritius, Mozambique, and South Africa are met by Dangote Sugar Processing Plants located in West Africa, Central Africa, East Africa and Southern Africa.

In 2010, the Dangote Sugar Processing Plant recorded annual turn-over of $580, 519,349 million and operating profit of $104,186.296milion and after-tax profit of $72, 788.645million. Dangote told the shareholders that the profits of the company had plummeted compared with the previous year's, ascribing the decline to "...increased cost of business and reduced level of activity occasioned by the high cost of sugar and foreign exchange that was experienced during the year (2010) in review." Continuing, Dangote believed that; "Though these challenges still persist (yet) we are committed to the effective management and application of our resources to ensuring that barring any unforeseen development in the cause of the current year, our pursuit of sustainable growth and dividend will yield the desired results."

After Mr. Dangote presided over the company's annual general meeting (AGM) in Abuja Nigeria's administrative capital in May 2011 where a dividend of ₦7.2billion (about $48.1million) was announced at the rate of ₦0.60 kobo for every ordinary shares of 50kobo, Mr. Aliko announced the company's merger with the Savannah Sugar Company. Today, the Dangote Conglomerate controls 60 percent of Nigeria's sugar industry. Incorporated on January 4, 2005, Dangote Sugar Refinery Company made its maiden entry into the Nigeria bourse on March 8, 2007 and instantly emerged as, *Africa Investor's "Best Africa IPO for 2007"* at a price of ₦18.90 per share (about $0.126). Organized as recognition of the performances of African Stock Exchanges by fund managers and equity research teams mostly based in London, UK, that analyze African companies listed on the various bourses, Dangote Sugar Refinery Company was the only Nigerian company nominated for the awards that featured in seven categories. That the "young" sugar company outperformed other older companies in Nigeria and Africa, and so soon only a year it was listed on the Nigerian Stock Exchange was a thing of joy for the arm of the group. According to Uzor Nwankwo, director of Dangote Sugar Refinery Company, who received the award in London, UK on behalf of the group, "That we beat some of the best companies in Africa shows that Nigerian capital issues have come of age."

The Dangote textile mills with ginnery plants in Kankawa, Katsina State in northern Nigeria is one of the largest in Nigeria and West Africa. The most dominant arm of the *Dangote Group* is the food chain of the conglomerate patronized by more than 150 million Nigerians daily.

The Dangote food group of Nigeria and West Africa

parade some of the best groceries in the world. Every day, over 50 million Nigerians drink *Mowa* bottle water; the same numbers of Nigerians drink *Ziza* pasteurized milk and over 150million Nigerian housewives, chefs and others use tomato paste from the factories of Dangote Foods Company. From rice, salt to sugar, flour, bread, macaroni, spaghetti, fruit juice and other edible products, millions of Nigerians, West Africans, and Africans including Indians, and Lebanese eat products manufactured, or refined, or distributed from the multi-billion Dangote Group. The expansive business conglomerate also extends to other service sectors of the Nigerian and African economies.

Dangote Group of Ivory Coast

The Dangote Group of Ivory Coast is helping to jump start the economic development of the West African nation. President Alassane Qattara of Ivory Coast, an international banker and former president of the World Bank (African Section), before he assumed the reins of power in Africa's largest cocoa producer is trying desperately to chart a new economic direction for his country. Towards this end, he is looking for reputable investors and business men and women, both from within and outside Africa to help in this economic drive. Shortly after his swearing in as president in 2011, he was in Abuja to thank President Jonathan in his capacity as chairman of the Economic Community of West African State (ECOWAS) for his leadership role in finding solution to the political crisis in the West African nation. Dr. Qattara also used the opportunity of his visit to appeal to the Organized Private Sector (OPS) in Nigeria to come to Ivory Coast to help his administration rebuild the nation. President Aliko Dangote of *Dangote Group* as usual, responded to President Qattara's call. Aliko Dangote announced that his billion dollar conglomerate would build a cement plant in Ivory Coast.

"We have got approval from the Central Bank of Nigeria (CBN) to invest about $3.9billion outside Nigeria, especially in neighboring African countries, and Ivory Coast is one of them. The cement factory was almost starting in Ivory Coast, but because of the war, we had to abandon it. Now that the war is over, we will start the business all over again. We will have a discussion with the Cote D'Ivoire minister of trade and see how we can go back there to commence the process of building cement factory in the country," Mr. Dangote informed President Qattara and his entourage at the Presidential Villa in Aso Rock, Abuja, Nigeria. The Dangote Ivory Coast Cement Plant is expected to create jobs and boost the socio-industrial development of the nation. The *Dangote Group* would be going to Ivory Coast, because of the veritable business opportunity created by the hasty departure of French-owned companies during the political logjam in the nation's presidential election crisis of 2010. Many of the French companies are returning, but Dangote's presence is a re-affirmation of his strong conviction that African business men and women are better placed to jumpstart investment drive in the continent than foreign investors.

Dangote Group of Zambia

The Dangote Group of Zambia is changing the economic outlook of the Southern African nation. History was made in the Southern African nation in the last week of July 2011 when the *Dangote Group* opened a $400million Dangote Cement factory in Masaiti near Ndola. The former President of Zambia, Mr. Rupiah Bwezani Banda, who led top government officials to the epoch-making event, commended the President of *Dangote Group*, Mr. Aliko Mohammad Dangote for his vision and belief in the economic potentials of Zambia and for contributing to its economic development through job creation. According to President Banda, "Zambia, indeed welcomes your decision to invest here as one of the continent's top global multi-national corporations. This is the largest investment into Zambia by a Nigerian company. I am glad to also note that besides the employment opportunities being created, the project will greatly benefit the people of Masaiti and the surrounding districts through transfer of technology and skills." President Aliko Mohammad Dangote of *Dangote Group* responded that, "Our choice of Zambia for this multi-million dollar investment is quite strategic. Last year (meaning 2010), the World Bank named Zambia as one of the world's fastest economically reforming countries. Earlier this year (2011), the World Bank reclassified Zambia as a middle-income country along with Ghana. The World Bank attributed the upward adjustment in Zambia's income growth to foreign aid-driven interventions and surging prices of copper in the last few decades." Continuing on the reason the Dangote Manufacturing Train berthed in Zambia, Aliko informed President Banda and other government officials including traditional rulers present at the occasion, "I am informed that our investment in the sector, which is outside the traditional mining sector, ranks as one of the highest in this country to date. This, no doubt, is a significant milestone for us as a company. But we are even more excited with the fact that an African company is making this investment in a sister African country. This indeed, shows that Africa is gradually taking its destiny in its own hands rather than wait for investors from outside Africa. Investment in the real sector of the economy is the only way that our continent can achieve the much-desired accelerated growth and development that we have yearned for."

Continuing, Mr. Dangote drew the attention of his audience to the report released on Africa's economic future by the US-based McKinsey Global Institute in June 2010, which said the continent needed about $46 billion in spending per year to meet infrastructural needs. He observed that the various governments in Africa's 53 nations (the latest is the newly-independent nation of South Sudan) lacked the capacities to meet these challenges, hence the much-needed support and partnership with the Organized Private Sector (OPS). He said it was in this spirit of Investment Promotion and Protection Agreement (IPPA), which the Zambian government signed with the *Dangote Group* in December, 2010 as a realization of Government / OPS African Economic Initiative that gave expressions to Dangote's presence in the Southern African nation. According to Dangote, "It is in this light that we have decided to invest in Zambia. We are motivated to create an African success story, because we believe that entrepreneurship, especially our own home grown African entrepreneurship, holds the key to the future economic growth of the continent. The fact that Africa offers one of the highest returns on investment (ROI) in the world is an additional incentive for any discerning investor, who can take calculated risks. While we are in the business of creating wealth primarily, we are also mindful of the need to touch lives of people. As a company, we have always been conscious of the need to give a little of our profit back to the society as a guarantee for sustainable business success. This has been our guiding business philosophy."

The Dangote Cement plant in Masaiti in Ndola, Zambia has the capacity to produce 1.5 million tons of cement annually. About 1000 and 6,000 full-time Zambians and indirect local employees respectively, would be given employment opportunities. In addition, as it is the tradition of the group in every locality it invests; schools, hospitals, road networks, electricity, water supply and housing estates for its workers are some of the social amenities that the people of Masaiti and their counterparts in Ndola would gain by the presence of the multi-million cement plant. Furthermore, the presence of the group in Zambia will not only strengthen bilateral relations between both countries, but will also signal the beginning of South-South economic cooperation, this time between two African nations.

The entry of Dangote Cement Company into the Zambian economy, notably the cement industry, according to Mrs. Vaida Bunda, the public relations officer of Zambia's Competition and Consumer Protection Commission, would enhance competition and lower cement price in the Southern African country. To her, "The price of cement in Zambia remains relatively high at over ZM K50, 000 (about $9.50) per 50 kilogram pocket of cement. It is therefore hoped that the new plant will lead to greater economies of scale, and enhance competition to a higher level, and assist in reducing the price of this key input in infrastructure development."

While the cement plant would create thousands of jobs for the natives, over 300 families in the areas would be displaced in Lupiya area of Kafulafuta Constituency in Kitwe, Zambia. Mr. Kampewa Nundwe, logistics manager at Dangote industries in Zambia said the group, in line with its corporate social responsibility, would not uproot the affected families from their ancestral homesteads. "There is land that is available with nobody there. If we find land that is inhabited, we will talk to the chief again, and if it is established that there are people doing farming activities, we will start a resettlement scheme on an alternative land for farming, and we'll dig boreholes, and we will also give them subsidies for them to start up their lives once again." The families that would not be rehabilitated would be adequately compensated. Before now, there has been wrangling among the Chiwala royal establishment but now that a new king has been crowned, the wrangling is over and a new king, Mr. Majaliwa has been installed. According to Mr. Nundwe, "the company had not yet sensitized villagers on the plans because they feared that everybody would rush to the new land in order to benefit from the scheme and other benefits that would come with the program."

THE STAFF STRENGTH OF DANGOTE GROUP

Mr. Aliko Mohammad Dangote once said: "I believe we have what it takes to create jobs in Nigeria. The main thing why we are not able to create jobs, one is that governments are not consistent in terms of policies; you know when you are consistent in terms of policies, then people will definitely invest." The largest private employer of labor should know. There are currently 25,000 Nigerian employees in the various arms of the Dangote Group. When you add the number with those in ancillary services, whose livelihoods depend on Dangote's salt, cement, sugar, noodles, spaghetti, bottle water, real estate, rice, pasta, bread, macaroni, milk, tomatoes, transportation and many more, the number of Nigerians tied directly, or indirectly to the group will be more than one million. In Nigeria and in most African countries, when you educate a child as the U.S Secretary of State, Mrs. Hillary Rodham Clinton once said, you educate a village. In the same vein also when you employed a Nigerian, or an African in the Black continent, you put food on the table of four, if not more Nigerians and Africans. This is because the hydra-headed monster of unemployment is biting so hard that an employed person has dependents: father, mother, brothers, sisters, relatives and friends to cater for as well. This is why kudos must be paid to Mr. Dangote for putting millions of Nigerians and Africans, including expatriates: Indians, Chinese, Japanese, Britons, Americans and several other nationals in his employ to work in Nigeria and Africa.

In summer 2011 as the prices of cement products skyrocketed compelling the President of Nigeria, Mr. Jonathan to summon Mr. Dangote and other stake-holders to Aso Rock Presidential Villa to crash the prices of the products so as to make them available to ordinary Nigerians, Mr. Dangote was the first to respond. Instead of ignoring the president, because he could so in the spirit of market forces and de-regulation, Aliko, who knows the cement industry like the back of his palms, said he knew how to crash the prices: more distribution networks. He imported 5,000 lorry trucks into the country within a month and put nearly 10,000 more Nigerians to work and true to his promise, the prices of cement products fell. His trick: eliminating too many middlemen and women.

How does Mr. Dangote co-ordinate all these menageries of businesses, starting from Africa's most populous nation, Nigeria, Togo, Ivory Coast, Liberia to Ghana, Sierra Leone, Senegal in West Africa; Cameroon, Democratic Republic of Congo, Uganda, Tanzania, South Africa and more than fifteen nations in the Black world? Again, Mr. Devakumar

Edwin, one of Aliko Dangote's longest and most trusted management staff and executive directors disclosed; "He has an extraordinarily brilliant mind. When you start working with him you will realize the real brilliance of his mind. He thinks very fast and has got a very quick, analytical mind. He looks at investment opportunities, makes a quick analysis and you will be surprised at his conclusions. He is also a phenomenally hard worker. He starts early in the morning and till late night, its work, work and more work. And number three, he has a phenomenal memory. You can't give him a figure today and maybe five or six years you come and give him something different. This helps him a lot. He is a very humble and understanding person. The other day we were driving in the jeep and I was sitting beside him. My subordinate who was sitting in the front suddenly sneezed. And immediately he (Dangote) said, "Mr. so and so, are you feeling cold so we can reduce or switch off the AC?" It's not that I am a person who doesn't have feelings, but I would not have thought about it. And this person was a general manager and not a director. But imagine Alhaji to have felt concerned about that person's cold right away. He is a very sensitive person. Once you start working with him, you will really appreciate the man. He is able to get the best out of his people, because they know that he treats a person not as just a human being, but almost like a family member."

According to Mr. Dangote, seven values defined his chains of businesses and on these seven values he leads the management team to greater heights. Cost advantage as a tool to corner the local market. In all his products and services, whether in making cement available, sugar, pasta, noodles, spaghetti, bottle water and other edibles available to Nigerian and African consumers, costs of productions and availability of such products and services are uppermost in the minds of Dangote and his management team. Take cement as an example. When President Jonathan summoned the stake-holders to the presidential villa shortly after he was inaugurated in summer 2011, and asked that the price of the product be reduced, Aliko, the magus of the industry agreed with the president. "We have made a pledge to ensure that the price of cement in Nigeria comes down, but that can only be possible if the product is available in the market through increased supply. We intend to keep this pledge," he told the journalists covering the meeting of the cement stake-holders with the president after the meeting. He does the same with his other products.

In this strategic advantage, Mr. Dangote has borrowed the templates of some renowned American manufacturers. For example, in 1953, Mr. K.R. Perry of Norfolk, Virginia saw that an earlier concept of selling each item in a retail shop for not more than $1 per item could still be achieved in the United States. He studied the retail market and decided to call his new concept *Dollar Tree*. He opened five stores with only $1.00. Today, there are 4,010 outlets of *Dollar Tree* in the nation's 50 states with total revenue of $5.23billion in 2000. The idea of marking each retail item at $1.00 was pioneered by Mr. Carl Turner. In 1939,Turner, the founder of the popular American retail chain, *Dollar General* began what is today a nationwide conglomerate worth $11billion in front of his house as J. L Tuners & Sons in Scottsville, Kentucky. In the 1950's, Mr. Leon Levine of Wadesboro in North Carolina visited Turner's home in Scottsville, Kentucky and saw *Dollar General.* He was only 22 years old, but knew that folk back home in North Carolina would love to see a store where no item was sold for more than $1.00 so in 1959, he established the *Family Dollar* retail outlet in Charlotte, North Carolina. His total revenue is about $8billion and unlike his two competitors, Howard Levine, Leon's son who took over from his father as chairman and chief executive officer in 1998 repositioned the company and chose to concentrate on food and clothing.

Both *Dollar General* and *Dollar Tree* exist side by side in many cities across the United States. While the latter concentrates more on food, snacks and party supplies, the latter prefers low cost general items, from toiletries, cheap electronics, toys, and perfumes to disposable kitchen needs. Looked at critically, these three retail companies provide identical products, but their management styles are markedly different. According to Mr. Levine, "More middle-ish income consumers are starting to shop with us...and we have a great opportunity here..." Aliko Dangote has used this style of entrepreneurship system in Nigeria too by taking on Indian, Pakistan, Arab and Chinese manufacturers of edible products such as macaroni, juice, tomato paste, spaghetti, noodles etc. "I began to manufacture those goods that I used to import after my visit to *Arisco* in Brazil in the 1980s," he disclosed. This move has driven down the costs of such staple items.

Competitive pricing: The *Dangote Group* is poised to make the group's products affordable through competitive pricing while simultaneously maintaining quality. There are few manufacturing companies that can achieve these twin objectives, considering the cost of doing business in Nigeria, especially manufacturers of groceries and edibles, which prices are prohibitive to many in Nigeria and Africa. But the group has been able to achieve both and the approach is similar to what Mr. Sam Walton, the founder of *Wal-Mart* and one of America's most successful businessmen was able to achieve. As Walton explained in *"Wal-Mart: A History of Sam Walton's Retail Phenomenon"* he devised a system whereby, each item in his stores is priced per item, while supplying large quantities at the same time thereby reducing the cost of each item and offering discount which ensure small profit, quick turn-over. "I found that by pricing an item at $1.00 I could sell three times more of it than by pricing it at $1.20. I might make only half the profit per item, but because I was selling three times as many, the overall profit was much greater," Walton disclosed.

This age-long standard practice of discounting prices to boost more sales and increase profits over a longer period has been the secret of Dangote's bottle water, pasta, noodles, spaghetti, sugar, salt, rice, canned tomatoes and other essentials that people cannot do without on daily basis. In fact, the profit-margin increases more for a manufacturer that sells both to retailers and wholesalers. Experience has shown that people value sophistication, style, and elegance when shopping for designer shoes, apparels, watches etc. and would not mind paying exorbitant prices for such products to maintain class status. However, when people want to buy groceries and edibles which are known all over the world as "essential commodities," the costs weigh heavily on consumers' minds. Although many Nigerians have complained that Mr. Dangote has become a virtual monopolist in some areas, especially cement as the Nigerian government has given his cement company a lot of waivers and preferential treatment. The *Dangote Group* has rebutted such argument. "In a de-regulated economy such as ours, it's impossible for government to dictate to consumers," a spoke person explained. "Can we be accused of two things at the same time; favoritism during government privatization and then the Nigerian government telling cement buyers, or sugar buyers to buy only our products? Can both be accurate at the same time? Can a government force its citizens to buy groceries from a particular chain store?"

Superior quality products as demonstrated by the Dangote Group in Africa. In the act of selling and marketing any product, quality and affordability of the product are essential. One of the most renowned motivational speakers of our time, and a leading authority in salesmanship; Mr. Hilary Hinton known worldwide as Zig Ziglar once said, customers patronize a product, or a service based on emotions. An accomplished author of some of the best-selling books on business success, Born on November 6, 1926 during the Hoover Administration and was only five years when, unarguably one of the greatest economic crises in America known as the Great Depression occurred, the late Zig Ziglar, one, out of twelve children, and the tenth child that grew up in rural Mississippi where the family was compelled to move to; from Alabama, when the Great Depression began in the United States; many of the nations of the world were also affected by the Wall Street stock market crash which was the genesis of the Great Depression. Like many Americans adversely affected by the global economic dislocation, Hilary lost his father to a stroke in 1932 at the height of the depression, and two days later, his younger sister died in Yazoo, Mississippi at a rural farm where his father had taken a job as a farm manager to feed his large family. Hilary decided to become a salesman after he left the U.S Navy, fought in WWII, and used the G.I bill to earn a degree from the University of South Carolina.

In his best-selling book; *"Zig Ziglar's Secrets of Closing the Sale"* which has sold millions of copies, he listed six secrets of effective sales strategies namely: the right mental attitude; the attitude of salesmen and women toward others; the attitude of salesmen and women to the sales profession; building reserves in selling; building a mental reserve in selling; and finally, showing love to your customers. The men and women at *Dangote* Group must have been trained to imbibe these Ziglar's success secrets of sales and marketing. All workers at the group ensured that all products offered to the public have superior qualities, while the men and women offering the products and services, whether at the cement section, foods and merchandize, haulage, real estate arm of the company, and many more demonstrate the six qualities of honesty, character, integrity, faith, love and loyalty which Ziglar listed as the six qualities of successful sales men and women.

This marketing strategy has been used by large retail stores to retain existing customers and win new ones. For example, to maintain its dominance in the merchandizing market in 2012, *J.C. Penney* went for Ron Johnson, formerly of *Apple*, as its new chief executive, and Mr. Michael Francis, formerly of *Target,* as its new president. Both decided to give *J.C. Penney* a thorough make-over: a new logo, massive price cut, and aggressive advertising and marketing strategies. According to *The New York Times,* the combination of the two men from two of the world's most successful companies was to re-position the merchandize retail giant. "We haven't given the customer enough reasons to love us. We want to be the favorite store for everyone, for all Americans, rich and poor, young and old," Mr. Johnson, the new helmsman revealed. This superior product quality ensures that Dangote's products can compete with imported goods in Nigeria and Africa.

Product availability and the spirit of laissez-faire in a de-regulated African economy which the *Dangote Group* exploited in order to achieve success are some of the business philosophies of the group. If it were left for Mr. Aliko Dangote, he would advocate the banning of certain imported products into Nigeria, and Africa, but the industrialist in him would not let him advocate for such anti-competitive and monopolistic policies. Of course, it would be oxymoronic for a foremost and successful industrialist like Aliko Dangote who believes in strong competition to canvass for banning of imported products. According to him; "We do not support the idea of any importation for now. When you import, you are increasing the employment opportunities in the producing nation. We are today suffering from employment problems, so it will be more viable for us to shun importation of cement." If importation is not desirable to economic development, then the banned products must be available domestically, and that has been the number one priority of Aliko in his economic nationalistic drive. Other marketing strategies that the Dangote Group has imbibed to maintain competitive advantages are; flexible terms to take advantage of emerging markets and investment opportunities; prudent financial management practices; and finally, accumulated capital for re-investment. Again, Aliko has borrowed the templates from many American companies on how to effectively compete.

For example, when the one dollar -retail giants: *Dollar Tree, Family Dollar* and *Dollar General* were competing few years ago, each began to re-innovate in order to become competitive. *Dollar General* capitalized on its brand name by focusing more on baby products than its customers. Then it did something remarkable as a way of attracting a particular segment of potential customers; it took control of the sponsorship of NASCAR –the motorsports in the United States. *Dollar Tree,* on its part decided to look outside the

United States for expansion. In November 2010, the Virginia-based retail company went to Canada and bought *Dollar Giant* Store of British Columbia for $52million in cash. According to Mr. Bob Sasser, the president and chief executive officer of *Dollar Tree;* "We now have an outstanding platform for significant expansion in Canada, with an experienced team of management and associates." *Family Dollar*, as its name depicts, concentrated on its base: family customers. The three still operate side-by-side in North America and cater to the eclectic tastes of their middle class customers.

Similarly, this ability to re-innovate was what Mr. Craig Herkert did at *Supervalu* when he was named the new president and chief executive officer of the Minnesota-based grocery chain in 2006. With vast experience in the retailing business, spanning over three decades, the former *Wal-Mart* chief executive rebranded the company with a new logo and catch-phrase, opened new retail outlets and slashed prices for customers. "We will be America's neighborhood grocer," Herkert promised. The third largest retail company in the nation with 142,000 work force and $44.05 billion in revenues, *Supervalu* has been expanding because of many new stores it had acquired, 2150 stores in 35 years. The weight was much and decline set in. Mr. Herkert was brought in to fix the problems. He unfurled his eight-point agendas which focused on customer satisfaction, price, fresh products, expansion, creating local and community relationship, maintaining competitive edge, and independence for wholesale outlets. Then he announced reduction in the salaries of top managers and out sourced the company's IT services to Tata in India. The measures worked and *Supervalu* regained its pre-eminent position.

The *Forbes* magazine that declared Dangote, the richest person in Nigeria and the richest black person in the world had also featured the Dangote Group of Companies among other companies in the world. The magazine featured Dangote Cement Company among the top global 2,000 companies in the world with a total asset of $2.1 billion in its 2011 edition. The company was ranked 1,434 in the world with a total market value of $12.5 billion and profitability of $384.4 million. It was the first time a Nigerian company would be featured on the *Forbes Global 2,000 Companies*. Altogether, 25 companies in Africa made the list, mostly dominated by South Africa. In the report, Egypt and Morocco were the other African countries that had companies featured in the special publication. In sub-Saharan Africa, *Standard Bank* of South Africa led the African category, while companies such as telephone communication giant; the *MTN Group, Sasol* and *First Rand* also made the list.

The *Forbes Global 2,000 Companies* is an annual ranking of the top 2,000 public companies in the world by the magazine. The ranking is based on four metrics: sales, profit, assets and market value. The list has been published since 2003 and is a useful indicator for rating leading public companies in the world. According to a statement from the magazine while explaining how the companies were ranked, "We compile our Global 2,000 list by screening Interactive Data, Thomson Reuters Fundamentals and Worldscope databases via Fact Set Research Systems for companies that were publicly trading as of March 11, 2010. Using these databases as our primary sources of data, we screen for the biggest companies in four metrics; sales, profits, assets and market value. Our market value calculation is as of March 11, 2010 closing prices, including all common shares outstanding," it added. Continuing, the magazine noted that, "Dangote Cement's emergence in the *Forbes* list barely a year of its listing on the Nigerian Stock Exchange (NSE) is a remarkable feat and attests to the company's drive and vision of becoming globally competitive."

In his reaction to the report, Mr. Dangote was optimistic about the economic future of Africa. According to the richest Black person in the world, "Africa has a lot of opportunities; the only thing we have to do is sit down and harness those opportunities. Aside from the few issues in North Africa, things are much, much better. You have less corrupt leaders;

we are having elections all over the place. I'm not saying we're 100 percent there, but we're getting there." According to one media analyst in one of the local newspapers in Nigeria, while describing the *Dangote Group*; "From any angle one chooses to look at it, 'Dangote' represents the face of emerging global brand from Africa and this has gone a long way to reposition the country as a nation of value. This explains why the handlers of the brand remained conspicuous in the subconscious of consumers while the celebration lasted. The *Dangote Group* is a diversified and fully integrated conglomerate with interests across a range of sectors such as cement production; sugar refining; flour milling; pasta production; sack manufacturing; salt production; port operations; and haulage. The group also has interests in oil and gas, real estate and other sectors of the economy. The president (of the group) has built a flourishing business empire with 13 subsidiaries spread all over Nigeria as well as nine African countries ...Little wonder, the brand Dangote is a household name. The group has four of its subsidiaries that are listed on the Nigerian Stock Exchange (NSE). They include Obajana Cement Plc (Dangote Cement Plc)/Benue Cement Company Plc (BCC); Dangote Sugar Refinery Plc; Dangote Flour Mills Plc and National Salt Company of Nigeria Plc)."

Mr. Bisi Ojediran, a columnist for *This Day* newspapers in Nigeria noted that the *Dangote Group*, more than any other groups of companies in Nigeria, is contributing immensely to the economic development of Nigeria through job creation and economic opportunities. According to him, "I get attacked by some readers anytime I commend Nigerians actively involved in Direct Domestic Investment (DDI). But I still believe that considering the harsh investment climate in the country that has consumed many entrepreneurs and millions of Nigerians, as well as governments that benefit from DDIs, our investors should be honored rather than demonized. Entrepreneurship is not the easiest way to make money in this country, and politicians who loot treasuries and keep their wealth in foreign banks don't contribute anything to the country they swore on oath to serve. I noted it when recently Aliko Dangote had Dangote Cement listed on the stock exchange after a merger with Benue Cement, making it the country's leading cement maker and the biggest company ever to (be listed) on the Nigerian stock exchange. From the thousands of Nigerians they employ, goods and services they provide the direct contribution in taxes (about N6billion-about $45m) from Dangote according to reports) and the confidence they generate in the economy, these investors should be encouraged." Mr. Segun Oshinaga, a pastor and business man in Lagos, Nigeria agrees with Mr. Ojediran. He says, Mr. Dangote "is a larger than life personality, a business icon, and perhaps the most successful business man in Nigeria and maybe in Africa today." According to him, "I haven't met him, but I know a few people who have met him, and they all speak well of him. He appears cool headed, humble and simple. His businesses have certainly enriched many lives by providing employment opportunities across Nigeria and Africa."

Good management, committed, loyal and hardworking employees are what define the Dangote Group. The men and women who sit on the management team of Dangote Group are tested hands, unarguably the finest and the brightest in their chosen fields. These are graduates of top notch local and foreign colleges and universities. Take for examples, Mr. Koyinsola Ajayi (SAN), one of Nigeria's foremost corporate attorneys, and one of the youngest Senior Advocates of Nigeria (SAN) equivalents to the British Queen's Counsel; Mr. Chris Atoki; Messrs. Abdullahi Sarki Mohammed of Dangote Flour; Suleiman Olarinde of National Salt Association, and now with the Dangote Salt; Audu Dantata-Dangote, a relative of Aliko, who also doubles as executive director of Dangote Industries; Uzoma Nwankwo of the Dangote Flour Mills; Ade Adeniji also of the Nigerian National Salt Company, who has equally pitched his tent with the Dangote Salt Company; Abdu Dantata, another of Aliko's cousin overseeing the Dangote Cement Company are top-notch professionals. The same can be said of Ms.

Benedicta Chimma-Molokwu with the Dangote Sugar Company; Mr. Samuel Laiye-Teidi, a former naval officer and now director of Dangote Flour; Mr. Shuaibu Idris also of the Dangote Flour; Mr. Asue Ighodalo of the Flour Mills Section; Ms. Folake Ani-Mumuney who, until recently, was responsible for co-coordinating the press and media relations of the group as communications officer; Mr. John Okonmah, who is the head of the groups' investor relations; Mr. Ekanem Etim who is the executive director of Dangote Cement Company, and many more who make day-to-day decisions in Nigeria's and West Africa's largest business empire.

These smart men and women look up to the groups' management team comprising of Mr. Aliko Dangote himself as chairman and president, ably supported by Mr. Marcus Olakunle Alake, the chief operating officer, Mr. Sani Dangote; Dangote's younger brother who is an executive director; Devakumar D. Edwin, who is executive director in charge of projects and industries and one of the earliest workers in the group. Others are Mr. Knut Ulvmoen, executive director in Dangote Cement Plc.; Mr. Sada Ladan Baki, executive director; Mr. Joseph Makoju, special adviser to Mr. Dangote; Mr. Tajudeen Sijuade, the group financial director; Mr. Paramji Pabby, the group human resources director and Mr. Kuzhyi Ravindran, the group's chief financial officer.

According to the management policy of the group; "We recruit for placement of competent people to actualize opportunities and enhance the potentialities of the business as well as identifying associated risks and to put in place a framework for managing such risks." How did *Dangote Group* achieve all these successes? Mr. Dangote, the man who put it all together has one word "Hard work" "It is only through hard work that we have come this far," he said. Aliko Dangote explained why he chose manufacturing at a time many Nigerian elites, and aspiring industrialists were running after the black gold-crude oil-through which many Nigerian rich men and women made their money. In addition, why did he go into manufacturing in a nation bedeviled by infrastructural problems hostile to local manufacturing? His answer: "There is money in manufacturing even though it is capital intensive. To achieve a big breakthrough, I had to start manufacturing the same product I was trading on; which is commodities. I am an advocate of manufacturing, because it does not only improve your business status; it also helps you give back to your community and country; with respect to job creation and economic development." The ability to withstand competition from multi-national corporations in the African market is the hall mark of the Dangote success story. Many Nigerian business men and women have given up trying to compete with companies controlled and owned by Indians, Japanese, Koreans, Britons, Pakistanis, Chinese, Arabs, Americans and other non-Nigerians. These are companies that have become household names in Nigeria but Dangote was not deterred. The *Dangote Group* was able to compete with these foreign-owned and multi-national corporations to win the local Nigerian market just as the 105-year old San Antonio-based *HEB* Grocery Stores has been able to withstand the stiff competition from other competitors in western United States and Mexico. Honored as the Grocer of the Year by Trade Publications, publishers of *Progressive Grocer* magazine in 2010, *HEB* was commended for its ability to withstand competition, maintain sound corporate culture and satisfy its customers. According to Craig Boyan, president and chief operating officer of the 329 strong retail chains in the nation and Mexico, *HEB* was able to achieve this feat, because of the remarkable performance of its more than 76,000 employees "who strive each day to provide our customers with a superior shopping experience." But in the beginning it was hard for what is today nearly a-$20billion retail chain.

Founded by Mrs. Florence Butt on the first floor of her home in Kernville, Texas in 1905, Howard, her youngest son took over the company from her mother in 1919, but his attempt to grow the company beyond Texas was an uphill task at a time WW1 had just ended. But he did not despair. Now in the hands of the fourth generation of the Butts family, Charles Butt, the youngest son of Howard, who became president and chief executive officer in 1971 has grown the retail company from a-$250million company to nearly $20billion to become the largest retail outfit in Texas and the 14th in the nation.

The *Dangote Group* is also a notable company for maintaining good corporate social responsibility in Nigeria and Africa. The group has been one of the major corporate sponsors of the popular annual Calabar festival and carnival for some time now in eastern Nigeria. Modeled after the popular Thanksgiving Day Parade marked every November 24 each year in New York City and sponsored by *Macy's*, the annual Calabar festival is becoming a popular event in Nigeria which attracts local and foreign dignitaries. *Macy's* has been sponsoring the Thanksgiving Day Parade for 88 years running in addition to the popular Fourth of July fireworks display marking the founding of the United States, which the popular department stores has been sponsoring for 36 years.

The ability of the *Dangote Group* to build a dedicated customer base and re-innovate for competitive edge in Africa is a secret of the group's success. Mr. Dangote's belief in, and demonstration of economic nationalism has earned his brand of products a strong client base and committed customers. From his bottle water, spaghetti, macaroni, tomato paste to noodles, pasteurized milk, salt, cheese and many more, more than 150 million Nigerians that consume his products daily take pride in Nigerian-made products. This ability to maintain a loyal clientele and dedicated customers are the secrets of some of the largest retail companies in the world. For example, how did the Kirkland, Washington-based *Costco* Wholesale Corporation become the largest membership-only warehouse club in America, the 6th in the nation and the 7th in the world? With more than 55million paid-up membership profile who renew their memberships and pay up-front annually in its 592 outlets in Australia, Canada, Japan, Mexico, South Korea, United Kingdom, the United States and Taiwan, the global wholesale giant employs more than 142,000 workers and generates $88.915

billion in revenues as at 2012. The benefits of the $55.00 annual membership fee are far greater than anyone can think of, and that has kept the wholesale conglomerate in its dominant position in the world.

The ability to re-innovate in the corporate world in order to remain competitive was displayed in 2010 by *Sobeyes* -the second largest food retail giant in Canada. The owners of *Price Chopper Supermarket* with 1,300 outlets in North America, more than 85,000 employees and nearly $16billon in revenues, the company closed some of its outlets in eastern Canada and moved its re-branded stores to the Atlantic in 2010 to maintain competitive edge. In early 2011, Bill McEwan, the president and chief executive officer of the Stellarton, Nova-Scotia-based food distributor company announced that the company had finalized arrangements with *Shell* Canada to use 250 of its gas stations in Quebec and the Atlantic as retail outlets. In the first quarter of 2012, the company posted an $87.1 million profit soon after those measures. These are examples of how corporations re-innovate, re-position and achieve competitive edge in the market.

With all the awards, accolades and recognition that the Dangote Group has achieved and the billions of dollars Mr. Dangote has made, when will the richest Black person in the world go on break? Aliko says he is just warming up. "We are still expanding," he said. "We are not slowing down at all. There is no economic meltdown." This philosophy of Dangote has led to the establishments of companies in some of the most volatile nations in Africa, where ordinarily, many investors believe are some of the most unstable and unpredictable areas of the world. According to Dangote "We are not a company that is owned by government. People are still doing business in troubled areas like Congo. In fact, Congo is one of the best countries to invest in. During the war in Liberia, people were still doing business. A friend of mine opened a flour mills six months ago in Cote D'Ivoire." In the Democratic Republic of Congo, the political instability and war in the central African nation has not deterred Mr.

Dangote to invest in the volatile nation as well. As one of his aides humorously said, "Even when people at war, they must eat; when nations fight, the people still wear cloth and when the war is over, cement will be needed to rebuild."

A savvy billionaire maximizing the power of New Technology in Africa.

Some of the everyday products that Dangote Group make available to nearly 400million consumers in Nigeria, West Africa and Africa: Top: Macharoni, Fruit Juice, Milk, candies, biscuit, crackers, donuts, © Dangote Group, Lagos

The Many faces of the Richest Black Person in the World All Photo Credits: Dangote Group Nigeria

THE FACES BEHIND THE DANGOTE GROUP

From top clockwise: Aliko Dangote, president; Sani Dangote, brother and vice-president; Abdu-Garba Dantata, cousin and executive director; Olakunle Alake, chief operating officer; Knut Ulvmoen, group executive director; Ladan Baki, group executive director; Devakumar Edwin, group executive director; Joseph Makoju, special adviser; Tajudeen Sijuade, financial director; Paramjit Paddy, director of human resources; and Kuzhyil Ravindran, chief financial director, Suleiman Olarinde, managing director, Dangote Sugar. Photo Credits: Dangote Group, Lagos, Nigeria

Dangote Group Office in London, UK. Photo Credit Dangote Group, Lagos Nigeria

From Top: The Dangote Group Offices in London, UK.

Dangote Obajana Cement factory, reputed to be the largest in Africa Photo Credit Dangote Group

Middle: Obajana Cement factory, owned by Aliko Dangote reputed to be the largest in West Africa

Bottom: Mr. Oladeinde Brown (middle) former special assistant to Aliko Dangote, now managing director & CEO, Dangote Pasta Nigeria Limited, Ikorodu, Lagos, Nigeria © Dangote Group, Lagos

278

Chief Oladeinde Brown (middle) formerly Special Assistant to Aliko Dangote, now Managing Director & CEO. Dangote Pasta Nigeria Photo Credit Dangote Group

SOME OF THE PRODUCTS PRODUCED BY THE DANGOTE GROUP OF AFRICA

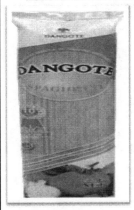

Dangote Spaghetti   Dangote Cement   Dangote Bottled Water

Dangote Sugar   Dangote Flour   Dangote Noodles

Some of the everyday products that Dangote Group make available to nearly 400million consumers in Nigeria, West Africa and Africa: Dangote Spaghetti, Dangote Cement, Dangote Bottled Water, Dangote Sugar, Dangote Flour, and Dangote Noodles © Dangote Group, Lagos

CHAPTER 9
RULING AND
DOMINATING
CORPORATE NIGERIA

IN THE FALL OF 2009, the man whose conglomerate controls about 38 percent of the Nigerian Stock Exchange zoomed into the apex leadership of the third largest bourse in sub-Saharan Africa as president. The election of Mr. Dangote as the president of the Nigerian Stock Exchange (NSE) by the stock market's council climaxed his contributions to making the exchange an important player in the nation's economy. Mr. Obafoluke Otudeko, another Nigerian industrialist was elated when he passed the baton of leadership to his good friend. It was time for clinking of wine glasses and felicitations at the ceremony watched by the *crème de la crème* of Nigerian industrialists and business class, supervised by Ms. Ndidi Okereke-Onyiuke, the exchange's erstwhile director-general. Mr. Dangote's election was unanimous and he delivered this acceptance speech:

"Distinguished colleagues in council, it is with great pleasure and humility that I accept your decision to become the 17th president of the council of the Nigerian Stock Exchange. I have no doubt whatsoever that without the conviction and support of all of you particularly that of the immediate past president, Mr. Oba Otudeko and our great director general who worked tirelessly for the last 10 days, I may not have become the president of the NSE. I want to seize this opportunity to thank all of you immensely, particularly the past presidents of council, our indefatigable director general Professor Ndi Okereke-Onyuike, all council members, stockbrokers, family, friends and well- wishers who lavishly gave their support and encouragement to ensure that the proper thing is done, and that the esteemed tradition of the stock exchange is pursued. I have no doubt that my tenure as the president of the NSE will be tough and challenging, especially, because of the global economic downturn, its effect on our economy and our capital market. However, I believe that these challenges will provide the opportunity for us to reposition our stock exchange, and capital market to become the leading stock exchange in Africa for capital formation driven by transparency, innovation, efficiency and liquidity.

During my tenure as president, I will be guided by the following five key themes: transparency and improved governance of the market; improving the liquidity, turnover and size of the market, enhancing market efficiency by ensuring clearer, and updated rules, processes and procedures, provision of world class infrastructure, and technology for our market, massive capacity building, and rapid skill enhancement of the staff of the stock exchange and investor education. The effects of the global financial meltdown and the subsequent massive outflow of investments from our stock market, (which) led to a precipitous slide in the value of securities in our market, have greatly shaken confidence in the market. One of my main tasks will be to begin to restore the confidence of our battered and disillusioned investors once again in the market. This will be accomplished by ensuring that we have a more open, and fair market, improving the disclosure standards, forging a closer and better collaboration with other regulators particularly SEC, (while still protecting the independence of the NSE). Our zero tolerance regimes will be emboldened to ensure speedy penalties on operators who flout our rules. Our surveillance, compliance and enforcement units will be further strengthened to ensure that they operate optimally. We will update our corporate governance rules not only for our listed companies, but also for operators and the council itself because charity must begin at home.

If the stock exchange and its dealing members must continue to remain viable economic units, we must make sure that we increase the liquidity and turnover in the market. One of my first missions will be to lead and intensify discussions with other relevant parties in the economy to put in place a plan to improve the liquidity and turnover in our market particularly in the secondary market. We have to discuss, and agree on what to do with the 'toxic assets' in our market, and very critically how to provide funding for our stockbrokers to refloat their businesses. If we are to compete with other market on the continent, then we have to begin aggressively marketing all the high quality companies in the sub region to make sure that they are listed in our market. I will make sure that we take very concrete steps to ensure that we further deepen, and expand our market by introducing other products, and attracting more investors. Working with the management of the NSE, I will make sure that we adhere to the timetable to dematerialize the market so that by January 2010 we do not have certificates in our market. I will ensure that we strictly implement the ongoing enterprise business transformation exercise, which is aimed at improving the efficiency in the operations of the market, and update the entire business processes of the stock exchange.

I am aware that the business transformation team is currently working on the detailed operating process for each business unit of the NSE. What is left is to ensure that market rules are reviewed, aligned, and harmonized with issuance, and trading practices, and technology. Given the recent world wide experience, risk issues have now come to the fore in all markets. We have no choice than to increase our focus on all risk issues that are likely to affect our market. Our technology infrastructure will continue to be central in our competitiveness as a market, therefore starting today, we commence work to decide on the new technology platform, which will take our market to the next level. It will include a world -class trading engine, a surveillance platform, and all other features required for the efficient running of a capital market. I am aware that the management of the NSE has done a lot of work to improve the physical infrastructure, and enabling environment of the NSE building in Lagos. I am informed that we have started fixing the power problems and the elevators in the building. The focus will now be to continue the renovation of the NSE building, so that we can give a proper facelift in readiness for our golden jubilee celebrations in a few years' time. Finally, we will make sure that the security in the NSE building is improved upon, and that we continually test our business continuity plans. Since the stock exchange business is driven by skills and ideas, our staff must at all times be abreast of development in global capital markets, and stay ahead of the market they supervise. Therefore, in line with the business transformation plan, we will improve the competency level of every staff of the NSE. Council will approve a capacity building blueprint covering not only our staff, but also other market operators before the end of the year. We realize that investors have options on where they can invest their savings; our challenge therefore is to ensure that our market is continuously competitive, and attractive to investors, and issuers alike.

My fellow colleagues, the task of taking our markets to the next level will undoubtedly be quite daunting, but I believe that with your cooperation, and that of the management of the NSE *In-sha Allah,* we will succeed. Once again, I thank you for giving me the opportunity to serve."

Founded on the eve of Nigeria's independence in 1960, there has been only one industrialist that has been unanimously elected as the president of the Nigerian Stock Exchange, and that was Mr. Louis Odumegwu Ojukwu in 1963 commonly referred to as Mr. Nigerian Stock Exchange. Mr. Dangote became the second person to the late Odumegwu Ojukwu in 2009 and the exchange's seventeenth president. Mr. Obafoluke Otudeko handed over an exchange with market capitalization, which opened in 2008 with ₦9.56 trillion (about $57.3billion), which closed on August 5, 2009 at ₦8.43 trillion ($50.9billion) due to excess supply over demand.

ALIKO DANGOTE, POLITICIANS AND POLITICAL LEADERS

WHICH COMES first: politics or wealth? Or let's frame it another way: which is more powerful and desirable: political power or economic power? The obvious answer is, both. As the late Ghanaian nationalist, politician and first president of independent Ghana, Mr. Kwame Nkrumah once said, every ambitious person should seek the political kingdom first, and the rest shall be added unto it. The great Osagyefo was right. Political power, as students of elementary political science know, is the instrument that regulates; who gets what, when and how, and which determines, and regulates the allocation of values in the modern society. However, since human wants are numerous, and there are inadequate resources to meet the sundry demands of every member of the modern society, every politician seeks wealth for security and comfort. No rich person would be insensitive to the political direction of the society or nation he/she lives. There is a symbiotic osmosis between politics and business in every nation of the world. Politics and economics are sometimes symbiotic; politicians, and rich men and women are likely buddies, and controversies normally trail rich people that befriend politicians.

Take for example, Mr. Bernard Arnault, the third richest man in Europe, and the 10th richest man in the world, and his "favors" to the daughter of former prime minister of the UK, Ms. Kathryn Blair. There were insinuations in 2007, when Kathryn was admitted to France's prestigious university at the Sorbonne for a French Language course for three months, and during her short stay at the elite institution, the young lady was provided with posh accommodation, first class transportation, and other conveniences valued at £80,000 Pounds (about $100,000) by Mr. Arnault. Did the French billionaire and Europe's third richest man do this favor to Kathryn, because her father was still a serving prime minister? Was there more than meets the eye in Mr. Arnault kind gesture? Why are rich men and women so close to politicians, and political leaders? To put it another way, why do politicians covet the friendships of rich people?

The late American billionaire and philanthropist, Mr. Walter Annenberg worth $4billion and once occupied Number 34 on the *Forbes* list of world billionaires was one of the closest persons, and an informal adviser to Mr. Ronald Wilson Reagan, former president of the United States (1980-1988). In fact, Mr. Annenberg was reputed to be a personal buddy to former US Presidents; from Eisenhower, Nixon to Reagan. The former first lady, Mrs. Nancy Reagan referred to him as one of "Reagan's closest friends for half a century." President Richard Nixon appointed Mr. Annenberg as U.S Ambassador to the U.K between 1969 and 1974. Mr. Annenberg was on the post for half a decade, even though many believed the billionaire didn't need the job. Mr. Joseph Kennedy, whose son, Jack, later became the president of the United States, was also US Ambassador to the UK (1938-1940).

In both advanced and developing nations, politics and economics have always intersected. In pre-colonial Nigeria, and during the struggle for political independence, indigenous African entrepreneurs could not stand idly by and watched the activities of the British colonial administration, which were inimical to the development of indigenous entrepreneurship. For example, when the Nigerian Youth Movement (NYM) was established in 1933, some of the initial funds and resources the organization was able to source for in order to prosecute its pro-democracy, pro-independence, and nationalist agitations were provided by three businessmen; Messrs. Timothy Adeola-Odutola of Ijebu-Ode, Joseph O. Fadahunsi of Ilesa and Sule Oyeshola Gbadamosi (S.O.G) of Ikorodu. They were more involved in pre-independence politics, because of the Cocoa Pool of 1937-38 law of the British colonial administration, which clearly disadvantaged indigenous Nigerian business men and women. Thus, rich people are interested in politics and befriend politicians in order to protect their business interests.

Mr. S.O. Gbadamoshi later used his company; the Ikorodu Trading Company, established in 1937 to assist in funding the defunct Action Group (AG) led by his good friend, the late Mr. Obafemi Awolowo (1909-1986), the first indigenous governor of defunct western region of Nigeria (1951-1958), leader of the opposition at the federal parliament after independence (1960-1966), and later finance secretary, and vice president of the federal executive council during the military regime of Mr. Yakubu Gowon (1966-1975). Mr. Fadahunsi later became a governor, between 1963 and 1966 in western Nigeria during the political crisis within the Action Group (AG). In eastern Nigeria, young Louis Odumegwu-Ojukwu was a great financier of the NCNC, indeed, he was part of the party's delegation to the London Constitutional Conferences held by the British colonialists prior to granting political independence to Nigeria. Mr. Adeola-Odutola, one of the most prominent pre-independence Nigerian industrialists, indigenous manufacturers and educators lived by certain code of tenets of business success. His twelve principles are: mission, vision, ambition, sense of direction, discipline, strength, frugality, determination, total commitment, tenacity of purpose, abiding faith in God Almighty and credibility. He said he defined his mission very early, which was to make enough money in life, in order to enjoy his popular delicacy; "*ikokore*" which is a very popular meal among the Ijebus of western Nigeria. According to him, the meal needs to be spiced with several condiments, which only a rich person could afford. The vision of Odutola was to break the back of poverty and emerge one of the richest Yoruba persons in Nigeria. He disclosed that his ambition to make money was anchored on his belief that money is a strong tower in the days of need. To Odutola, credibility is important, because it brings out the true character of a businessman. According to him, "character is power." Mr. Odutola, the first indigenous president of the manufacturers association of Nigeria, lived by those timeless principles. He succeeded in creating one of the largest business conglomerates in Nigeria, including retailing, tire manufacturing, farming, a cattle ranch, educational institutions, and thriving exporting business throughout the British colonial period, and throughout forty years of Nigerian nationhood till 1995 when he bowed to the inevitability of death,. But, in spite of his amazing business exploits, Mr. Odutola was also a politician. In 1956, the traditional council of Ijebu-Ode in western Nigeria unanimously chose him as the *Ogbeni Oja* of the kingdom (literally the prime minister of the Ijebu-Ode traditional council), according to the *Time* magazine.

Mr. Odutola led the agitation for the creation of the Ijebu-Ode town council during the British colonial period, arguing that the population and entrepreneurial spirits of the Ijebu people qualified them for a self-autonomous county. The agitation led to the creation of Ijebu-Ode town council, which later morphed into Ijebu-Ode local government area. Mr. Adeola-Odutola was rewarded by the Ijebus as an adviser to the native authority for his activism. Between 1945, and 1951, he contested, and won a parliamentary seat into the western legislative council, and later became a member of the western region house of assembly between 1945, and on the eve of Nigerian political independence in 1959. He was also a member of the federal House of Representatives in Lagos, between 1952, and 1954, and a senator in Nigeria upper house at independence until 1964 when he left active politics. In some countries, the richest person is also the president or prime minister. The richest person in Ghana, Mr. Kwame Addo-Kuffuor estimated to be worth about $1.2 billion is both a politician and a businessman. As the younger brother of former President John Kuffour (2001-2009), the second democratically-elected president of Modern Ghana in the 4th Republic after President John Rawlings; Kwame, a physician by training was defense secretary for eight years under his elder brother. He was a Member of Parliament representing Manhyia district. Today, Mr. Addo-Kuffuor has successfully combined his thriving medical and business careers with his political career. He has served as the interior secretary, while still pursuing his presidential ambition as the flag bearer of the New Patriotic Party (NPP). Mr. Silvia Berlusconi of Italy, who is the richest man in Italy, was also his country's prime minister at a time. In Ivory Coast, the richest man in the nation, Mr. .Alassane Dramane Ouattara is also the president of the country.

In addition to the proximate relationship between politics and business at the level of actors, there is also institutional nexus between both sectors. The confidence that organization, and successful business corporations such as *Dangote* Group and other local manufacturing concerns instill in foreign investors to come to Nigeria to invest, and the positive image that Mr. Dangote gives to Nigeria in the global community cannot be over-emphasized. If the richest Black person in the world can be found in Nigeria, the obvious logical deduction is that Africa's most populous nation is conducive to conduct business, in spite of the misanthropic activities of the Islamic terrorist Jihadist group, *Boko Haram*. Within Nigeria, the activities at the Nigerian Stock Exchange (NSE) suddenly became bullish immediately after the successful conclusions of the 2011 presidential elections and the election of Mr. Jonathan. Although there were some skirmishes in the northern part of Nigeria shortly after the elections, yet the positive impact on the stock market could not be diminished. As Ms. Arumah Oteh, director-general of the Nigeria's Security and Exchange Commission (SEC) noted, "While effective governance is key to a well-functioning capital market, the Nigerian capital market has, in the last two years, been characterised by governance weaknesses that led to improper behaviours and sharp practices such as insider trading and share price manipulation. We must, therefore, implement the SEC zero tolerance policy in a decisive and far-reaching manner. I am therefore determined to eliminate sharp practices, deter malpractice and change behaviours by ensuring that both the institutional and personal costs of any wrong doing is extremely high. We will ensure high standards in regulatory oversight and enforcement and will name and shame where necessary."

When Dangote cement company, a member of the Dangote conglomerate made a profit of ₦54.51billion (about $369.5million) alone in just three months of 2010, and the same arm of the company recorded a turnover of ₦49.87 billion (about $311.167million) the previous year, then any foreign investor still thinking that Nigeria is a difficult nation to invest in must be kidding. Mr Joseph Makoju, special adviser to Dangote was elated about the impressive turnover of the *Dangote* Group. "This impressive result for 2010 financial year when viewed against the background of the relatively stable environment of 2010 is not unexpected as the supply and cost of major input of cement manufacture such as natural gas, LPFO and diesel were relatively stable."

Here in the United States of America, there is a thin line between politics and business and between politicians and rich business people. It was President Calvin Coolidge, who once stated the obvious osmotic relationship between business and politics when he said, "The chief business of the American people is chiefly business" and the 30th president of the United States was right. Nearly all the 100 U.S Senators are millionaires. American politicians crave the support of rich people, because they need their money for campaign expenses, while business people on the other hand, get access to power and favorable legislations in return. For examples, the lists of the rich people who gave money to the Obama Presidential Campaign Organization in the 2008 elections were a list of; Who's Who in America business and corporate world, even from far-away Africa, politicians gave out to President Obama in the 2008 presidential election.

In the United States, where Nigeria copied the presidential system of government, billionaires are applauded when they give out campaign donations to political parties. Mayor Michael Bloomberg of New York has doled out a total of $784,000 equally to both the Democrats and Republicans for the past ten years. So are billionaires like; Warren Buffet ($127,400); Ted Turner ($391,624); New York financier, George Soros ($1,777,837); real estate mogul, Donald Trump ($813,633); Oprah Winfrey ($19,300); and many others. The largest campaign donations to a political party in the United States today came from the Walton Family, owners of *Wal-Mart*. The five billionaires from the same family; Alice, John, Jim, Robert and Helen have contributed a total of $5,584,951 to both the two political parties, with over sixty-percent of their campaign contributions going to the Republican Party. For instance, Mrs. Linda McMahon, co-owner, World Wrestling Entertainment-(*WWE*) of Stamford, Connecticut will never donate a cent to the Obama Presidential Campaign or Democratic candidates as a matter of principle. All her $53m donations went to the Republican Party. She gave $30,000 in August 2011 to Mr. Mitt Romney toward the 2012 Presidential Election. She spent $40m of her own money to become a Senator under the Republican Party in 2010 and failed. Just as Mrs. McMahon is passionate about the Republican Party, so also is another billionaire; Mr. George Zimmer, founder and chairman of popular clothier; *Men's Warehouse* is passionate about the Democratic Party. His entire $307,000 campaign donation in 2008 went to Mr. Obama.

It is also a known fact that virtually all Hollywood celebrities: actors/actresses, singers, musicians, artists, authors, writers, television producers, fashion designers, film producers etc. are the backbone of the Obama campaign donations, and the Democratic Party in general. From Madonna ($41,000); Eddie Murphy ($30,800); Bruce Springsteen ($24,000); powerful Hollywood couple: Will and his wife, Jada Pinket-Smith ($101,600); to Barbra Streisand ($740,775); Denzel Washington ($30,800); Hollywood mogul, Laser Wasserman ($1,736,400); Quincy Jones ($248,475); and fashion designer, Calvin Klein ($342,350) and many others. These are the Hollywood financial powers of the Democratic Party. In the 2012 presidential elections, billionaires; the Koch Brothers and

Sheldon Adelson made history when they jointly bankrolled the presidential candidacy of Mr. Romney of the Republican Party to the tune of $1billion and their candidate lost to incumbent Barack Obama.

The list of Nigerian millionaires, who have understood the symbiotic relationship between politics and business, especially those in the United States of America; and have played the rules decently through campaign contributions, is long. Take Nigerian-American oil magnate, Mr. Kase Lawal, chairman and chief executive, CAMAC International, Inc. based in Houston, Texas for example. He is a major contributor to the two political parties; Democratic and Republican parties in the United States. In 2011, he cut a hefty check for $35,000 to President Barack Obama Presidential Campaign toward the 2012 presidential campaign. In 2008 presidential election, he gave Mr. Obama $28,000 while he had earlier supported Senator Hilary Clinton presidential campaign with $10,000 during the Democratic Party Presidential Primary. Lawal's political campaign contributions alternate between Republican Party candidates for the state of Texas, and Democratic Party candidates for national elections. In all, the Texas-based multi-millionaire has given out more than $256,000.00 in campaign contribution to state senators, state assembly members, national senators, and presidential candidates of the two parties.

Another Nigerian-American multi-millionaire and "heavy hitter" for President Obama and the Democratic Party is New York-based investment banker, and currently, chairman, Global Investment Partners, Mr. Adebayo Ogunlesi. He has given over $163,600 in campaign donations to President Obama and Democratic Party candidates. Another major political contributor is Mr. Lawal's wife; Eileen Lawal, in the state of Texas. She has given out over $50,000 in political contribution to date, while Kamoru, Mr. Lawal's brother too is also a major campaign fundraiser. There are also other wealthy Africans in the United States, who have contributed significantly to political campaigns. Even Nigerians resident in Nigeria and maintain homes in the United States have contributed to Obama Presidential Campaign; former Governor Orji Kalu of Abia State gave out $10,000.00 from his Potomac, Maryland residence; Senator Ayo Arise donated $2,500.00 from his Lawrenceville, Georgia home; Mr. Mike Adenuga gave out $2,500 toward the presidential campaign of his state of Texas governor, and later President George W. Bush (2000-2008). The second richest and wealthiest man on earth, Mr. Bill Gates of the United States understood the power of wealth to determine public policy when his company, *Microsoft* was under the radar screen of the United States Department of Justice in the 1990's. The billionaire cut two hefty checks for $1m each to the two political parties. The case was amicably resolved between his company, and those corporations accusing the computer giant of violating anti-trust law of the United States.

No wonder billionaire Aliko Dangote too has been heavily involved in the lives of most Nigerian politicians. As he openly admitted, "I am close to people in government, because I am one of the big businessmen in Nigeria. If we don't have the right people there then all the money I have is useless. If the country turns into another Zimbabwe, for example, then I will become a poor person." Although Mr. Dangote cannot be poor anymore in life, but what he was alluding to was that, a government that is anti-business and a country that is not conducive to business, like Robert Mugabe is doing in Zimbabwe, could be very calamitous to every responsible business person in Nigeria. It makes business sense for Dangote to pay more than scant attention to the political direction of Nigeria. He is actively involved in courting the friendships of political leaders, while many aspiring Nigerian politicians also court the friendship and support of the richest Black man in the world. In every plural and participatory democracy; from the United States, UK, Italy, France to India, Brazil, South Korea and Russia, there is a mutual and symbiotic relationship between the corporate and the political worlds.

It was this reality in the world that politicians can, and

should be financially supported by wealthy business people, as is the custom here in the United States, and elsewhere that made Aliko to donate a hefty ₦50million (about $350,000) to the presidential campaign of President Olusegun Obasanjo in 1998. Similarly, in 2003, he gave out ₦1billion (about $7m) and a private aircraft toward the re-election bid of the former president. Other causes of President Obasanjo that Aliko has given out generously included; the former president's presidential library at Abeokuta, western Nigeria; ₦201million (about $1.3million), and another ₦1billion (about $7million) to the building of the national headquarters of Nigeria's ruling party, the People's Democratic Party (PDP), Abuja. To Aliko, every Nigerian should be involved in the nation's democratic process. In many of the world's enduring democracies; the USA, UK, Germany, France etc., there are many advantages for any nation, when rich people participate, either directly or remotely in the democratic process, either as political supporters, campaign donors, or as direct political participants. The advantages that rich people derive from political campaign contribution range from; networking, strong connections, drawing attention to their corporate social responsibilities and philanthropic activities, avenues to enter into joint ventures with other business people to creating opportunities for partnership deals and strategic alliances. Others are; buying influences through visits to political shakers, and movers of the society, fun and displaying our human behavior and unique characteristic as part of the larger social biological organism of the modern society. But it also demonstrates the patriotic zeal and love of rich people toward their nations.

Rich people have a stake in the survival of their nations, because they have a lot to lose in the event of crises, political upheavals and economic dislocations. In Nigeria as elsewhere, the political elites and their business and economic counterparts have a lot at stake in the corporate existence of the most populous nation in the world. According to Aliko; "I believe in Nigeria. I believe there is always going to be Nigeria. My faith and belief in this country is unshakeable. We have to live together in peace and not in pieces." When you own some of the largest companies, own some of the beautiful houses, and you are the largest employer of labor in a nation of 180 million inhabitants, you must be on the qui vive to ensure those who decide who gets what, where, when and how are people of honor who will not upset the status quo ante. "Why are we-(Nigeria) - important in the world today?" Mr. Dangote asked. He provided the answer to his question; "It is because of our population; population and our oil. It is not because the world loves the name Nigeria. No. When was the last time you heard about Kuwait or Brunei? The importance of Nigeria is the market. The population is there. The money is there. It is just a matter of having good entrepreneurs who can push this thing forward..."

This is one of the reasons a wealthy man like Aliko maintains strong relationships with his fellow wealthy Nigerians and political leaders so that Africa's most populous nation will be able to produce nationalistically-committed and patriotically-motivated business/political leaders to provide jobs for Nigerians. No wonder former Nigerian military leader and later re-elected twice as civilian president, Mr. Obasanjo once remarked that, if Nigeria could produce ten Aliko Dangotes, the hydra-headed monster of youth unemployment would be drastically reduced. "Then, I can go to bed and sleep soundly as president," Obasanjo said. Dangote ruffled feathers of the schizoid Nigerian ruling class when he told truth to power at the presidential palace in Abuja the other day; never mind he is part of the infinitesimal powerful Nigerians. Idle hands create opportunities for mischief, he said, and in a nation of nearly 200million where almost half is either unemployed or underemployed, it may degenerate to a level where powerful Nigerians may be too scared of public Nigerians. Because the streams of unemployed Nigerians are idle and hungry and stay awake at night, people like him and Mr. Obasanjo may not be able to go to bed and sleep soundly as Obasanjo would love to. That will be a great migraine for a billionaire who, according to him; goes to bed at 2am and is up at 6am. With much discomportment to his fellow ruling elite, Dangote wanted the Nigerian government to produce more Dangotes so that jobs will be available to many Nigerians and ladders of opportunities will be created for social opportunities and economic justice.

Mr. Dangote says Nigerian politicians need to learn the secrets of business successes from successful Nigerian entrepreneurs, because; both politics and business are not mutually exclusive. When successful business people say, politics is a dirty game and decide not to get involved, the people and the nation suffer, and the ripple effects would be felt by everyone, including business people who maintain stoic aloofness "That is why you end up having wrong materials in politics," according to Dangote. He disclosed that he must befriend politicians in his home country and in Africa, because such synergistic relationships between members of the organized private sector (OPS) and political leaders lead to the business development of the black world. "That is the main reason why people like me should be very friendly with them (politicians and political leaders)," he asserted. His relationship with political leaders, he says is co-terminus with his leadership role in the Nigerian and African society as a foremost industrialist and business mogul. Mr. Dangote, expatiating further, tried to link business people as managers of human beings, while politicians and political leaders are leaders of people. According to him; "...when I come out, it is to assist in running the business of the country. If we do one business, we would be contributing, because we would always be together with them, and I think that is enough; because for a businessman to leave his business for politics is not a good thing for him."

Mr. Dangote, like every Nigerian citizen says he is a political animal, but he is apolitical. Although he supports politicians and those aspiring to lead in Nigeria and other parts of Africa who approach him for support as long as their policies are not anti-business. But not all the aspiring leaders get his support after scrutinizing the political and economic philosophies of such politicians. "The need to create an enabling environment for private enterprise is non-negotiable for any politician wishing to get the financial support of Aliko," a source informed the authors.

A natural political go-to-guy in Africa, but as politicians nuzzle up to him, Dangote disclosed he will never be tempted into dabbling into Nigerian politics, because that is not his calling. "We cannot all be the same thing," he said. "That is why a lot of people are running into business. You have to define whether you want to be a good coach or a good player. It is much better for me as a person to run my business, because everybody cannot be in government," he repeated again. He railed against politics of poverty and personal pecuniary gain, which has manifested since the de-militarization of Nigeria twelve years ago, warning that such a trend, if allowed to continue would destroy Nigeria's nascent democracy.

That sounds like the political philosophy of Oprah Winfrey, the popular African-American woman billionaire and eminently politically-influential American media mogul. Reputed to be, unarguably one of the most influential "go-to" rich people in American politics, the billionaire was once asked why she has not considered direct involvement in American politics, even with calls by some admirers and well-wishers, especially women, on Ms. Winfrey to give the US presidency a try. "No, I think I could have a great influence in politics..." she told editors of *Good Housekeeping* magazine in an interview in October 1995, "But I think that what I do every day has far more impact. I see my TV show as a great forum for teaching; it's the biggest classroom you could ever imagine." After all, who would want to be president when you can make people president and stay behind as a powerful "king (queen)-maker!

As John Travolta, the American actor once said, if Ms. Winfrey asks you to come and see her, you go, no questions asked. She is the queen, the woman president of the United States, period! Aliko Dangote is unquestionably, and an undisputable political "kingmaker" not only in his native

Nigeria, but in other West African and African countries. He is a close chum to virtually all the political leaders in Nigeria. Since Africa's most populous nation returned to participatory American-style presidential democracy twelve years ago, Mr. Dangote has chaired the fundraising committees of the presidential campaigns of all the three post-military administrations of Nigerian Presidents: Mr. Olusegun Obasanjo (1999-2007); the late Mr. Umaru Musa-Yar'Adua (2007-2010), and current Goodluck Jonathan (2011-2015). It is not only Nigerian business that catches cold when Mr. Dangote sneezes; Nigerian politics too catches cold as well. In Nigeria, when it comes to raising cash for political campaign, who you going to call? Mr. Aliko Dangote, of course!

In 1999, shortly after the late Nigerian military dictator, General Sani Abacha was eased out of the way, his then chief of defense; General Abdusalam Abubakar took over as Nigeria's new military strongman. It was Abubakar who conducted another general election after the annulled June 12, 1993 presidential election won by the late Mr. Moshood Abiola. Both Abacha and Abiola died in summer 1998 and former military dictator, retired General Olusegun Obasanjo, who had ruled Nigeria between 1976 and 1979, was brought out of prison to become an elected president on My 29, 1999. Mr. Obasanjo had contested the 1999 presidential election under the platform of the People's Democratic Party (PDP) against his main challenger, Mr. Olu Falae, a retired technocrat, who flagged the presidential candidacy of the Alliance for Democracy (AD). It was obvious that Mr. Dangote would be a major player in the administration of Mr. Obasanjo in post-military Nigeria. After all, the paths of both Obasanjo and Dangote had crossed in the past when young Dangote was learning the ethics of business from his late uncle, Mr. Usman Amaka Dantata. In his second coming as head of state, this time around as an elected president, Mr. Obasanjo decided to make privatization the major fulcrum of his economic policy. It was this economic policy that renewed the old friendships between President Obasanjo of

Nigeria and President Aliko Dangote of *Dangote Group*.

At independence in 1960, Nigeria was at quandary on her economic philosophy at a time the world was bifurcated into two economic systems: capitalism or socialism. The East-West ideological war known as the Cold War dominated the global system as both the United States and Old Russia known as Union of Soviet Socialist Republics (USSR) jostled for influence around the world. As a former British colony, Nigeria seemed to adopt a mixed economic system where public utilities such as water, electricity, telephone, etc. were run by the government, while the private sector provided some services as well. The first six years of Nigerian independence, between 1960 and 1966, a federal government existed in Lagos, which was the nation's administrative capital, while three regional governments operated in the north, west and east. The Northern People's Congress (NPC) led by Mr. Ahmadu Bello with administrative capital in Kaduna controlled much of the then northern region with minority parties, such as the United Middle Belt Congress (UMBC) led by the late Mr. Joseph Tarka of Benue, the Northern Elements Progressive Union (NEPU) led by the late Mr. Aminu Kano of Kano and few others in the northern east zone. In western Nigeria, the Action Group (AG) led by the late Mr. Obafemi Awolowo was in control with the ancient city of Ibadan as administrative capital. The National Council of Nigeria Congress (NCNC) led by the late Mr. Michael Okpara controlled much of eastern Nigeria with the seat of government in Enugu.

The 1959 general elections held to usher Nigeria into political freedom did not produce a majority winner in the federal elections, between the three main dominant parties: NPC, AG and NCNC. Since Nigeria adopted the Westminster parliamentary system, Mr. Abubakar Tafawa-Balewa, leader of the NPC in Lagos was chosen as the nation's prime minister, while Mr. Nnamdi Azikiwe, leader of the NCNC became the nation's president, because of the political alliance entered into by both the NPC and NCNC. Mr. Obafemi Awolowo's AG decided to lead the opposition in the federal parliament with Awolowo as leader. The three regions literally operated as semi-autonomous entities and they ran their governments from the natural resources they sold as exports in their various regional zones. The AG was led by Mr. Akintola as regional governor in Ibadan immediately Mr. Awolowo moved to Lagos as leader of opposition. The government was able to transform the region from the revenues realized from cocoa, the dominant economic mainstay of western Nigeria. The AG government introduced free primary education for all children in the zone, free medical care, awarded scholarships to well-deserving and brilliant young men, and women in local, and foreign institutions of higher learning. The NPC government of Mr. Ahmadu Belo in Kaduna relied on groundnuts, mostly in the ancient city of Kano referred to as the famous Kano groundnut pyramid, tin ore in Jos and cotton as some of the export products to run its affairs. In eastern Nigeria, palm oil, timber and other commodities and natural resources were the sources of government funds by the Michael Okpara-NCNC regional government. In 1963, the NPC and NCNC federal coalition government teamed up to break the monopoly of Awolowo's AG in western Nigeria by creating the mid-western Nigeria with administrative capital in Benin City. During this period, oil had not become the mainstay of Nigerian economy.

The 1964 general elections led to nationwide crises, especially in western Nigeria. Mr. Samuel Akintola, as the regional governor rebelled against the leader of his party, Mr. Awolowo after Akintola lost his nomination as the AG candidate in the 1964 general elections. Mr. Akintola decided to break away from the AG, and set up his own political party known as the United Democratic Party (UDP). To ensure he remained in power as governor, he formed an alliance with the federal government of NPC of Mr. Abubakar Tafawa-Balewa which gave him tactical, logistic, and security support. At the end of the exercise, Akintola's UDP "won" the regional elections in western Nigeria. The AG cried "foul" and resorted to violence which threw the nation into political

299

turmoil. Meanwhile, the Balewa federal government cracked down on the leaders of the AG accusing them of planning to unseat the federal government. Some of the AG leaders were arrested, prosecuted, and sent to jail with all of them serving various prison sentences. Mr. Obafemi Awolowo was sent to a -10-year jail term, and was sent to Calabar prison in eastern Nigeria. Mr. Anthony Enahoro, who ran to London, UK on political asylum after alleging he would not receive fair trial at the treason case was repatriated back to Nigeria by the British government, and handed over to the Balewa federal government to face trial. He bagged ten years prison sentence. Other AG leaders were tried and sent to prison with Mr. Obafemi Awolowo. It was the crisis ignited by the western Nigerian political topsy-turvy that led to the military *coup d'état* of January 15, 1966, the counter coup of July 1966, and the installation of General Yakubu Gowon as Nigeria's second military head of state.

We have gone into these details in order for reader to understand, and know how privatization of public utilities began in Nigeria, which led to cozy relationships between businessmen and women, and politicians. Following the discovery of oil, the military regimes that ruled Nigeria between 1966 and 1979 operated a highly regimented and centrally-controlled administrative system, whereby the Nigerian federal government controlled virtually everything; from electricity, water, telephone, airlines to universities and colleges, public transportation, even sewage collection. For example, the Gowon military regime anchored its resolve to control virtually every sector of the Nigerian economy on the need to maintain Nigeria's fragile unity following the three-year Nigerian-Biafra civil war of 1967-1970. For nine years, the Gowon military regime controlled everything, literally everything in the Nigerian economy. By 1975 when Gen. Gowon was ousted, his military successor, General Murtala Ramat Muhammad went over the top in centralizing everything in the hand of the federal government; the regime acquired the Nigerian Television Authority *(NTA)*, the Nigerian *Daily Times*, all colleges, polytechnics, regional schools and universities in the country. As every elementary student of economics knows, when government controls everything in an economy, inefficiency, bad management and corruption set in. The mindset of workers in government-controlled and government-owned industries is that, such companies belong to the "government"-that nebulous concept that most Nigerians still do not understand-and what belongs to the government belongs to all of us, and what belongs to every citizen apparently does not belong to no one. This is the genesis of the nation's crippling, chronically-run and inefficiently-managed public utilities: water supply, telephone, electricity etc. By the time Mr. Olusegun Obasanjo came to power twenty years after he ruled Nigeria as military head of state, his first priority was to animate some of the foundering public and government-owned companies, and offer them for sale to private investors in Nigeria, and foreigners under strict guidelines to be followed by the newly created Bureau of Public Enterprises (BPE).Mr. Dangote became a major beneficiary of some of the government-owned corporations sold to private entrepreneurs during the privatization exercise.

As it has been indicated earlier on, Mr. Dangote has challenged anyone to prove there were any under-the-table deals in the whole exercise. "We are large and have been in business for long. If there was any corruption, the Nigerian media would have discovered it," he asserted. "Many people may be thinking that we would not be where we are today, if not for government, but we have been in this thing for over thirty years."

By 2010, it was obvious that President Jonathan would throw his hat into the presidential race. In September 2010, he made his intention known and, on Saturday September 18, 2010 at the Eagle Square, Abuja, President Jonathan officially declared his decision to contest for the 2011 presidential election. Thereafter, President Jonathan set up his presidential campaign finance and fundraising committee and chose Mr. Obafemi Otudeko as chairman, retired Nigerian Police Boss; Mr. Mike Okiro headed the security committee with Mr. Ebenezer Babatope as head of inter-arty relations committee. The committee that would raise money for Jonathan's campaign, known as donor committee was headed almost expectedly by Mr. Aliko Mohammad Dangote with the following rich Nigerians as members; Mr. Mike Adenuga, chairman of *Glo* and Nigeria's second billionaire according to the *Forbes* list of world billionaires in 2011. Mr. Tony Elumelu, a retired banker, another Nigerian billionaire, Mr. Femi Otedola worth $1.2billion; the founder of *Zenith* Bank and its first chief executive, Mr. Jim Ovia, Sayyu Dantata, and Mr. Dangote's cousin, Mr. Kola Salako, a businessman, Mr. Kashim Bukar, Mr. Emeka Offor and Mr. Dahiru Mangal, a friend of the late President Umaru Musa Yar'Adua. Just as he gave money to the presidential campaigns of Obasanjo in 1999 and 2007 and supported his administration, Mr. Dangote also supported the administration of the late President Umaru Musa Yar'Adua, and he is doing same to the current Nigerian President, Mr. Jonathan. To Aliko, it is the Nigerian nation that is uppermost in his calculations and not a particular individual, or a particular political party. "We need peace and stability in Nigeria, we also need justice and equity," Mr. Dangote said. "Nigeria can be greater than she is right now, if all hands are on deck to re-position the country, by installing good, and transparent people in government, and support them to deliver. I have no doubt that Nigeria is the best place to invest in the world. We have the resources and everything it takes to lead the Black world."

CHAPTER 10
ALIKO IN THE COMPANY OF RICH MEN AND WOMEN

THERE ARE many rich people in Nigeria. Nigeria is acknowledged as one of the richest nations in Africa, and one of the medium economies in the world, because of her abundant oil deposits. There are three Nigerian businessmen that have appeared in the *Forbes* list of billionaires. One Nigerian woman, Ms. Folorunsho Alakija, an oil magnate, fashion designer and philanthropist has also been identified as a billionaire, the first Nigerian-born, black woman billionaire. For examples, Mr. Mike Adenuga, the Lagos-based telecommunication magnate has appeared with Aliko as a billionaire worth $2billion, while Mr. Femi Otedola, a close chum of Aliko appeared once, and has since disappeared from the *Forbes* list. There are many Nigerians on the *Forbes* list of millionaires. But in spite of the resources of the Nigerian nation, the wealth has not trickled down to the vast majority of the Nigerian people. According to available statistics, an average Nigerian lives on less than one dollar a day, while a tiny elite, about one percent, controls more than 90 percent of Nigeria's wealth. Mr. Aliko Dangote has riled against the inequality in the Nigerian society in many of his speeches. He is also seen among the tiny plutocratic elite to change the ugly situation in one of the most volatile nations on earth. So why is Aliko seen among fellow rich men and women in Nigeria and around the world?

Mr. Dangote has demonstrated that making money does not lie in other places of the world but in Nigeria- his country- and business opportunities abound in Africa. When he surrounds himself with fellow Black (African) millionaires, he is indirectly calling on them to partner with him to develop the nation and the African continent. There is a local adage in Nigeria that says, "What you are fretting to go and purchase in Sokoto town is already in your *sokoto* which is your pocket." In every nation, community, society, village or hamlet, there is always a group of people that determines what goes on in that locale. This elite is called a "class" by political scientists and political economists. Those who do not belong to this tiny minority, but powerful group also constitute a "class" and from the time human beings introduced commerce, and the use of money into their affairs, and instituted what today is referred to as "government" these two "classes" have always butted heads. This is evident, because the interests of both groups are mutually exclusive though academicians have identified a third group, which exists between the two groups known as the; "middle class." Every society in the world, no matter its level of political and socio-economic development comprises these three groups, and they coexist together, albeit in tense and sometimes adversarial atmosphere. Every member of the three groups gravitates towards each other, and this has been so since the advent of human society. In hierarchical feudal society, there was a line that demarcated these three classes, especially in Western Europe where marriage was even forbidden between members of the different classes. In other words, members of the rich upper crust consort among themselves, while those who belong to the lower rung of the social order also consorted among themselves. Those dividing lines seemed to have disappeared in many societies of the world, and Nigeria too.

In Africa, there were some certain demarcations too and different social, political and economic ladders exist among members of the society. Among the Yoruba, no one could be a king, if the person was not born into royalty, and there are distinguishing names for scions of the royal class. Names among Yoruba people depict either the political, social, or economic pedigrees of members of the society. Among the Hausa-Fulani, class matters when it comes to choosing an emir, or king; while religion too also plays a major part in social class relations. The *"talakawas,"* or poor peasants are always in the majority in many Hausa-Fulani states. However, these class distinctions today are not much pronounced, because of productive activities which have created level playing fields for all members of the modern society. Nevertheless, there are extant structures that still divide societies into class categories, even though such bifurcations are fast disappearing. In the United States for example, there are many classes, yet those who have impacted on the growth of the largest economy of the world are not scions of the nobility but naturally-gifted people who put their creative ingenuities to use. This is what defines America's exceptionalism.

There is trust among the rich; and rich people tend to blend easily among themselves. The rich do not want to let off their guards that there is no animosity between the different classes in the Nigerian society. There is tension in the inequitable distribution of wealth in the Nigerian society that often scares the rich. The poor in Nigeria work at cross-purposes, and do not have, or share the same characteristics, and hold to shared benefits. Nigeria is still deeply a religious and highly superstitious society. Finally, the political class has succeeded in bonding with the members of the economically privileged few, who know it is better to maintain organic linkages for shared beneficial interests, or they would perish together. Consequently; there is shared affinity between both classes. In Aliko's world, he envisages a Nigeria where the upper crust and the middle class can work together for the benefit of all members of the Nigerian society. He has started this in his vast business empire where every member of the Nigerian disparate ethnic groups and religious affiliations work together for the common good.

MONEY IS GOOD, POVERY IS A CURSE

"I think I have to be rated by the *Forbes* magazine first before I can be called the richest man in Africa,"---*Aliko Dangote*

SOME MILLIONAIRES and billionaires live cheaply. You see some of them and wonder if truly, they are millionaires and billionaires. Take Mr. Howard Hughes for example. One of the richest men in America in the last century, but his eccentric attitudes to wealth pissed a lot of people off. Aliko Dangote is a billionaire. He has worked hard for his wealth and he is not a nerd. Consequently, it is not all work, work, and work but no play for the richest Black person in the world. The rich people of the world have money, and plenty of it, which affords them the opportunity to indulge their fancies within reasonable limits as their crowded engagements afford them to spend their precious time. Mr. Branson has some wacky sense of recreation which he indulges in that mystifies many people. He is an aviation enthusiast, and has carried his passion to a ridiculously high level by planning to circle the earth four times as a balloonist. He has already laid a world record as the only person in the world to cross both the Atlantic and Pacific Oceans as a balloonist. On Christmas Day in 1998, he would have added another feather to his cap as the first human being to circumnavigate the world with his team, but the voyage was aborted at the Pacific Ocean by bad weather. His main rivals and balloonists in this weird "sport" are; Bertrand Piccard and Brian Jones. Billionaire Soros envisages a world of human rights, open discourse, and eradication of inequality through his "Open Society;" Oprah is monomaniacal in her aggressive empowerment of women, especially in the developing world. Warren Buffett wants his co-billionaires to sign pledges to give away their several billions for worthy causes around the world.

Mr. Billionaire Aliko is a not social hermit. In spite of having his hands in numerous business pies, the richest Black man on the face of the planet still socializes. Aliko attends night parties across Nigeria thrown by select members of the Nigerian upper class. He also attends weddings of few elites with political connections and business potentials. The favorite sport of Aliko is the sport of Polo. Polo is often referred to as the past time of the superbly rich, and in Nigeria, the sport, called "sports king," for its sheer extravagance, is mostly played by the well-heeled who can afford to buy ponies from abroad, especially Argentina. A typical pony goes for about $30,000.00 and when you add the overhead expenses for taking care of the expensive animal, you realize that playing polo in Nigeria is for the superbly-wealthy folk. You need at least three servants to take care of the horses, and of course they have to be fed, groomed and looked after including the monthly salaries of the trainer/groomers. Do not forget too that medical attention is needed for the horses to keep them fit.

Mr. Dangote is one of such rich men in Nigeria who could afford these expensive animals, and also many other Nigerians who have taken the sport as their past-time. The game of polo runs in the veins of the Dantatas and of course, Aliko Dangote still maternally carries the DNA of the Dantatas. His uncle, the late Usman Amaka Sanusi Dantata, was an avid polo player during his life time. He once bought 70 Argentine ponies to Nigeria. Initially, he wanted just 10 of the beautiful animals, but the Argentine seller/owner insisted that all the seventy ponies had bonded and became one family so he did not want them separated. Usman bought all the 70 and brought them to Nigeria. Most of them graced several polo games in Lagos, Kaduna and Kano before he decided to re-sell 60 of the ponies for good money. It is no surprise then that the favorite pastime of Africa's richest person and the richest Black person in the world is polo. What is polo as many novices in the world would ask? Polo was introduced into Nigeria by the British colonial authorities in the 1930s and for a while, it was the exclusive preserve of the British colonialists. The Nigerian Polo Society did not admit any Black Nigerian, until two years to the granting of political independence when Nigerian millionaire,

"Baba Olomi" Mr. Oladele Da Rocha Afoda was granted membership. The colonialists were going home anyway, so the indigenous rich Nigerians took over in 1960. Today, the negligible few rich Nigerians who want to announce their arrivals into millionaire club do so by joining the elite Lagos Polo Country Club.

As Dangote is competitive in the business world, so also he displays his competitive spirit on the Polo playing ground. In 2011, he assembled a formidable team of Messrs. Ahmadu Umar, Hakeem Ashiru, Obafemi Otudeko and Bowale Jolaosho known as the *Team Dangote Quartet* and toughened it out with *Team Churchward* comprising Messrs. Adamu Yaro, Baba Dangote, Aliko's younger brother, Tunde Karim and Tobi Edun. It was during the Lagos Polo President's Cup which took place before a capacity crowd of polo enthusiasts, the rich and famous of the elite game at the Ribadu Road Polo Ground, Obalende on Lagos Island. Though Aliko led *Team Dangote,* but just as he sometime does, he yielded the captainship to his fellow rich man, the chairman of *Honey Well* Corporation, former chairman and managing director of *First Bank* of Nigeria, former president, Nigerian Stock Exchange (NSE), Mr. Obafoluke Otudeko. The trio of Ahmadu, Hakeem and Bowale held the back for the "Field Marshall," while Aliko was the charging bull in the fiercely contested game. *Team Churchward* gave a good account of the team during the contest. Mr. Adamu Yaro was the captain of the opposition squad, charging and raging against *Team Dangote,* ably supported by the trio of Baba Dangote, Tunde and the youngest athlete in the pitch, Tobi Edun. In the competition, Mr. Dapo Ojora, another magus of elite sport in Nigeria was the commentator at the fiercely-contested tournament. The sport's enthusiasts watched the tournament, which included Senator Tokumboh Ogunbanjo, Audu Oshogwemoh, Sani Dangote and Bayo Amusan, past presidents of Lagos Polo Club. At the end of the competition, *Team Dangote* managed a razor-thin victory of five- and -a - half –over- five against *Teach Churchward.*

On the social scene, Dangote is a member of the exclusive

boat club known as *Aquamarine* owned by his friend, the former chief executive officer, and managing director of *Zenith* Bank Mr. Jim Ovia. The richest Black man is also a member of one of the oldest indigenous socio-cultural clubs in Nigeria, the *Ikoyi Club*. An ardent supporter of the *Arsenal Football Club* of England; there were reports sometime in 2010 that he was planning to buy some shares in the popular English football club. But Aliko debunked the rumor, "I'm a fan of Arsenal and the owner is a friend, but I am not planning to have a stake in the football club for now." Billionaire Aliko Dangote is a natty dresser like Oprah Winfrey. As a TV personality, Ms. Winfrey maintains expensive wardrobes, designer clothes, and some of the most expensive and largest homes in Chicago and California. Mr. Aliko has homes in Lagos, Abuja, Kaduna, Kano, Port Harcourt, London, and the United States, and in other choicest capital cities of the world. His choice property in the exclusive Maitama area of Abuja, Nigeria is a sight to behold. He owns properties also in Dubai, Saudi Arabia, and in many of the cities where he owns companies; from Abidjan, Ivory Coast, Accra, Ghana to Lusaka, Zambia, Johannesburg, South Africa and other places. Mr. Dangote has several aircrafts in his fleet, which help him to meet deadlines while crisscrossing Nigeria, Africa and other parts of the world where his many businesses are located. There are two of such expensive aircrafts. He owns a yacht, which is counted among his several "toys." Some of his children live in Atlanta Georgia, New York and Miami Florida. He maintains offices in London, the UK; Jeddah in Saudi Arabia, South Africa, Dubai and many other places around the world. He is a Jazz enthusiast and drinks red wine occasionally.

One of Aliko's "toys" a customized Bombadier private jet worth $45million purchased in May 2010

Aliko and one of his daughters at an event in Lagos, Nigeria. © Ovation,
Lagos

Top: Fatima, the eldest
daughter of Aliko the
US$billion Babe who
currently lives in the
US.

○ Fatimat Aliko Dangote, the USS Babe now lives in the United States with her husband
and child Photo Credit Phe

Bottom: Aliko bought
himself this $45m toy
as a birthday gift in
2010

Aliko's Bombardier, one of his "toys" delivered to Lagos April 2010 Photo Credit Dangote Group

The Billionaire stepping out of one of his "toys" in style. All Photo Credits: Dangote Group, Nigeria

Inside Aliko's Bombadier: Money is good

o   Money is good, especially inside a US$50m Bombardier jet

Inside Aliko Dangote's US$50m Bombardier Private Jet Photo Credit Dangote Group

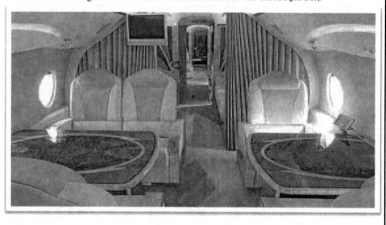

o   Inside Aliko's Bombardier private jet

More from inside Bombadier. Life is even better when you have money and plenty of it like Aliko.

o   Bombardier Jet worth US$50m that Aliko bought for himself as a birthday gift at 50 years old. Photo Credits by Dangote Group

Top: Bombadier, the costliest private jet in the world. Bottom: Aliko with Mr. Jonathan Dimbleby of British Broadcasting Corporation inside his Bombardier flying to Obajan Cement Factory, the largest in West Africa. ©BBC of London, UK

Aliko and Dimbleby at Obajana Cement Factory in central Nigeria.
©BBC of London, UK

CHAPTER 11
ALIKO THE FAMILY MAN

THE MEMBERS of the billionaires club of the world have certain behavioral characteristics about marriage and children. Most have few children, which makes one to wonder why they maintain small family when they can easily support harems and large families. The ten richest men of the world all have not more than five children: Mr. Helu was married to his late wife Soumaya Domit for 32 years, until her death in 1999, and the marriage was blessed with six adult children. Since his wife's death, the 71-year old richest person on earth, worth $74billion has not re-married. Bill and Melinda Gates have three children. The Oracle of Omaha, and the second richest person in America, and fourth richest person in the world got married to Susan Thompson, his first wife of 52 years until she died in 2004. The first marriage was blessed with three children: Susan, Howard and Peter. The 81-year old billionaire remarried in 2006 to Astrid Menks but Buffett has stopped having children. Mr. Arnault, the tenth richest person in the world, and the third richest person in Europe, has five children. Mr. Larry Ellison, co-founder of *Oracle* worth $39.5billion has two children.

The richest man in the UK, Indian-born Lakshmi Mittal, and second richest in Europe, and sixth richest in the world is not even married; but has two children. The seventh, eighth, ninth and tenth richest persons in the world; Spanish fashion businessman, Amacio Ortega; Brazilian oil and gold magnate, Eike Batista worth: $30 billion; the 54-year old richest man in India, Mukesh Ambani worth: $27 billion; and the only woman billionaire worth $ 26.5 billion among the top ten billionaires of the world, Mrs. Christy Walton, the widow of John, the first son of Sam Walton, the founder of *Wal-Mart* who died in a plane crash in Jackson, Wyoming in 2005 have 3, 2, 3 and I children respectively. The German billionaire, Michael Otto has two children. Even among African-American (Black) billionaires, they share the same lifestyles of, one or two wives and few children. For instance, Oprah Winfrey, the richest Black woman in the world does not have a child. She is not even "married," (but has a male companion, she is not gay, mind you!) with all her wealth, and never regrets a bit. All the 14 billionaires in Africa; eight Egyptians, four South Africans, and two Nigerians also keep to this tradition, thus deconstructing the notion that most Africans keep large families. Even those of them that are Moslems do not have large families: maximum of four wives and many children- which is permitted by their religion. Take the Three Sawaris Brothers of Egypt- Nassef, Naguib, and Sannih - all billionaires worth total of $13.8billion. They are Coptic Christians, and they keep small families. The Three Mansour Brothers of Egypt; who are also billionaires: Mohammed, Yassen and Yousseff-worth total of $6.1 billion have 2, 4 and 5 children respectively, while Mohammed Al-Fayed worth $1.2 billion has 5 children. These are all Moslems. Mr. Patrice Motsepe, the only Black billionaire South African worth $3.3billion has three children.

It is not surprising therefore that Mr. Dangote; with his billion dollars wealth has consistently maintained one wife at a time. He has three grown up children from his fourth wife. Since his marriage to his first wife in May 1977, Aliko Dangote has been married to three other women in 35 years. He is permitted by his religion to have a maximum of four wives. He could have more, if he is able to provide for them, and you bet; he is capable of providing for all his wives and children, but unlike most polygamists in Africa and elsewhere, Aliko is a serial monogamist rather than being a polygamist. Although investigations by the authors revealed that Aliko

Dangote also has other children in addition to Halima, Fatima and Sadia "officially" listed as his three children, he does that when referring to his current wife. There are also; Salma and Zainab, who are currently living in the United States. Aliko's second daughter, who wedded in Kano two years ago, has since given Aliko his first grand-daughter. The daughter and her family live in the United States too, while some of Aliko's biological children live in the United Kingdom. In all, the richest Black man currently has 15 children. He has also been rumored to have fathered some children from other women in Nigeria and the UK.

Why do most rich men have small families? Ms. Sarah Curman is the founder, owner and chief executive officer of the UK-based *My Wardrobe* which caters to the fashion taste of elite professional women. As she narrated her story to Richard Quest on *CNN the* Boss on Sunday July 31, 2011, her family suffered while she was setting up the successful Internet-based retail outlet. "My relationship suffered, my love life suffered and I had to decide which of the two most important engagements in my life: Jake, my son and my other 'baby,' mywardrobe.co should be my focus." Rich men and women of the world make a lot of "sacrifices" especially their relationships with family members. Dangote has been able to achieve the balancing act of juggling business, family and parenting at the same time, but more than anything else, his love life has suffered considerably as he is always on the go all the time. This is why he has not been able to manage his love life and that has accounted for his marriages to 4 women.

With all his billions, it has not been smooth-sailing for Nigeria's first "official" billionaire and richest black man. Dangote has tasted life's adversities like the rest human beings on planet earth. He has been sorrowful and sad. Equally, he has his own share of life's ups and downs. Like the near aircraft mishap that occurred a cough away to his 51st birthday in 2008 over the Angolan air space on his return trip from South Africa, where he had gone to sign some business deals. It was a period the verdict had just come out from the *Forbes* magazine celebrating the richest man in Africa. He was worth "only" $3.3billion then.

He was returning from a business trip to Johannesburg, South Africa in one of his private jets when trouble started. Aliko and his business team had barely left the South African airspace when his private pilot announced that one of the aircraft's engines had developed faults. Traveling at over 40,000 feet above sea level as they entered into the Angolan airspace, every member of his entourage began to pray. Mr. Dangote narrated the ugly incident; "The plane was coming from South Africa. The engine problem developed about 138 miles away from Luanda, because we were passing Luanda to come to Nigeria. The plane was vibrating. It was terrible. It was a very bad experience. The pilot was calm. We were all calm." He said he directed the pilot to make an emergency landing at the Augustino Neto Airport, Luanda. Luckily, they were able to make it safely to the Angolan capital, but two minutes after landing, the second engine of the private jet stopped working. The attitude of Aliko Dangote to the inevitability of death is philosophical. Like every mortal, who faces the distinct possibility of death one day, he said, death does not scare him. "Death can come any time. Even if you are in your bedroom, once it is your time to go, you will go," he said.

Ironically, Aliko has had two bouts with near-fatal air crashes in the past, making the Angolan near-tragedy his third experience. Again, he narrated the earlier two incidents. "I have experienced plane crash twice. We had one in London, I think in January or March 1983. We landed at the end of the runway. Everybody escaped, apart from the co-pilot. The co-pilot got paralyzed. That was actually my first aircraft. We had a crash-landing, and the plane got burnt actually. But we all escaped. Nine of us escaped. According to aviation experts, we were very lucky, because it was one of the bad (air) accidents that people hardly escaped from. The second plane crash involved *Hamzair* when they (the now defunct airline) newly started operation. It was the first flight in Kano. And ironically, it was their last one." On those occasions, Aliko did nothing, but pray. He said as a businessman, he travels frequently, and there is no fear of death in his veins, once he has taken all precautions to ensure his personal safety, and those who accompany him on his numerous business trips. "What can you do other than to pray? In such a situation you have nothing to do than to pray, and you think of your family. As a businessman, if you put a lot of fear inside you, then you won't be able to transact any business. In modern day business, you have to travel quite extensively," he said. The ugly incident made headlines news, but Aliko Dangote took the incident in its strides, preferring not to comment. In his philosophical calmness, he has always insisted that "Life is transient and unpredictable." The attitude of Dangote to life and the inevitable mortality of every human being are similar to what his grandfather, Sanusi Alhassan Dantata believed. According to the iconic industrialist and renowned West African kola nut merchant during his 82 years on earth; "Our destiny lies in the hands of Allah; we don't know when our time would come, but once it comes, there is nothing you can do, but submit to it."

Aliko is a realist. He has been bereaved, betrayed and disappointed and suffered unhappiness too like other humans. He lost one of his younger brothers in a plane crash on January 17, 1996. The presidential aircraft was conveying the first son of the late Nigerian military dictator, Gen Sani Abacha from Lagos to Kano. The young man, Ibrahim Abacha, 28, was killed with fourteen of his friends on board, including Aliko's brother. His grandfather's death the following year was also painful. Mr Sanusi Dantata died at the age of 82 in 1997. Aliko also felt some pains when he was removed in March 2010 as president of the Nigerian Stock Exchange barely a year to his tenure. Similarly, he was deeply touched by the tragic death of former President Umaru Musa Yar'Adua in 2010. With all his billions, his love overtures to one of the daughters of the late President Umaru Yar'Adua of Nigeria was rebuffed in 2009, and the billionaire did not take kindly to being spurned by women. But the lady, Miss Nafisa Yar'Adua rejected Aliko's offer, because she claimed to have been a close friend to Halima, one of Aliko's daughters. The president's daughter later got married to Mr. Isa Yuguda, the governor of Bauchi State in northern Nigeria.

Mr. Dangote was very embarrassed few years ago by the news reports that he was a debtor to some financial institutions during a high profile publication by Nigeria's apex bank; the Central Bank of Nigeria. It is very difficult for the *Iroko* tree to suddenly fall, according to an African adage. Its tap root is so deep on the soil, and its sheer size could withstand all kinds of adversities. Indeed, the *Iroko* tree is compared to the elephant in the jungle, so many Nigerians were aghast when, in the fall of 2009; Nigerian newspapers reported that Mr. Dangote owed billions of loans to some indigenous banks. To its rue, the Central Bank of Nigeria later retracted the publication. It made a mistake by assuming that the name of the "golden child" of Nigeria was on the board of a company of someone with similar name on the board of another company owned by one of his relatives, where Aliko was not a shareholder. "We don't owe a dime, zany, nothing to any bank, any financial institution, either here in Nigeria, or anywhere in the world," Aliko thundered furiously, warning the Central Bank of Nigeria of the error in the publication. "This is not a company built on bank loans. They better straighten out their books." The CBN ate the humble pie later by apologizing to the Richest Black man in the world for the slip-up after the billionaire threatened to sue the newspapers and the CBN for libelous publication.

According to Dangote while reacting to the embarrassment; "For the *Oceanic* Bank debt, we've sent a check to the bank, and they've collected it and have given us a receipt that they have it." Dangote officials later clarified that Dangote Industries Ltd. had paid *Oceanic* Bank ₦3.1 billion (about $22m) for its debt plus other fees. The time the debt was paid was not disclosed by the officials of *Oceanic* Bank, as some of the spokes persons in the bank insisted it was not their custom to discuss personal details of their customers on the pages of newspapers. An official with the Nigerian apex bank said that there may have been mistakes in the debtors list, and that as it was for debts not paid through the end of May, some debtors may have settled their loans in the interim. "I don't think they understand the consequences of what they've done," Mr. Dangote said. "The Central Bank should have at least checked with people before going to press. For a group like ours, two and a half billion N aira, that is actually just about 10% of our cement turnover per month. We're a well-diversified organization," he said. One complication that emanated from the so-called list of bank debtors released by the Central Bank to Nigerian newspapers was that, Aliko Dangote was linked with another company owned separately by one of his family members with the same last name. He was also pained by the media war ignited by his disagreement with his business pal, Mr Femi Otedola, a fellow billionaire according to the *Forbes*. The feud between him and his billionaire pal, Femi Otedola soon turned into a raucous meme in Nigeria's social mediascape. Aliko, media shy and humble to a fault, the various news reports flying in the local newspapers, especially on the Internet touched his raw nerves, but as it is his custom, he shrugged it off and made up with Mr Otedola. Both are billionaires!

THE RELIGIOUS ALIKO MOHAMMED DANGOTE

ALIKO MOHAMMED Dangote was born a Moslem. His religious obligations date back to the first generation of his great grandfather, the legendary Mr. Alhassan Dantata, who built the wealth of the Dantata family. He died two years before young Aliko was born, but his religious piety runs in the veins of his first great grandchild, and the richest person in Nigeria, West Africa, Africa and the Black world. Mr. Dangote takes his religion very seriously. He prays five times daily in accordance with the fundamentals of Islam. Curiously, in all his business undertakings, and with his hands in virtually all Nigeria's and Africa's business pies, Dangote has steered clear of conventional banking.

Since he shut down his merchant bank-Liberty Bank- in the 1990's during the regime of former Nigerian military dictator, General Sani Abacha, he has deliberately chosen not to open his own bank. Although he mentions three Nigerian banks he is closely associated with, but according to him, "I do not go to all the banks, only some. And if you find me in any function organized by any of these banks, it is a testimony that such a bank is strong and has good growth prospect." It is an open secret that many of the bank chairmen and directors are his friends. Many are wondering if this "aversion" to investing in the banking sector is because of his religious beliefs, because come to think of it, Dangote believes in lending out money without charging interest. He does not charge interest for money loaned to people, in accordance with his Islamic belief. It stands to reason why Dangote is one of the supporters of the introduction of Islamic banking by the Central Bank of Nigeria. Islamic banks do not charge interest on loans, which makes the unique banking system attractive to business people all over the world, and hopefully, in Nigeria too. As someone once said, money has no color or religion, and as it has happened in Europe and elsewhere, Islamic banking has been embraced by Christians and Moslems, including adherents of other religions.

Mr. Dangote has also discharged other religious obligations as a devout Moslem. He has embarked on Holy Pilgrimage to the holy lands of Mecca and Medina numerous times, in accordance with the Islamic injunction on Hajj. His great grandfather was one of the earliest Moslems to embark on Hajj as far back as the 1900's. It is an open secret in Kano that Aliko's great-grandfather was the first Kano industrialist to set up the Kano Trading Company, an association that served as a platform for all Hausa-Fulani traders in Old Kano toward presenting a common front to protect their business interests. In addition, the association was also responsible for making funds available to prospective traders in the ancient city. One of the achievements of the association was the establishment of a weaving mill in Old Kano during the lifetime of the great industrialist. Aliko Dangote has imbibed these sterling qualities from his great-grandfather, both as an industrialist, who has assisted many Kano indigenes to find their financial and business footing; in addition to supporting the development of Qur'anic education. The Kano Pilgrims Society, the brain child of his great-grandfather continues to benefit from financial assistance from the billionaire.

Every year, Aliko Dangote sponsors many Moslem pilgrims to Mecca and Medina, a tradition he inherited from his great-grandfather; Mr. Alhassan Dantata and his grandfather, Mr. Sanusi Dantata. Every year during the annual celebration of the Moslem Eid-Il-Kabir, a herd of cattle are slaughtered at the houses of Aliko Dangote at Karim Kotun in Lagos Island, his mansion in Abuja and his houses in his ancestral home of Kano. During these celebrations, Moslems come from far, and near to eat, and pray without discrimination, and adherents of other faith are welcome.

The open-handedness and large-heartedness of Aliko Dangote are rooted in his strict Islamic upbringing. The corporate social responsibility of his company was also derived from the religious background of Africa's richest man. The *Dangote Group* was awarded the, "Sponsor of the Year in Africa," in 2011 in recognition of the various projects the conglomerate had sponsored across the African continent by the South Africa-based *African Investor*. Other winners presented with awards were; the Zambia-owned Copper belt Energy Corporation (CEC), Plc which bagged, *"Developer of the Year in Africa,"* Stanbic IBTC Bank was presented with the, *"Bank Arranger of the Year Award;"* while the Development Bank of Southern Africa won the, *"Regional Project of the Year Award,"* because of the bank's Outstanding Kasumbalesa Border Post Project.

323

Being decorated with the highest honor in Nigeria by President Goodluck Jonathan © Vanguard, Lagos

Stressing a point during an interview in Nigeria.

Aliko with another Nigerian rich man, Femi Otedola.

Aliko and his many lovers: Clockwise: Miss Nafisa Umaru Yar'Adua, daughter of late President Umaru Yar'Adua, Miss Bisi Ibidapo-Obe, a Lagos-baed actress, Ms. Mariya Rufai Muhammad, first wife, Ms. Oluwatosin Coker based in the UK and late Ms. Josephine Kuteyi. Also Ms. Jamila Nuguda (not pictured here). © Author's file

o   With Mr Ovia, Elumelu and Ndidi Okereke Onyiuke Picture Credit: Photo File

o   With Obafoluke Otudeko as 17th president of the Nigerian Stock Exchange Photo Credit: NSE, Lagos

Top: With Mr Ovia, Elumelu and Ndidi Okereke- Onyiuke and Bottom; with Obafoluke Otudeko as 17th president of the Nigerian Stock Exchange. ©Nigerian Stock Exchange, Lagos

With Evelyn Oputu, Aganga and Sanusi Photo Credit: Ministry of Trade, Abuja

Aliko with President Obasanjo and Femi Otedola Photo Credit: Photo File

Top:With Evelyn Oputa, Aganga and Sanusi © Ministry of Trade, Abuja , Nigeria Bottom: Aliko with President Obasanjo and Femi Otedola

Top: With fellow African billionaire and countryman, Mr. Mike Adenuga, chairman, Globacomm ©: This Day Newspapers, Nigeria
Bottom: With Vice-President Mohammad Sambo and President Jonathan of Nigeria ©State House, Nigeria.

Top: With former President Rupiah Banda of Zambia   ©Lusaka Times Bottom: With Mr. Luc Maglorie, Minister of Trade, Republic of Cameroon. © News Agency of Nigeria

○ Dangote (2nd from right) with State Governors and a Senator in Nigeria Photo Credit: The Vanguard Newspapers, Lagos.

◇ Aliko at a social event in Lagos, Nigeria Photo Credit: The Vanguard Newspapers, Lagos, Nigeria

Top Aliko Dangote (2nd from right) with State Governors and a Senator in Nigeria and Bottom: Aliko (first from right) at a social event in Lagos, Nigeria. ©The Vanguard Newspapers, Lagos

Top: With President Bai-Koroma of Sierra Leone in Freetown. ©
President's Office, Freetown. Bottom With Mr. Femi Otedola and Mr.
Lamido Sanusi, Nigeria's chairman of the Reserve Bank in Abuja.
©Aso Rock Presidential Palace, Abuja, Nigeria.

Aliko with his management team and Sinoma Chinese investors in Lagos, Nigeria Photo Credit File

With Prof Klaus Schwab at the World Economic Forum in South Africa Photo Credit Credit Reuters

Top: Aliko with his management team and Sinoma Chinese investors in Lagos, Nigeria © Dangote Group File, Lagos Bottom: With Prof Klaus Schwab at the World Economic Forum in South Africa © Reuters

Signing a multi-million Dollar deal in Cameroon with, Mr. Atagana Commerce Secretary and Mr. Marcel, Head, Cameroon Port Authority Photo Credit News Agency of Nigeria (NAN)

Arriving for the swearing in of President Goodluck Jonathan with Andy Uba and Godsday Orubebe in Abuja May 2011 Photo Credit: The Vanguard Newspapers, Lagos

Top: Signing a multi-million Dollar deal in Cameroon with, Mr. Atagana Commerce Secretary and Mr. Marcel, Head, Cameroon Port Authority © News Agency of Nigeria, Abuja Bottom: Arriving for the inauguration and swearing in of President Goodluck Jonathan with Senator Andy Uba and cabinet secretary of Niger Delta Affairs, Mr. Godsday Orubebe in Abuja May 2011 © The Vanguard Newspapers, Lagos

o   With fellow billionaire Dr Mo˙ Ibrahim of Sudan Photo Credit: Mo Ibrahim Foundation

⸫   Being decorated by President Goodluck Jonathan with the second highest honor in his country in 2011 Photo Credit: The Vanguard Newspapers Lagos

Top: With fellow billionaire Dr Mo Ibrahim and Bottom: Aliko being decorated by President Jonathan with the second highest honor in his country in 2011©: The Vanguard Newspapers Lagos

Top: Dangote with Marilyn, the popular Liberian singer © Dangote Group, Lagos Bottom: Aliko (middle) with businessmen; Messrs. Jegede, Thompson, Mederer and Olusanya © Reuters

CHAPTER 12
ALIKO THE
CHEERFUL AND
GENEROUS GIVER

"Truly those who believe, and do deeds of righteousness, and perform As-Salat (Iqamat-as-Salat), and give Zakat, they will have their reward with their Lord. On them shall be no fear, nor shall they grieve..."

--- The Holy Qur'an, Surat Al-Baqarah 2: 2777

"...believe in what has been sent down to you (Muhammad SAW) and what was sent down before you, and those who perform As-Salat (Iqamat-as-Salat), and give Zakat and believe in Allah and in the Last Day, it is they to whom We shall give a great reward"

---The Holy Qur'an, Surat An-Nisā' 4:162

MONEY IS GOOD when you have it. When you have plenty of it like Dangote; life is even better and well lived. The beauty of having money and plenty of it is that, you can snap your finger any time, and under any circumstance and buy whatever you want without qualms. You do not think about where your next meal will come from, and where to keep your head. If you are a millionaire, you prioritize your expenses, but when you are a billionaire, living just on the bank interests that accrue from your wealth are enough for you to spend for the rest of your life. So, besides the joy in meeting all of one's personal needs, what gives joy to a rich man or woman? What benefit does one derive from being a billionaire? When you do not worry about life's needs, what do you do with money?

At the elementary stage of one's life, some rich people come to realize that money does not provide real satisfaction that runs deep. Money can surely buy you the biggest and most expensive mansion, but you only stay in one room. You need more than money to enjoy the peace in the house. Sure, money can buy you happiness, but it cannot buy you joy. Money can buy you happiness, especially when you make sure every activity of your life is full of events, but money does not give real joy. When asked in the 1970's what satisfaction he derived from his millions and the meaning of his stupendous wealth, the Greek –American shipping magnate, Mr. Aristotle Socrates Onassis (1906-1975), replied that all the money in the world would have no meaning without women. Mr. Onassis had just presented Mrs. Jacqueline Kennedy-Onassis (nee Lee Bouvier), wife of the late President John Fitzgerald Kennedy, and former first lady of the United States with a $700,000 40-carat Marquise Lesotho III diamond wedding ring when both tied the nuptials in October 1968 in New York City. The wedding ring, which was sold for $2.59 million at a public auction in the Big Apple later in 1996, should be worth triples that amount in today's market value. Mr. Onassis did enjoy life to the fullest.

Many of the rich people in history, and also those still living have different reasons for the joy, and satisfaction they derive from their wealth. The most important satisfaction they said they derive from their abundant wealth is charity; that is, the number of lives they have been able to touch with their stupendous wealth. People do not even know who is rich, until the rich does something that touches the lives of men and women around them. It was Mr. John Rockefeller, who once asked the greatest question of all; "The only question with wealth" he said, "is; what do you do with wealth?" He answered his question by donating two-third of his wealth, valued at $663.4billion in 2007 by the *Forbes* magazine to charity during, and after his death in 1937 at the age of 97. Mr. Rockefeller donated the land that currently houses the United Nations in Manhattan, near East River, New York to the world for $8.5million in 1945 shortly after WWII. He began by practicing the Christian rule of tithing from the age of 18, by giving generously to his church. His philanthropic activities extended to civil rights causes, endowment of the arts, and generous donations to education and hospitals. The $80 million donation he gave to the University of Chicago was instrumental in turning the university into one of the best in the world today. He funded Spellman College in Atlanta, Georgia-a renowned African-American college for Black women- to honor his in-laws, who were ardent abolitionists, and civil rights crusaders-among some of his numerous philanthropic activities. His greatest legacy to the world was his $250million Rockefeller Foundation which he founded in 1913, which is now active in promoting knowledge in all areas of human endeavors across the globe.

Mr. Robert Edward, who the whole world knows as Ted Turner, the founder of the world's first 24-hour cable news network television –*CNN* -gave billions of dollars away by donating his fortunes to the cause of humanity through the United Nations Foundation. The proud owner of the largest bison-herd in the world, and one-time owner of the largest real estate in the United States, Turner has opened his generous hands to supporting worthy causes, ranging from; the arts, environmental protection, and peace initiatives in the world. With all his achievements and generosity, Turner ruefully remarked at a time that, he is inflicted by one ailment: pride. As he once confessed; "If only I had a little humility, I'd be perfect." But Ted doesn't know that generosity of the heart through giving is an act of humility too. Mr. Bill Gates, the second richest man in the world has made the eradication of malaria his top priority, and most of his billions have gone into the cause of combating the scourge of diseases, especially in developing nations. Together, he and his wife,

Melinda through the William Henry and Melinda Gates Foundations, have given out a total of $28billion as at 2007 in charity to supporting all menageries of causes around the world.

In 2005, Ms. Oprah Winfrey gave out over $250million to charitable causes in the United States and around the world, thus becoming one of the 50 greatest philanthropists in America. This generosity was in addition to several hundreds of automobiles she had given out during her phenomenally-successful *Oprah Winfrey Show* in Chicago, including her orphanages in many developing countries, and her school for girls in South Africa. The name; Willie Durant, will probably not ring a bell in many parts of our world today, and even in the United States where he should be a celebrated icon. Many will ask; William Durant who? Well, Mr. Durant was the founder of *General Motors GM* at Flint, Michigan. His name doesn't ring a bell, because he gave away all his fortunes after leaving the company and retired to a small community; where he owned a small bowling alley and became a coach to many young kids before his death in 1947. It was Mr. Barack Obama, the president of the United States of America, who aptly pointed out the over-riding joy, and the motive behind the successes of some of the biggest founders of companies and successful outfits in the United States while addressing the graduating students of the University of Arizona as commencement speaker in summer 2009. According to the 44th president of the United States; "The leaders we revere, and the businesses that last are generally not the result of narrow pursuit of popularity, or personal advancement, but of devotion to some bigger purpose. That is the hallmark of real success. The other trapping of success might be the by-product of this larger mission but it can't be the central thing."

The greatest orator of the 21st century was right, because every real and legitimate rich person had something greater than self, when they set out to create their businesses. Their altruistic motives to solve a problem, proffer a solution to an issue in their small corner of the world, put people to work, provide a service, manufacture a product which will make life easier, better, and well-lived, and in the process leave behind a legacy, or an institution; are greater goals greater than self that defined real success. The generous hearts, charitable acts, and philanthropic activities of the real rich in the world are testimonies to their altruistic motives which gives meaning to their stupendous wealth. The fact of the matter is that, the intense desire to have money, plenty of money, soon evaporates immediately one has plenty of it in terms of billions. You begin to realize that, perhaps, you don't really need plenty of these things, just as Bill Gates discovered as the richest man in the world for thirteen consecutive years. It was this realization that made him to give half of his fortunes away.

No one can spend $1billion in his, or her entire lifetime, so when you have $16.1 billion like Nigeria's Aliko Dangote has, what do you do with such stupendous wealth, but to give plenty of it away? Dangote is generous, he is open-handed, and he is a cheerful giver. He gives to worthy causes that he is passionate about, but he also puts smiles in the faces of the poor, the unfortunate, the underprivileged, the little guys, and the poor. Prior to coming to Obajana where he now builds what is perhaps the largest cement factory in Africa, the entire place was barren. "Nothing, absolutely nothing when we came here; no schools, no light, no drinkable water, no roads but we provided the villagers with all these amenities now, including schools, because we are here and they are our neighbors," he said with a re-assured mien of satisfaction during an interview with Isha Sessay of *CNN*.

Mr. Dangote is real. It is erroneous to say he is only putting his money where his mouth is. He could choose to look the other way like some corporations have done in many developing world, especially the way some of the oil-prospecting companies have done in many parts of Nigeria, and around the world, which have become causes of incessant skirmishes between these companies and their host communities. But did Aliko put his money where his mouth was when rainfall and water flooded, and submerged parts of Sokoto State in north-western Nigeria, and he quickly rushed ₦100million (about $645,000), and other aids to the flood victims? No, Aliko did it from his heart, for, as an associate disclosed; "Aliko did not just believe it was his religious obligation as a practicing Moslem to come to the aid of the Sokoto flood victims in 2010, but he also sincerely believed it was the right thing to do." The victims of the Sokoto flood were not the only beneficiaries of the large-heartedness of Africa's richest person and the richest Black man.

There are seven sources that gave rise to the motivation of Mr. Dangote to open his hands to others, namely: his religion, his upbringing which made charity as hereditary; the joy of giving; the business philosophy of manufacturing; the sheer quantum of his wealth; spirit of empathy, and generosity, and the rightness of giving back. Every Moslem is enjoined to observe the spirit of zaka'at (giving), which is one of the five pillars of Islam. It is both an obligation and a rule to fulfill this Qur'an injunction by any Moslem desirous of entering al-jana (paradise) and it must be taken seriously, consequently; every Moslem strives to fulfill this holy injunction. There are copious references on the need to fulfill this major pillar of Islam in the Quran, including the two verses quoted above, and those who abide by this injunction will be rewarded by Allah. In addition to zaka'at, the Holy Prophet Mohammad taught every Moslem to practice zada'qat or what is known as "free will alms giving." While the former is compulsory, the latter is obligatory. Alms giving recognize that, every rich person on earth is fortunate to be blessed by Allah and the blessing should also extend to the rest of humanity. When a practicing Moslem goes to mosque every Friday to perform, yet another compulsory pillar of Islam; salat or five times daily prayer, the believer should set aside a portion of his or her paycheck or salary, which must be deposited into the offering plate at the mosque. On Friday, in particular, this should be done during juma'at worship service. The Quran specifies certain percentages of such compulsory giving to the offering in a mosque based on the believer's paycheck. The higher your salary, or the richer you are, the more the amount of your zaka'at. No matter your financial status in life, it is compulsory to discharge this religious duty and fulfill it. However, for those practicing Moslems who want to have more rewards from Allah, free-will alms giving, generous acts, and opening one's hands to the less privileged in the forms of zada'qat are highly encouraged. There are many hungry, homeless, unemployed, sick and ill people that need help and assistance. Consequently; it behooves those who are more blessed than others to come to the aid of these less fortunate and underprivileged people. Every religion of the world recognizes this act of giving and the eternal rewards that follow. Mr. Dangote discharges this compulsory pillar of Islam with single-minded devotion as a practicing Moslem. He has come to the aid of several less fortunate Nigerians and Africans. He has opened his hands, and continues to open his hands to victims of flood, earthquakes, and diseases in Nigeria, and in many areas of the world. He has sponsored thousands of practicing Moslems on pilgrimage to the holy land and his various contributions to his religion are legion.

Charity, generosity, alms giving, and the inability to look the other way to people's sufferings and needs in one's immediate surrounding are in the DNA of the Dangotes. The same spirit of charity could be observed in the veins of his maternal family members; the legendary Dantatas of ancient and modern Kano. Aliko's maternal great grandfather, Alhassan Dantata was a philanthropist per excellence. Aliko's grandfather, Sanusi Dantata also continued with the philanthropic spirit of his father, which he later passed on to his elder daughter; Madam Mariya Sanusi Dantata-Dangote, Aliko's mother. She is still alive, and currently lives in the ancient city of Kano, northern Nigeria. This simple, humble, and unassuming mother of the richest Black person in the world does not flaunt the stupendous wealth of her first son. She too is a millionaire in her own right. She supports worthy causes that have uplifted many downtrodden, and brought succor to many underprivileged Nigerians in Kano, and other parts of Nigeria. The majority of Madam Mariya's generosity is concentrated on the areas of providing basic health care delivery to rural dwellers, especially poor rural women; provision of clean water, and building of nurseries and schools to educate young girls in many remote areas of Kano, and northern Nigeria. She has built six nursery schools for girls, in at least six local government areas of Kano state, primary schools and women education center to demonstrate her commitment to child education. The most equipped and well-modernized rural hospital in Rijiya Lemu local government area of Kano donated to the Kano state government during the first administration of Mr. Rabiu Kwankwanso (1999-2003) was built by Madam Mariya. "I believe that privileged individuals who are blessed in our society should consider assisting government in supplementing their efforts to solve the problems of our communities, whether in the education, health and other sectors. These donations and projects are my little contributions in this regard," she said in 2003.

The generosity and numerous acts of kindness and philanthropic activities of the woman philanthropist have not gone unnoticed by Nigerians. She was conferred with the Doctor of Letters (Honoris Causa) by the council, and senate of Bayero University, Kano on Saturday January 12, 2002, at the institution's 19th and 20th convocation (Commencement) ceremonies. At the august event, two other distinguished Nigerians were also honored, the late General Murtala Ramat Mohammad who ruled Nigeria as military head of state between, July 1975, and February 13, 1976, who was honored posthumously with Doctor of Law (Honoris Causa) for his indefatigable leadership, and for being, unarguably the best military head of state Nigeria has ever produced. He was assassinated in an abortive coup d'état on Friday, February 13, 1976. The third honoree was Mr. Alexander Ifeanyichukwu Ekwueme, former vice-president of Nigeria in the second republic (1979-1983) during the Shehu Shagari Administration, who bagged Doctor of Law (Honoris Causa) of Bayero University, Kano. In his speech at the ceremony on behalf of the three honorees, the former vice president paid glowing tribute to Madam Mariya Sanusi Dantata-Dangote for "her own special and inimitable way, (which) symbolizes the selfless individual sacrifice and philanthropy needed to solve the educational problems (of young girls) in Northern Nigeria..."

Like other rich people of the world, who enrich life more when they open their hands to the less fortunate, instead of turning their eyes to the plights of the less privileged, Dangote firmly believes that, there is joy in the heart of rich people who practice charity. Aliko's generosity is both at the personal and corporate levels. He, as a billionaire businessman gives out generously, while his company adheres strictly to sound corporate social responsibility. For instance, Mr. Oluka Ngofa, community and public affairs manager of Dangote Bail, the cement arm of the company located in Port Harcourt and Onne in Rivers state, south-eastern Nigeria disclosed that, the Dangote Group made it a corporate policy to recruit most of their workers from the communities they operate, and also provide social amenities in the areas. "We engaged majority of our workforce from the host community and within the state. They are usually given priority consideration, and also, in terms of infrastructure development, we have two projects which we have done in this community. We have built a youth development center, and we have also put a scholarship scheme in place, because we knew providing the infrastructure without the human capital development, does not amount to anything," he disclosed.

Mr. Devakumar Edwin is executive director of Dangote Group responsible for projects and industries. An Indian, he has been with the conglomerate for more than two decades. He disclosed that the generosity of the company towards its host communities is taken seriously. Consequently, when Dangote Industries operate in any part of Nigeria or Africa, the company goes the extra miles to establish infrastructural facilities and social amenities that some of African governments cannot provide for the people. "We don't invest dependent purely upon the government, either regarding infrastructure or its policies. Take Obajana Cement for example. We had to build our own dam, a 90-kilometre access road, gas pipeline, power plant, a housing estate, everything. When we started, there was not even mobile telephone in the area. So we had to set up satellite communications," he disclosed.

The sheer amount that the Dangote Group is worth and the personal fortune of Nigeria's, and Africa's richest person, are enough reasons why Dangote continues to give. There is too much poverty in the land, against the backdrop of Nigeria's abundant human and natural resources. In spite of the nation's petrol-dollars, it is estimated that an average Nigerian lives on less than US$1 per day. This should not have been the case, yet extreme poverty lives side-by-side with stupendous wealth in Africa's most populous nation. If Aliko Dangote was to retire at his age, and says, he does not want to work for the rest of his life; his personal fortunes would still be enough for him to live comfortably for the rest of his life, and still remains for his children, grandchildren, and great grandchildren to live on. So what continually drives him to expand? What continues to motivate him to give generously to others? Love for the Nigerian people, because of his desire to provide employment opportunities for able-bodied and energetic Nigerian striplings roaming the streets. According to Dangote, "If you give me $5 billion today, I will not invest any abroad; I will invest everything here in Nigeria. Let us put heads together and work."

In furtherance of this commitment, the Dangote Group has established a school to teach African youth on how to supplement their college education with entrepreneurial education. The business school, named Dangote Leadership Academy, was set up to teach African college graduates how they can think with the right attitude and positive spirit, so they can contribute to the growth and development of Nigeria. Established at Obajana cement plant, Kogi state, central Nigeria, the academy, according to Aliko Dangote was founded; "to train young local talent to boost the manpower needs of our nation's industries. This initiative is largely driven by our corporate social responsibility (CSR) to the nation. All of us understand that we cannot bring in expertise from outside continuously. There is therefore an urgent need to develop skills in our local talent through knowledge transfer, and sustained training, and development efforts to drive growth in our industries." The academy would consist of a dormitory, and all other conveniences for the training of the students at the centre. Addressing the pioneering students at the centre in Kogi state, Dangote gave them some templates they need to succeed, as future business men and women, and in life. These are: focus, determination, utilization of power of prayer, the ability to "think outside the box," the need to think innovatively, and the virtue of hard work. Mr Dangote admonished the young men and women to remove negative thoughts about doing business in Nigeria. He said Nigeria is a good place to conduct business; citing his own success story as a classic example. According to the industrialist; "There is perhaps no better way to drive this point home than to cite the example of Mark Zuckerberg, owner of Facebook a youth like you, who is currently the 52nd richest person in the world. (2010)"

Mr. Dangote believed that, if the students at the academy are able to exploit the resources at the school, his companies will be able to draw from the pool as future employees. "We believe that if we have the right mix of manpower and other resources, we will churn out quality products that have always been our hallmark of success. Our ultimate aim is to have highly-trained and committed workforce to drive our businesses and also beef up the nation's industrial manpower needs." According to him; "We believe the youths are the future leaders and as much must be empowered to enable them to function effectively in this role. We have a new crop of highly talented young Africans, who are championing generational change, gender equality, social entrepreneurship and good corporate governance." Addressing world leaders at Davos, Switzerland during the economic summit of world leaders in summer 2011, Mr. Dangote took his message for the empowerment of African youth to the forum by appealing to the developed world to invest in Africa, instead of giving aid to African leaders insisting that; "We cannot always build the future for our youths, but we can build our youths for the future" borrowing the words of President Franklin Delano Roosevelt of the United States during the Great Depression in the 1930s.

Mr. Aliko Dangote, the businessman and Dangote Group, the corporate giant, are two Siamese twins in displaying their milk of human and corporate kindness and generosity to victims of natural disasters. Dangote once donated ₦50m (about $300,000) to the Jigawa state government in northern Nigeria to alleviate the suffering of flood victims. The Dangote Foundation had earlier donated ₦355m (about $2.1 m) through the United Nations World Food Program (WFP), to assist survivors of flood that ravaged Pakistan. The donation was made through the Dangote Foundation. Dangote believes in the ingenuity of the Nigerian/ African youth, if given the opportunity. He sincerely and earnestly shares the aspirations, vigor, and optimism of African youth. Towards this end, he is exploring all avenues, starting with his foundation,-one of the largest in Africa- to empower African youth to be self-sufficient and break the back of endemic poverty in Nigeria, and the African continent.

Dangote knows the power of western education in national development. Consequently, he is committed to the development of education right from the moment his companies began to turn around dilapidated educational institutions beginning from his home state of Kano. He has demonstrated his unwavering commitment to supporting the development of education in Nigeria. No wonder, the Kano state government realized the contributions he could make toward education, and consequently decided to install him as the pioneer chancellor of the state-owned university of science and technology located in Wudil. The state university has now been re-named after his late great-grandfather as Alhassan Dantata University of Science and

Technology in Wudil. The then state governor, and presidential candidate in the 2011 presidential election in Nigeria, who is now Mr. Dangote's in-law, Mr Ibrahim Shekarau implored the newly-appointed chancellor to use his enormous resources to help develop the infant tertiary institutions into one of the best in Nigeria. According to Dr Aisha Ismail Tofa, the state's education secretary, and the governor's representative at the institution's ceremony where Mr. Dangote was installed the new chancellor, Dangote would bring his enormous resources to develop the new institution. In his citation at the ceremony, the institution's president, Professor Ibrahim Garba paid glowing tribute to Dangote for his financial assistance to the new college and announced the institution senate's decision to confer an honorary doctorate degree on Mr. Dangote.

In his acceptance speech at the occasion, Mr. Dangote, in his characteristic humility, expressed gratitude to the institution's principal officers, teachers, and students for the honour done to his family and to him personally. He promised to assist in developing the new college to one of the best in Nigeria. He announced that his company would build ₦400 million (about US$2.8m) student hostel facility in the university, and automatic scholarships and automatic employment to the best graduating student every academic session. Other pledges announced at the installation ceremony by Dangote were; fixing of the epileptic power-electricity- situation in the institution, and other developmental needs promising, "I will work diligently to transform this university, to make it compete with any other university in the world in infrastructure and academic performance."

The areas of Nigeria's socio-economic and educational developments that Mr. Dangote has silently touched, but has been under-reported, or unknown to many, is in the areas of art promotion and book publishing. There are many authors and writers in Nigeria whose books would have remained just mere manuscripts, because of lack of funds but for the financial lifeline of Dangote. (By the way, this biography was not commissioned by Dangote; we never asked for, nor received any money from Mr. Dangote, or any of his companies in the research and printing of this book). Mr. Lawrence Olufemi Obisakin would forever be grateful to billionaire Dangote for the financial assistance he received while writing; *On the Wings of Time* in 2007. Mr. Bola Akinterinwa, former director-general of the Nigerian Institute of International Affairs, and former chairman, editorial board of *This Day* newspapers, Lagos/Abuja has disclosed that Mr. Dangote assisted him financially in 1999 when he was writing his book: *"Nigeria and France: The Dilemma of Thirty-Five Years of Relationship,"* prompting the former university professor to dedicate his 2001 book: *"Nigeria in the world: Issues and problems for the Sleeping Giant,"* to Mr. Dangote. The Nigerian Union of Journalists, Lagos state council has acknowledged the contribution of Mr. Dangote to the council's annual publication series since 2005 titled: *"Nigerian Media and Challenges of Democracy"* with Mr. Dapo Olorunyomi, as its editor/author. At the launch of the book; *"Marwa in the Eyes of the Press,"* written by General Mohammed Marwa's erstwhile press secretary, Mr. Sina Ogunbambo which was launched in 1998; Mr. Dangote launched it with ₦1million (about $10,000). Mr. Wale Folarin, author of: *"The Beaded Crown: A biography of the Timi of Ede, Oba Oladokun Oyewusi Agbonran II,"* written in 1996 would also be included among the list of Nigerian authors whose creative works have been supported by the generous funding of artistic works by billionaire Dangote.

Aliko Dangote is noted for standing up for the economically less privileged. He opens his generous hands to the needy. In a nation where there is no medical insurance scheme, no social security benefit, no government-assisted student loan, and everyone is virtually on his or her own, it can be very tough. That was the pathetic situation of Ms. Khadijat Oluwatoyin Sanya, a mentally-ill and emotionally disturbed student at the state-owned university in Lagos, Lagos State University (LASU), in south west Lagos. One day in 2010, the sophomore at the college just went insane. She threw every member of her family and neighbors into panic at the congested area of Arowojobe community area of Oshodi, Lagos. No one knew what bewitched the 32-year old college student, but according to a source who knew, and witnessed what happened, Khadijat just ran out of her parent's house berserk. She was on the verge of madness-let lose like a street lunatic- until members of the Adeyemi-Arowojobe community development association (AACDA), and the Aiye-Gbesin central mosque where her parents worshipped ran after her and rescue her. Khadijat was taken to a private hospital for treatment, but the indigent parents could not afford the cost of treatment. This forced them to go public by appealing to kind-hearted Nigerians to assist in the cost of treatment.

The Nation newspapers carried the story of the college student in its June 13, 2011 edition, and set up an appeal fund titled: "Khadijat Oluwatoyin Sanya Trust Fund." What complicated Khadijat's condition were the physical injuries, and bruises she sustained the day she was mentally unbalanced and ran out of her parent's home before she was rescued. Mr. Dangote was reading the daily newspapers as his usual morning routine on his way to his office in Ikoyi, Lagos when he saw the story, and unable to restrain himself in such situation as this, he sent a check of ₦850,000.00 (about $6,000.00) to the fund. *The Nation* newspapers promptly notified the trustees of the fund and the secretary of the CDA, Mr. Sunday Akani Alade, the general overseer of Christ Light House Church, Rev. Joshua Oguntulu and the Imam of Aye-Gbesin Central Mosque, Alhaji Abdurrahman who collected the check. Applauding Mr. Dangote for his generosity, Alhaji Abdurrahman said: "We thank Dangote so much for this gift of life. We did not know that help will come this quick. He will be successful in all his business. His business will continue to grow. This kind of sickness will not befall any member of his family. The community decided to take responsibility of the girl when it was discovered that there was no one to take care of her. We are appealing to other good- spirited Nigerians to assist in emulating Dangote." Ms. Khadijat was on the verge of recovery, but needed money for further therapy and final rehabilitation after discharge. She soon recovered and went back to school.

There are thousands, if not millions of Nigerians in Ms. Khadijat's situation who have benefited from the milk of Dangote's human kindness. Mr. Dangote's generosity extends to several individuals, and organizations both professional, and voluntary that have sought, and received his financial assistance in writing a book, promoting a cause, or one thing, or the other. The list is just too long. For the past two decades in the history of Nigeria, there is no Nigerian author who has not benefited from the financial assistance of this kind and generous Nigerian, either through direct solicitations to defray the costs of print production or invited as chief launcher, or one of the launchers of such creative works.

The same could be said of professional organizations in the academia, media, architecture, gender promotion, medicine, law, business, sports, and in the sciences just name it. They have solicited, and most often definitely receive financial donations from Aliko Dangote the businessman, and, or from the Dangote Group as corporate sponsor. It is often said in Nigeria that if there is any occasion, a ceremony, or an event where Aliko Dangote is present during fundraising -which are plenty and occur regularly in Nigeria-then the event would be a financial success because, head or tail, the organizers will win-money will be realized. There is not a single non-governmental organization (NGO) in Nigeria that has asked for financial assistance and has not received, either personally from Dangote, or from his business conglomerate; Dangote Group, or from his foundation, the Aliko Dangote Foundation; the largest foundation in Nigeria, in West Africa, and one of the largest in Africa. Traditional rulers, community organizations, tribal unions, and religious organizations both from the two dominant religions of Christianity and Islam have benefited from one form of financial assistance from Mr. Dangote, the billionaire or the Dangote Group. In virtually all

Nigerian colleges and universities, solicitation letters pour into the Dangote Group offices across Nigeria, and the West African sub-region and other parts of Africa regularly requesting for financial assistance and Dangote obliges them all. At its corporate headquarters in commercial Lagos, the authors observed firsthand, how these solicitations are handled by the conglomerate.

The Nollywood industry, which is now Nigeria's version of Hollywood-the world's entertainment epicenter-has also benefited immensely from the large-heartedness of Aliko Dangote and the Dangote Group of Companies. The Nigerian sporting world cannot be left out, so also the Nigerian students' body; the national association of Nigerian students (NANS) and many more. Mr. Dangote is now Nigeria's foremost philanthropist and number one generous giver. When veteran Nigerian actor Mr. Usman Baba Pategi, known by his stage name as Samanja took ill and needed eye surgery, he took his plight to the Nigerian media which is common in Nigeria. The 60-year old man had glaucoma, and even though he has retired from acting, Nigerians still continue to enjoy his rib-cracking jokes from his sit-com re-runs. The grandfather needed ₦1.5m (about $10,000) for the eye surgery, and Dangote gave out the money. The donation was handed to Mr. Ladan Salihu, zonal manager of the federal radio corporation (FRCN), Kaduna, northern Nigeria was given to Mr. Pategi to enable him travel to India for the eye surgery. The old man was effusive in his thanks, gratitude and heartfelt appreciation to Mr. Dangote for saving his eyesight. These types of charities and giving by billionaire Dangote are commonplace in Nigeria, in West Africa and around the world. Many of these kind-hearted gestures are not reported, and the amiable giver does not open his hands to assist people, and support worthy causes for personal aggrandizement or for grandstanding applause, and media attention or publicity. Dangote does these, because he is a kind and generous man.

Every year during the Muslim holy month of Ramadan, Dansa foods limited, a subsidiary of the Dangote conglomerates normally donate food items to Muslim faithful. In 2010, items donated on behalf of the company by Mr. Olajide Oni, who was represented by the Abuja marketing executive, Mr. Aderibigbe Olayiwola amounted to 3,000 cartons of assorted products of the company, which included; fruit nectars, juice, dairy products, sugar, powdered milk, and soft drinks. According to Mr Olayiwola, the gesture was part of the company's community relations and corporate responsibility. Alhaji Yusuf, chairman of Ansar-Ud-Deen society of Nigeria (AUDSON) who received the food items at the mission's mosque at Wuse Area II, Abuja was full of appreciation for the company's kind gesture. The food items were shared among ten mosques in the federal capital territory (FCT), while similar food distribution was carried out in the rest thirty-six states of the Nigeria federation. Several causes that are dear to his heart, and also geared towards promoting various developments of Nigeria have also received financial support from Dangote. For example, at the launch of Sir Ahmadu Bello Memorial Foundation in Kaduna in the fall of 2009, Mr. Dangote donated ₦150 million (about US$1m); the second highest donation at the epoch-making event, where incidentally his uncle, Mr. Aminu Dantata, gave the highest donation of ₦250million (about $1.8m) as the chief launcher. The ever smooth operator and humble man he is, Dangote did not physically show up at the event so as not to steal the show from his uncle, Mr. Aminu Dantata, who announced the donation on behalf of his nephew at the event where over ₦5.5billion (about $40m) was realized. Billionaire Dangote has also supported the pet project of the first lady of Benue state, Mrs. Yemisi Dooshima Suswan by donating ₦10 million (about $60,000) to her Sev-Av Foundation established to enlighten women and children about HIV/AIDS, and also empower them to acquire skills so as to contribute their quotas to the development of Benue state, central Nigeria.

Similarly, in summer 2009, Mr. Aliko Dangote and his uncle, Aminu Dantata effectively "double-teamed" and surpassed every one, individual, state government, corporate bodies just name it, when they gave generously to the pet project of former Nigeria's first lady, Madam Umaru Turai's international cancer centre Abuja, Nigeria. Launched at the international conference centre, Abuja and attended by the who's who in Nigeria and chaired by former President Olusegun Obasanjo, Uncle Aminu Dantata wrote a check for a princely sum of ₦1.2billion (about $7.5million) while Nephew Aliko Dangote tagged along with a modest sum of ₦1billion (about $7million) on behalf of the Dangote Foundation. Realizing the meeting of minds between the former first lady's pet project and the Dangote Foundation, Mr. Dangote announced that his financial support for the international cancer centre Abuja (ICCA) project would be a continuous one with a second round of cash donations that would facilitate synergistic efforts between the federal ministry of health, all the state's ministries of health, including the federal capital territory (FCT), Abuja toward providing vital health services in the country.

When the Lagos state government floated the state's trust fund in 2011, the Dangote Group led the pack with the highest donation of $326m. The governor of Lagos State, Mr. Babatunde Raji Fashola, could not hide his joy, and was full of thanks to Africa's richest man "On behalf of the good people of Lagos State," he told the company's representative who delivered the check at the launch of the trust fund, "I sincerely thank you for this noble and voluntary gesture on the part of Dangote Group. We also express our delight and pleasure for the recent prosperity of Dangote Group and the defining success of Alhaji Aliko Dangote, who has made all of us proud. His success is a reflection of the character and dynamism of Nigerian youth, because he is still a young man."

In summer 2011, in Cape Town, South Africa, Aliko Dangote stunned the world at the World Economic Forum (WEF), when he announced the establishment of the young African leader's fellowship program. The price tag: a hefty $2million. Prof. Klaus Schwab, the president of the WEF, who sat beside Africa's richest person, could not hide his excitement after Dangote announced the establishment of the fellowship program. Addressing the press at the forum, Mr. Dangote disclosed that he was moved to introduce the program so as to spur young Africans to aim higher in achieving laurels in non-business sector, but more importantly, he wanted young Africans to be engaged in the world's young global leader's community. Billed to run for five years in the first place, 35 young Africans would be chosen annually to compete with their counterparts across the world toward competing for young global leadership. The successful young African competitors would be provided with the relevant training in some of the best institutions in the world to adequately prepare them to participate in the fellowship- through young global leader's competition. Prof Schwab said he was very proud of the announcement and expressed appreciation to Mr. Dangote for his generosity as he signed the agreement for the formal take-off of the program on behalf of the WEF; the managers and trustees of the fellowship program.

In fall 2009, it was the turn of the people of Iyin-Ekiti, Ekiti state, in western Nigeria to benefit from the philanthropic gesture of Mr. Dangote. For those who may not know, Iyin-Ekiti is the birth place of retired General Robert Adeyinka Adebayo, first military governor of the defunct western region of Nigeria between 1966 and 1975. His son, Mr. Niyi Adebayo later became the first democratically-elected civilian governor of Ekiti state after the creation of the state from the old Ondo state by the military regime of the late General Sani Abacha. Like other Nigerian towns and cities, Iyin-Ekiti needs development and progress; so the indigenes gathered together and formed Iyin progressive federal union (IPFU), an umbrella organization of the town's prominent sons and daughters saddled with the task of spear-heading the development of the town through self-efforts. The IPFU set a target of ₦100million (about $800, 000) at an endowment fund which drew guests from far and near including the UK and the United States. Mr. Dangote sent ₦5million (about $33, 00) through a representative toward the appeal fund.

In a country where the local rich men and women cut corners, and do not hold their fair shake of the nation's tax burdens, Mr. Dangote is the highest tax payer in Nigeria. Every year he cuts a check for ₦50billion (about $49million) to Nigeria's tax collection agency, the federal Inland Revenue service (FIRS), Abuja. That is not surprising for the richest man in Nigeria and the largest private employer of labor in Africa's most populous nation. But in Nigeria, there are whispers of other equally rich Nigerians-although there is no rich Nigerian in the league of Aliko Dangote-but nevertheless they are rich, but do not discharge their tax obligations. As Aliko Dangote is living up to his tax obligations, so his numerous companies continue to assist many nations of the world.

In the nearby Republic of Niger, Nigeria's neighbor to the north, desertification and starvation hit the land in 2011 leaving devastation of great magnitude in its wake. The famine was so bad that people were dying in the streets, prompting the Dangote Foundation to come to the rescue of the victims of the natural disasters. Since food materials, water and other basic essentials of life were direly needed, fifty truckloads of food items valued at ₦100million (about $650,000) were rushed to the arid nation. Food items donated to the Nigerien included 3,000 bags of salt (50kg); 3,000 bags of sugar (50kg), 6,000 bags of flour (50kg), and 30,000 cartons of Dangote noodles, donated through the Dangote Foundation. "The relationship between Nigeria and Niger Republic is like that of brothers," Dangote said. "We cannot sit back and watch our brothers suffer. It is in line with our corporate social responsibility that we are making this donation to alleviate the suffering of the people," Sada Ladan-Baki, executive director at Dangote Group presented the relief materials to Colonel Garba Maikido, a regional governor in the Republic of Niger who received the food items from the Dangote Foundation. The kind gesture, according to Ladan –Baki was part of the guiding philosophies of the largest foundation in Nigeria to wit: maintain good corporate social responsibility and assist the needy. The media, both local and foreign, have been awash with news of displaced Nigerians that became refugees in their own country, because of incessant tribal clashes, and perennial religious disturbances in Nigeria since 2009. Many of these displaced Nigerians need food items, housing and other basic things. These communal clashes and religious violence are common in towns such as; Jos and Bauchi in central Nigeria, and at times the crises often spill over to neighboring states and towns. The Dangote Foundation has been commended for the way and manner it has come to the aid of these internally-displaced Nigerians. According to Dangote, "Our mission at the Dangote Group has always been to touch the lives of people by providing their basic needs. Our vision is to be a world-class enterprise that is passionate about the quality of life of the general populace and high returns to stakeholders." The foundation supplied relief materials to these internally-displaced Nigerians estimated to cost more than ₦200million (about US $1.2 million). At the same time, while these various humanitarian activities of Dangote Foundation were providing succor to needy Nigerians, the foundation continues to distribute food items to poor people across major towns in Nigeria, including sinking water boreholes in many rural communities in the country. Established about 18 years ago, Dangote Foundation is involved in several areas of Nigerians' lives: health care, provision of social amenities, community development efforts, community grants, grassroots' empowerment for rural women, and scholarship support, road construction, culture promotion, educational opportunities and numerous activities bordering on the welfare of ordinary Nigerians

In the past, Africa used to be the main beneficiary of relief materials and donations from non-governmental organizations (NGOs) when disasters strike. Such disasters are; water flood, desertification, famine, ecological and other natural and man-made disasters. The richest man in the continent is determined to change this trend through his foundation. "The Dangote foundation and the entire management and staff of Dangote industries limited feel a real need to make a modest contribution to help make life a little more bearable for the survivors in Pakistan," Aliko Dangote, chairman of the Dangote foundation said when he cut a hefty check for the sum of ₦300million (about US$2million) as aid assistance to victims of flood which devastated the Asian nation of Pakistan in fall 2010. Commiserating with the victims, Dangote said, "The hearts of all Africans go out to the people of Pakistan as they go through this ordeal. Africa is not only a recipient of humanitarian aid, but is also able to help her brothers and sisters in Pakistan and elsewhere where there is suffering. Helping our family, in this case our global family is part of Africa's traditional values." He specifically directed the World Food Program to use the money to "provide life-saving food relief to the millions of Pakistanis whose lives have been turned upside down by this disaster. It will also help with the logistics of the entire humanitarian community working to supply urgent food and other supplies to the estimated six million Pakistanis that WFP is (are) serving who have lost their homes and livelihoods due to the heavy monsoon rains that have hit the country."

The philanthropic activities of Dangote foundation cut across national, regional and continental borders. Ms. Sandy Westlake received the donation on behalf of the World Food Program (WFP). She was full of thanks and appreciation to the richest person in Africa. "We are completely humbled by the Dangote Foundation's generous donation on behalf of WFP and the people of Pakistan. Your contribution will make a life-saving difference and allow WFP to continue its important work on the ground. The funds for Pakistan are absolutely critical and will do a lot to further WFP's focus on saving lives in the flood zone." On his part, retired Major-General Asif Duraiz Akhatar, the United Nations High Commissioner in Pakistan was full of gratitude to the Dangote foundation for the generous donation with assurance that; "...the people and government of Pakistan will forever remain grateful to the Dangote foundation for this big sacrifice that will greatly address the needs of the people."

The activities of the Dangote Group in discharging its unalloyed corporate social responsibilities run almost throughout the year, 365 days of the year, because in every holiday observed in Nigeria, and every festival celebrated, the group has been heavily involved. From New Year day on January 1, Valentine holiday and celebration on February 14 each year, Christian Lenten season, Easter celebration, May Day-workers rally, Children's Day, Mother's day, Father's day, Nigerian universities sports and games festival, Nigeria's Independence Celebration Day every October 1, Moslem's Ramadan fast, Eid-il Fitri (Break of Moslem Fast) celebration, Moslem Hajj or holy pilgrimage, Christmas celebration and others are fully, or partially or co-sponsored by many of the subsidiaries of the Dangote Group in many communities across Nigeria. The boldest initiative so far from the stable of the group to tackle youth unemployment in Nigeria was the launching of a whopping ₦5billion (about US$35million) fund called micro, small, and medium enterprises business development fund by the Dangote foundation in conjunction with the Bank of Industry (BOI), Nigeria. The Dangote foundation will make available the sum of ₦2.5 billion (about US$17.5million), while the remainder of the fund will be made up by the bank. The aim is to make money available for aspiring Nigerian youth with entrepreneurial drive toward self-employment.

There are several thousands, if not millions of able-bodied, energetic and focused young Nigerian men and women looking for people to mentor them. These Nigerians and Africans are full of ideas, and if given the opportunities, they would change the course of history in Nigeria and Africa. These young minds should not be neglected by those who have reached the top. The greatest satisfaction any rich man, or woman can derive from his or her wealth is how such wealth has impacted on the lives of others. There is a wry saying among some youngsters in Nigeria that when a Nigerian, or an African has struggled to get to the top, once he or she reaches there by climbing the ladder of success, he/she throws away the ladder so that others would not use the same ladder to climb and join him or her at the top. But in other climes, some successful men and women are ready, willing and have been known to assist others in climbing the ladder of success.

We hear, listen to, enjoy, dance to, and appreciate the artistic works and performances of great African-American / Black musicians like the legendary Jackson 5, the late Marvin Gaye, Stevie Wonder, the great Michael Jackson, The Temptations, The Miracles, The Supremes, Diana Ross, The Four Tops, Smokey Robinson of KC & Sunshine, even Queen Latifah, and numerous others who have enriched, and still continue to enrich humanity with their prodigious artistic talents. But someone discovered all these great men and women of American music scene: the legendary Berry Gordy, a young African-American/Black ghetto boy from Detroit, Michigan who rose from the nadir of poverty to the pinnacle of American music world. He went through a lot in life but did not waver, and built *Motown Records* from the scratch to become, at a time, one of the largest and most stunningly successful music record companies in the world. He achieved success, but was not content in existing as an oasis of success in the desert of failure, and in the midst of misery and poverty. He lifted up many talents, erected many ladders for other aspiring young African-American/Black talents to climb up and join him in success land. As Mr. Ben Murray-Bruce, Chairman and CEO, *Silverbird* Inc., one of the few Nigerian industrialists heavily involved in manufacturing and youth empowerment told Zaki, the musician in an interview on the Nigerian television authority NTA 2, Abuja on Saturday June 25, 2011 "Those Nigerian leaders who are not contributing to this country, who refuse to grow the economy but causing trouble are not truly Nigerians. I don't care what anybody may say, such leaders are demented, they are psychopaths, and they do not belong to this country but should go to their country."

Billionaire Dangote genuinely believes in the empowerment of Nigerian youth. Imagine what Nigeria will look like, if other equally rich Nigerian men and women would emulate him, and join in growing up the nation's economy! African-American foremost filmmaker, business man, and activist; Shelton Jackson (Spike) Lee told the Black community in America that there is only way the Black race can endure and make it in the world, and that is; through self-empowerment and empowering others. No other race will develop Nigeria or Africa. "We've got to start grooming people to own businesses. That's the only way. Then you can start doing what you want: keep the money in the community; provide jobs for (our) people," Mr. Lee said. It is a message and advice Nigerians, indeed Africans all over the world should take to heart.

Nigerians and Africans should be able to get it by now that non-Africans and non-Black people will not go to Africa and develop Africa. It isn't going to happen! The Europeans were in Africa for almost four hundred years and they bled the Black race dry. For those students of colonial history, it wasn't far-fetched to figure out why Europeans colonized Africa and other parts of the world. Looking for cheap labor, they headed to the Dark Continent and carted the best, the powerful, and the noble of African men and women away to the Americas, and other parts of the world. The trans-Atlantic Slave Trade was described as the greatest injustice and dehumanizing act ever perpetrated against the Black race as nearly 500 million able-bodied African men and women were forcefully uprooted from their ancestral land, and taken to sugar cane plantations to work as slaves. After the nervous systems of the Europeans were tormented by the degrading act, and they were compelled to scrap the inhuman trade, a new way of making money was found: raw materials for industries after the Industrial Revolution. Where again did they come to obtain these raw materials? Africa of course! Africa was exploited, ravaged, and despoiled; Africans were treated as less than human and like mere beasts of burden.

When the British got to Nigeria and Africa during the colonial days, they didn't want any local company to compete with any British company. The local market was virtually theirs. While they were content with buying the local raw materials, it was also theirs too to set the prices of cocoa, cotton, coffee, palm kernel, etc. They bought these raw materials cheaply, and took them to Europe which they refined and returned back to Africans as finished products, but they also set their prices, so head or tail, Africans suffered. Take the case of imported British dry gin for example. The British colonial authorities discovered that Nigerians had their own version of local dry gin called, "ogogoro" which was competing for the domestic market with their imported dry gins, and so enacted a law banning the local dry gin. Anyone caught drinking the local dry gin was arrested and sent to jail. The late Mr. Tai Solarin, one of the early educationists in western Nigeria and co-founder (with his late British wife, Sheila) of Mayflower Schools, Ikenne, Ogun state looked at the law and knew something was wrong. Mr. Solarin could not fathom the reason behind the ban on "ogogoro" by the British colonial masters, while they allowed imported British dry gin into Nigeria. The colonialists so demonized "ogogoro" that to drink the local stuff was like taking poison, yet there was no fundamental difference between the locally-made "hot drink" and the British dry gin, so Solarin defied the order and instead offered to go to jail.

If there was any nation that should not have developed, or even given up to rise to the top but defied all obstacles that littered its path, it is the modern state of Israel. Imagine what the Israelis went through in the hands of foreign domination and the number of them that were slaughtered by Nazi Germany in WII. Imagine the odds that confronted them when they returned back to their homeland in 1945! The whole of the place was barren. No one gave them a chance of survival, but their rise to world power has demonstrated the ingenuity and indomitability of the human spirit. They turned a desert into a lush green savannah, and today they have come to stay as a people, and as a nation.

How about the Indians? They went through colonialism just like Africans although they were not commercially enslaved, but the way the Europeans treated them was basically the same. They fought hard to gain their independence, and millions of them were slaughtered but the British would not let go. When it became obvious that the Indians would not give up, the British decided to go home rather grudgingly, but not until they made sure that a newly-independent India would collapse, so they bled the nation dry. India at independence in 1945 started the tortuous journey to freedom with nothing, virtually nothing. But they didn't give up. An independent India was buffeted from all sides by the departed colonialists: psychological assault, international sabotage, and trade embargo, name it! At a time, the British colonial propaganda machine went to work feeding young Africans with lies that the degrees obtained from Indian colleges and universities were inferior and sub-standard. It was all lies! We see the results today. As Mr. Devakumar Edwin of the Dangote Group said, "You see, countries have not grown being dependent upon importation." Edwin is an Indian and has been with Dangote Group for over 20 years. He gave examples of the rise of the two most populous nations on earth; his native India and its Far East behemoth; China. "Take India, take China. Industrialization takes root through production. So, we knew that though in the short term we may lose, the Nigerian government and people would eventually realize that people need to have employment and the country ought to develop. Nigeria ought to stand on its own legs and not on importation." These are the twin pre-occupations of Mr. Dangote, and what he is doing with his companies and wealth.

In spite of his busy schedules and numerous business commitments, Mr. Dangote still finds time to serve others in numerous capacities. He serves on the boards of the national council of Nigerian vision, Mohammed Bello endowment for justice and jurisprudence, Kano foundation, the Nigerian economic summit group, African Petroleum Plc., National investment promotion council, and the heart of Africa (a management group on Nigeria image project) etc. He has served as a director of transnational corporation of Nigeria. He is a graduate of business studies from Al-Azahar University Cairo, Egypt and thus participates actively in the affairs of the university's alumni association. For his generous heart and support for worthy causes, Mr. Dangote has received numerous honours, laurels, awards and recognitions all over the world. These recognitions are either for the generosity of any of the Dangote chains of businesses, or for the personal generosity of Mr. Dangote as a businessman but either way, the name Dangote is respected and eulogized both at the personal and corporate levels. In an unscientific survey conducted for the European media outfit in 2009, the *BBC*, veteran journalist and correspondent Mr. Sola Odunfa, asked Nigerians at home and abroad to send in the name of their favorite five Nigerian legends of all times. Mr. Aliko Dangote expectedly appeared among the list of Nigerian legends for his impact on the economic development of Nigeria, and his generosity, which has touched several lives in Nigeria, Africa, and many other people around the world.

In 2010 when Nigeria marked its 50th Anniversary of nationhood from its former colonial masters, the British; the federal government of Nigeria decided to honour fifty prominent Nigerians, who have contributed to the development of Nigeria in all fields of human endeavours. Mr. Aliko Dangote was expectedly one of these prominent Nigerians. He shared the honour with three other prominent Nigerians from his home state of Kano: his maternal grandfather, and the patriarch of the Dantata Family; the late Alhassan Dantata, the grandfather of his mother, Madam Mariya Sanusi-Dantata, former Nigerian permanent representative at the United Nations, Mr. Maitama Sule, Dan Masani Kano, and the late Mr. Aminu Kano, national leader/founder of Northern Element Progressive Union (NEPU) in the first republic (1960-1966), and presidential candidate of the defunct People's Redemption Party (PRP) during the second republic (1979-1983).

Other awards that Mr. Dangote has won include: Zik

prize for leadership in business management in 1998, Sir Ahmadu Bello international award by Arewa research and publication, Kano, 1999, for outstanding contributions to economic development, Best entrepreneur and philanthropist of the year by Governor Donald Duke of Cross River state, 2002; and the first ever fellowship award by the Lagos State Polytechnic, 2002 for his role in economic development of Lagos State, and Doctor of Science in business management of the University of Calabar, Cross River state, Nigeria. The list of laurels continues with: *This Day* newspaper of Nigeria business man of the year award; *The Sun* newspapers of Nigeria business man of the year award, and numerous other awards from the various media organizations in Nigeria, the West African sub-region and the African continent. The crowning glory of Mr. Dangote was summer 2011 when he emerged as the African business man of the year and was presented with the award by the *African Business* magazine based in London, UK in conjunction with the Commonwealth Business Council (CBC), and *Business Africa*. At the star-studded event in June 2011 which had the President of Namibia, Mr. Hifikepunye Pohamba in attendance, including Baroness Lynda Chalker, Ms. Evelyn Oputa, chief executive of Nigeria's Bank of Industry, Mr. Pascal Dozie, chairman of CBC, and other important dignitaries and government ministers, Mr. Omar Ben Yedder, publisher of the *African Business* magazine said, "The exciting news story today is the expansion of groups such as MTN, Shoprite, Ecobank, Standard Bank, Oando and Dangote into other neighboring and far-away African countries. They are paving the way in creating African giants which the world will no longer be able to ignore."

The award-winning magazine instituted the award to showcase the best of African business men and women that are behind the rapid economic transformation of Africa. Mr. Dangote was declared the African business leader of the year 2011, because of his drive and efforts as a change agent, who displayed the necessary courage and imagination in making difficult decisions according to media reports " ...with long term value and sustainability in mind which can ultimately transform corporations." Among African business leaders nominated with Dangote for the prestigious award were Vima Shah of *Baker Oil* refineries of Kenya, Nizar Juma of *Jubilee Holdings* Limited of Kenya, Mr. James Mwangi of *Equity Bank*, Pluthuma Nhlekho of South Africa, and *MTN Group* of South Africa. Dangote Group Nigeria Limited also emerged the African business company of the year 2011.

Mr. Dangote was present at the ceremony to receive both awards. He informed those present that, "Reforms are changing the face of doing business in the (African) Continent. Over 84 percent of economies in sub-Saharan Africa have implemented reforms making it easier to do business." Dangote continued, "There are still challenges to doing business in Africa but there is hope. This is a new Africa. Governance is much better. Yes, there is corruption and it is still an issue. But looking at where we have come from, things are getting better and fast." The annual event is fast becoming a platform to celebrate business excellence in Africa, especially the business men and women that are driving the economic development of Africa. In addition to the company of the year award and "business leader of the year award, won by the Dangote Group and Mr. Dangote respectively; other categories that awards were presented included; award for corporate governance in African business, investor of the year award, green award of the year, and the best corporate social responsibility and outstanding business woman of the year award" for 2011. In fall 2010, the Nigerian investment promotion commission (NIPC), in conjunction with the CBC in Abuja presented Mr. Dangote with the investor of the year award as parts of activities lined up to celebrate Nigeria at 50.

In the same fall 2011, the Nigerian government took the novel step of conferring the nation's second highest national honor on Mr. Dangote. The award; grand commander of Nigeria (GCON), which was traditionally bestowed on the nation's vice-presidents was given to billionaire Dangote. Nigeria's highest national honor; the grand commander of the federal republic (GCFR) is normally conferred on the nation's president. President Goodluck Jonathan explained his administration's reason for conferring the nation's second national honor on a private person. "Aliko Dangote deserves more honors than even those of us holding political offices," said Jonathan, almost gooey when presenting the award to Mr. Dangote and pointed out the giant strides a business man such as Dangote has made in Nigeria's economic development. Aliko Dangote thanked the Nigerian government for the national honor and many Nigerian commentators said it was a well-deserved honor to Mr. Dangote.

CHAPTER 13
DANGOTE'S
TEMPLATES FOR
BUSINESS SUCCESS

THE GREAT BOOK, the Holy Bible says no one should despise the days of small beginnings. What starts like a small project, if cleverly and methodically nurtured, can end up becoming a big and mighty project. The Qur'an in Surat Al-Baqarah enjoined all Muslims "...not to be [too] weary to write it, whether it is small or large, for its [specified] term. That is more just in the sight of ... it is [grave] disobedience in you. And fear Allah. And Allah teaches you. And Allah is Knowing of all things" (2:282). Native wisdom in virtually all cultures of the world emphasizes the power of beginning from small beginning, and then gradually transiting to something big. Small drops of water they say make a mighty ocean. Those who pride themselves as born to run in the journey of life soon crash out. There is no easy road to freedom as Nelson Mandela said, and the great Madiba should know. The South African leader and pan-Africanist gave quarter of a century of his life to liberate a nation. Great successes require great sacrifices, and only those who are ready to make sacrifices win the eternal prize and laurels of heroism. No struggle comes without any demand

As it is in politics so also it is true of real business success. The world's household soft drink giant, Coca-Cola started small. Mr John Pemberton of Columbus, Georgia in the United States began his idea, for what later became the most popular beverage drink of billions of human beings in more than 150 countries with only US$500 in May 1886. Mr Dangote began from small beginnings at the age of fifteen, and did not doubt for once his mission in life. Dangote adheres to the principle of planting an acorn to become an oak. As he noted, "I built a conglomerate and emerged the richest Black man in the world but it didn't happen overnight. It took me thirty years to get to where I am today. Youths of today aspire to be like me, but they want to achieve it overnight. It's not going to work. To build a successful business, you must start small and dream big. In the journey of entrepreneurship, tenacity of purpose is supreme." Expatiating further the power of small beginning, Dangote disclosed that, "You have to start from somewhere. No business is too small to do. As they say, Rome was not built in a day."

The same principle of starting small was used by Messrs. Dmitry Igorevich and Segei Galitsky, chairman and chief executive of Magnit Stores, the largest retail stores in Russia. Shortly after the fall of communism in 1985, the two business men knew that food and household goods would be the priorities of Russian workers. In 1994, they opened their first grocery store in Krasnodar, and when they saw the reception they got from customers, they opened one more branch. Watching how receptive customers were patronizing them, they adopted the Wal-Mart style of distribution-one retail outlet for each city or town with large parking space, menageries of household products and groceries at affordable costs. Mr. Igorevich, now known as Mr. Sam Walton of Russia has succeeded in creating a- $7.7billion food chain in eighteen years, employing 79,000 workers, 3,228 retail outlets in 57 regional branches serving customers in 974 cities/towns in Russia. The food chain opens a new retail store weekly. Both Messrs. Igorevich and Galitsky are billionaires and credited their success from starting from small beginnings.

Another trait of Aliko Dangote which brought him to the top is simplicity. He does not shout. Simplicity is the way of many billionaires of the world which Mr. Dangote also imbibes. Mr. Li Ka-shing, the son of a refugee, is the richest man in Hong Kong, and the richest man in Greater China. He built the two largest companies in Greater China, the popular Hutchison Whampoa and Cheung Kong Holdings to become the 8th richest person in the world with an estimated personal fortune of $31billion. But when you see this rich man, who has given out more than $10 billion in donations, pledges and philanthropic activities, you will not believe his sense of simplicity. A widow with two adult sons; Victor and Richard-both work in their father's expansive business empire. Mr. Ka-shing wears a Seiko wrist-watch, and at times a- $50 Timex wristwatch. He does it the old school and guards his wealth with simplicity and discipline. He refuses to wear designer shoes. It took prodding from his two sons to wear ties. He insisted on just plain ties. How about the richest man in Spain, Mr. Amancio Ortega, the founder and chief executive of Inditex Group, the popular fashion company? A quiet and unassuming man, he dresses in simple T-shirts and denim jeans trousers. He refuses to wear ties, even with his $57billion wealth which made him the richest man in Spain, the richest man in Europe, and the 3rd richest man in the world. For nearly twenty years, he refused to grant press interviews. He still works in the production line in his company, and has refused to be photographed. He only had his small picture on his company's website until 2000, when he appeared publicly, because he was planning to take his company to his nation's bourse. Spain's photojournalists and admirers were jostling to take his photograph. Just like simplicity defines the rich men and women of the world, so also is a trait of Aliko Dangote of Africa. It is a trait common to those, who have climbed the mountain and have seen the top, and want to remain there.

Mr Bill Gates, the richest man on planet earth for thirteen years was in Nigeria few years ago. These days, he comes regularly as he promotes his foundation's cause of eliminating malaria from Africa, but when he first came, a group of Nigerian elected state governors were asked to see him. He was waiting for them and when the politicians entered the room one by one, it took someone to introduce the richest person in the world to the politicians. Many of the state governors wore skin shoes, Rolex wrist watches and flowing grand boubou, but the man who could buy everything and will not feel a dent in his wallets was his simple self with casual wear. No ostentation, no outlandishness but in Nigeria, people blow their trumpets above the rooftops. The only hint that an important global citizen was in the room were the presence of U.S Secret Service agents that accompanied Mr Gates to Nigeria. Empty barrels make the loudest noise. Dangote's humility, as he once revealed, came from his grandfather, the greatest salt merchant of West Africa Pa Alhassan Dantata. "His humility is the type I have never seen anywhere. He was a very humble person. He never looked down on anybody," Dangote recalled.

Every successful business person who has made their mark in our world live by certain principles and those who have followed their footpaths replicate the success of these successful businessmen and women. Sam Walton, the late founder, first chairman and chief executive of the largest retail conglomerate in America and the world built and lived by Walton's ten principles as revealed in his biography; "Made in America, My Story." They are: be committed to your goals; share your rewards; energize your colleagues; communicate all you know; value your associates; celebrate your success; listen to everyone; deliver more than you promise; work smarter than others, and blaze your own path.

Mr. Warren Buffett, the fourth richest man in the world who recently gave out $31 billion of his wealth to charity once granted a one- hour interview to the CNBC and gave ten rules on how to make money and build wealth. It will be apposite to refer to the rules as the Buffett Rules. Rule one: develop the habit of savings. He explained that although inflation can eat up into one's saving, but the culture of putting some money aside on a consistent basis is good for creating wealth. He advised parents to develop this spirit in their children. Mr. Buffett has company in Michele Singletary, the celebrated and syndicated columnist for the Washington Post. Rule two: do not spend your money on what you don't really need. Again, he implored all parents to inculcate this culture into their kids very early in life. As Mrs. Singletary says, differentiate between your needs and wants as secret to money making. Rule three: always think of how you can accomplish things most economically. Rule four: when or if you run your own company, or business, make sure you assign the right people to do the right jobs. According to Buffett, if you put square pegs in round holes, you are courting disaster. Rule five: you are the man or woman with the vision in a company, so set the goals and make sure everyone follows the goals. Rule six: make sure you manage your shareholder's money and lose none of their money. Rule seven: cultivate the spirit of investment, and inculcate the same spirit into your kids very early in life because, what you sow early grows more than what is put in and thus double your initial investment. Rule eight: live frugally and avoid ostentatious lifestyle, live within your means, and buy what you need and avoid your wants. Rule nine: be your own boss and set your time. Finally, rule ten: be yourself and do not pretend to be what you are not. In other words, simplicity should be the watchword of any man or woman who wants to be a business success.

We examined the life of Mr. Dangote closely from interviews with close associates and family members for this biography. We were able to piece together six secrets of the richest Black person in the world. See the six secrets of his success, or what we call the Dangote's secrets to successful business and money making in Africa.

The ability to take risks; life is a risk; everything we do since the fall of humanity from yore has always been experimental. When one embarks on anything in life, its success in not guaranteed; from marriage, running a family, setting up a business to just about any human activity in life; nevertheless, you plod along anyway, and anyhow, believing somehow that with faith you will become successful. Life therefore is a big risk. Those who do not try because of fear of failure are cowards. History does not celebrate lily-livered people, but only the daring and risk-takers are memorialized. Where the faint-hearted shrinks away for fear of failure, the risk-takers braced all odds and come out successful. How many years did it take Henry Ford to create and invent the automobile? He failed several times but he did not give up. He was booed, derided, jeered at, and made fun of as he worked in his garage refusing to give up until he had a breakthrough, almost in his mid-life. According to him; "Failure is a chance to begin again more intelligently. It is just a resting place. We learn more from our failures than our successes." As an engineer and a machinist at Detroit Edison Company on a monthly salary of $125 in 1892, none of his contemporaries shared his optimism of a motor car with combustible gasoline engine. His idea was considered a stupid idea. His colleagues saw him as an insane person who should give up, but Henry Ford didn't give up. In 1896, he met the great inventor, Thomas Edison and told him about his idea. Edison himself, who had endured all kinds of failures in life, and knew what risk-taking in life was all about looked at Henry and said; "There is a big future for any light-weight engine that can develop a high horsepower and is self-contained...Henry, keep on with your engine. If you can get what you are after, I can see a great future." Henry Ford later disclosed that the encouragement he received from Edison was the defining moment in his life which really spurred him never to give up. Edison lived long to see Ford's success before Edison died in 1931.

In the 1970s, a Lebanese immigrant at the University of Southern California entered the university library, and saw how fellow students lined up to use the university photocopying machine. He felt there should be an efficient way to serve the students. In his mind, he thought how cool it would be for someone to go to the dormitories of the students, collect the books they wanted to photocopy, did the copies, and return the finished copies back to their dormitories. He had the idea but needed money to buy his own photocopying machine so he went to his father and begged him to give him a loan of $5,000 for his business start-up. His father didn't believe him, or shared his optimism, because of his son's natural disabilities: he was an immigrant with a foreign accent in America. He is also dyslexic, and such speech impairment would turn fellow students away, who would find it difficult to understand what he was saying. "You're just an average student, you do not have flair for anything mechanic," his father told him. Actually his father was right, because the young man graduated in finance from the University of Southern California as a "C" student or third class as it is called in the British-modeled education system. But the young man persisted telling his father what he saw at the campus library, "Dad, this thing here is going to go for a long time" -referring to the long lines of students waiting in the library to make photocopies of books. Because of his persistence, his father agreed rather grudgingly, but took him to the nearby Bank of America and said he would only co-sign for the $5,000 bank loan.

Elated and ecstatic, the young man returned back to campus and printed leaflets announcing new services to students, and staff. But this time around, he would go to student's dormitories and staff offices to collect the photocopy materials, and still charged the same price as the university libraries. The new service saved time for students and staff. Words of mouth quickly went round, and soon, he extended his reach to the nearby University of California at Santa Barbara and told some of his class mates to join in the "fun." He made $2,000.00 (two thousand) in his first month. He paid back some of his bank loans, and ploughed the rest back to his new business all the while attending classes. One of the problems he encountered at the University of California, Santa Barbara was how to secure an office. He didn't have money for rent, so he told one of his friends who had a Volkswagen Beetle. They entered into a deal; the friend would make his jalopy available when he didn't have lectures and meanwhile, he had sent flyers out at Santa Barbara when the "mobile office" would be on campus to pick up books for photocopying and when to return them. As he told the *Forbes* magazine later in an interview: "If you can't fix things and can't read things, then you can't get a job and I'm sort of unemployable. I'm basically a peddler." Twenty years later, the business grew to 830 outlets in the United States, Japan, Canada, South Korea and the Netherlands. Today, that company "... is the largest retail provider of document copying and business services in the world." The name of the young Lebanese man is Paul Orfalea and the name of the company is Kinko's. By the way, the name: Kinko's was the nickname –actually a pejorative alias- that fellow students gave to him, because of his hair and manner of speaking as a dyslexic immigrant at the University of Southern California! Orfalea has refused to disclose the sales figures of his company, but the *Forbes* magazine estimated that with 20,000 employee workforces worldwide, each of his 830 outlets around the world grossed about US$750,000.00 annually. You do the math! In February 2004, Mr. Frederick Smith, chairman, founder, chief executive and owner of Federal Express Corporation FedEx bought 1200 retail outlets of Kinko's from Mr Orfalea for $2.4billion cash. The company was renamed FedEx-Kinko's.

The nerve for adventure is a secret to Mr. Dangote's business success. In many advanced capitalist nations of the world, those who succeeded in amassing fortunes beyond their wildest dreams did not set out initially to become wealthy entrepreneurs. In other words, the billionaires of the world did not put money-making in the front burner as motivating factor, or overriding motive for venturing into business. The Wright Brothers-Wilbur and Orville- of North Carolina were sons of a church pastor desirous of adventure when they conceived the idea of building an aircraft. The Wright Brothers got it right when they changed the course of human history in 1903. Today we owe much to them in their invention that has revolutionized human history. Mr. Henry Ford of Michigan was not thinking of making money when he continuously tinkered with the novel idea of building an engine as human wagon. He said his main objective was to see a car in every garage in the United States, and the car must be cheaper, easy, and affordable to own by every American. Bill Gates he and his buddy; Allen that co-founded *Microsoft* said their motivation was to ensure every home and office in America have access to computer, and every business will be able to use it to make their works faster and efficient. But plenty of money and wealth were the results of the altruistic motives of these great men.

Aliko Dangote has turned around many moribund corporations with the sole aim of saving the jobs of the employees in those corporations while ensuring there is no disruption in the services that such corporations provide for the people. In the process of pouring his own money into such corporations, profits are the results that naturally come with such efforts, for, even as the Holy Bible says, every labourer deserves his or her wage. Rich people and great inventors did not set out to be rich. Many of them just wanted to make life better, improve people's living conditions, and provide a service for the people. His visit to *Arisco* Stores in Brazil was the turning point in his business life. The spirit of adventure to the South American nation in the 1980s moved Mr. Dangote from importation to manufacturing and Nigeria, indeed Africa have become better for it.

One of the secrets of Mr. Dangote for business success is the ability to spot a talent, and put such talent at the helms. He knows how to identify people with rare distinguished skills and dedicated talents. This has accounted for the growth of his corporation in leaps and bounds. For example, Mr. Joseph Makoju is former managing director and chief executive of West African Portland Corporation (WAPCO) makers of Ewekoro cement at Ewekoro in Ota, Ogun State in western Nigeria. His brilliant performance at the former moribund cement company which he turned around in few years netted the once comatose company staggering profit of ₦5.1 billion (about $35million) in 1995. Former President Olusegun Obasanjo was so impressed by Mr. Makoju's feat at WAPCO that he quickly drafted the first class graduate of mechanical engineering to the nation's epileptic power company, then known as Nigeria Electric Power Authority (NEPA), which Nigerians had humorously dubbed; Never Expect Power Always, because of the poor performance of the government-owned power company, which gave more darkness than light to its numerous customers. Mr. Makoju did not disappoint as he went to work replicating the same feat at NEPA. In his short spell at the electricity company, he increased Nigeria's electricity production from 1,750 megawatts to 3,700 megawatts, but because he did not stay long, the electricity supplies fell to 2,500 immediately he departed the government-owned power utility company.

Seeing the Midas touch of this brilliant man, Mr. Dangote went after him. He tapped into his wealth of experience, and today Mr. Makoju is the managing director of Dangote cement and special adviser to Africa's richest man. Makoju also doubles as the chairman of cement manufacturers association of Nigeria (CMAN). There are many unique advantages Mr. Joseph Oyeyani Makoju has brought to the table that no one else would have been suited for his position at the Dangote Group. In addition to his intimidating credentials: first class honors in electrical and mechanical engineering from the University of Nottingham, UK; fellow, Nigerian academy of engineers; Nigerian society of engineers, Nigerian institute of management, grand commander of special order of merit from Niger Republic, and pioneer president of the Federal University of Petroleum Resources, Effurun, Delta state mid-western Nigeria, winner of John F. Kennedy memorial essay competition while in college, and recipient of the prestigious Commonwealth Scholarship in 1974, Joseph was born in the very land Dangote has his cement factory in Obajana, central Nigeria. Makoju knows the community like the back of his palms. The meaning of his middle name, "Oyeyani" in Yoruba Language and in his native Ebira dialect are; "The one destined for laurels" and "The man who knows how to get things done" respectively. Many of such men and women born to win laurels, and know how to get things done are plenty in the Dangote Group.

Mr. Dangote believes and lives by the credo that there is

dignity in hard work and labour. Today's rich men and women have been used to hard work right from their youth, and hard work is not alien to them. As Patrice Motsepe, the third richest man in South Africa and one of the richest Black persons in South Africa disclosed to the *Sowetan* newspapers, "I must have been about eight years old when my father said one day; 'We make so much money when you're behind the counter so you should take over the business when you grow up.' But it was hard work, from 6.00am to 8.00pm." Patrice's father was a liquor seller in Johannesburg during the apartheid regime in the erstwhile laager. Patrice later went to college, graduated as a lawyer, and today owns the majority shares in African rainbow minerals ARMgold -the 5th largest gold mining corporation in the world- where Patrice has a personal fortune of $3.3 billion.

The Albrecht Brothers; Theo and Karl, watched their mother handled money at her grocery store while growing up in the 1920s in Essen, Germany. Theo soon applied as an apprenticeship in his mom's grocery store. His brother became the delicatessens attendant, and both brothers later grew up to own the popular *Aldi* Grocery Stores operating all over the world. Although Theo died in 2010 at the age of 88 years, his 91-year old elder brother, Karl Hans Albrecht continues to manage the largest grocery retail store in Germany which made him the richest man in Germany with staggering fortunes of $26 billion and the 18th richest person in the world. Ms. Liliane Bettencourt, the richest woman in the world's Top 20 Billionaires and French entrepreneur began her journey to billionaire land at the age of fifteen when her father made her work at the company's cosmetic company, *L'Oreal*. She began her apprenticeship by mixing hair shampoo chemicals, affixing labels, and an apprenticed cosmetologist even though Liliane lost her mother at the relatively young age of five. That virtue of hard work, diligence, and honesty built strong character in the woman, who later emerged as the ninth richest person in the world with her fortune put at $30 billion. While little Liliane was working for her father, many of her friends would be hard-pressed to believe that the future heiress to one of the largest cosmetic companies in the world would "descend" so low to be a factory worker. That early exposure to work ethics showed Liliane the power of hard work, diligence and responsibility on how to make money.

Mr. Dangote disclosed that he learned the power and spirit of hard work from his grandfather, the legendary Pa Sanusi Dantata; "I leaned hard work from my grandfather. I learnt that it pays to work hard. Hard work is the key to success in life. Once you are ready to work and consistent, you would make money." Every rich person in the *Forbes* list of world billionaire shared this timeless principle.

The power of "can- do-anything," and the spirit of not giving up which was what made us Americans some of the most ingenious human beings on earth. In Nigeria, many have given up because they have tried, either in politics, or business to give their best, or turn things around; tackle headlong the problems of corruption, graft and other political debilities confronting Nigeria. They have exasperatedly thrown their hands up. In business, too many have also resigned themselves to fate insisting that it is impossible for a Nigerian business man, or woman to emerge as the richest person in Africa without cheating, or cutting corners. Dangote's success de-mystified all these assumptions. In a chaotic ambience hostile to business, he did not give up. When the nation's business climate did not support manufacturing as far back as the 1970s, and the 1980s, and Nigerians imported virtually everything including toothpicks, Dangote knew the future belongs to locally manufactured goods and products, and didn't waver. Time eventually proved him right. According to him, "A smart business person should manufacture, and don't just trade. There is money in manufacturing even though it is capital intensive. To achieve a big breakthrough, I had to start manufacturing the same products I was trading on. I am an advocate of manufacturing, because it does not only improve your business status; it also helps you give back to your community and country; with respect to job creation and economic development." Continuing, Dangote disclosed that, "The whole thing is that you have to really be very determined. You have to believe that, yes, there's a future in this country of ours and I can tell you right now, I don't believe we have even started doing anything in Nigeria, because the opportunities are so enormous. I don't even know where to start from."

As Mr. Rasheed Gbadamoshi, Lagos industrialist and chairman of Ragolis Waters Nigeria, Lucky Fibre Nigeria, among others; former public servant in Lagos state, economist and former secretary of national planning in Nigeria once said, resilience is the ability to stand against adversities, and the ability to do things which are of benefit to people and society. Mr. Gbadamoshi cited Mr Barack Hussein Obama, the first African-American President of the United States, and the iconic Madiba Nelson Rohlahla Mandela, first President of a de-segregated South Africa, who spent 27 years behind bars for the freedom of his people as two of his inspirations, and those he admired in life. According to the Ikorodu-born industrialist, and writer / author and art enthusiast, "When I was in America in the 60's, carrying placard (against racial discrimination) and singing: "we shall overcome someday.....' I never believed that in my lifetime, a Blackman would emerge as president in America. Also, Mandela, the indestructible human spirit, he was caged for 27 years for standing against apartheid. He came out and was still able to provide leadership not only to his people but also to the African continent, leaving example for the whole world to emulate."

Resilience permeates Mr. Dangote's life and his business where he has phenomenally excelled. No one knows the power of perseverance in our contemporary business world than the late Mr. Steve Jobs, the co-inventor of *Apple* Computers. The success story of one of the most remarkable "business-come-back-kids" is an epitome of the resilience, and long-suffering of the two men behind today's success story. Steve Wozniak and Steve Jobs began the company in a garage in Cupertino, California in 1976 and within twelve years had grossed \$1.5billion in sales and was rated number 234th on *Fortune 500*. The vision of the two "computer nerds" as both were called by the US media, was to make computer smaller, affordable, and portable in every home in America just as Henry Ford dreamt of a Ford automobile in every American garage. The duo sold their personal effects to raise the initial capital of \$1,300 they started the business with, but in 1981 at the height of their business potentials, Steve Wozniak had an accident in a plane crash which he survived, but his injuries prevented him from continuing at the company. He cashed out leaving Steve Jobs to continue with the dream. Meanwhile, computer giant, *Microsoft* was sucking the oxygen out of the strongest competitor in town. Steve Jobs needed help, more so when customers began to complain that his products had small hard drive and other "defects."

The new chief executive he brought in to replace his partner apparently didn't share Jobs' vision and soon began to scheme for Jobs' removal. In 1985, Jobs was fired by the board he had constituted in a boardroom political move orchestrated by the man he had hired as chief executive. The business world thought Jobs was toast but the irrepressible man didn't give up. He named the company "apple" when he dropped out of Reeds College and went on a summer vacation to India and converted to Buddhism by shaving-of his head so the concept was his brainchild. After he lost his company, he moved on and set up *Next* and began to put in place all the ideas he had for the company he had lost. Meanwhile, those who orchestrated his removal were battling with competition from *Microsoft*: sales plummeted; managers began to leave and *Apple* was bleeding profusely. The new owners knew who to go to: Steve Jobs, so they approached him to buy his *Next* but he insisted he must come on board as chief executive. A decade after he lost the company which he co-founded, Steve Jobs lived up to his name like the Biblical Job and stopped the hemorrhage. Jobs introduced two new "inventions:" laser writer and page maker which became instant success. He made up with the company's bête noire- *Microsoft* and within two years, Jobs brought *Apple* from the red. He introduced *Apple* Store where customers buy directly from the company's several outlets around the United States and the world. The first quarter of 1997 when Jobs returned, the company that was on financial life support made after tax profit of $44million. The rest as they is history. Before he died in 2011, Steve Jobs was a billionaire with estimated personal fortunes of $8.3billion according to the *Forbes* magazine. When Jobs was asked later during an interview what kept him going during those giddy years, especially after he lost his "baby," and people thought he was finished, he had one word: perseverance. "I'm convinced that about half of what separates the successful entrepreneurs from the non-successful ones is pure perseverance," he said. At his death in 2011, Mr. Jobs left behind a -$338billion company.

And lastly is the power of vision to see beyond the immediate and into the future. Vision is the vehicle that drives ideas and without it a people perishes, so also a business organization. Vision in leadership is very important, because it answers vital questions such as: where is this company or corporation going, who will be going with us and how do we get to where we are going? Journalists and media practitioners define news as what is happening, where, who, when and how of events and people, while political scientists define politics as, the art of who gets what, when, where and how? In leadership, it is vision that defines who, what, why, when and how of business and its success. Jack Welch, former chief executive of one of the largest corporations in the world, General Electric *(GE)* knew the powerful weapon of the right vision for a successful company. He ran the Schenectady-based industrial giant in Up-State New York at a time the "beast" that was giving the company nightmares was Japan, and the dire prediction for *GE* was sure disaster. A decade after he defeated the "beast" and returned the largest company back to its pre-eminent position, Mr. Welch was asked by Piers Morgan on CNN at primetime on Thursday June 09, 2011 how he was able to break the back of the monster tormenting *GE,* Jack had one word: "Vision."

According to Mr. Welch, "In order to lead a nation, or a business corporation, you must have a vision; the head who is the chief executive must put everything on the table and put everyone on the same page; a leader must explain to his subordinates how to re-innovate." He disclosed that the very day he drove out to downtown Syracuse and saw cheap Japanese television sets being sold; he knew that he must do something and do it fast if *GE* must survive. He said America was still the world's global economic giant, and the American Dream was still well and alive but now that the "beast" tormenting America is China, what the Lone Super Power in the world today needs is political vision. He concluded by saying, "How do we–Americans-become more competitive again? How do we out-innovate China and our competitors? Which innovative policies do we put in place as a nation? How does America close tax loophole and tax havens so the money could be repatriated back to the United States and what winning policies does America need to put in place, and does America restrict the temptation of erecting a wall around itself? To make America become the most competitive nation in the world as it was, everyone must not be freewheeling." Welch gave his first elixir for America's success again and soaring to greater heights: "Vision."

It all boils down to powerful insight into the future which is anchored on brands. In the Dangote Group, Mr. Dangote is the visionary man at the helms. When virtually all companies were tanking at the height of the world economic slump in 2010, his company, according to the *Forbes* magazine recorded the highest net profit of over 550 per cent amid complaints, hand wringing, and anguished souls from other corporate chief executives in Nigeria, Africa and around the world.

Whatever Dangote does, he does it in style. He needs to; his brand is the best in Nigeria, and he has the money, plenty of it to hire the smartest, the best and the brightest. But most importantly, the name Dangote is a brand and everything directly, or remotely connected to that brand name must be topnotch. According to the richest Black person on earth, "One of our core brand values as a group is to be customer-centric; we continually seek to ensure that the consumer drives our everyday operations, from research and development to sales and marketing. We are gratified to note that our numerous consumers are keeping faith with our product offerings. As we make plans to make Dangote a global brand, we pledge to work even harder to retain the confidence and support of our consumers in Nigeria." No wonder, whatever new product the Dangote brand releases into the African market, it does it with, élan and panache as it was when he decided to unveil another baby from the Dangote Empire: the popular Dangote Noodles.

This customer-centric philosophy was what motivated *CVS Caremark Corporation*, America's drug retail giant for example, to put so much value on its coupons to retain its loyal customers, while attracting new ones. The rebate coupons, exclusive to more than 67million of its loyal customers under CVS Extra Care loyalty program, according to *The New York Times* normally appear at the bottom of member's receipts. When redeemed, it all adds up, according to Ms. Melissa Studzinski, the drug store's vice president for customer relations. "There are tens of millions of shoppers that realize this and take advantage, yet there are still millions of customers who don't," she disclosed in one of her several email to customers. "We wanted to do something fun and irreverent to help draw attention to the savings that people are "trashing"...and drive more customers to redeem their rewards."

These are the stellar qualities and unique attributes of most *Forbes* billionaires and their companies. Even those who are not in the billionaire club but live by these principles, they are sure to excel wherever they are in any part of the world. These are timeless principles that work beyond geographical boundaries, because when all is said and done we are human beings. We eat, sleep and clothe ourselves. We want to remain in good health. We want to be respected, have our basic needs met and find employment to take care of our needs and the needs of our children and families.

The authentically rich people of the world that began from the scratch, and through diligence, hard work, dedication and strict discipline worked their ways to the top and succeeded in building brand names, have certain values and ethics. These ethical values define their attitudes to how they handle money, their approaches to businesses and life generally. The first trait that is noticeable in their lifestyle is frugality. The common adage, "The empty vessel or drum makes the loudest noise" is seen in the lifestyles of those who are phony rich men and women but pretend to be rich.

Mr. Walton, the founder of *Wal-Mart* - the largest retail network and the second richest man next to Bill Gates in America in the 1990's- rode an old *Ford Lincoln* car. He chose to drive himself just as Aliko Dangote chooses to drive himself from his Karim Kotun house in Ikoyi to the Boat Club in Lagos Island. Mr. Warren Buffet, the Oracle of Omaha, Nebraska and the fourth richest man in the world today, lives in the same house –a three bedroom house- he has been living with his wife for 50 years. He once said, "I have no need for another house because this three- bedroom house has all that I need." Mr. Buffet does not travel by private jet though he owns the largest private jet company in America. Mr. Buffet lives by ten ethical rules: don't try to show off but be yourself, and do what you enjoy doing. Do not go on brand name; just wear those things in which you feel comfortable. Do not waste your money on unnecessary things but just spend on those things you really need. Do not give chance to anyone to rule your life for after all, it is your life. Stay away from loans and credit cards but remember to invest in yourself. Remember money does not create man, but it is man that created money. Live a simple life as simple as you are. Set goals and make sure you and your subordinates follow those goals. Do not do what others say but just listen and do what you feel is good. And finally, live frugally and economically. Examine the lifestyles of the real rich men and women of the world and you will see the twin traits of frugality mixed with elegance.

Frugality is the ethical way of doing things in moderation; elegance is the portrayal of class. As early as the 1950s, the late Mr. Shafi Lawal Edu of Lagos was a proud owner of a *Rolls Royce*. He built his business empire on oil tankers. As the president of Lagos chamber of commerce and industry in Nigeria in the '60s, he used to go about with his *Mercedes Benz* car and when asked why he hardly rode in his silver-blue *Rolls-Royce,* he replied that it would be too ostentatious for him to go about with the world-class automobile. Those who really work for their money, and know the value of genuine hard work and wealth do not flaunt it. Mr. Branson, one of the richest men in the world has a trademark in his attire: blue jeans and sweaters over simple suits and ties. Jeans pants for a man sitting atop a $3billion conglomerate. He told his employees at *Virgin* not to call him "Sir" even though he was knighted by the Queen of England, but to simply address him as Richard. Mr. Dangote is an epitome of simplicity and frugality.

Another Nigerian business man I-Moshood Fayemiwo-saw display this attitude of simplicity and humility was Mr Jimoh Ibrahim that one of the authors ran into at the local wing of the Murtala Mohammed Airport, Ikeja, Lagos in early 2011 during the field work for this biography. We were flying from Lagos to Abuja, Nigeria's administrative city. We queued up to board the local *Aero Airways* and Mr. Ibrahim also took his turn on the queue like the rest of us. He could ask to be treated differently for after all, he bought Virgin Nigeria Airways from Branson and renamed it; *Air Nigeria* but he took his turn and was checked-in like the rest passengers. There were only few of the passengers that recognized the publisher of *National Mirror newspapers, Newswatch magazine, Global Fleet* Group of Companies and several others, including the author. When we arrived at the Nnamdi Azikiwe International Airport in Abuja, Nigeria, someone the author recognized went to him for a discussion. "Who was that man?" I asked and was told who he was. That was rare in Nigeria because the bigger your grand bobou, the bigger your personality which entitles you to live above the rules and law in Nigeria. The locals refer to such impunity as "The big man syndrome."

Mr. Aliko Dangote believes in becoming his own boss very early in his business life and that is one of the secrets to business success. It is a fact of life that those who control their work, control their lives, and ultimately determine their own destiny. One of the secrets of business success is the ability to see into the future by owing your own business. No one makes money, plenty of it as we see in the narratives of billionaires of the world by working for others. Even in the spiritual realm, if you work for others, you have to pray first to God Almighty to bless your employer before you can be blessed. After all, your employer writes your pay check and if your employer does not make profit you can't get paid.

Every phenomenally rich person imbibes this secret of wealth-making in their lives and business ventures. In 1990, Mr. Jeff Bezos was named the *Banker's Trust* youngest vice-president and was given a beautiful plaque to show for designing the best computer systems that helped his employers; *Bankers Trust* of New York managed the company's assets valued at over US$250 billion. Although he was given an award but remained an employee. A graduate of electrical engineering and computer science from the prestigious Princeton University at Princeton, New Jersey; Bezos moved to *D.E. Shaw & Co* on Wall Street and replicated the same feat he had performed at *Bankers Trust,* but received the same plaque and a small ceremony for his brilliance. No one knew about Bezos until he founded his own company, *Amazon* and within two years he had built a global company which stock climbed to US$1.75billion from 1997-1999 while Jeff himself was worth $2billion with 45 per cent stake in the conglomerate. There is a local proverb in Africa, which says; "This thing belongs to all of us is not as good and impressive and as when you say 'this thing is mine." And until "it is yours," you may not be able to give it all your best. As Mr. Dangote disclosed, "I don't like business partnerships or joint ventures, they create a lot of problems."

The power to have the insight into the reality of life that no one can make money, plenty of money to the tune of a billion dollars by working for others was brought home to Ms. Oprah Winfrey in 1984. She was working for the Chicago-based *WLS-TV*, an affiliate of *ABC* on annual salary of $230,000.00. Now when you earn that amount in the United States, you belong to a negligible few of less than five percent Americans that make that amount yearly. Ms. Winfrey never knew she was actually being under-paid by her employers, because her show had the highest ratings in Chicago, even more than Phil Donahue who was then referred to as the king of talk-show in Chicago, Illinois. Then Oprah heard from the station's executives that her paycheck had been increased by $23,000.00 because her agent was good. That revelation made her thinking that she must be very good for the television station to agree to the pay increase, which meant she must have been worth more than she was actually being paid. So Ms. Winfrey fired her agent and hired another agent, Mr. Jeffrey Jacobs. It was Jacobs who opened the eyes of Oprah.

As the queen of television talk-show later disclosed to the *Forbes* magazine during an interview in its October 16, 1995 edition; "I'd heard that Jeff is a piranha and I like that. Piranha is good." Jeff told Ms. Winfrey to look at herself first and foremost as a business woman, and not an entertainer. Second, he told her to re-negotiate her initial contract with the television station to include a clause that she would henceforth hold the copyright to all her editions/episodes. Thirdly, he said she should look beyond the local Chicago media market. And lastly, he told Oprah to open a new company that would handle the distribution and syndication of her shows. That was how *King World Production* began to handle the distribution of the popular *Oprah Winfrey Show*. The change was dramatic; two years later in 1986, the popular show was showing in 138 television stations across the continental United States. That year *Forbes* estimated Ms. Winfrey's fortunes at $400million. Five years later, the ratings soared, and the show was being aired on 200 television stations across the world and two years later, Ms. Winfrey became the first African-American/Black woman to appear on the *Forbes* list of world billionaires. Oprah Winfrey had worked for others for 15 years, but she became a billionaire after working for herself for only 7 years!

The above are the basic fundamental principles that some of the superbly rich men and women of the world live by to reach money land. These principles have been tested and found to be working. Anyone who puts them to use will also record business success, breakthroughs and financial success, whether the person is a Black or White person, it doesn't matter.

Mr. Dangote's templates for business success in life should equally be matched with his templates for business failure. Just as Dangote's recipes for business success can be applied by aspiring young business men and women for business success, indeed to other areas of life; it is also important that the richest person in Nigeria and the richest black person in the world also live by some Don'ts. Here are some of them; actually they are seven things to avoid if you want to become another Aliko Mohammad Dangote of Nigeria, or Aliko Mohammed Dangote of Africa and possibly Aliko Dangote of the world.

Do not waste your time; learn how to manage your time judiciously. Time is precious. The first thing to learn is the way to manage your time. Your time is your greatest asset in life. You waste your time, and you waste your life. Actually time is life. Who knows more about the value of time management than one of the greatest and popular chief executives of our time, Mr. Lee Iacocca? Mr Iacocca, the man who turned around the fortunes of *Chrysler Motors* in the 1980s and served as president and chief executive officer, and later chairman of the auto company after he was fired by the *Ford Motors Corporation* and succeeded in positioning *Chrysler* into an auto giant throughout most of his thirteen years at the helms. He once said, "If you want to make good use of your time, you've got to know what's most important and then give it all you've got." Described at a time as the

18th greatest American chief executive of all time, Iacocca explained how he was able to prioritize his time in his popular autobiography co-authored with William Novak titled: "*Iacocca: An Autobiography.*"

It is not only in business that the act of skillful management of time is essential but in all ramifications of life. God Almighty or Nature, (whatever your belief), has given each and every one of us in the world equal opportunities which no one can deny, and that is the number of hours that make up our day in the world. Those are the 24 hours we all have to decide how we manage those hours of the day. Mr. Benjamin Franklin, one of the founding fathers of the United States, a man of many parts who invented the lightning rod, the bifocals and other scientific inventions including participating in other political activities once said, "Time is money." He was right. The way one spends his or her time determines how much the person is worth. Time management is very essential in the life of a business man and woman. As Aliko Dangote once disclosed, his time is so important that he goes to bed most times at 2:00am and is awake by 6:00 in the morning. Several studies have shown how one can easily maximize the use of time. So like Aliko, use your time wisely and get a firm grip on your life.

Another "don't" to avoid: do not bring emotions to management and financial decisions. Emotions stretched to the limits can destroy successful businesses. Good, successful, and smart business men and women are not weighed down by emotions. They reward every employee according to their productivity and contribution to the overall success of their companies. They do not have favorites; neither do they build personality cults around themselves. It was said of John D. Rockefeller, the richest man in the United States and the world in his day that he extracted a promise from each of his children that they would not touch cigarette in their first eighteen years of life and made sure they lived by that sworn oaths. When it comes to employee's promotions, you get to the top not because you are slick, know how to curry favors, or have "god fathers" in high places within the organization, but because you are hardworking and trustworthy. If a smart business man, or woman has some of his, or her relatives in the workforce, they are treated just the same way as other employees. Such level-playing fields for all employees bring the best out of all workers and reinforce the spirit of constant strive by every worker to give their utmost to the company, or corporation. There is a general belief that what is good for the goose is also good for the gander.

Mr. Charles *Walgreens,* founder of the popular Walgreens pharmaceutical chain stores followed this credo to the letter during his lifetime. Charles Walgreens Jr. the heir to the popular drug store chain *Walgreens* in the United States should have easily stepped into his father's shoes but was forced to work his way from the bottom up. His father, Charles W. Walgreens, who founded the renowned drug stores in 1901, made him a delivery boy at nine years old. Later, he became a store keeper, and served in many capacities for 33 years before he became president of his father's company. When Chuck died in 2007 at the age of 100, he had succeeded in nurturing the company to greater heights. His father did not favor him because he was his son. Chuck was initially planning to study architecture in college, until his father told him he would not turn over the company to him if he did not read pharmacy. He changed his mind and went on to study pharmacy at the University of Michigan. He still works three days a week even in his '90s at the company's headquarters in Deerfield, Illinois.

In many developed nations of the world, there are laws prohibiting any forms of discriminations, either because of a person's race, sexual orientation, religion, age or sex. In the largest private company in Nigeria and West Africa known as the Dangote Group, associates from virtually all tribes, ethnicities, religions, men and women including expatriates work as a team. According to Dangote, "The fact that I, a humble Kano boy, can reside peacefully in the south-west, do business in the south-east and build one of the biggest cement plants in the world in the middle belt, is a testimony to how great Nigerians are and Nigeria truly is. Nigeria has given so much to me. I stand before you today and renew my commitment to give much more back to Nigeria," while addressing a group of young Nigerian graduates at the Dangote Business Academy and School of Entrepreneurship which he established to re-train young Nigerian university and college graduates on how they could use their classroom theories to excel in the real business world. The Dangote Group with nearly 25, 000 workforces in Nigeria alone is like a mini-Nigeria and his other subsidiaries in West Africa and other parts of Nigeria are a mini-African Union.

Another "don't" in the Dangote principle: Do not hang around with the wrong crowd. Watch those you hang around with and the company you keep. It is said that those at the top, either in politics or business often find that they are lonely up there. It is true. There are plenty of rooms at the top, but unfortunately only few would make it to the top. At the bottom rung of the ladder of life are many people struggling to climb to the highest rung to reach the top. Those few people able to reach the top and etch out discover that their few contemporaries may not belong to their geographical areas, or they do not share a lot of things in common thus unable to interact, they find themselves lonely and wish they could interact with the crowd down below. But unfortunately, there are plenty of people down below who want to cultivate their friendships. This is where trouble starts, because many of those down below angling to befriend those few at the top are doing so, in most cases not out of love, or affection but for them to supplant the few at the top. This is why it is very dangerous for anyone at the top to make the mistake of befriending any of the numerous people down below. This is the way life is exactly is; if we are to be frank with ourselves. Simplicity does not mean carelessness! It is enough to care for those down below but careless for those at the top to let off their guards.

How many billionaires do we have, say in Nigeria? How many billionaires do we have even in Africa and in the world? The 1,200 or thereabout billionaires that are in the world collectively control more than 15 percent of the wealth on planet earth. It will be a lie to say the rest of the world is happy, but there is nothing anyone can do about it. So what is the attitude of the rest of the world? We pretend that we love and cherish these select rich men and women of the world. But in reality we "hate" them, period! We call them all sorts of names: criminals, oppressors, capitalists, cheaters, fat cats, oligopolistic blood-suckers, monopolists, and all kinds of derogatory names. The same in politics; how many presidents can a nation have but only one? We scrutinize their lifestyles; we poke noses at how they conduct the business of governing and statecraft, and hold them to high standards which we ourselves do not live by. We see them as privileged, outstanding, lucky and advantaged people who are more than lesser mortals. But in reality, these few top class guys, whether in politics, or in business are very much like the rest of us, and we should view them that way. But in reality they are different. That is why they are few. This is why rich people and the powerful of the world erect security barricades around themselves, because there are only two types of people they should hang around with: their peers, who are also after them and their positions, and those at the bottom who also want to be like them. It is up to the successful, the famous, and the powerful to select who to hang around with and make a wise decision on whom to really and truly trust and hang around with, because such decision will either make or mar his/her business, wealth or position. It is a no brainer! It is said by geographers that the higher you go, the cooler it becomes but in the journey of life's race to the top, the higher you go the lonely you find yourself because your circle of friends begin to shrink. It was said of President Bill Clinton by one of his aides; Mr. Dick Morris on the Fox News that, Mr. Clinton complained it was loneliness that drove him into the waiting arms of Ms Monica Lewinsky during his presidency (1992-2000) which led to the Monica Lewinsky sex scandal of 1997.

Here again is another "don't:" do not take people's loyalty for granted. Any business person who desires to be successful must not take the loyalty of his, or her subordinates for granted. It is essential to attend to the welfare of employees promptly and with dispatch. Some employers have the erroneous belief that employees come to work every day, because of their salaries and wages. That may be partially true but sociologists and some economists have also argued to the contrary, insisting that the workplace is more than a place for just paycheck. For example, Professor Flora Gill of the University of Sydney, Australia conducted a research, and discovered that the overriding motive why people work transcends just paycheck. According to her, people work because; it brings the creativity in human beings; workers first look at the workplace as an avenue for bonding and interact, which money cannot buy. Indeed, there have been instances of workers that have turned down job offers from other employers, even with higher paychecks and perks, because of their inability to get away from co-workers they have bonded with over a long period of time. This is why knowledgeable, and smart employers, and businessmen / women do not treat their employees as mere numbers, but as human beings which they truly are. As it is in politics so it is in business.

According to Dangote while addressing the presidential national job creation committee in Nigeria which he is the president, he was keenly aware of the political and socio-economic ambience he operates in his native Nigeria. He told the Nigerian government not take Nigerian citizens for granted warning that, "As we have seen in the Maghreb countries of Tunisia, Egypt, Libya and now spreading to the Emirate of the Middle East, youth unemployment is a very effective catalyst for social unrest that has brought down entire government." In the presence of President Goodluck Jonathan, his deputy, Mr. Namadi Sambo and top echelons of the Nigerian government, Dangote, who an average citizen would think must be out of sync with his fellow Nigerians, majority of whom live on less than 90 cents per day in a nation awash with petro-dollars was hardly ensconced in his billionaire land.

He knows what happens to ordinary Nigerians on the

streets and said it as it is supposed to be: youth unemployment is a worrisome issue. It is a time bomb which the Nigerian government should fix otherwise, the privileged positions of the nation's political and economic elites would be threatened. Mr. Dangote the industrialist didn't stop at that but went further to impress it on the Nigerian government the need to create the enabling environment for private enterprise to thrive. He stressed that in the spirit of free enterprise, it is the private sector that can put unemployed hands to work. If the Nigerian government stands in the way, things may get out of hand. Even though a status-quo potboiler, Aliko is no hagiographer of Any Government in Power- AGIP- on the issue of unemployment. When he went out on a limb and warned the Jonathan administration on the ticking bomb of youth unemployment, he was reacting to the trove of letters that bombard his offices on daily basis.

This is a great lesson for any ambitious entrepreneur: avoid burying your head in the sand like the proverbial ostrich to urgent and critical matters, either in your own company or in the local community or in the nation where you operate. An entrepreneur, or an industrialist does not necessarily have to be a politician, but that does not mean you should pretend not to know what is happening in your environment. What requires your presence should not be delegated to subordinates; you need to come out of your high horse and nip such potential and highly combustible issues such as worker's grievances, bad community relations, customer's cares, needs and worries in the bud.

This sensitivity to corporate consciousness has accounted for the relative peace that the Dangote Group enjoys with communities in all parts of Nigeria, especially in the Niger Delta areas of south-eastern Nigeria where no single community agitations and demonstrations have been waged against the company. In addition, while expats in the employment of other companies in the Niger Delta areas, both local and foreign have been routinely kidnapped by local militias and disgruntled local urchins for ransoms, not a single expat working for Dangote has suffered similar fate. There are some simple things called "inconsequential things in business," yet, as a successful business starts from small beginnings and systematically becomes conglomerates and corporations, "inconsequential things" that are left unattended can also cause the downfall of such corporations. Research into failures of big corporations and famous brands began from neglecting these "inconsequential things." No simple things are simple in managing businesses.

Another "don't which Mr Dangote has taught future and aspiring business men is behaviour to women. This "don't" is very powerful and must be taken seriously by any entrepreneur, or anyone aspiring to be one: Do not be a womanizer. Be careful with women. Human beings are confronted by many life's choices. In personal life choices, we are confronted with legionary binaries. One of the most effective ways of making sensible life decisions is living by strict ethical codes. No matter one's calling in life, individuals must live by certain disciplinary values to be successful in life. One of the pitfalls in life that every sensible man including any business man should watch out for is womanizing. Life has no meaning without women. God Almighty or Nature (again pick your choice), created women to complement men. There are few successful men in history, or out there, who would not credit their Significant Others as pillars of support. As the popular saying goes; "Behind every successful man in life, there is a supporting woman" or as some women would like to say, "Beside every successful man there is a woman by his side." However, to womanize is to be married and still engages in philandering and adulterous relationships. Who would ever believe that in the Nigerian culture, a man as rich as Mr. Dangote is a serial monogamist? He has the means and wherewithal to marry more than one woman at a time. He is a sensible man, and that is why he is where he is today. It is an important factor in the list of Don'ts in Aliko Mohammad Dangote's success templates.

Another lesson that Mr. Aliko Dangote learned from his

maternal grandfather on the "secrets" of business success is Spartan self-discipline which does not mix business with pleasure. According to him, "I learned strict discipline from my grandfather, I learnt first things first: that hard work should not be mingled with pleasure, with enjoyment. I am not saying people should not relax but too much enjoyment creates distraction for those who want to make it in life. Make the money first. Money is difficult to make but easy to spend. You must love and respect money. If you respect money, you would spend it wisely and not recklessly."

The list of great men in history, and in our contemporary world that have been brought down, or diminished by philandering, bad choices about the opposite sex and extra-marital affairs is legion. The world is full of men with great careers, and promising futures cut down by extramarital sex and "strange" women. The Mayor of Detroit in Michigan, Kwame Patrick was disgraced out of office, and sent to jail in 2008 for having illicit affairs with Christine Beatty, a city council official. Both were found guilty of using state funds to finance their secret amoral affairs. In March, 2008 a promising and energetic young Governor of New York, Elliot Spitzer humiliated himself, his family, and New York State when it was revealed he was having secret affairs with a call girl named Ashley Dupre. He resigned and left the Government House at Albany, NY in public obloquy. Here was a man already being speculated as a future president of the United States, because of his brilliance and political success beginning from his days as New York attorney-general and an anti-corruption czar, especially the way he cleansed the fat cats on Wall Street. Mr. Mark Sanford, former Governor of South Carolina had his political career cut short, because of extra-marital affairs when he abandoned his family, wife, chidden, and state duties for Argentina to meet a paramour in 2009. In Italy, former Prime Minister Berlusconi fought for his political life, because of sex scandal. In India, 86-year old Governor of Andra Pradesh, Mr. Narayan Dutt Tiwari was forced to resign from office in late 2009 when sex tapes of him with three naked Indian prostitutes making love were exposed by Indian newspapers. *The Times of India* reported that Mr. Tiwari admitted to the sleaze and quit his position and Indian political scene in shame and disgrace. The powerful rich French man and former head of the International Monetary Fund (IMF), New York, Mr. Dominique Strauss-Kahn lost his job, reputation, and dignity because of sex scandal in 2011. According to TIME, 30% of U.S military commanders lost their job between 2005 and 2012 because of sex-related offences, ranging from adultery, sexual harassment to indiscretion and improper relationships. In December 2012, David Howell Petraeus, a five-star military general, war hero and director, Central Intelligence Agency (CIA) ended his eventful military and public career abruptly in disgrace because of sexual indiscretion.

The largest sex scandal in world history involving almost $2billion law suit surfaced at *Dresdner Kleinwort* in 2006 in Germany when six female workers brought a law suit against top executives of the company when it was exposed that they were in the habit of bringing prostitutes and porn stars to offices at night. The head of the Royal Bank of Scotland RBS -one of the most powerful and largest banks in the world- Sir Fred Goodwin, lost his job when members of the British Parliament discovered he had been having illicit and extra-marital affairs with a female subordinate. The list is endless.

No matter how rich, famous, powerful and successful you are, extra-marital sexual affairs and womanizing can bring your career, wealth, fame and position crashing down before your very eyes. Some American political analysts once said that President William Bill Clinton would have been one of the greatest presidents in US history, if not for the blemish brought on his presidency by the Monica Lewinsky Scandal in 1998. Mr. John Edwards, a former senator, vice-presidential candidate, and presidential aspirant from North Carolina has been reduced to political nothing, because of extra-marital affairs. Not only is his political career over, he has lost his wife, his children, his reputation, his job and narrowly escaped imprisonment when he was not found guilty for misappropriating campaign contributions during his 2008 presidential campaign.

Next to womanizing is this other "don't:" which is, do not be a drunkard. Steer clear of illicit drugs. Do not cultivate the habit of cocaine, or heroin. Another "don't" in business success is too much wine and drunkenness. It is not a bad idea to take sweet, or red wine once in a while but for any business man, or woman to take to a life of drunkenness means the business he, or she owns cannot survive. Drunks have distorted sense of reality, and even employees who are drunk can never give their best to any organization. Workers who are in top management positions, and are functioning alcoholics can never take the department to greater heights. It is because of the deleterious effects of drunkenness that every company and corporation in America insists potential and newly-recruited workers, and employees must go for drug test before resuming work. Many workers lose their jobs every day around the world because they failed drug tests. As with womanizing, so also is with drunkenness and business men and women who engage in illicit drugs cannot build reputable companies and corporations that would outlive them. Many lives have been ruined; some people have lost their careers, families, dignities, and virtually everything they have toiled, laboured, and worked for all their lives because of drug addiction. According to David Rockefeller, the second son of John D. Rockefeller, "Success in business requires training and discipline and hard work but if you're frightened by these things, opportunities are just as great today as they ever were."

Do not hire mediocre and avoid those employees who do not buy into your company's objectives to be on decision-making part of your business. In other words, do not appoint or promote such people into management positions. The ambition of Dangote's expansion project is "to create an African champion that can compete with the largest cement companies in the world." A very laudable, and an ambitious dream but Dangote meant it. What he did was to hire the best in cement production who bought into this goal from Day

One. Today, Dangote cement has captured virtually all the West African sub-regional cement market, and has branched into other areas of Africa, and beyond the continent. The magic wand is that he surrounds himself with experts and not mediocre employees but smart people who are working on the same page with him. In addition, he pays his employees well. When a business outfit ensures no mediocre exists in its ranks and file, it is possible and beneficial to introduce, and practice what in politics is called "groupthink" which has been adapted into business decision-making process.

When Irving Janis coined the phrase, "groupthink" in the 1970's, he had studied major policy decisions of certain political figures; from Chamberlain's appeasement of Hitler pre-World War 11, President Kennedy's Bay of Pigs fiasco of Cuba, invasion of Pearl Harbor and many defining historical moments. He defined groupthink as; "A mode of thinking that people engage in when they are deeply involved in a cohesive group, when the members' strivings for unanimity override their motivation to realistically appraise alternative courses of action." When applied to organizations' decision-making process as in politics, it simply means, subsuming one's personal decision for group decision or in street lingo; "just go with the crowd." Organizations and political leaders often engage in groupthink to legitimize their authority, remove oppositions to pre-conceived policy decisions and use it as followership recruitment. In addition, groupthink assists leaders and managers to engage in blaming game in the event of policy failures and debacles. Followers and employees, who groupthink in organizations are afraid to dissent because of losing patronage, suffer from independent thought process or reluctance "not to rock the boat." Raven in, "*Groupthink,* Bay of Pigs, and Watergate Reconsidered," surmised that groupthink may indeed be beneficial to organizations as it promotes collective wisdom. In addition, it allows for unanimity of purpose in corporations and big business conglomerates.

Do not let power diffuse in any shape or form. Let every member of your company's management knows where power lies. Let the buck stops at your desk. Let your management team knows who calls the shots. The boss is the leader, even though you allow every member of your management to contribute to policy decision-making, and be a team player but do not let any of them lose sight of the fact that you are the boss. One of the things a business person who really wants to succeed should avoid is to allow power to diffuse in his, or her organization. Simply put, power is diffused when subordinates do not know who calls the shots and have no clue who, and who, are the bosses whether laterally, or vertically. Of course, no big corporation should allow every worker to have access to the founder or chairman, especially in corporations that have been diversified. But what we mean by power diffusion is for every top shot to be calling the shot. In politics for instance, Mr. Henry Kissinger, former secretary of state of the United States under two Republican administrations; Presidents Nixon and Ford (1973-1976) made this vital point on global security that the major concern of the United States during the Cold War was the mistaken reality that humanity would have that every nation wants to become a Super-Power and plunge the planet earth into unnecessary crisis. Henry Kissinger in his books, *"Diplomacy," "American Foreign Policy" and "A World Restored*: Metternich, Castlereagh and the Problem of Peace" explained that the plan of the United States was to give the world a Lone Super Power, and that Lone Super Power would be the United States, who would be calling the shots, and through that emergence of a global Super Power, global security would be guaranteed. And 70 years after the Old Union of Soviet Social Republics (USSR) engaged the United States of America- the capitalist world -in a global ideological war and crashed, the United States of America eventually won, and ushered the world into what is essentially a Uni-Polar world as we know today.

In business, the easiest way not to let power diffuse, according to Schein in *"Classics of Organizational Theory"* is by formulating organizational behaviour. When we say organizational behavior, or culture, we mean; workers know how things are done according to the laid down tradition, and ethical cultural values system prevailing in that organization. It speaks about an "in-house style" of the organization. The top management cadre right down to the bottom understands that, although elsewhere in another company in a different setting, a particular issue would be dealt with this way; however, in the organization they are, there is a unique and distinct way an issue is dealt with in line with the traditional values of that particular company. In short, organizational culture as defined by Peterson and White; "is the deeply imbedded patterns of organizational behavior, and the shared values, assumptions, beliefs, ideologies that members have about their organization." It is also the "...rules for being a member of an organization, and the climate or atmosphere that brings from both the physical elements and the structure of the organization," according to Schein. There are certain realistic yardsticks to measure managerial and worker organizational acculturation processes as enshrined in the organizational behaviors and cultures of a company or corporation. This organization culture is well and alive in the Dangote Group.

Good ccommunity relations and sound corporate social responsibility. Organizations do not exist in a vacuum; those that produce products need customers, ditto for those that produce services. In short, organizations and companies are social organisms that affect the way people live and are affected by people as well. As President Obama said on Saturday May 5, 2012 in Columbus, Ohio and Richmond, Virginia while flagging off his re-election campaigns for a second term; "Corporations are not people, people are people." The organizational cultures of companies become organizational behaviors in the way staffers are told, trained, and prepared to deal and interact with customers, and the outside world. Internal Discipline: How workers are disciplined and fired is dictated by the company's culture. Some company's culture says a worker must have been written down thrice, before a query can be issued and then the worker will be allowed to respond to the allegations before a decision is reached. Some companies do not have patience for such elaborate "in-house democracy." Some organization's culture specifies only the president or chief executive can fire a staff, others have different methods. The list is inexhaustible.

Organizational culture is very, very important in the success of any organization, because if workers work at cross-purposes, disaster looms. This is what we do, this how we do it, and this why we do it for we are what we are. That sums up the ways, do's, don'ts, rules, and etiquettes of an organization and that is the culture of the organization. Families have certain beliefs, communities subscribe to certain communal creed, and nations have national ethos. People in tertiary educational institutions have codes of behavior translated into the culture of the academy; sports men and women live by certain beliefs called team culture. Societies, sororities and organizations prescribe peculiar behaviors for membership and members, encapsulated in club cultures; members of the Armed Forces: marine, infantry and, naval personnel live by the culture of *esprit de corps*, and organizations, whether private or public live by organizational culture. Before you step into an organization's premises, you may not know its organizational culture, but you will recognize it when you see it. Consequently, organizational culture as Becker and Geer said, "is a set of common understandings around which action is organized . . . finding expression in language whose nuances are peculiar to the group" or as Louis saw it; "a set of understandings or meanings shared by a group of people that are largely tacit among members and are clearly relevant and distinctive to the particular group which are also passed on to new members."

If you want to be a successful business person, develop, and cultivate organizational culture very early in the life of the outfit and as the business continues to grow, make sure these organizational cultural traits are imbibed by the ranks and file of the company.

Every organization, including the Dangote Group has

developed these organizational behaviors and culture for, according to Mr. Oluka Ngofa, community and public affairs manager of Dangote cement in Port Harcourt, Rivers State, south-southern Nigeria when asked how the Dangote Group has succeeded in maintaining peace and harmony with the local communities it operates in Nigeria, especially in the once volatile Niger Delta areas of south-eastern Nigeria, he disclosed that "As a responsible corporate citizen, we try as much as possible to abide by the regulations as regards government and community relationship. And outside of those rules, as an organization, we also go ahead to engage our communities in such a way that we see them as stakeholders. We are not just out to pacify them but we make them part of our business so that they have stakes in what we are doing. That is the main secret and that is why we have been having peaceful operations despite other challenges."

With 600 employees on their payroll who are 100 percent Nigerians in the Niger-Delta area, Ngofa disclosed that all the workers are engaged full-time and hail from the host communities, either far or near which make them to see the company as "one of their own." "We engaged majority of our workforce from the host community and within the state. They are usually given priority consideration, and also, in terms of infrastructure development, we have two projects which we have done in this community. We have built a youth development center, and we have also put a scholarship scheme in place because we knew providing the infrastructure without the human capital development, does not amount to anything." Dangote has been at its location since 2003 and none of its workers has been harassed or threatened by the host communities.

Mr. Abdullahi Bada is the general manager in charge of operations at the Dangote cement factory in Port Harcourt and said that, "As local capacity increases in terms of production, what we are looking at for Dangote Bail Limited is to become an export hub." Mr. Timothy Age is the acting production manager at the Dangote Port Harcourt cement factory and his views aligned with that of his management colleagues. This is organizational culture at work at the Dangote Group.

The Power of Grandparents in the success of Aliko Dangote of Africa and in the lives of successful people of the world.

Making money and becoming a multi-millionaire and a billionaire have rules and if you followed those rules, you will make it like these rich men and women presented here no matter where you live: Africa, Asia, Europe, and North America or anywhere in the world.

The talent of Jeff Bezos, worth $25.2billion and founder of online retail giant, *amazon* was discovered by his grandfather in Cotulla, TX at age 6.

Oprah Winfrey, first African-American/black woman billionaire worth $2.7 billion was raised by her aged grandmother, Ms Hattie Mac Lee in rural Mississippi in the 1950s.

Barack Obama's political success could be traced to his late mother and single parent; Ann Dunham and his maternal grandparents; Madelyn and Stanley Dunham

Mr. Carlos Slim Helu, Mexican and richest person in the world worth $73billion learned trade and business ethics from his Lebanese parents; Khalid and Linda at the age of 14.

Late Sam Walton, founder of *Wal-Mart,* largest public corporation in the world worth $258billion learned how to trade and conduct business from his mother in Missouri in the 1920s

Late Timothy Adeola-Odutola, described by TIME in 1963 as a millionaire and the Harvard Business School as "pioneer in manufacturing business in Nigeria," in 2006 owed his business success to ethics and skills gained from an uncle at 13.

Late Johnson Olajide Fagboyegun, a multimillionaire indigenous businessman described by *The Financial Times* of London as "Nigeria's foremost cocoa magnate" and the man, *Africa Today* journal published by Indiana University, USA called "foremost indigenous produce buyer in Nigeria" grew under the mentoring of his uncle, Pa Daniel.

Ms. Louis Ciconne a.k.a Madonna, famous singer and described by the *Guinness World Records* as "the most successful female artist of all time" worth nearly $1billion was raised in Bay City, Michigan by her grandmother, Madam Elsie Mae Fortin.

Prodigiously-talented Eric Bishop a.k.a. Jamie Fox worth nearly $100million was brought up by his grandparents; Mr. and Mrs. Mark and Estelle Talley in Terrell, Texas.

Comedian George Lopez, the genius behind the successful *George Lopez Show* on *ABC* was abandoned by his father at 2months old and deserted by his mother at 10 but was raised by his grandparents; Mr. Refugio and Mrs. Benita Gutierrez of Mission Hills, California.

Certain traits Billionaires of the world share in common, including Aliko Dangote of Africa

All these successful men and women have a lot of things in common which they tapped into to make money, plenty of money irrespective of circumstances of birth and region of the world.

These billionaires epitomized the seven laws of business success and making money, plenty of it: God's favor, prudence and simplicity, charity/philanthropy, discernment, risk-taking, hard work and habit of saving.

Prof Cheriton of Stanford University, CA and *Google* investor is worth $1.4billion but lives a simple lifestyle "These people who build houses with 13 bathrooms and so on, there's something wrong with them."

John Caudwell, British billionaire and former auto repairer-turned wireless cellular investor is worth $2.6billion but an epitome of frugality and simplicity. According to him, "If you throw money around like confetti, it just becomes shallow and meaningless

Ted Turner, founder of *CNN* is worth $2.2billion and a great philanthropist "Over a three- year period, I gave away half of what I had. To be honest, my hands shook as I signed it away. I knew I was taking myself out of the race to be the richest man in the world."

Rupert Murdoch, an Australian turned naturalized US citizen, worth $11.2billion seized the opportunity offered by an alternative press in America and launched the *Fox News Corporation* in 1986.

Azim Premji, worth $11.2 billion, Indian richest man and credited with transforming his nation's industrial life is so simple and ordinary, he rides a fairly-used *Ford Escort*.

Richard Branson, worth $4.6 billion was a college drop-out but a risk-taker who made substantial profits from his *Virgin* investment in Africa

America's Jim Walton, worth $26.7 billion inherited life of simplicity and contentment from his late father, Sam, founder of *Wal-Mart*. He chooses to drive a-15-year old Dodge Dakota truck

Ingvar Kamprad, the Swedish billionaire, worth $3.3billion rides a 1993 made *Volvo*, does not fly first class and eats in drive-through take-away

America's Warren Buffet, fourth richest man in the world lives in the same house for nearly 30 years

George Soros, Hungarian-American hedge fund investor and philanthropist made $1billion in a day from an investment on Wednesday September 16, 1992. His net worth: $19billion

Aliko: "It is passion that drives me to go to bed at 2am and wake up at 6am." Hard work pays.

Aliko Mohammad Dangote of Nigeria $16.1 billion

The Richest Black Person in The World

Johann Rupert of South Africa worth $6.6Billion

Nicky Oppeheimer of South Africa of South Africa worth $6.5Billion

Nassef Sawiris of Egypt worth $6.5Billion

Naguib Sawiris of Egypt worth $2.5Billion

Mike Adenuga, Nigeria's second richest man worth $4.7Billion

Onsi Sawiri of Egypt worth $2Billion

Miloud Chabi of Morocco worth $2.1Billion

Othman Benjalloun of Morocco worth $3.1Billion

Patrice Motsepe of South Africa worth $2.9Billion

Oprah Winfrey of the United States worth $2.8Billion

Christofell Wiese of South Africa worth $3.5Billion

Mohamed Mansour of Egypt worth $2.2Billion

Anas Serfrioui of Moroco worth $1.3Bilion

Yasseeen Mansour of
Egypt worth $2Bilion

Youssef Mansour of
Egypt worth
$1.95Billion

Mohamed Al-
Fayed of Egypt
worth
$1.4Billion

Mo Ibrahim of
Sudan worth
$1.1Billion

*There are other three African/Black Billionaires worth between
$1Billion and $1.2Billion not pictured here

CHAPTER 14
WHAT IS NEXT FOR THE WORLD'S RICHEST BLACK PERSON?

ALIKO DANGOTE is not satisfied with his remarkable success in life. Every day, he strives to reach greater frontiers, and swim in uncharted waters. His knack for taking business risks continues unabated, even as he is considered "the richest black person in the world." In 2010 after his sugar refinery plants (DSR) recorded profits that fell below his expectations, he announced merger plans with Savannah Sugar Company which should take three to four years to materialize. His plan took some analysts by surprise considering the fact he doesn't like business mergers, but his plan is to take the company to greater heights by setting his eyes on local production of sugar, rather than being content with importing into the Nigeria economy to refine. According to him; "What we have to do to continue to give shareholders value is to try and grow the sugar here locally, rather than using foreign exchange to import it. Our projection is that in the next three to four years, we should try and grow at least a million tons of sugar locally here in Nigeria, which will provide 40,000 jobs and that is really the target of the company after the merger." The merger made business sense and so Aliko violated his personal view against sound business decision.

In all his business subsidiaries, Aliko Dangote is setting higher standards. He is racing to the top, and broadening the horizons. He is determined to ensure more cement production in Nigeria to make the commodity more available locally. He is also aiming his sights towards the West African sub-region, and the African continent at large.

Algeria: In North Africa, Algeria is beckoning as the Dangote business train moves to the Maghreb. Aliko Dangote is setting his eyes on the North African nation of Algeria. The Dangote Sucreine Algeria SPA, which is one hundred per cent owned by the continent's "richest person" will take-off with ₦972.337 million (about $6.274million), and is currently building a multi-million dollar sugar plant that will supply the North African market. At the annual general meeting of Dangote Sugar Refinery in Lagos in 2010; he disclosed that the sugar arm of the Dangote Group; reputed to be the largest in sub-Saharan Africa, and one of the largest in the world, has the capacity to produce 600,000 metric tons annually. Listed on the Nigerian Stock Exchange (NSE), the sugar quality of the group is reputed to be one of the best, because it contains ion exchange resin (IER). The new sugar plant in Algeria is expected to be completed in 2014. Aliko Dangote told the shareholders that "In the 2010 business year, we recorded a turnover of ₦89.980 billion (about $566.6million) while our operating profit and profit- after taxation stood at ₦16.148 billion (about $101.8million) and ₦11.282billion (about $70.04 milion) respectively. Though challenges still persist, we are committed to the effective management and application of our resources to ensure that, barring unforeseen development in the cause of the current year, our pursuit of sustainable growth, and dividend will yield the desired result. Further to our determination to satisfy our shareholders' expectations, in line with our dividend pay-out policy, we are proposing a total dividend of ₦7.2billion ($44.5million). The dividend represents the sum of 60 kobo for every one ordinary share of 50 kobo held in the company, payable net of withholding tax not later than May 25th, 2011 if approved by our shareholders at this meeting."

Aliko Dangote also disclosed why the North African nation of Algeria is ripe for investment. "We will be opening a refinery in Algeria. This is because Algeria is a high sugar consuming country. The new EU policy in the removal of subsidy on sugar will result in a decline in the competitiveness of sugar industries in the EU nations leading to a decline in the production of sugar in the region. This will shift their attention to Africa. Since Algeria is close to them, it will be beneficial to us when we are situated there," he said.

The Republic of Uganda: Next is the Republic of Uganda. When Aliko Dangote said his greatest wish in life is to be remembered as the greatest African investor and foremost industrialist, it is not an empty boast. In virtually all the 53 African nations, Dangote has either made his presence felt, is about to enter a new territory, or has already sent an advanced party to go and explore a new virgin land. When Dangote's business exploits are reported, few commentators and reporters are yet to cover all of Dangote's accomplishments, because the "richest black person" on the face of the earth is setting his sights right now on the "Pearl of Africa" as British Prime Minister Winston Churchill once referred to Uganda during his vacation in the East African nation. The man with the "Midas touch" in Nigeria's business has discovered that there are no limits of investments on the black continent. "Africans are always calling on foreign investors to come and invest in the continent. African leaders spell out all manners of incentives to attract foreign investors but do you think any foreigner would invest in Africa if African business men and women do not invest in their own continent?" Dangote once asked. He answered his own question: "That is why I am investing in Africa and like I have said before, Nigeria and Africa are the best places to invest. We need such international expansion to grow at a similar rate or outperform the BRIC nations: Brazil, India and China. At Dangote Group, our aim is to achieve global operational excellence, enlarge our footprints through cross-border acquisitions, build a global brand and in five years, be number one cement company in Africa."

In Uganda, East Africa, Mr. Dangote came to town in 2010 with $500million (in Uganda Shillings, that is roughly Shs1.24 trillion), not to invest on cement but to boost the East African nation's power project. The political history of Uganda is well known. It was here that one of the most notorious military tyrants and buffoons once held court as military head of state. At the height of his infamy, Mr. Idi Amin Dada, known as the Butcher of Kampala, turned this beautiful land into a basket case. But that was forty years ago! Today, President Yoweri Museveni, who changed the destiny and reputation of the country, has succeeded in building a stable and economically advanced nation within African standards. Mr. Dangote, Africa's foremost industrialist, said he was spurred to invest in Uganda because of the political stability that President Museveni has achieved in the once volatile and unstable nation. In the 1980s, and early 1990s Uganda under Museveni was reported to be the fastest-growing economy in Africa. Welcoming the chairman of Dangote Group and his entourage to Uganda, Mr. Patrick Bitature, head of Uganda Investment Authority said the investment of Dangote in Uganda would not only add to the rapid transformation of the nation's economy but complement the government's job creation and employment drive. According to him, "Dangote's investment ambition, if successfully implemented will go a long way in supplementing the on-going $500 million (Shs 1.24 trillion) Bugajali power project in curbing the power problem the country is experiencing. This will mean more industries coming up, job creation thus economic development of Uganda." The Republic of Uganda has been wooing foreign investors for some time now to help cushion the nation's rate of unemployment put at 45 percent. Dangote also informed the various stake-holders in Kampala that he would equally be interested in investing in Uganda's food processing industry, cotton, coffee and fruits. According to the local media, Uganda currently earns $1.7billion (about Shs 2.8 trillion Uganda shillings) from her export products which are a far cry from the abundant natural resources the Pearl of Africa is endowed with and, undoubtedly this is the area the Dangote Group will make a major difference.

The Republic of Zambia: The Dangote Group lands in Zambia. The Southern African nation, formerly known as Northern Rhodesia has been experiencing steady economic growth since 2005. This was made possible when the nation had all her foreign debts written-off, because the country qualified for debt forgiveness under the World Bank reprieve for highly indebted poor country initiative (HIPCI) in 2005. The $6billion foreign debt relief assisted the Zambian government to re-position the country's economy for growth, especially its privatization program. With the plummeting prices of the nation's two foreign exchange earners: copper and maize in pre-2005, and the prices of both commodities picking up thereafter, Zambia has continued to experience steady economic growth of 8 percent annually from 2005, and up to 2008. The nation's GDP real growth increased to 7 percent in 2010 against the backdrop of the nation's bad climatic and weather conditions, which affected copper and maize production. But the average per capital income has increased from $1,400 to $1,500 in the same period, which has led to a small increase in economic activities, especially in the area of retailing, and infrastructural development. Consequently, it was not surprising why Mr. Dangote set his eyes on Zambia as another African nation ripe for expansion. With 13 million population and though landlocked, the economy of this Southern African nation is booming, and Dangote, as shrewd as ever, is poised to spread his tentacles to the nation and reap bountifully.

Like other developing nations in Africa, trading is a very lucrative business in Zambia. But the country's public corporations-those owned and managed by government- are badly run. This has forced the Zambian government to consider privatization. In the Copper Belt area of the country, mining activities are commonplace, and it is in this area that Dangote wants a piece of the Zambian pie. In 2010, Dangote Group signed Zambia Kwacha 2.04trillion (about

$400million) business deal with the Zambia Development Agency (ZDA) toward jumpstarting the Zambian economy in the cement sector to be located in Makati, Copper Belt area of Zambia. Dangote applied for a license in 2008, and the Zambian government approved the deal, which would create about 1,600 jobs. At the Inter-Continental Hotel in downtown Lusaka, the Zambian capital where the deal was signed in fall 2010, ZDA chief executive, Mr. Luke Mbewe disclosed that all legal, and investment paper work had been signed, and the Dangote Group had already commenced works at the cement processing plant with an estimated projected production capacity of 1.5 million tons annually. Because the ZD-Dangote Industries cement deal was above the $10millin foreign investment drive in the nation, a special incentive package would be added under Item 58 of the ZDA Act. The proposed Dangote cement plant will complement the efforts of three other existing cement plants in Zambia: Lafarge, Oriental, and Zambezi Cement Plants, thus driving down the price of cement in the country.

On his part, Mr. Dangote said he was spurred to invest in Zambia because of the macro-economic policies recently announced by the administration of former President Rupiah Banda, and his implicit confidence in the prospects of indigenous manufacturing in Africa. He chose Ndola in the Masati area of the Copper Belt region because of the seriousness of the Zambian government to diversify its economy instead of concentrating solely on the mining sector. While at its construction stage, 1,600 local workers would be needed, and after the cement processing finally comes on stream, there would be rapid transformation in the local community as it did for the Obajana community in central Nigeria. The Dangote Group expects a $70million return in its first year of operation in Zambia.

The three elements, or incentivizing measures put in place by the administration of former President Banda made the Republic of Zambia attractive to Aliko Dangote for investment. First is the stability of economic legislation which provides for continuity in policies irrespective of change in government through the nation's investment promotion and protection agreement (IPPA). As most foreign investors know, there is political instability in many African nations, which scares prospective investors from investing in the continent. But Zambia, in its desire to douse investors' fear of the safety of their investments, against the backdrop of incessant change of political guards now enter into agreements with foreign investors through the IPPA legislation with assurance that nothing in any agreement entered into between foreign investors, and the Zambian government will be affected by political instability. Mr. Dangote has entered into this landmark agreement with the Zambian government under ex-president Banda. It is expected that the new Sata administration will uphold this agreement.

The second reason that spurred Mr. Dangote into investing in Zambia is the encouraging report of the World Bank Group on investment potentials of the Southern African nation. In its 2010 Report on Investment Climate in Developing Nations of the World for 2011, Zambia was named by the apex global bank as one of the fastest economically reforming nations in the South. In addition, the report disclosed that the Southern African nation is one of the most highly urbanized nations in the world with over 44 percent of its population living in urban center. For any potential investor, that means Zambians need more urban infrastructure, and other amenities to keep up with this rapid urbanization growth. Thirdly, another important report released in June 2011 by the McKinsey Global Institute based in the United States, disclosed that the African continent would need more than $46billion every year to meet the infrastructural demands of a rapidly growing urbanized population.

These three reasons convinced Mr. Dangote that the Republic of Zambia was ripe for investment. He said this as much in Lusaka, the nation's administrative and political capital during the signing ceremony in 2011. According to him "It is in this light that we have decided to invest in

Zambia. We are motivated to create an African success story because we believe that entrepreneurship holds the key to the future economic growth of the continent. We are spurred on by the fact that the rate of return on foreign investment is higher in Africa than in any other developing region. We are also particularly encouraged with the Zambian government's robust economic diversification program designed to reduce the reliance on the copper industry, which is the mainstay of the economy."

To Aliko, every inch of the African land the Dangote business train has not berthed is still a virgin land, hence the richest black man on earth is just warming up to control the black continent. Continuing on the Zambian deal, Dangote revealed that: "The plant should be up and running by 2013 which means in all, we have presence in about 14 African countries." Mr. Dangote disclosed that the eliminations of trade barriers such as ubiquitous and bureaucratic paper work for importers and investors, ports' congestions, and cumbersome procedures, stability in government policies, conducive atmosphere for doing business, and other artificial problems by the various governments in the West African sub-region are the catalysts needed for the economic transformation of the region. Apart from Nigeria, other parts of Africa remain a potential goldmine for investors, Aliko further disclosed. "That is why we have moved beyond ECOWAS to other nations in East, South and North Africa, which have opened their doors to us. Boston Consulting Group (BCG), an international rating agency based in the United States, rated us among the Top 40 African Challengers last June, based on our size, international expansion drive and revenue."

The report Aliko was referring to was released by the Massachusetts-based Boston Consulting Group, which analyzed the economic growth of African countries and disclosed that the black continent, which had been written-off by foreign investors in the past may after all be coming up on its own. The report listed Botswana, Morocco, Mauritius, Algeria, Egypt, South Africa and Libya as the new emerging economies in Africa dubbed, "The African Lions." Libya made the group before the civil war that toppled Muammer Ghaddafi broke out and the beginning of the Arab Spring Revolt. But the kernel of the report was that these African nations seemed to follow the patterns of the BRIC nations of Brazil, Russia, Indonesia and Chile. The report listed indices such as: political stability, investment in education, and social services, the rule of law, and property rights; surmising that, as at 2008, the African Lions recorded GDP per capital of $8,800 whereas, the BRIC nations similarly recorded GDP per capital of $10,000 thus drawing commonalities in economic growth of both blocs. As for corporations and conglomerates that would continue to shape the economic futures of Africa, two conglomerates; the Dangote Group and United Bank of Africa-UBA were listed for Nigeria. In addition, the report listed the Dangote Group among 25 Corporations in Africa that would continue to shape the economic future of the continent.

The Far East and Orient: The prospects of the Dangote Group in the Far East and the Orient are brighter. The Chinese are coming; indeed they are already in Nigeria and in every parts of the African continent. In international business, especially in many developing nations, it's very important to know how things work, the economic climate, and the go-to guys to show you the way. The Chinese have now known how to navigate the economic topography of Africa and they don't want to be losers, so it is not surprising that the richest man in Africa is the natural go-to guy in Nigeria and the West African sub-region. Yes, the Chinese are coming and Mr. Dangote is partnering with them in transforming the continent.

The Dangote Group is making its presence felt in the United Kingdom. With the local Nigerian market in his pocket, and as the largest private employer of labor in Africa's most populous nation, Dangote is on a roll. With the market of the West African sub-region as his backyard, and with presence in virtually all the business zones of the African continent: east, north, and south; it is not surprising

Mr. Dangote is taking his chains of businesses to the United Kingdom. The Dangote Group is planning to be listed on the London stock exchange. He explained why he is taking his companies to the London bourse in an interview with William Wallis of The Financial Times of London. "We are creating a foundation on which Nigeria and African markets can grow. We now have the capital, the profile and the expertise to move into new businesses and new markets." Indeed, the Dangote Group wants to enter Europe in a grand style by being listed in the London Stock Exchange for starters. With the cement arm of the conglomerate estimated at over $1.2billion which is the largest company in the West African sub region, coming to the LSE is cheery news and mutually beneficial move for peoples on both sides of the Atlantic. "The proposed listing on the London Stock Exchange," as Mr. Makoju disclosed "will provide foreign investors with the opportunity to invest in Nigeria" adding that "the reality of the Nigerian business environment is far better than its perception. Although doing business in Nigeria can be quite challenging but it is rewarding as well." This is Nigeria's largest and most capitalized company by market value, which Aliko Dangote is taking to the United Kingdom by 2012.

Mr. Dangote unfurled his plans at the world economic forum in Cape Town, South Africa after Mr. Makoju had spoken. He said his group planned to increase cement production from 20 million tons in 2010 to 50 million tons by 2013. Similarly, plans were afoot to take Nigeria's largest conglomerate to the British stock market to shop for between $3bn and $5billion. But to make the sales attractive, Dangote will pump over $3.9billion into the company between 2010 and April 2012. According to Dangote; "We have a major infrastructure deficit in Africa, in Nigeria, we have an 18 million-homes deficit. This will continue to grow because growth in population in Nigeria is 3 per cent per annum. Definitely, we need cement to drive that growth. Right now, our own area of business and focus is Africa. We are not indebted, and have a lot of room to expand. We are looking at organic growth first and if there's any opportunity outside Africa that will be secondary. We'll look at it on merit." Currently, the Dangote Cement Corporation is worth a market value of ₦1.9 trillion (about $12.3 billion) making it the largest company in Nigeria and West Africa.

Mr. Dangote is committed to making cement cheaper for Nigerians, even before President Goodluck Jonathan gave the marching order in summer 2011 to the sector's stakeholders to crash the price of the commodity. The price of cement should be affordable to Nigerians because of its importance to the nation's infrastructural and industrial development. As a magus of the industry, Dangote has vouchsafed the impediments confronting the industry, and one of such impediments is the cost of transporting the precious product to far-flung areas of the country. Consequently, his company is partnering with relevant stakeholders to significantly ameliorate this major problem. One of the strategic partners in this regard is with the Nigerian inland waterways authority (NIWA).

The Dangote Cement plant at Obajana in Kogi state is exploring ways to dredge the River Niger with a view to making cement distribution easier and cheaper in eastern, central and northern parts of Nigeria. If jetties can be constructed at Lokoja in Kogi state, according to Mr. Ahmed Aminu Yar'Adua, managing director of NIWA, not only will it be easier for Dangote Cement at Obajana to transport and distribute its cement products effortlessly, the Nigerian government can turn the jetties into commercial use for other companies in the area. "We have, by now, finished the dredging of the River Niger. We are now working with a transport company and an oil company to move cement and oil products through the channel. We are trying to start our own transport services in collaboration with some private individuals. We want to buy a 45-seater boat to carry passengers from Onitsha through the river. We want to dredge the Benue River and we intend to construct jetties along the river. We also hope to buy our own dredgers and work with some consultant engineering companies to maintain the dredged channel," he disclosed. To achieve these economic objectives, the Nigerian government awarded a- ₦35 billion (about $245million?) contract in 2009 to handle lot 5 area between 7.7million cubic meters of silt from an estimated 900,000 cubic meters covering the northern cities in Kogi and Niger States while additional ₦10billion (about $70million) contract covering 6.1 million cubic meters of silt in the same lot area must be removed between Jamata and Baro towns under the dredging scheme on the River Niger end of the scheme. When these schemes are finally completed, there is no doubt they would accelerate economic development of the areas. Not only the Dangote Cement Factory at Obajana would be main beneficiary, already companies such as Sterlion Oil Company and Ninon Transport Limited based in Warri have signed up to use the jetties for faster transportation of petroleum products and cement in northern Nigeria.

But while the Nigerian government is partnering with Dangote Cement Company at Obajana to bring down the price of cement in the country, the Dangote Group is also looking beyond the immediate by exploring hi-tech methods in cement manufacturing and distribution. This could be achieved if the nation's energy supply is radically improved, which the group is also a major player in Nigeria. Mr. Knut Ulvmoen, the Norwegian group managing director of Dangote Cement Company has a unique perspective into the root causes of high costs of cement in Nigeria. According to him, "the current cost of a 50-kg bag of cement, which is between ₦1,500 (about $8.50) and ₦2,000 (about $12.50) in the market, is on the high side because of the low level of importation due to the distress in some of the exporting countries and unfavorable government policies on importation." In addition "... the recent tsunami in Japan has reduced exportation of cement from the country; they now import cement instead of exporting. The Nigerian government's policy on importation is also a factor. So, by the time we totally depend on local production, it will definitely reduce price generally." The costs of energy and ancillary overhead expenses, including servicing the machines at the company's factories due to unstable electricity supply in Nigeria were also cited by Mr. Ulvmoen. He said that sourcing alternative energy at 600,000 liters of diesel annually, which pushed overhead expenses to more than 60 percent, would undoubtedly add to the company's overhead expenses. However, he disclosed that the Dangote Cement Company was exploring ways to reduce the costs of production and in turn, the retail price of cement. "All things been equal, we are going to be producing 28 million metric tons annually to meet the whole market demand of 80 million as at today, and we are also aware that more production capacity will be needed in the long-run, maybe three to four years." In addition to lowering the price of cement and make it more affordable, Dangote is concentrating on bringing his Ibeshe Cement Plant located in rural Lagos/Ogun State into full operational capacity and early, 2012; the plant was officially commissioned. Mr. Ved Prakash Sarkari is the plant's deputy managing director while Mr. Bolu Aladeniyi is the project engineer and the two men face the task of achieving the arduous task of making cement available at affordable reach of Nigerians. With a projected annual capacity of six million tons from six cement silos when at full capacity, the Dangote Cement Plant at Ibeshe will crash the price of cement again by further 25 percent from the 20 percent achieved in 2011 after President Goodluck Jonathan pleaded for further slash in the price of the product.

According to Mr. Sarkari, "The factory is billed to have 300,000 metric tons storage capacity, six cement silos, roto packers that can pack 2,400 bags per hour and about 18 trucks at a time. The factory site has limestone deposit capacity of about 240 million metric tons and is being constructed to ensure environmentally friendly operations." However, Sarkari provided a caveat just like other industrialists in Nigeria: improved power supply. This is because the Dangote Cement Group alone spends more than ₦1billion (about $7million) annually to generate power supply to its cement production plants across the country. Definitely this additional overhead costs would affect the market price of cement to distributors and end-users. But that is not the only disenabling environment notching up cement price in the country. Another problem is Nigeria's bad road networks which affect distribution and the wear/tear of lorry trucks from the plant to distribution centers in Lagos, Ogun and other states in its distribution zone.

To Mr. Aladeniyi, the Dangote Ibeshe Cement plant has been undergoing test runs and the three turbines of 37 megawatts in addition to a pipe gasoline from nearby Itori, which is about 22 kilometers from the town of Ibeshe. Built with the latest modern technology, Aladeniyi disclosed that the top-notch technology-12 packing machines, 18 T-loading bays, mining license for limestone and other additives- will drastically reduce the cost of cement when the plant fully came on stream in; 2012. With 800 lorry trucks and 24,000 bags with capacity for 600 bags each in 2,000 hectares of land as factory, Ibeshe Cement plant will add 760 million tons to the national cement output guaranteed to last for 105 years. "Our equipment is of the latest technology which has given us the opportunity to achieve a pollution-free environment. The national standard for dust emission is 50 per cent but we have targeted and achieved 30 per cent surpassing the national standards," Aladeniyi disclosed. The Ibeshe Cement plant is the first of its kind in Africa because, according to Aladeniyi, a cement production expert, it has the ability to employ surface mining techniques that are environmentally-friendly and avoid blasting thus pollution-free. Like the retail giant *Target* has done in the United States by using modern technology to attract customers, Aliko has introduced cutting edge technology to maintain the Dangote Group's dominance in the Nigerian and West African markets. For example, the Minneapolis-based retail company re-engineered its e-commerce site in 2011 to be more user-friendly and also create multi-channel platforms for its customers. According to Mr. Steve Eastman, president of *Target* e-commerce site, the innovative idea was to place the company in a better position to "satisfy our guests constantly evolving preferences- whenever, wherever- in the same way we have earned their loyal support in our stores for decades."

The concentration of *Target* on e-commerce is understandable: most of its customers are affluent, educated and young; those that are often referred to as the "new technology generation."

Mrs. Abimbola Windapo is a fellow of the Nigerian institute of building (NIOB), and fromer professor at the University of Lagos in south-western metropolitan city of Lagos, the hub of economic activities in Nigeria where Mr. Dangote has his corporate headquarters. She weighed in on the debate on the price of cement. She disclosed that, if the infrastructural disabilities affecting cement production in Nigeria such as; epileptic power supply, transportation costs, currency fluctuations and oligopolistic tendencies of supply cartel are fixed, the price of cement would fall and most Nigerians would be able to afford the product. According to her, "The high cost of cement undoubtedly has an adverse effect on the construction industry and the Nigerian economy. Higher cement costs will obviously result in a decrease in demand for cement and construction services as individual and corporate developers and investors will be deterred by exorbitant prices. The government should fund research, which could lead to discoveries of alternative materials that could be cheaper to mine and produce – which would not be dependent on imported machinery / parts. Architects / building professionals should consider other more sustainable ways of building design/construction that would require the use of less cement. The Nigerian government should also offer incentives to companies or individuals that initiate research and incorporate local technology/materials into their construction activities. Improved infrastructural development is also recommended to counter rising fuel costs. If materials can be transported quicker and efficiently, this would mitigate the effect that rising fuel costs have on transportation costs and hence, the final costs of the building material." On sugar, Dangote Sugar Company is raising the bar with the plan of the arm of the company to introduce new sizes into the market. This is in the bid to achieve two objectives that have defined the Dangote Group: accessibility and affordability. Mr. Sai Prakash, acting managing director and chief executive, Dangote Sugar Company disclosed that 1gram, 500 grams and 250 grams are meant to bring Dangote sugar to virtually all Nigerian homes. According to him, "Apart from making the product affordable, our plan is to turn it into household goods that would appeal to people at the lowest segment of the (Nigerian) market. There is no gainsaying the obvious fact that Dangote sugar has contributed immensely to industrial growth in the country. After thorough research, we realised a vacuum that needed to be filled in the interest of our teeming consumers and we are striving to fill it and arrangements have also been concluded to take Dangote sugar to other West African markets." One of the executive directors of Dangote Sugar Company disclosed that, as Dangote Group is the Cement King in Africa, their ultimate aim is to achieve the same feat in sugar production and supply in Africa.

As one Abuja-based economic and business analyst quipped, "This man is involved in everything! It's amazing that one man has such potpourri of menus in his industrial and economic plates. You would expect him to say yes, "I have now achieved my aim of being the richest black person in the world and so let me relax," but no. Aliko Dangote is expanding more and more, which means; the man is more interested in creating more job opportunities and developing the Nigerian and African economic growth and by implication the world. I am sure; this is more than making -money." Which is true because Aliko has said that his greatest wish in life is to be referred to as the greatest industrialist to have lived in Nigeria" but at the rate he's going with his hands in virtually all pies in Nigeria and Africa, who knows; his achievements may surpass his greatest wish in life for, already he has achieved the feat of the greatest industrialist in Nigeria, the greatest investor in Nigeria and the greatest and largest private employer of labor in Nigeria and the richest black person in the world right now." As Mr. Uzo Nduka, managing director and chief executive of Domino Information Company, owners of business manager patent, which was signed in 2011 by the Nigerian government said, "An entrepreneur is a person who solves practical problem in the society and in the same process gets rewarded financially, having solved the problem that existed before offering a solution. You are not an entrepreneur if you are not solving a problem. Making money and becoming wealthy is not the end result of entrepreneurship... I ask you to wonder where Nigeria would be if we have 100 of Aliko Dangotes."

Mr. Aliko Dangote has surely taken over the nearly 100 million Nigerian consumers who cannot do without the foremost industrialist for their food, clothing and shelter. Now he is going after 300 million consumers in the West African sub-region. He said it himself as much with excitement, "Although there are challenges in doing business in the sub-region and elsewhere, discerning investors see a range of opportunities for business and economic growth. We should see these challenges as opportunities because no serious investor, particularly in the non-oil sector will establish heavy industries in our region unless they see us doing so. This will show the world that we believe in our region. Eliminating obstacles to trade, transport and free movement of goods, services and capital would greatly enhance inflow of investment into a country. It is my hope that the Governments of Economic Community of West African States (ECOWAS) countries would urgently review their policies to remove identified obstacles to free trade to enable us reaps the full benefits of economic integration." But Dangote is not content with just limiting himself to the West African sub-regional market. According to him, "Apart from Nigeria, other parts of Africa remain a potential goldmine for investors. That is why we have moved beyond ECOWAS to other nations in East, South and North Africa, which have opened their doors to us." Well said from a man who is still in his fifth decade and five years and has already conquered Nigeria, West Africa and his setting his sight to "own" Africa. Argosies of honors, slews of awards, and numerous recognitions, plenty of rewards and menageries of success benchmarks have come in the way of the richest Nigerian, the largest employer of labor, Nigeria's number one business man, foremost industrialist and the richest black person in the world. From northern Nigeria, Mr. Aliko Mohammad Dangote has been bestowed with award for excellence in leadership and entrepreneurship by the Conference of the Northern States' Chambers of Commerce, Industry, Mines and Agriculture (CONSCCIMA) of Nigeria in May 2011. The Nigerian industry reporters and commerce correspondents association gave him award of Nigeria's commerce and industry ambassador in summer 2011 in Lagos. Mr. Dangote, the nation's foremost industrialist and astute business man was conferred with the man of the year 2011 award by *The Sun* newspaper of Nigeria "in recognition of his leading role in industrial development of the country."

For the Dangote Group, the accolades have come in torrents from within Nigeria where the companies are supporting all manners of causes; and from the African continent, where the various African governments are grappling with the time-bomb issue of youth unemployment which the presence of Dangote companies has been able to reduce. From other parts of the world, all of a sudden, more people now pay more than scant attention to business and economic activities in Nigeria and Africa. Foreign investors are increasingly aware that African economies are growing in leaps and bounds. Of course; Nigeria and indeed African economies must be reckoned with, if the richest black person on earth has now been found in the African continent. The Boston-based Boston Consulting Group (BCG), an international economic rating agency based in New York/Massachusetts, in the United States recently examined the size, revenue, expansion and international drive of Dangote Group and rated it among the 40 African Challenger Companies of the world.

The Super brands Awards for the years 2010/2011 presented by super brands Nigeria, which adjudged the Dangote Group and its brands of products as quality products that have succeeded in winning and earning the trust and confidence of the Nigerian consumers. The *New Africa* magazine of London, UK, awarded the Dangote Group the biggest quoted companies in West Africa. The New York-based *Forbes* magazine in its *Forbes* Global 2000 Companies in 2010 listed the Dangote Cement Company as one of such companies in the world. Similarly, the *African Business* magazine awarded the four arms of the Dangote Group listed on the Nigerian Stock Exchange (NSE) as the biggest and largest quoted companies in West Africa.

Mr. Mathew Pearson, strategist for the UK-based Standard Bank's head of equity product in Africa told international business men and women during the *Reuters* Investment Outlook Summit in 2010 that the bank's forecast for stock in Nigeria was less than sanguine. This was because of the crisis that bedevilled the nation's banking sector, but quickly disclosed that any optimistic forecast for Nigeria would be because of the stability of the Nigerian stock exchange anchored on the presence of the Dangote Group in the bourse, which was initially dominated by Nigerian banks prior to Dangote Cement listing, which represents more than half of the bourse's total market capitalization. According to Pearson, "Nigeria has had its own banking crisis, where almost 50 per cent of local banks were put into effective liquidation. Nigeria has significantly underperformed frontier market peers as well as emerging markets, but from a valuation point of view it is now very cheap," adding that the intervention of the Central Bank of Nigeria has renewed confidence in Nigeria's banking sector and few sure-footed companies, foremost of such liquid companies being the Dangote Group seemed to have restored confidence in Nigeria's banking and financial sectors. No wonder, financial analysts that say, when Mr. Dangote sneezes, the Nigerian economy catches a cold may after all be saying the obvious. By taking his companies to the London stock exchange, Mr.

Dangote is boldly announcing the presence of African companies on the global stage. Traditionally, the African continent has long been neglected and scorned by investors but things are now changing. With the emergence of Mr. Dangote as the richest black person in the world from Africa, economic analysts are predicting that Africa is the new continent for world investors. According to Mr. Ferdinand Dum, the country managing director of *Ernest and Young* for the Republic of Ghana; "Africa is making progress! A report stated recently that the continent has remained the most attractive for investment in the last three years. And in West Africa, Ghana and Nigeria, which both held successful elections recently, also boast of impressive Gross Domestic Product (GDP) figures. There are calculations that both countries' GDP growth will be over 10 this year (2011), compared to that of China and India, which experts said would be 9.8 and 8.2 respectively. EOY (Ernest and Young Report) is yet another proof that we are making progress." It was in the realization of the good tidings coming out of Africa that made *Ernest and Young* to institute the entrepreneur of the year award with its maiden edition for 2012. A highly prestigious globally-recognized economic award established in 1986 in the United States, the award was intended to spur industrial and management capabilities of managers and entrepreneurs across the world except Africa. According to Mrs. Zanele Xaba, program director of the award, "Currently, the programme is held in over 50 countries and 140 cities around the world (but now) it's Nigeria's and indeed West Africa's turn to showcase its entrepreneurship worth to the world by nominating worthy achievers for the award." According to her, the award is categorized into four broad areas: master entrepreneur, emerging entrepreneur, lifetime achievement award and social entrepreneur. But, only the first two were in focus in 2011.

According to Mr. Henry Egbiki, the awards' chief executive officer for West African sub-region, nominees for the prestigious award must be innovative, hardworking and shrewd business men or women who, through perseverance and resourcefulness have succeeded in creating successful enterprises that have impacted significantly on the lives and living standards of the African people. Other qualifications that potential nominees must possess are; nominees must have been in business for a minimum of a decade as a manager of a private company with at least ₦75million (about $476,000) turnover and several employees in its staff strength. The aim of the award is to encourage innovation and entrepreneurial spirit in Africans so as to curb youth restiveness and unemployment in that part of the world. Said Egbiki, "How do we channel the energy of our youths to productive ventures remain a major challenge for us"? One can then understand the importance of any kind of support to entrepreneurship."

Going into production and manufacturing in an oil-based and import-oriented economy such as Nigeria was very difficult for Dangote in the beginning. He disclosed as much, "Running a factory here is very difficult. What we did was backward integration. So instead of worrying about the market, and who is going to buy the stuff, you just have to worry about production." For those belittling the rapid transformation of Nigerian economy through Dangote's bold moves and jeering at his success ascribing it to his political connections, Dangote snapped back, "If things were easier, you would have seen 20 Alikos doing business here." That is true; for in a country where the enabling environment in terms of infrastructure and political stability until 1999 were problematic, going into manufacturing business where cheap imported Asian goods flood the market can drive the most well-meaning local business man or woman from the market insane and hope of success could be nightmarishly suicidal. But Dangote did not and has not despair.

As for political connection, Mr. Dangote told William Wallis of the *Financial Times* of London that it was a no brainer and had no apology to make. According to Mr. Dangote, all over the world, sensible and smart business entrepreneurs know it is wise to be interested in the political affairs of the nations where they operate. For Africa and

African entrepreneurs, it is even more significant to be keenly interested in the actions and policies of political leaders because of political instability, disruptions in policy formulations and implementations, bureaucracy and the menace of corruption. As he explained, he is interested in the political direction of his native Nigeria because he does not want Nigeria to turn into another Zimbabwe. Since 1999, Nigeria has enjoyed twelve years of uninterrupted representative democracy and as it is the practice all over the world, Nigerian politicians want the support of rich people because democracy is expensive. Consequently, there is a symbiotic relationship between politicians and rich and money men and women in Nigeria, like in other democracies in the world.

In Nigeria, hearsays, rumors and lies are the past-times of some people and this should not be surprising in a nation where millions are unemployed and are idle hands. One of the rumors is that Mr. Dangote would not have become the richest man in Nigeria, if not for the Nigerian government making any perceptive mind to wonder why is it that those who are in government and have amassed fortunes beyond their wildest dreams have not used the money for the betterment of the Nigerian people. In a nation where the economic environment is so chaotic to embark on manufacturing, why is that the Dangote Group has to construct its own road network, provide its own power supply, dig water boreholes, erect telephone satellites network, build schools, construct health care centers and medical facilities, provide recreational facilities; indeed virtually everything that ordinarily the government should provide to propel commerce and business? Someone once said the political class in Nigeria should coalesce and work together to make the current President Goodluck Jonathan a success through a government of national unity. To replicate the political gesture, President Jonathan should give Nigerian politicians their dues. But in Nigeria, the local politicians are not like the Roman Caesar as Lord Jesus Christ admonished. Nigerian politicians are not content with their dues; rather they want to gobble everything without caring a hoot for anyone. So how did a person like Dangote, who has never been in government, succeed in acquiring his staggering fortunes through government? What is difficult to understand in the illogicality of those rumor-mongers is that; where and how did multi-national oil companies operating in Nigeria amass their billion dollar fortunes from in Nigeria and other countries in Africa? Did they also make their fortunes from governments? Mr. Dangote replied to the rumor-mongers; "If you are successful in Africa, you are bound to be attacked from here and there; there will be people who say that, without government support, there is no way this guy can make money." When you have to build your own gas pipeline, dams, power plants and your rail networks to the potentially largest cement plant at Obajana, Kogi state as Mr. Dangote is currently doing, then so much from amassing fortunes from government! A consumer nation such as Nigeria cannot develop without a sound manufacturing base, and as Dangote disclosed; "If things were easier, you would have seen 20 Alikos doing business here," but because doing business in Nigeria is very difficult, that is why there is only One Aliko Dangote in Africa's most populous nation. Does Aliko Dangote want more Aliko Dangotes to emerge? You bet!

In summer 2009 while Nigerians continued to bemoan the state of the nation's refineries which are not running at full capacity, the management team of Dangote Group comprising Messrs. Olakunle Alake, COO, Knut Ulvmoen, a director; Joseph Makoju, COO, Dangote Cement Division- one of Alhaji Dangote's "brain-trusters;"- and Mrs. Folake Ani-Mumuney, former chief marketing and communication officer of the group jointly addressed a world press conference in Lagos. They disclosed the conglomerate was putting finishing touches toward building Nigeria's first private refinery to be cited in Nigeria's economic hub; Lagos. According to the foot soldiers of the largest company in Nigeria and West Africa, the proposed Dangote refinery would have the capacity to store 300,000 barrels of crude oil per day. That would be a feat no single black man has ever achieved anywhere in the world, but for the man who is always first in everything concerning the black race; Dangote's surrogates were not boasting. Mr. Knut Ulvmoen, who explained at the press conference that the Dangote Group definitely had the financial might to pull the feat, though the spokesperson disclosed that a lot of work still needed to be done to make the refinery become a reality. At the same press conference, Mr. Makoju also disclosed yet another "first" from the Dangote Group in accelerating Nigeria's economy: a partnership with the Nigerian government toward constructing the first "private" rail line at Obajana and Itakpe where the Dangote Cement Factory-the largest in the black world-is located in central Nigeria. Shortly thereafter, another big one from the richest black person in the world: Nigeria's and Africa's first wholly indigenous fertilizer manufacturing plant is on the way too.

As Mr. Dangote continues to make forays into untapped markets in many African countries outside Nigerian shores, his sharp and eagled-eyed business exploits have not escaped fallow business lands within Nigeria. In other words, manufacturing business opportunities abound within Nigeria and such opportunities to put people back to work, accelerate Nigeria's production base and thus reap bountifully as a savvy investor have not escaped Aliko Dangote. Consequently, Edo state in mid-western Nigeria will soon have the largest fertilizer manufacturing plant in black Africa, courtesy of a joint venture between the Dangote Group and Saipem Group-a Chinese conglomerate. The proposed fertilizer plant, according to Messrs. Dangote and Giuseppe Surace, the managing director of the China-based company in Nigeria, will have the capacity to roll out 7.700 MTPD of granulated urea, (two trains with a production capacity of 3,850 metric tonnes each per day. The Chinese company will build Nigeria's and Africa's largest fertilizer plant which will drastically cut down the importation of fertilizer into the country. Nigeria currently imports all its domestic fertilizer needs mostly from the United State. The fertilizer plant is coming at a time Nigeria is exploring ways to make money from its abundant gas reserves much of which is currently being flared.

"There is no reason why Nigeria should be importing fertilizer," Aliko Dangote said at the signing of the documents between both companies. "I am happy that with this agreement, by the time our plant is completed and commissioned, the country will become self-sufficient in fertilizer production and even have the capacity to export the products to other African countries. Right now, farmers are forced to utilize whatever fertilizer that is available as they have no choice, but we need to know that the fertilizer that will work in Jigawa state (in northern Nigeria) may not be suitable in Adamawa State (north-eastern Nigeria), as they may not have the same soil type and composition. The same fertilizer you use for sorghum may not be the fertilizer you will use for sugar cane." He disclosed the reasons why he has decided to go into local manufacture of fertilizers and the road map his proposed fertilizer plant will take to be able to meet local needs of Nigerian farmers, which are not currently being met by imported fertilizer products "There is no way we can on an annual basis be able to import over 1 million tons of fertilizer through the port. There are issues of the capabilities of the Nigerian ports and transportation and the capability of the ports. But where are the ports? Even where you have the ports, where are the modern equipment for their operations? We don't have a good network of roads for evacuation anytime you have two or three ships of fertilizer docking (at the Nigerian Ports); transporters will capitalize on the situation and continually increase the freight charge."

There is no doubt that the fertilizer plant, when completed in 2014 and operating at full capacity, according to the memorandum of understanding (MOU) between the two companies will employ several hundred Nigerians. If the proposed plant follows the usual pattern of Dangote Sugar, Cement and the rest products from the Dangote Group which began from Nigeria and over the years has spread their tentacles to other parts of Africa, then the Dangote Group is on a roll. The cheery news about the proposed plant is that currently, the only fertilizer plant serving Africa has only a capacity to produce 1,000 metric daily and only 1,500 metric tons of urea per day. The Dangote Fertilizer plant slated for 2014 will up the ante and double both daily metric production and urea per day. The Edo state government which will host the fertilizer plant is already celebrating!

If Mr. Aliko Mohammad Dangote boasted that by the year 2018, his estimated fortune would be between $68 billion and $72 billion, where did this optimism come from? Is there any person that has accomplished that feat before, which could serve as a template for Dangote's buoyed optimism? Yes and that is Mr. Bill Gates, the richest man in the world for thirteen consecutive years, and now the second richest man on planet earth with estimated fortune worth $67billion. As we pored over books, reports, interviews and life history of Mr. William Gates III, we discovered startling similarities between him and Aliko Dangote. Here are the similarities.

Mr. Gates was born on October 28, 1955 in Seattle, Washington State, while Mr. Dangote was born on Wednesday April 10, 1957; which made the two of them contemporaries. With two years separating the two billionaires, and in spite of the different locales they grew up, there are similarities in the manners and trajectories of their lives. In 1968 while he was 13 years old, Bill had begun to master computer programming while at the age of 13 in 1970, young Aliko had begun to trade in commodities and edibles at the Dantata family business in Koki Quarters in Kano while a student at the Kano capital secondary school. By the time Bill was 18 years old, he had already developed BASIC for microcomputers as an undergraduate at the Harvard University in Cambridge, Massachusetts, United States. Similarly, just as Bill Gates attended but later dropped out of Harvard as a sophomore, Aliko Dangote attended the oldest university in the world- the renowned Al-Azhan University in Cairo, Egypt- but did not drop out. At 23, Mr. Bill Gates had become a millionaire so also Mr. Aliko

Dangote in 1976 even before he got married, he was already worth ₦1.5 million-and going by the foreign exchange of the Nigerian Naira in 1976 when ₦1.00 was exchanging for $0.75 cents. Mr. Gates developed *Microsoft* in 1975, while Mr. Dangote set up his manufacturing and trading company in 1977-again the two years difference as if Dangote were Mr. Gate's "business running mate" in life.

By the time Mr. Gates was 24 years old in 1989, his company was worth $20 billion, and Gates was worth about $5billion, and two years later, the fortunes of *Microsoft* and Gates had soared to $22billion and $7billion respectively. That year, at the relatively young age of 36, Mr. Gates became the richest person in the United States. Similarly, Mr. Dangote was already worth $1 billion through his trading in commodities but the Nigerian media didn't get it because, by the nature of Nigerians, they wait on the foreign media to point out the best and brightest in Nigeria and Africa. No wonder Mr. Dangote once said that until the *Forbes* magazine went to town with the news, which those who had their ears to the ground as far as the 1990s had already suspected that Aliko Dangote was already a billionaire by world standards, his country fellow citizens would not consider him a billionaire. But he had to wait for another decade, thanks to the power of globalization, and when he was declared to be worth $3.3billion in the 2008, it was just mere formality.

In an interview with the editors of the *Forbes* magazine in 2011, Aliko disclosed that after he has finished planting his businesses in virtually all African countries, which hopefully would be by 2016, and when he would be celebrating his 62nd birthday in 2019, his projected net worth should be in the neighborhood of $65billion to $70 billion. That is a realistic target for a man whose fortunes grew by 544% in just three years! No one needs a mathematical whiz kid to do the math: if in three years, Mr. Dangote's fortune grew by 544 %; by the time he will be celebrating his 58th birthday in 2015, he would be worth between $69 and $71.4 billion if he continues at the rate he is going in his business over-drive. This is business success on steroid for all things being equal; Mr.

Dangote may become the richest person in the world in the next six years.

At 56 Mr. Dangote is just warming up. He has his hands in virtually all pies, and with presence in nearly twenty African countries: Republic of Benin, Togo, Ghana, Sierra Leone, Cote d'Ivoire, Liberia, Senegal, Cameroon, The Gambia, Mali, Gabon, Sao Tome and Principe, Algeria, Democratic Republic of Congo, Zambia, Uganda, Tanzania, South Africa, Ethiopia, Guinea and more still coming, Aliko Mohammed Dangote of Nigeria is no more the golden child of Nigerian business. He has become the golden child of African business and the black world. With his eyes set on the Orient, with plans to storm Europe, with synergistic alliances with the Chinese, with presence in the Arab world and with the Americans angling for a part of the Dangote pies, which areas of the world remain for Dangote to take on? Who and who are still not yet signed in on the Dangote business success train? With age on his side, good health his asset, business feisty his passion, discipline his watchword, prudence his desideratum, altruism his goal, generosity his style, hard work his mantra, sporting good talents his knack, simplicity his way, and religious piety his faith, who knows Mr. Aliko Mohammad Dangote, the economically rambunctious young lad from the historic city of Kano born 56 years ago this year 2013 may emerge the first black person, and the first African to emerge as the richest person in the world. And it may not be long. The world is watching.

CHAPTER 15
ALIKO IN THE EYES
OF THE WORLD

"In person, Aliko Dangote does not come across as a member of the super-rich... He appears shrewd and ambitious but unassuming..."

---The Financial Times of London, UK.

"The President of Dangote Group towered above others on the list with his unrivalled strides in the nation's economy. Beyond being the first Nigerian to create an international conglomerate and the highest employer of labor outside government, Dangote brought his companies to the capital market in 2010. The Dangote Group, which *Dangote* sat atop as president, was noted as having an unmatchable contribution by any singular Nigerian company to the stock market and the economy."

--The Sun Newspapers, Lagos, Nigeria.

"The (Dangote) Group's core business focus is to provide local, value-added products and services that meet the 'basic needs' of the populace. Through the construction and operation of large scale manufacturing facilities in Nigeria and across Africa, the Group is focused on building local manufacturing capacity to generate employment, prevent capital flight and provide locally produced goods for the people."

--- The Woodlawn Post Detroit MI, USA.

"Dangote built up a leading position as an importer in these markets, before investing in manufacturing. Along the way he has become the biggest private-sector employer in Nigeria"
--- *The Financial Times London, UK.*

"Aliko, the Nigerian billionaire, and Africa's wealthiest man began early in life to carve his business niche. He is a visionary leader. Alhaji Dangote has become one of the most powerful business and power brokers in the region."
--- *Energy & Corporate Africa Houston, TX, USA.*

"Nigerian tycoon Aliko Dangote -- one of the world's richest men and the African continent's most successful men with business interests in oil and gas, food processing, mining and telecoms..."
--- *The Mail & Guardian newspaper, Johannesburg, South Africa.*

"Aliko Dangote, Pieter Fourie, the chief executive of Sephaku Cement said, its investment was the largest foreign direct investment into South Africa by an African company and the new plants were an important milestone in South Africa. This was because they would be the first new clinker projects to come on stream since 1934. Dangote was a strong believer in growth in Africa because cement was one of the key building blocks as governments tried to address backlogs in infrastructure. He said it was Dangote's intention to consolidate all its cement interests into a single firm that had the scale to compete globally"
---*Sunday Independent newspapers, Johannesburg, South Africa.*

"Aliko Dangote makes his fortune from trading and his interest in sugar, cement and food has propelled Dangote to the top of the pile in Nigeria. Dangote represents a break from this tradition as a man who has created his wealth in a comparatively transparent manner"
--- *Daily Observer Banjul, Republic of Gambia.*

"During the 2010 Africa Investor projects summit in South Africa, ... Sponsor of the Year was presented to Dangote Group in recognition of the various projects they have sponsored across the (African) Continent"

---The Post Newspapers, Lusaka, Zambia.

"ZAMBIA Development Agency (ZDA) has signed an Investment Promotion and Protection Agreement (IPPA) with a Nigerian Company Dangote Industries worth US$400 million (about K2 trillion) which will facilitate for the establishment of a cement processing plant in Masaiti area on the Copper belt Province. The project to be undertaken will create 1,600 jobs for the local people and was one of the largest investments in Zambia this year outside the mining industry..."

---The Times newspapers, Lusaka, Zambia.

"Aliko Dangote... In recognition of his contributions to the growth of the Nigerian economy and his philanthropy, he has been conferred with several awards including the prestigious ZIK award for professional leadership (1992), the international award of Sir Ahmadu Bello, the Cross River state roll of honor award (2002) and the *Thisday* newspapers award for chief executive officer of the year (2005). He was conferred with the national honor of officer of the Order of the Niger (OON) in 2000 and commander of the order of the Niger (CON) in 2005"

---The Herald newspapers of Harare, Zimbabwe.

"In a calculated move aimed at promoting intra-African trade and investment, Dangote Industries of Nigeria has invested US $ 400 million in a cement plant in Kafue on the Lusaka-Chirundu road. At the helm of Dangote Industries is Aliko Dangote who is believed to be Africa's richest man."

---The Monitor newspapers, Gaborone, Botswana.

"Africa's richest man Aliko Dangote (and).... one of Africa's most influential business leaders..."

-- *Business Day newspaper, Lagos, Nigeria*

With estimates of an additional 500 million African consumers in the next 15 years and the recent success of African entrepreneurs, such as Aliko Dangote who has amassed a personal wealth of $14bn through companies targeting the Nigeria consumer, (Africa is coming of age)"

---*Investment Week, London, UK.*

"Aliko Dangote's fellowship is great news as Africa continues to make strides in amassing more leaders in business and entrepreneurship, which will ultimately strengthen the continent's economy"

--- *The Atlanta Post, New York, NY, USA.*

"This man Aliko Dangote is the richest man in Africa"

---*Mr. Femi Otedola in Business London, UK.*

"Make way Donald Trump, here is the richest African: Aliko Dangote. The Nigerian is the richest African, whose fortune is equivalent to the entire value of all companies listed at the Nairobi Stock Exchange. Actually, he is richer than American property impresario Donald Trump, who is worth $2.7b (Shs 6.5 trillion) and whom he can buy out and tell: "You're fired!"

Dangote can acquire Sir Richard Branson's Virgin Group and employ him as a flight attendant on Virgin Air. Branson is worth $4.2b (Shs10.2 trillion). That is not all. He makes Oprah Winfrey's $2b (Shs4.8 trillion) read like pocket change, meaning Dangote can buy out Oprah and make her his secretary..."

--- *Daily Monitor newspaper, Kampala, Uganda*

"Aliko Dangote, Africa's most successful businessman..."
--- *The International Business Times, Sydney, Australia.*

"It may not be a wild assumption to say that every Nigerian has heard of his name because of the impact of his business. His products are in most homes across the country. Those who may not use his products would have passed some of his trailers by the way. He is into export, import, manufacturing, real estate and philanthropy. All these are rolled together into what is known as the Dangote Group. At the helm of its affairs as president and chief executive officer is an unassuming man named Aliko Dangote. The focus of his investments is food, clothing and shelter."
---*African Success, Paris, France.*

"Aliko Dangote is the richest African, black man... in the latest list, (of *Forbes* in 2011) surpassing a whole lot of bunch like Abramovich, Richard Branson, Oprah, just name it and followed closely by Mark Zuckerberg of *Facebook*. And he is still scratching the surface, because his massive investments are just coming up, like the cement factories he is building all over Africa even in Europe, believe me before he reaches 60 years he should be in top ten.."
Nigeria Daily News, Cumming, Georgia, USA

"It may not be tasteful to a lot of people what this achievement entails due to certain prejudices they hold against him (Aliko Dangote), however you look at it, whether he received favor from government or not, he has kept the favors within and not away"
---*Mr. David Attah, former chief press secretary to General Abubakar Abdusalam, military head of state (1998-199), Nigeria.*

"Aliko Dangote, Africa's most successful businessman, controls about two-thirds of the Nigerian cement market and seeks to

expand his interests in the (African)...Continent... "
---The Next newspapers, Lagos, Nigeria.

"Nigeria's Aliko Dangote is now the world's richest black person."
---The Nazret Online, Washington, DC, USA.

"Africa's billionaires on the *Forbes* list made records this year with a few surprises...Topping the list is Nigeria's Aliko Dangote our new richest man, Dangote who made US$10.7 billion, putting him at the top of the list..."
--- The African Vibes magazine, Los Angeles, California, USA.

"Dangote is now the richest African alive, richer than South African billionaires Nicky Oppenheimer of DeBeers and Johann Rupert of luxury goods group Richemont, which owns Cartier, Dunhill and other premium brands. He is also richer than Chelsea Football Club owner, Roman Abramovich "
---PM News (Evening) Newspaper, Lagos, Nigeria

"Dangote represents a break from this tradition as a man who has created his wealth in a comparatively transparent manner. His interests in sugar, cement and food have propelled Dangote to the top of the pile in Nigeria."
---The Standard Times News, Freetown, Sierra Leone.

"By his own declaration, he has surpassed his expectations. Not in wealth – that has become a pedestrian accumulation – but in national honor, individual fulfillment and service to humanity."
---The News Magazine, Lagos, Nigeria.

"In a calculated move aimed at promoting intra-African trade and investment, Dangote Industries of Nigeria has invested US $ 400 million in a cement plant in Kafue on the Lusaka-

Chirundu road. At the helm of Dangote Industries is Aliko Dangote who is believed to be Africa's richest man. "

---*The Monitor Newspapers, Gaborone, Botswana.*

"The huge investment into Sephaku Cement of South Africa by Dangote is the largest ever foreign direct investment (FDI) by an African company into South Africa,"

---*The Daily Trust newspapers, Abuja, Nigeria.*

Dangote Industries to acquire power generation assets in Nigeria. The African firm, led by billionaire Alhaji Aliko Dangote, has qualified to bid for two hydropower generation assets put on block by Nigeria... Dangote Industries is present across real estate, food and beverages, telecommunication, port operations, steel, cement, oil and gas and packaging sectors"

--- *The Times of India, New Delhi, India.*

"The Dangote Group is the largest industrial conglomerate in West Africa and has been successful in cement, flour and sugar production..."

--- *African Business Review, San Diego, California, USA.*

"...We recall that the Dangote Foundation has always been a dependable ally of Nigerians in times of adversity. It had identified with all kinds of humanitarian gestures in Nigeria and beyond, especially in the areas of human capital development, education, nutrition and public health. This is the least responsible organizations should do to give back to the society. They should come to the aid of the governments to complement their developmental efforts, since governments alone cannot shoulder the responsibilities. How, for instance, could the state governments that benefited from Dangote Foundation's milk of human kindness have handled the disasters in their domain, considering the magnitude, without assistance from outside? The wealthy in our society should emulate this gesture of selfless service to mankind. At least this is what all religions, from Christianity to Islam and even the traditional religions preach. They enjoin us to be our brother's keeper. And we do not have to be super rich to help in such hours of need. Our widow's mite might just be all that the victims need to get back on their feet..."

--- The Nation newspapers, Lagos, Nigeria.

"Africa's richest man wants his continent to grow -- and some say his project to build its largest fertilizer plant could provide relief to farmers and help put a dent in food shortages. The project, set to come on stream in three years, may also serve as an example of how Nigeria, the continent's largest oil producer with massive untapped gas reserves, can put its often-squandered natural resources to good use. Of course, Nigeria-based Dangote Group, headed by Aliko Dangote, once dubbed Africa's richest man by Forbes, could stand to rake in yet another small fortune along the way... "

---Agence France Press- (AFP), Paris, France.

"The Dangote Cement Plc has emerged as Africa's best cement manufacturer company with the presence of its plants in 14 African countries. The countries include; Zambia, Tanzania, Congo (Brazzaville), Ethiopia, Cameroon (Grinding), Sierra Leone, Ivory Coast, Liberia, Ghana among others..."

---The Construction Business Review magazine, Nairobi, Kenya.

"The richest man of African descent in the world is making huge investments in establishing various factories in Sierra Leone. The Nigerian billionaire and founder of the Dangote Group, Alhaji Aliko Dangote briefed President Ernest Bai Koroma on the status of his business venture in the country at State House during a courtesy visit."

---The Exclusive newspaper, Freetown, Sierra Leone.

"President Ernest Bai Koroma (of Sierra Leone) will be hosting West Africa's richest man on Sunday 6th and Monday 7th April 2008. The special guest, Nigerian-born business tycoon Alhaji Aliko Dangote, is coming to explore the possibility of investing in Sierra Leone, while Sierra Leonean businessmen would have an opportunity to learn from his experience."

---Awoko newspaper, Freetown, Sierra Leone.

POSTSCRIPT

THE PHENOMENAL success of Mr. Aliko Mohammad Dangote is an inspiration to all Africans and the black race in the world. For long, the contribution of the black race to world civilization has been consigned to the limbo of forgotten things, especially the natural endowments of Africans of old. These had been denigrated as magic and African voodoo, in spite of the powers of such natural gifts and Divinely-inspired endowments to make life better for the African peoples. But more importantly, Mr. Dangote's business success is a testimony to the power of hard work and deep conviction for any one, whether black or white, who sets his or her mind to make a difference in his or her part of the world. From his story, it is crystal clear there is no magic bullet to attain financial success in life, except some of the proven ingredients that have been revealed in this book.

We have written this book to celebrate a business icon of immense proportion. Mr. Dangote is a trail-blazer, who has made Africans all over the world proud of their ancestry. We were conscious of criticisms that may emanate from certain quarters about the business practices of Mr. Aliko Dangote which some newspapers, especially from Nigerian-owned, foreign-based Internet publications, but as we explained in our opening words overleaf; we did not set out to do a critique of our subject and we have succeeded in objective portrayal of Mr. Dangote as much as possible. This is a biography of a successful man in every sense of the word. We compared the phenomenal success of this great son of Nigeria and Africa, with the successes of other rich people of the world with a view to drawing out certain commonalities in their life trajectories and how they made their billions. For Nigerians in particular, the success story of Mr. Dangote is significant for several reasons.

First, that Nigeria is the most populous nation in the black world is no longer news. That Nigeria is also prodigiously blessed with crude oil as its major foreign exchange earner is also an open secret. Similarly, Nigerians are scattered all over the world and known for being hardworking, aggressive, highly educated and gregarious. These known traits of these groups of Africans have also come with drawbacks. There is the menace of what is commonly referred to as "419-scam letters" emanating from Nigerians, offering business and other bizarre phony money-spinning ideas to people-which has brought low the reputation of the nation. The menace got to a ridiculously-embarrassing level that ordinary parcels and letters coming out of Nigeria often face special scrutiny at airports and outposts in many Western nations. The few bad eggs that continue to diminish majority of Nigerians open the rest of their country men and women abroad to embarrassments, targeted discriminations and racial profiling, but with the emergence of Mr. Dangote as the richest black person in the world, the rest of the world may now begin to look at Nigerians as a people and Nigeria as a country rather differently.

Secondly, the notion that one has to be sneaky and dubious in order to conduct business in Nigeria has been debunked by the business success of Mr. Dangote. Granted, the words of the Irish essayist and political commentator, Mr. Oliver Goldsmith who once said that where commerce is involved, honor and morality sink to the bottom may still ring true in our world of today, the fact that all the business arms of the *Dangote Group* operating in Nigeria, West Africa and all over Africa appear on the stock exchanges of all the nations they operate debunk these accusations against free enterprise. The message of Dangote's success to the world is simple: Nigeria and Africa are safe for foreign investments. The business success of Dangote has sent a clear message to the rest of the world. That message is simple: Africa is rising.

Finally, it is time Nigeria began to exploit the business success of Mr. Aliko Dangote to jump start Nigeria's industrial growth and economic development in the age of globalization. The influential *Forbes* magazine has its unique in-house style of looking at the business investments of rich people of the world, in computing its annual list of world billionaires. It is gratifying to note that with his heavy concentration on manufacturing and commodities, trading and groceries such as food, clothing and shelter, Mr. Dangote has shifted the focus of the world on Nigeria as a land of oil and free money. No wonder, retail giant; *Wal-Mart* is now exploring ways to open outlets in Africa's most populous black nation. We hope the current Jonathan administration and successive Nigerian governments will build upon the gains of Aliko Dangote success story to re-position Nigeria as an economic giant in the next two decades. If Nigeria could harness its vast natural and human resources, legislate strict laws that would regulate business and commerce, unleash the creative ingenuities of Nigerians at home and abroad, Nigeria would not truly be the giant of the black world only in populations but also in economic power. As Mr. Dangote aptly remarked; "(Nigerians) can even be bigger than Aliko Dangote. The whole thing is that you have to really be very determined. You have to believe that, yes, there's a future in this country of ours and I can tell you right now, I don't believe we have even started doing anything in Nigeria because the opportunities are so enormous. I don't even know where to start from."

There are many Aliko Dangotes in Nigeria, in West Africa and Africa. The world is waiting for these Africans to stand up and change Africa for the better and make the black race proud.

ALIKO MOHAMMAD DANGOTE ON MARBLE

The richest black person in the world has enriched our world with evergreen words, clichés, words of wisdom and expression on virtually all areas of life which are commended to all and sundry. Here are some of the sayings of Mr. Aliko Mohammed Dangote on various areas of life:-

ON GOD ALMIGHTY:

I am a very prayerful person, I believe so much in God Almighty.

ON BELIEF AND FAITH:

Hard work counts quite a lot in business but at the same time you have to have luck and divine favor. Because if you don't have luck and divine favor, whatever you touch might turn out to be bad.

ON HARDWORK:

I learnt that it pays to work hard. Hard work is the key to success in life. Once you are ready to work and consistent, you would make money."

ON HOW NIGERIA AND AFRICA CAN BE GREAT:

"Agriculture is where the nation's wealth and job opportunities are. Whether we like it or not, we must face agriculture; not only to sell and make money but to feed the nation because by 2025, the nation's population will be hitting over 250 million."

"Fellow Nigerians who are materially well endowed should join me in the necessary but difficult tasks of industrializing Nigeria. It is from this kind of most worthy self-help that outsiders may take a cue and complement our local efforts with the much needed foreign investment. We must always remember that without leading, nobody will come to invest in our country."

ON BUSINESS SUCCESS:

"I can remember when I was in primary school, I would go and buy cartons of sweets (candies) and I would start selling them just to make money. I was so much interested in business. Even at that time, I was very used to buying and selling. It is in my mind all through. I did that on a part-time basis. I usually bought packets of sweets (candies) and gave some people to sell for me. I would join them whenever I closed from school. I would collect my profit and give them something out of it."

"The family had many servants. So, some of them were selling things. I would say, 'Please, sell these for me' and he would sell and render accounts afterwards. That was what I was doing. It was not as if I established shops."

"You must have passion. Passion is what drives me forward. Passion is what makes me go to bed at 2am and wake up at 6am..."

"There is money in manufacturing even though it is capital intensive. To achieve a big breakthrough, I had to start manufacturing the same product I was trading on; which is commodities. I am an advocate of manufacturing because it does not only improve your business status, it also help (sic) you give back to your community and country; with respect to job creation and economic development."

"To succeed in business, you must build a brand and never destroy it. One competitive advantage I had when I ventured into manufacturing was my brand "Dangote," which I diligently built in the course of my trading commodities."

"I built a conglomerate and emerged the richest black man in the world in 2008 but it didn't happen overnight. It took me thirty years to get to where I am today. Youths of today aspire to be like me but they want to achieve it overnight. It's not going to work. To build a successful business, you must start small and dream big. In the journey of entrepreneurship, tenacity of purpose is supreme."

"To build a successful business, you must start small and dream big. In the journey of entrepreneurship, tenacity of purpose is supreme."

DANGOTE ON DANGOTE GROUP:

"I always make sure I hire people smarter than me."

"It's just a matter of time, One day; Dangote Cement will be number one in the world."

"We believe that if we have the right mix of manpower and other resources, we will churn out quality products that have always been our hallmark of success. Our ultimate aim is to have highly trained and committed workforce to drive our businesses and also to beef up the nation's industrial manpower needs. The job of industrializing the nation should not be left in the hands of the government alone but should be a partnership between the government and the private sector."

"We already have operations in Nigeria, Ghana, Benin, Zambia and South Africa. We are looking for opportunities in emerging markets like the Middle East and Asia. I think the time has come for us to go global."

"We are not a company that is owned by government…"

"When the Dangote Group embarked on an unprecedented program of diversification and transformation from a commodity trading concern to a manufacturing conglomerate; it is a platitude to say that when we started nobody could have known or predicted the outcome as 1997 was a very trying period in Nigeria's political history."

"We are working towards making Dangote the biggest conglomerate in Africa. Now that we are training youths in this Academy, we are targeting that by 2015, Dangote will have $60 billion market capitalization. When you look at the equivalent, the total reserve of Nigeria is about $35 billion, by the next four years. Our own market capitalization should be somewhere around twice the reserve of Nigeria, and that means in the cement side, by this time 2014, we should be producing more than 50 million metric tons in more than 14 countries excluding Nigeria. And in sugar, we are trying to do the same thing. The same thing we did in cement, we are going to replicate in sugar."

"Our plants and factories are producing 750,000 metric tons of refined sugar, 360,000 metric tons of flour, 600,000 metric tons of salt, 2 million cartons of pasta (spaghetti), 180,000,000 poly-propylene bags and 5,000,000 tons of cement out of installed capacity of 9 million annually."

ON DOING BUSINESS IN NIGERIA:

"If you give me today $5 billion, I will not invest any abroad; I will invest everything here in Nigeria. Let us put heads together and work."

"(Nigerians) can even be bigger than Aliko Dangote. The whole thing is that you have to really be very determined. You have to believe that, yes, there's a future in this country of ours and I can tell you right now, I don't believe we have even started doing anything in Nigeria because the opportunities are so enormous. I don't even know where to start from."

"Nigeria is really the best place to invest. It is one of the best places to make money. You know all over the world it is the best kept secret actually in terms of investment."

"The importance of Nigeria is the market. The population is there. The money is there. It is just a matter of having good entrepreneurs who can push this thing forward."

"What we are trying to do is to ... broaden the base of our revenues, those who are investing in banking, who are doing several other things, so that by the time oil starts going down ... oil will no longer constitute the major factor in our national economy..."

"All of us understand that we cannot bring in expertise from outside continuously. There is therefore an urgent need to develop skills in our local talent through knowledge transfer and sustained training and development efforts to drive growth in our industries. That is why we took up the strategic decision to set up an institution called the Dangote Academy of Learning and Development to train young local talent to boost the manpower needs of our nation's industries. This initiative is largely driven by our corporate social responsibility (CSR) to the nation."

ON BEING A NIGERIAN:

"I feel great. I'm feeling fulfilled that at least you are doing something great for your country."

"I believe in Nigeria. I believe there is always going to be Nigeria. My faith and belief in this country is unshakeable."

ON DOING BUSINESS IN AFRICA:

"Reforms are changing the face of doing business in Africa. Over 84 per cent of economies in sub-Saharan Africa have implemented regulatory reforms making it easier to do business. There are still challenges to doing business in Africa but there is hope. This is a new Africa. Governance is much better. Yes, there is corruption and it is still an issue, but looking at where we have come from, things are getting better and fast."

"...we are big in Nigeria and outside. We have invested in cement factories outside Nigeria and we have got the approval of the CBN to invest about $3.9 billion outside Nigeria..."

"Africa is gradually taking its destiny in its own hands rather than wait for investors from outside Africa. Investment in the real sector of the economy is the only way that our continent can achieve the much desired accelerated growth and development that we have yearned for."

"I have built the biggest cement company in Africa. Now I'm setting out to build the biggest cement company in the world."

"People are still doing business in troubled areas like Congo. In fact, Congo is one of the best countries to invest in. During the war in Liberia, people were still doing business. A friend of mine opened a flour mills six months ago in Cote D'Ivoire."

"There is no way to invest in Africa without coming to South Africa. We want to be a pan-African company, the champion in the sector. Africa is the only continent with a cement supply deficit. Many countries rely on imported products and pay a price premium..."

"The credit crunch works better rather than worse for Africa in terms of investment. It means there is a lot of money that needs to be invested somewhere and the best place is ... developing countries like Africa..."

"African countries have a lot of resources like iron ore, manganese, oil. They are all right at the top. Even cocoa, cashew nuts, the prices have hit the roof."

"Africans are always calling on foreign investors to come and invest in the continent. African leaders spell out all manners of incentives to attract foreign investors but do you think any foreigner would invest in Africa if African business men and women do not invest in their own Continent?"

"...Nigeria and Africa are the best places to invest. We need such international expansion to grow at a similar rate or outperform the BRIC nations: Brazil, India and China. At Dangote Group, our aim is to achieve global operational excellence, enlarge our footprints through cross-border acquisitions, build a global brand and in five years, be number one cement company in Africa."

"There is no reason why Nigeria should be importing fertilizer. I am happy that with this agreement-,(signed by Dangote Group to build Africa's largest fertilizer plant in Nigeria)- by the time our plant is completed and commissioned, the country will become self-sufficient in fertilizer production and even have the capacity to export the products to other African countries."

"We are motivated to create an African success story because we believe that entrepreneurship, especially our own home-grown African entrepreneurship, holds the key to the future economic growth of the continent. The fact that Africa offers one of the highest returns on investment (ROI) in the world is an additional incentive for any discerning investor, who can take calculated risks."

THE PRICE OF SUCCESS:

"If you are successful in Africa, you are bound to be attacked from here and there. There will be people who say that, without government support, there is no way this guy can make money."

ON JOB CREATION IN NIGERIA:

"I believe we have what it takes to create jobs in Nigeria. The main thing why we are not able to create jobs, one is that governments are not consistent in terms of policies; you know when you are consistent in terms of policies, then people will definitely invest."

"The National Job Creation Committee was inaugurated by the National Economic Management Team in response to a dangerous paradox that was emerging in our national economy – impressive economic growth but with high and rising rates of unemployment. Most worrisome in this emerging paradox is that the highest rate of unemployment was in our rapidly expanding youth population. In other words, our youth are under employed, unemployed or unemployable at the peak of their productivity."

"As we have seen in the Maghreb countries of Tunisia, Egypt, Libya and now spreading to the Emirates of the Middle East, youth unemployment is a very effective catalyst for social unrest that has brought down entire governments. Unrest in the Maghreb region was apparently sparked by a single unemployed youth who took his own life in a very public manner rather than face a lifetime of being unemployed and not being able to meet the basic human needs of food, shelter and clothing not to talk of the dignity of productive labor."

ON GOVERNMENT:

"When taxes are increased, the people may initially grumble, but when they see that the money is being used judiciously, they will be happy ready to pay without prompting. That is what is happening in Lagos and the business community is happy with the government. We can see the development in many areas, schools, hospitals and roads."

"...Wealthy Nigerians should come out to help. Government cannot do it alone. Government cannot create jobs but only create the enabling environment. Nigerians should invest in agriculture. By 2030, our population will be about 280 million, with the population of other West African countries about 140 million. How do we feed our people if we are finding it difficult to feed ourselves now that we are only 150 million?"

"Policies that allow the outflow of our hard earned reserves to pay for the imports of manufactured goods that we have comparative advantage for producing in this country only helps not only to create jobs in the exporting nations but create job losses back home here with the close down of factories attempting to produce the same goods."

"We are not an export nation. We import quite a lot of what we are using today. And if we devalue our currency, it will have quite a lot of effect. By just devaluing, everybody will increase his price. Even somebody, who is producing local products such as boli and co (roasted plantain), will tell you they are doing devaluation. So, we have to be very careful. I even support the Governor of Central Bank that devaluation today is not the best of reasoning."

"I am close to people in government because I am one of the big businessmen in Nigeria. If we don't have the right people there then [all the] money I have is useless. If the country turns into another Zimbabwe, for example, then I will become a poor person."

ON RECREATION AND LIFESTYLE:

"I like exercising a lot; I go to the gym almost every day and I do about 15 km at least 6 times a week."

"I enjoy myself a lot but I derive more joy in working. I believe in hard work and one of my business success secrets is hard work. It's hard to see a youth that will go to bed by 2am and wake up by 5am. I don't rest until I achieve something."

"I happened to be the first grandson of Sanusi Dantata. So the person I truly see as my father is my late grandfather, Sanusi Dantata. I learnt a lot from his hard work, from his simplicity. People always talk about my humility but nothing can compare with him. When you see him you would think he doesn't have anything."

ON AFRICAN YOUTH:

"We believe the youths are the future leaders and as much must be empowered to enable them to function effectively in this role. We have a new crop of highly talented young Africans who are championing generational change, gender equality, social entrepreneurship and good corporate governance."

"Youths of today aspire to be like me but they want to achieve it overnight. It's not going to work."

"Power (electricity) should not be an excuse before the government sorts out the power issue; you should also try and do your own. In most of our own companies, we generate our power, so it is not really an excuse. We need to also look at long-term funds and interest rates. Interest rates are getting a bit high, even though the current governor of CBN has done very well, by providing about N500 billion, which has never been done before. Now, if you want to generate your own power, or even if you have your own power, you can go and re-finance by borrowing money for 15 years, which we have never seen before at seven per cent. At seven per cent, you cannot complain."

ON HIS PHILANTHROPIC AND HUMANITARIAN GESTURES:

"We share in the agonies and pains of those who lost their loved ones (to crises in Kaduna, Gombe and Bauchi states, northern Nigeria) and those who lost their property and have been displaced. We at the Dangote Group are deeply touched by this development. This is why we decided to assist the government in the resettlement efforts aimed at alleviating the psychological trauma and pains suffered by the displaced victims who have been taking refuge in various camps..."

"While we are in business of creating wealth primarily, we are also mindful of the need to touch lives of people. As a company, we have always been conscious of the need to give a little of our profits back to the society as a guarantee for sustainable business success. This has been our guiding business philosophy."

ON HIS LOVE FOR FOOTBALL (SOCCER):

"My interest in Arsenal started in 1980 when I forged a relationship with Mr. David Dein, former vice-chairman of the board of Arsenal. However, I can say categorically at this time that I have no intention of investing in the club and will not be acquiring a stake."

Aliko Mohammad Dangote

ON LEAVING A LEGACY:

"If you look at our generation, we have done extremely well [in business]. The generation before ours hasn't done well at all, In fact, they were the worst ones. And the generation before that was just concerned about local issues because there was no such thing as globalization back then."

"After my death, I want to be remembered as Africa's greatest industrialist."

PRAISE FOR THE RICHEST BLACK PERSON IN THE WORLD

"I have been in a place where Aliko had already arrived and people were still asking 'when will this Alhaji Dangote come?' because he is unassuming, shy and humble. That is why people hardly know whenever he is around anywhere and the only way you see him everywhere is through his numerous investments."
---President Olusegun A. Obasanjo of Nigeria (1999-2007).

"Zambia, indeed welcomes Aliko Dangote's decision to invest here as one of the continent's top global multi-national corporations. This is the largest investment into Zambia by a Nigerian company. I am glad to also note that besides the employment opportunities being created, the project will greatly benefit the people of Masaiti and the surrounding districts through transfer of technology and skills,"
—President. Rupiah B. Banda, of Zambia (2008-2011).

"Aliko Dangote deserves more honors than those of us holding political offices."
---President Goodluck E. Jonathan of Nigeria (2010-)

"Dangote is not only the richest black man but he is also richer than Mark Zuckerberg, (in 2011), founder of *Facebook*.

The Nigerian spirit is an excellent spirit. Believe it today and always"
---Mr. Nassir A. El-Rufai, minister of federal capital territory, Abuja, Nigeria (2003-2007).

"Apart from the foreign investors from Europe and other parts of the world, Dangote Group is the first wholly owned African company to commit huge investment to our country and we are proud of him and urge other African companies with similar financial and technical capacity to tow the path that Dangote has initiated..."
Mr. Serigne M. Ndiaye, special adviser to ex-President Abdoulaye Wade of Senegal on foreign investment, Dakar, Senegal.

"...Which of the rich men have established factories and employ the people? Thank God for Dangote. But how many of these big men have established factories for uplifting the young ones in Africa?"
---Dr. Thomas A. Adaba, broadcaster and former director-general of the Nigerian Broadcasting Commission.

"Alhaji Aliko Dangote is a shining light in Nigeria"
--- Ms. Evelyn N. Oputu managing director and chief executive officer, Bank of Commerce and Industry, Abuja,, Nigeria.

"Alhaji Aliko Dangote is a trail blazer in Nigeria."
---Senator Jubril Martins-Kuye, minister of commerce and industry, Abuja, Nigeria (2010-2011).

"We should produce and manufacture goods and make foreign exchange from it... before this country can move forward, we need 200 Dangotes, not 200 rich men because there are so many rich men in Nigeria that produce nothing. But people who provide jobs like Aliko Dangote are few. We need job creation if we really want to move Nigeria forward. We need a lot of people who can do what Aliko Dangote is doing in

Nigeria, creating jobs regularly and creating room for economic progress in Nigeria."
---Prof. Patrick O.Utomi, founder, Lagos Business School (LBS) and presidential candidate, Social Democrat Mega Party (SDMP), Lagos, Nigeria

"The name Dangote has for long become a household name and a story of hard work and discipline."
--- Gov. Aliyu M. Wamakko, Sokoto State, Nigeria (2007-

"Alhaji Aliko Dangote- a rare breed Nigerian whose passion for entrepreneurship and entrepreneurial development knows no bounds and thus not restricted or guided by class or creed"
--- Gov. Sanusi L. Sanusi, Central Bank of Nigeria Abuja, Nigeria (2009-

"We also express our delight and pleasure for the recent prosperity of Dangote Group and the defining success of Alhaji Aliko Dangote, who has made all of us very proud. His success is a reflection of the character and dynamism of Nigerian youth, because he is still a young man."
---Gov. Babatunde R. Fashola, Lagos State, Nigeria (2007-2015).

"The richest African, Alhaji Aliko Dangote is a northerner. So, you don't have problem of bringing resources. The problem is whether there are structures on ground to take advantage of the human capital. There are so many scholars, so many educated people of northern extraction that can give us development..."
---Speaker Oladimeji S. Bankole, House of Representatives, 7th Assembly (2007-2011), Abuja, Nigeria.

"We are completely humbled by the Dangote Foundation's (US$2million) generous donation on behalf of WFP and the people of Pakistan..."
---Ms. Sandy Westlake, head, private sector partnership, World Food Program, (WFP), Islamabad, Pakistan.

"...the people and government of Pakistan will forever remain grateful to the Dangote Foundation for this big sacrifice (US$2million aid) that will greatly address the needs of the people"

--- Retired Major-General Asif Duraiz Akhatar, United Nations High Commissioner, Islamabad, Pakistan.

'When billionaire Aliko Dangote sneezes, the Nigerian Stock Exchange catches a cold..."

---Mr. Mfonobong Nsehe the African Chronicles, Lagos, Nigeria and contributor, Forbes magazine, New York, USA.

"Alhaji Aliko Dangote has not only raised his profile on the international scene, he has also helped in boosting the positive impression about Nigeria as a safe investment haven"

--- Mr. Oluwadamilare Okunola, major cement distributor, Lagos, Nigeria.

"The beauty about Dangote's investments is that he generates jobs for several thousands of Nigerians in an environment that is very hostile to business. He has proved that business can flourish in Nigeria at a time that several industrialists are fleeing to neighboring countries because of challenges"

---Dr Shuaibu Jegede, economist, University of Lagos, Nigeria.

'In the land of the Big Man, Aliko Dangote is the biggest...the richest businessman..."

---Mr Jonathan Clayton, The Times newspaper London, United Kingdom

'Dangote Cement now has a market value in excess of $13 billion, and accounts for a quarter of the Nigeria Stock Exchange's total market capitalization"

---Ms. Tatiana Serafin, Eurasian Intelligence, New York, USA.

"Dangote has made a fortune by providing cement to Nigeria and other African countries that otherwise would likely have to pay to import much of the materials. In December, he consolidated his previously public cement holdings with his private investments across 14 African countries into newly listed Dangote Cement. The new group has a market cap of around $17 billion, more than one fourth the entire capitalization of the Nigerian market..."

> *---Ms. Luisa Kroll, Forbes magazine, New York, USA.*

"The Nigerian businessman's fortune surged 557% in the past year, making him the world's biggest gainer in percentage terms and Africa's richest individual for the first time... "

> *---Ms. Keren Blankfeld, Forbes magazine, New York, USA.*

"Aliko Dangote has made us proud, and I believe that he is going to keep on getting better "

> *---- Mr. Segun Akande, chief executive officer, SBA Interactive Data Limited, Lagos Nigeria.*

"I want the government to continue to encourage Dangote in his business "

> *---Mr. Ajisafe Ishola, major distributor of Dangote products, Lagos, Nigeria.*

"Aliko Dangote has been able to meet the essential needs of most Nigerians and reduced the problem of unemployment by establishing manufacturing industries that have employed a large number of Nigerians both directly and indirectly "

> *---Mr. Henry Nwokide, major distributor of Dangote spaghetti, Lagos, Nigeria.*

"No matter detractors' or competitors' allegation of embarking on business intrigues that will ensure he dominates the market, Dangote has contributed a lot to the economic development of Nigeria through employment creation"

> *---Ms. Ngozi Ughagwu, major distributor of Dangote products, Lagos, Nigeria.*

"Aliko Dangote is the best thing that has happened to the Nigerian economy. Nigerians are crying foul of Chinese domination yet they won't encourage Dangote who has stood up against foreign domination of business in Nigeria"

---*Alhaji Muhammad Tukur, executive director, Afrijet Airlines, Lagos, Nigeria.*

"Aliko Dangote is out to help build Nigeria's economy through local production"

---*Mr. Habeeb Salami, major distributor of Dangote products, Lagos, Nigeria.*

"I am impressed by Dangote's humility in spite of his affluence; it's a rare quality among Nigerians"

---*Mr. Nenye Kocha, banker, Afribank Nigeria Plc, Lagos, Nigeria.*

"I do not see anything wrong with Aliko Dangote's doggedness, as any businessman worth his salt will always strive to dominate the market"

---*Mr. Otio Nathaniel, banker, Afribank Nigeria, Plc, Lagos, Nigeria.*

"I extend my congratulations to *Dangote* Group and its president Alhaji Aliko Dangote for this massive investment initiative in Cameroon. It will certainly change the industrial landscape of Cameroon We salute the determination of Dangote who believed so much in this project,- ($115 million investment agreement for the construction of a composite cement production plant, which will result in the production of 1.5 million metric tons of cement in Douala, Cameroon yearly)- who has done so much for the African community and has stopped at nothing to make it happen"

---*Mr. Philemon Yang, the prime minister & head of government of Cameroon, Doula, Republic of Cameroon.*

"Through his various subsidiaries, Mr Aliko Dangote has touched lives in many ways, especially in an era where Nigerians have bemoaned the nation's unsustainable consumption pattern and import dependency,"

---Alhaji Mohammed N. Umar, director-general, small and medium enterprises development agency of Nigeria (SMEDAN), Abuja, Nigeria.

"The ($2milion) donations from Dangote Industries (to the Pakistani flood victims) makes the first time WFP receives a major contribution from a company based in Africa"

---The United Nations World Food Program, (UNWFP), Rome, Italy.

"We didn't have to vote. Dangote was elected by a unanimous acclamation. He was the second to be so voted as the chairman of Nigerian Stock Exchange (NSE) after Sir Odumegwu Ojukwu who succeeded Mr. E. C. W. Howard, an expatriate"

---Dr Ndidi Okereke-Onyiuke, former director-general, Nigerian Stock Exchange, Lagos, Nigeria.

"I sincerely want to commend the (Dangote) company for making the (cement) product more affordable for the people. I recalled that the company's price before devaluation in June 2008 was ₦1,380 ($8.78) per bag. So for the company to change its ex- factory price to ₦1,350 ($8.59) per bag is highly commendable,"

...Mr. Yinka Adebisi, cement distributor, Lagos, Nigeria.

"I commend Dangote for bringing the price (of cement) down. You know property business is the most reliable business. The price reduction is a good development. This will help in the achievement of housing provision in Abuja, Kaduna, Port Harcourt and other places with high demands. This will also reduce demands and housing rents. So it's good but he should do more"

---Mr. Shehu Liman, property developer, S.D. Ventures, Abuja, Nigeria.

'Nigeria's Dangote Group, for example, is still run by its founder, Aliko Dangote, who has built an empire spanning food processing, cement manufacturing, and freight over 30 years. His company now has $2 billion in sales, operating in nine countries, and is the second-largest global sugar producer..."

---The Boston Consulting Group, the African Challengers: Global Competitors Emerge from the Overlooked Continent, 2010; Boston, Massachusetts, USA

"Aliko Dangote, the president and chief executive officer of Dangote Group of Companies is a case study of Africa's private entrepreneurship that has emerged from trading and branching into diversified unrelated business units...The story of Aliko Dangote and the Dangote Group illustrate entrepreneurial strategies suitable in the concept of a developing economy..."

---Mr. John O. Ogbor, in "Entrepreneurship in Sub-Saharan Africa: A Strategic Management Perspective," Bloomington, Indiana, USA

"Aliko Dangote is a business mogul...with interests in virtually every sector of his country's economy. By all standards, he is a business magnate of international repute...he has his hands in textile, property, shipping, oil service, mining, fishing, manufacturing and banking..."

---Mr. David S. Flick in "Entrepreneurship in Africa: A Study of Successes," Westport, Connecticut, USA

"The Dangote Group is a leading and responsible organization in West Africa, and is one of Nigeria's foremost diversified business conglomerates; with a hard-earned reputation for excellent business practices and product quality...The Dangote

Group also has its own foundation dedicated especially on the development of education in Nigeria. Dangote Group is the brainchild of Alhaji Aliko Dangote..."

---Ebiz Guides, Dublin, Ireland

"Aliko Dangote began his career as a trader, at age 21 with loan from his uncle, built his Dangote Group into a big conglomerate with interests in sugar, flour milling, salt processing, cement manufacturing, textiles, real estate, and oil and gas..."

---Mr. Emeka L. Ogazi in "African Development and the Influence of Western Media," New York, USA

"The Dangote Group of Companies, with headquarters in Lagos, is one of the largest trading organizations in Nigeria and has diversified into textile, banking, property, shipping, fishing and services..."

--- Mr. Tom G. Forrest, International African Institute, University of Edinburgh, UK.

"Dangote Group is an industrial and manufacturing group whose interests include cement, energy and foodstuffs... "

---The OECD 2011 Report Belgium, Brussels, the European Union.

"In Nigeria, Dangote Group has finalized plans to build a steel mill in the commercial hub of Lagos with the help of Indian consultancy Meacon... "

--- The OECD 20006 Report Belgium, Brussels, the European Union.

"Nigeria's Aliko Dangote is a Nigerian who started a highly successful company known as the Dangote Group. In 2008, he was ranked the richest person in Nigeria by the *Forbes* with an estimated net worth of $3.3billion. "

---Dr Comfort Babalogbon in "Beyond Being Black," Bloomington, Indiana, USA

"...Dangote Group of companies owned by Alhaji Aliko Dangote, who is a northerner yet the company recruits anyone who is qualified to do the job including Lebanese..."

---Dr James G. Olusoji, London, UK

"The Obajana cement factory is not only important to the Dangote Group, but it is important to Nigeria... The Dangote Group has always operated as a socially responsible organization"

----The Nigerian Investment Promotion Commission, (NIPC), Abuja, Nigeria.

"The Dangote Group is currently the largest industrial conglomerate in West Africa and one of the largest in Africa. It generated revenue in excess of $1.25 billion in 2005. The group is one of the leading diversified business conglomerates in sub-Saharan Africa..."

---The Wikipedia, the Free Encyclopedia, in San Francisco, California, USA

"I want to thank Dangote for his philanthropic gesture. May the good Lord reward you abundantly? I also want to thank all our religious leaders, royal fathers, all security agencies and all the good people of the state who did all that were possible at ensuring a sustained peaceful atmosphere within Kaduna. May all your efforts never be in vain and may God reward us all"

---Gov. Patrick Ibrahim Yakowa, Kaduna State, Nigeria (May 2010- December 15, 2012).

"Dangote caused a revolution in the cement industry by consolidating the group's concerns across Africa into Dangote Cement Plc recently, in line with his vision of creating a pan-African conglomerate. Dangote Cement, one of the quoted subsidiaries of the group, is currently the biggest company quoted on the Nigerian Stock Exchange (NSE)"

---Mr. Idris Ahmed, Daily Trust newspapers, Abuja, Nigeria

"With Ibese Cement Plant coming on stream with 6 million metric tons, Obajana expanding to 10 million metric tons, and Book at 3.5 metric tons, Dangote is already geared towards meeting local demand for cement (in Nigeria)."

....Dr Bala Ahmed, financial secretary, real estate development association of Nigeria (REDAN), Lagos, Nigeria

"(The) United States –based rating agency, Boston Consulting Group (BCG) had listed the Dangote Group among the top 40 African Challengers, which are companies of African origin that have the potential to rival *Fortune 500* Companies. Some of the criteria used in making the selection include size, growth and international expansion. Dangote Group has 13 subsidiaries spread all over Nigeria."

---Mr. Crusoe Osagie, ThisDay newspapers, Lagos, Nigeria

"The huge investment into Sephaku Cement of South Africa by Dangote is the largest ever foreign direct investment (FDI) by an African company into South Africa,"

---Messrs. Idris Ahmed & Sunday Williams, Daily Trust newspapers, Abuja, FCT, Nigeria.

"Aliko Dangote is the founder and president of Dangote Group. He is currently the richest man in Nigeria and the richest black man in Africa..."

The Financial Freedom Inspiration, Lagos, Nigeria

"The Dangote Group, the largest manufacturing conglomerate in West Africa..."

Facebook, Internet social media, Menlo Park, California, USA

"Dangote Group is Nigeria's premier diversified business conglomerate with a reputation for excellent business practices and product quality... "

Twitter, Internet social media, San Francisco, CA, USA

"Dangote Group has unveiled its plans to invest approximately $3.9 billion (about ₦585 billion) in the construction of additional cement lines both within and outside the country within the next few months. Dangote Cement currently accounts for more than 50% of the Nigerian market share..."

WorldCement.com, London, UK

"I must say that much has been achieved by Dangote Cement in an attempt to meet local demands. And government would like to replicate these exploits in the production of rice, sugar and wheat... The *Dangote* Group is a success story... "

---Mr Olusegun Aganga, minister of trade and investment, Abuja, Nigeria.

"Dangote Group has brought new state of the art technologies in cement production into the country. The nation's industrial sector is now better with the new technologies as Dangote's efforts will result in technological transfer. The building profession is being kept abreast of new developments in the industry through technology transfer... "

---Prof. Akin Akindoyeni, chairman, council of registered builders of Nigeria (CORBON), Lagos, Nigeria.

"The significant jump from 2010-2011 which is the largest jump in the *Forbes* ranking indicate the huge potential for growth which Nigeria hold for highly disciplined man like Aliko Dangote. I will not be surprised if he is ranked as one of the top 20 richest men the world in the next three years. "

---Mr. Godwin Obaseki, vice-president, Afriinvest, Lagos, Nigeria.

"This news to me by the *Forbes* magazine that Aliko Dangote is the richest black person in the world is just the beginning for a very intelligent entrepreneur"
---*Mr. Bismarck Rewane, managing director and chief executive officer, Financial Derivates, Lagos, Nigeria.*

"Dangote -- whose business empire in Nigeria has led to his fortune being rated at $3,3-billion by the *Forbes* -- has built up diversified holdings in a country whose wealth mostly derives from its position as the world's eighth-biggest oil exporter..."
---*Ms. Katrina Mansion, Reuters, Freetown, Sierra Leone.*

"This man should be an inspiration to every entrepreneur in Nigeria. In a country where a lot of people have lost their way and believe the only way forward is via embezzlement or outright theft, he remains a shining example of what can still be achieved in Nigeria the old fashioned way through hard work, dedication and a remarkable display of business savvy that rivals any global business icon"
---*Mr. Philip Ideh, Abuja City Online, Abuja, Nigeria.*

"Dangote is not in the habit of extravagant display of opulence, like some elderly moneybags who still behave boyishly and organize *owambe* parties with roadblocks to the discomfort of the ordinary citizens. He resists the temptation of participating in highly lucrative, fast money yielding ventures like oil business, GSM, hotel business and even airlines, probably to discourage destructive competition with indigenous entrepreneurs..."
---*Mr. Yushau Shuaib, public affairs commentator, Abuja, Nigeria.*

"Those who rule Nigeria do not believe in the country. Yet there is hope. In the last few years, four new developments have taken place. Oil has diminished in power, and other forms of wealth are emerging. Aliko Dangote, said to be Nigeria's richest entrepreneur, made his billions from cement and transport..."

--- *Mr. Richard Dowden, London, UK*

"Dangote's investment ambition if successfully implemented will go a long way in supplementing the on-going $500 million (Shs850 billion) Bugajali power project in curbing the power problem the country (of Uganda) is experiencing. This will mean more industries coming up, job creation thus economic development of Uganda"

---*Mr. Patrick Bitature, chairman, Uganda investment authority and Australia's honorary consul in the Republic of Uganda.*

"Alhaji Aliko Dangote's plan to build Africa's largest fertilizer plant in Nigeria will boost agricultural production in the country and tremendously increase the yields of farmers since more fertilizers will be available to them"

--- *Alhaji Ahmed R. Kwa, executive secretary, fertilizer suppliers association of Nigeria (FSAN), Abuja, Nigeria.*

"Whatever happens here (with Alhaji Aliko Dangote's plan to build Africa's largest fertilizer plant in Nigeria) will have a multiplier effect on the rest of Africa. Once there is food sufficiency in Nigeria, other African countries, including the famine-ravaged Horn of Africa, will benefit."

--- *Mr. Benjamin Odoemena, country program officer, International Fund for Agricultural Development, Abuja, Nigeria.*

"We are encouraged by Alhaji Aliko Dangote...; his companies have been creating jobs and feeding Nigerian families. All Nigerians should emulate him..."

--- *Alhaji Mukhtar Mukhtar, chairman, shareholders' trustees association of Nigeria, (STAON), Kano, Nigeria*

"The most important thing ever said by Alhaji Dangote when he came to donate relief materials to the victims of Ibadan flood disaster, was to site (sic) a big production company in

Ibadan, the Oyo State capital, as a means of contributing his own quota to the development of Oyo State. I was deeply moved by the statement made by this noble businessman poised to use his personal wealth to create jobs in Oyo State. The people of Oyo State, particularly unemployed youths, should thank their stars as Alhaji Dangote is reputed as being a man of his word..."

> ---*Mr Jimoh Mumin, Ibadan, Oyo State, the Nigerian Tribune newspapers, Ibadan, Oyo State Nigeria*

"May Allah give Aliko Dangote more health and wealth. I hope that people would emulate him."

> ---*Malam Yahaya Dahiru, 70-year old beneficiary of Aliko Mohammed Dangote succour to displaced persons of communal strife and political violence in Kaduna, resettled in Bauchi, Bauchi State, Nigeria.*

"Dangote Cement represents a new class in the Nigerian capital market. It will diversify the domestic capital market. The listing by introduction of the shares of Dangote Cement will expand the market from about \$40 million to \$55 million. Banking sector share in the market will shrink to about 30 percent. Foreign investors coming in now will see a more diversified market"

> ---*Mr. Ike Chioke, managing director, Afriinvest Limited, Lagos, Nigeria.*

"I want to thank Aliko Dangote and pray for Dangote Group that Allah should continue to bless them abundantly. May God protect Alhaji Aliko Dangote and bless him for all that he has done to reduce the suffering of the downtrodden in the society, especially for those that were once comfortable, but lost everything in the April post-presidential election violence"

> ---*Alhaji Adamu Mohammed, chief imam, Nabordo Mosque, Bauchi State, Nigeria.*

CREDIT ACKNOWLEDGMENTS

* Abubakar, Sanni Lugar (2004). Katsina College. Katsina: Lugga Press

* Ade Ajayi, J.F. (1995) Africa in the nineteen century until the 1880s, Oxford, UK: Heinemann Publishers.

* African Success Online, Paris, France.

* Allaire, Yvan & Firsirotu, Y. Michaela (1984) Theories of Organizational Cultures. Journal of Organizational Studies, 5 (3), 193-226.

* Alexander, L.M. & Rucker, W. C. (2010). Encyclopedia of African-American History, Volume I. Santa Barbara, California: ABC-CLIO, LLC.

* BBC Network (2008, 2006, 2005) London, United Kingdom.

* Becker, H. & Geer B. (1960) Participant Observation: the analysis of qualitative field data. In R. N. Adams and J. J. Preiss (editors), Human organization research: field relations and techniques. Homewood, Illinois: Dorsey Press.

* Branson, Richard (2007) Losing my virginity: How I survived, had fun, and made a Fortune doing business. New York: Random House Publishers.

* Broad Street Journal Weekly Newspapers, Ikeja, Lagos, Nigeria.

* Business Day Newspapers, Apapa, Lagos, Nigeria.

* Channels Television Network, Ikeja, Lagos, Nigeria.

* CNN International Network, Atlanta, Georgia, United States of America.

* CNN-Cable News Network (2011). The CNN freedom project: Ending modern-day slavery. Atlanta, GA: CNN International Network.

* Coyne, Kate (2011) Dr. Phil & Robin's Do-it-yourself marriage makeover; the famous couple on how to cope with the 5 biggest relationship busters, and their stay-together secrets for no-longer newlyweds. *Good Housekeeping*,

* Delissa, Jeanette (1997). The songs of Berry Gordy; the music, the magic, the memories of Motown,

* Weston, Randy (2010), African Rhythms, composed by Randy Weston and arranged by Willard Jenkins, NC: Duke University Press. Excerpts taken from Randy Weston's autobiography "African Rhythms, composed by Randy Westen, arranged by Willard Jenkins

* Fluehr-Lobban, Carolyn, Richard Lobban, and John Obert Voll (19992). Historical dictionary of the Sudan, Metuchen and London: Scarecrow.

* Gates, Bill (1995) The road ahead. New York: Penguin

* -------------- (1999) Business @ the speed of life. New York: Warner Books

* Gill, F. (1999). The meaning of work: lessons from sociology, psychology and political theory. *Journal of Socio Economic*, 28 (6); pp.725-743

* Grouley, Catherine (1997) Wheels of time: A biography of Henry Ford. CT: Millbrook's Press.

* Gumi, Sheikh Abubakar with Ismaila A. Tsiga (199). Where I stand? Ibadan: Spectrum Books Limited.

* Haskins, Jim (1997). Spike Lee: By any means necessary. New York: Walker and Company.

* Heyman Saly Jody and Barrera, Magda (2010). Profit at the bottom of the ladder: Creating value by investing in your employees. Cambridge, MA: Harvard Business School.

* Hofstede, Geert (1991) Cultures and Organizations: software of the mind intercultural cooperation and its importance for survival. England: McGraw-Hill Book Company Europe.

* *Iacocca, L. and William, N. (1986) Iacocca: An autobiography.* Peterson, W. M. & Company

* International Business Times Newspapers of Sydney, Australia

* Irving J. (1989) Crucial decisions: leadership in policymaking and crisis management, New York: Free Press

* Irving J. (1972) Victims of groupthink. Boston, MA: Houghton Mifflin

* Irving J. (2nd ed. 1982) Groupthink. Boston, MA: Houghton Mifflin

* Jackson, Tim (1998) Richard Branson, Virgin king: Inside Richard Branson's business empire. New York: Prime Lifestyle

* Johnson, H. John (1993) Succeeding against the odds, New York: Amistad Press.

* Kwande, Yahaya (1998). The Making of a Northern Nigerian: An autobiography of Yahaya Kwande, Jos, Nigeria: Quarhess,

* Lee, Spike and Ralph Wiley (1998) Best seat in the house: A basketball memoir, New York: Three Rivers.

* Mahajan, Viyay (2008). Africa rising: How 900million African consumers offer more than you think. Upper Saddle River, New Jersey: Pearson Prentice Hall.

* Manes, Stephan and Paul Andrews (1994) Gates: How Microsoft's mogul reinvented an industry-and made himself the richest man in America. New York: Touchstone.

* Mark Moring (2008). Hollywood fighter: elusive billionaire Philip Anschutz used to bemoan the lack of family-friendly values. Not anymore. Carol Stream, IL: Christianity Today

* Mariotti Steve, Castin, Mike & DeSalvo, Debra (2000).The very, very rich and how they got that way, and how you can too; Profiles of phenomenal entrepreneurs. Franklin Lakes, New Jersey: Foundation for Teaching Entrepreneurship, Inc.

* Marrs, Dave (March, 2010). Ackerman retires but keeps hand in. South Africa: Business Day, March 11.

* Marsick, J. V. & Watkins, E. K. (2003) Demonstrating the value of an organization's learning culture: the dimension of the learning organization questionnaire. Journal of Advances in Developing Human Resources, 5 (1), pp.132-151 Shafritz, J.M Hyde, A.C.

* McGilligan, Patrick (1994) Jack's Life. New York: W.W. Norton & Company,

* Muffett, D.J.M., (1982). Let truth be told: the Coups d'état of 1966. Zaria: Hudahuda Publishing Company.

* Olawoyin, J.S. (1993). My Political Reminiscences *1948-1983,* Ikeja: John West Publications Ltd.

* Ostwald, M. (Trans.1962) Aristotle, *Nicomachean Ethics.* Indianapolis, Ind.: Bobbs-Merrill

* Oxford Dictionary of National Biography (2004). Oxford dictionary, Oxford: Oxford University Press

* Paden, John N., (1986). Ahmadu Bello, Sardauna of Sokoto: Values and Leadership in Nigeria Zaria: Hudahuda Publishing Company.

* Pastin, M. (1991). The hard problems of management: gaining the ethical edge. San Francisco, CA: Jossey-Bass Publishers

* Next Newspapers, Ikoyi, Lagos, Nigeria.

* Next on Sunday Newspaper, Ikoyi, Lagos, Nigeria.

* Newswatch Magazine, Ikeja, Lagos, Nigeria

* Oprah Winfrey and Bill Adler (1999). The uncommon wisdom of Oprah Winfrey: A portrait in her own words. Bel Air, CA: Citadel Publishing.

* Pasternak Judeth Mahoney (September, 1999) Oprah. New York: Metro Books.

* Parkinson, Gary (2006). A day in the life of John Caudwell: How to make your first £1bn: start planning at the age of eight. The Independent, London, UK January 21.

* P.M Newspaper, Evening Newspaper, Ikeja, Lagos, Nigeria

* Raven, B.H. (1998). Groupthink, bay of pigs and Watergate reconsidered. Organizational Behavior & Human Decision Processes, 73(2-3)

* Richardson, Sam Scruton (2001). No Weariness: The memoir of a generalist in public service in four continents, 1919-2000, Wylye, Wiltshire: Malt House Publishing.

* Niger State (1999) Royal roots: Foundation history of emirate councils in Niger State Nigeria Minna: Ministry of Local Government, Community Development and Chieftaincy Affairs, Niger State,

* R. Brown (1896). Leo Africanus. London, UK: Hakluyt Society.

* Rosenbloom, D.H. (1981) Personnel management in government: politics and process. New York: Marcel Dekker, Inc.

* Saunders, Rebecca (1999) Business: The Amazon.com way; secrets of the world's most amazing web business. UK: Capstone Limited.

* Schein. H. E. (1987).Defining organization cultures. In classics of organizational theory, 2nd ed. Edited by Jay M. Shaffritz & J. Steven Ott. Chicago: Dorsey Press.

* Smith David (2006). The story of Bangalore Bill. The Guardian Newspapers, London. August

* The Weekly Trust Newspapers Abuja, Federal Capital Territory, Nigeria

* The Daily Trust Newspapers Abuja, Federal Capital Territory, Nigeria

* The Daily Sun Newspapers, Lagos, Nigeria.

* The Sun of Sunday Newspapers, Lagos, Nigeria.

* Tell Magazine, Lagos, Nigeria.

* The Leadership Newspaper, Abuja, Federal Capital Territory, Nigeria.

* The News Newspapers, Ikeja, Lagos, Nigeria.

* The Times of Nigeria Newspapers, Ikeja, Lagos, Nigeria.

* The Punch Newspapers, Ikeja, Lagos, Nigeria.

* National Compass Newspapers, Lagos-By Pass, Ogun State / Ikeja, Lagos, Nigeria.

* The Nigerian Tribune Newspapers, Ibadan, Oyo State, Nigeria.

* The Sunday Newspaper, Ibadan, Oyo State, Nigeria.

* The Guardian Newspapers, Oshodi, Lagos, Nigeria.

* The Guardian on Sunday Newspaper, Oshodi, Lagos, Nigeria.

* The Voice Newspaper of London, United Kingdom.

* The Times of London, United Kingdom.

* The Guardian Newspaper of London, United Kingdom.

* The Belfast Telegraph Newspapers, Northern Ireland, United Kingdom.

* The New York Times Newspapers, New York, United States of America.

* The Washington Post, Washington, United States of America.

* The Atlanta Post Newspapers, New York, Unite States of America.

* The Atlanta Journal Constitution (AJC) Newspapers, Atlanta, Georgia, USA.

* The Daily Mail Newspapers of London, United Kingdom

* The Independent Newspapers of London, United Kingdom.

* This Day Newspapers, Abuja and Lagos, Nigeria.

* The Daily Monitor Newspapers, Gaborone, Botswana.

* The Standard Times News Newspapers of Freetown, Sierra Leone.

* The Nazret Newspaper

* The African Vibes Newspapers, Los Angeles, California, United States of America.

* The Daily Monitor Newspapers of Kampala, Uganda.

* The Edmonton Journal (2006). Just an 'ordinary' hometown billionaire: Edmonton's wealthiest son is hardly a household name, and the Google billionaire couldn't care less. Alberta, Canada, April 3.

* The Business Spectator Newspapers of Australia.

* The Financial Times Newspapers, London, United Kingdom.

* The Forbes Magazine, New York, United States of America.

* The Herald Newspapers of Harare, Zimbabwe.

* The Daily Observe Newspapers of Banjul, The Gambia.

* The Times Newspapers of Lusaka, Zambia.

* The Post Newspapers of Lusaka, Zambia.

* The Woodlawn Post Newspapers of Michigan, United States of America.

* The Nation Newspapers of Lagos, Nigeria.

* The Energy and Corporate Africa Magazine, Houston, Texas, United States of America.

* The Mail & Guardian Newspapers of Johannesburg, South Africa.

* The Sunday Independent Newspapers of Johannesburg, South Africa.

* The People's Daily Newspapers, Abuja, Federal Capital Territory, Nigeria.

* The Nigerian Pilot Newspapers, Abuja, Federal Capital Territory, Nigeria.

* The Nigerian Tide Newspapers, Port Harcourt, Rivers State, Nigeria

* The Nigerian Observer Newspapers, Benin City, Edo State Nigeria.

* The New York Times, January 25, 2012 in an interview with Mr. Ron Johnson, CEO, J.C Penney

* The Wall Street Journal, September 30, 2010 for interview with Mr. Levine, Chairman and CEO, Family Dollars.

* Time Magazine, volume 170, No. 27, 2007, for Sir Richard Branson Interview/Quote on Page 12.

* This is Lapai (n.d) Minna: Minna, Niger State: Director of Printing Niger State

* Tracy, Brian (2001). The 21 Success Secrets of Self-Made Millionaires: How to Achieve Financial Independence Faster and Easier Than You Ever Thought Possible. San Francisco, CA: Berrett-Koehler Publishers.

* Urdu Encyclopedia (1968). New Edition, Lahore: Feroze Sons

* Uwechue, Ralph ed. (1991). Makers of Modern Africa: Profiles in History London: Africa Books

* Vanguard Newspapers, Apapa, Lagos, Nigeria.

* Wal-Mart (197). Wal-Mart: A history of Sam Walton's retail phenomenon, New York: Twayne Publishing

* Walton, Sam (1993). Sam Walton: made in America: my story. John Huey, Bantam House

* Whitaker, C.S. Jr. (1970). The politics of tradition: Continuity and change in Northern Nigeria 1946-1966, Princeton: Princeton University Press

* White, H. T. (1992). Faculty and administrative perceptions of their environments: Different views or different models of organization. Journal of Research in Higher Education (33), April

* Who is Who (1982). An annual biographical dictionary, London: Adams and Black Publishing Limited, 1982). 26

* Zakaria, Fareed (October, 2008). Economic crisis becoming psychological problem; explaining the crisis; George Soros interview. Atlanta, GA: CNN, GPS aired on October 12, 2008 Eastern Time, USA.

INDEX

Z

ABOUT THE AUTHORS

MOSHOOD ADEMOLA FAYEMIWO is a former publisher and editor-in-chief of popular *Razor* magazine and *Evening News* in Nigeria between 1992 and 1998. A former reporter with the defunct *National Concord* news papers; senior reporter, *The Herald* newspaper, Ilorin; staff writer, with the defunct *New breed* magazine; staff writer, *Sunday Champion* newspapers; special project staff writer, the defunct *African Guardian*; and senior special project writer/reporter, the defunct *Times Week* (*Daily Times*). He is an alumnus of the University of Lagos, Nigeria; the University of South Florida, and the State University of New York. He holds a doctorate degree in Public Policy and Public Administration.

Fayemiwo is author of *Who's Who of Africans in USA* and four published books in the United States. He was contributing editor for *The Informed Constituent* news paper in Albany, New York. He has written for news papers in Tampa, St Petersburg in Florida, New York and has authored / co-authored academic articles for scholarly journals in the United States and the UK. He writes a weekly column for the Charlotte, NC-based online news website; *Nigeriaworld* and the New York-based online website; *Diasporascope* and the MG Media Group in The Netherlands.

He is a member of several professional organizations: Association of American University Professors (AAUP), Society of Professional Journalists (SPJ), Investigative Reporters and Editors (IRE), National Association of Black Journalists (NBAJ) among others. Listed in Stanford

Who's Who and Worldwide *Who's Who* Directory, he is a writer, author, and commentator on local and international issues, policy consultant and a businessman. He is CEO, Alternative Lifestyle Communication, DBA – a publishing and public relations outfit based in Chicago (www.allternativecommunication.com).

MARGIE MARIE NEAL is a former university professor, an education consultant, and a reading coach/classroom teacher with the Chicago Area School System in Illinois, United States. A graduate of State University of New York (SUNY), the Chicago State University, American College of Education , Indianapolis and the University of Illinois at Urbana-Champaign where she earned her doctorate degree in Educational Leadership. She was formerly, president, Chicago Area Reading Association and committee member, International Reading Association, United States. She is a member of several professional organizations on reading and educational development in Chicago, USA; including the Illinois Reading Council of President Obama Reading Award, and Association for Supervision and Curriculum Development. Listed in Stanford *Who's Who* and Worldwide *Who's Who* Directory, She is president, Alternative Lifestyle Communication DBA, and lives in Chicago in the United States of America.

CPSIA information can be obtained at www.ICGtesting.com
Printed in the USA
LVOW13*0521050813

346237LV00001B/1/P